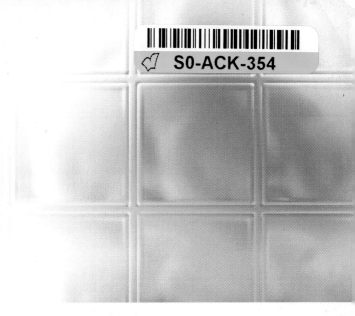

The Essential Elements of Public Speaking

Third Edition

Joseph A. DeVito

Hunter College of the
City University of New York

PEARSON

Boston   New York   San Francisco
Mexico City   Montreal   Toronto   London   Madrid   Munich   Paris
Hong Kong   Singapore   Tokyo   Cape Town   Sydney

Editor-in-Chief: Karon Bowers
Associate Development Editor: Jenny Lupica
Series Editorial Assistant: Jessica Cabana
Marketing Manager: Suzan Czajkowski
Editorial Production Service: Tom Conville for Nesbitt Graphics, Inc.
Composition Buyer: Linda Cox
Manufacturing Buyer: JoAnne Sweeney
Electronic Composition: Nesbitt Graphics, Inc.
Interior Design: Nesbitt Graphics, Inc.
Photo Researcher: Nesbitt Graphics, Inc.
Cover Administrator: Linda Knowles

For related titles and support materials, visit our online catalog at www.ablongman.com.

Between the time website information is gathered and then published, it is not unusual for some sites to have closed. Also, the transcription of URLs can result in typographical errors. The publisher would appreciate notification where these errors occur so that they may be corrected in subsequent editions.

ISBN-13: 978-0-205-54300-7   ISBN-10: 0-205-54300-6

Library of Congress Cataloging-in-Publication Data
DeVito, Joseph A.
  The essential elements of public speaking / Joseph A. DeVito. — 3rd ed.
      p. cm.
  Includes bibliographical references and index.
  ISBN-13: 978-0-205-54300-7
  ISBN-10: 0-205-54300-6
  1. Public speaking. I. Title.

  PN4129.15.D48 2009
  808.5'1 — dc22

                                    2007040333

Credits appear on page 330, which constitutes an extension of the copyright page.

Printed in the United States of America

10 9 8 7 6 5 CRK 11 10

New to This Edition

There are three major reasons for this new third edition of *The Essential Elements of Public Speaking*. First, the principles and skills of public speaking can only be appreciated when seen operating in today's world, when they deal with contemporary issues, and when they are presented by today's speakers. Hence this revision adds new speeches and speech excerpts to illustrate the principles and to demonstrate their application to issues relevant to today's college students.

Second, our knowledge of culture, audience analysis, language, and persuasion, for example, all grow regularly from the research and theory in communication and related areas. Hence, this revision adds new research findings and theoretical perspectives.

Third, no matter how hard an author and editors may try, there are always things that can be improved—sometimes little things like word choice, examples, and photo captions and sometimes big things like new topics, reorganization of material, or clarification of the text's main focus. This revision aims to fine tune the presentation of public speaking in all of these ways. A major effort was made in this revision to focus more clearly than in previous editions on the *essentials* of public speaking.

To achieve all three of these revision goals, a variety of both general and specific changes were made. Pages xv–xxii of the Welcome section present detailed information on what is new to the third edition. Here's a quick (and abbreviated) view of some of the most important changes:

- This edition includes new speeches and speech excerpts. The major speeches and outlines now appear throughout the chapters (rather than at the ends of chapters) in Public Speaking Sample Assistant boxes.

- Each of the chapters has been revised to include materials instructors using the text requested and to incorporate new research and updated examples.

- Chapter 1 includes an expanded discussion of communication apprehension to deal with perhaps the number one problem in a public speaking course. Chapter 1 also discusses plagiarism to address this crucial issue right at the start.

- The material on Preparing and Presenting a Public Speech (in Brief) is now its own chapter (Chapter 2).

- The chapter on Speaking in Small Groups has been deleted and the material most essential to public speaking, "presenting the group's thinking," has been moved to Chapter 12. For those who want to cover small group communication in more detail, two chapters from the 6th edition of *Essentials of Human Communication* (2008) are available on the Web on this book's MySpeechLab at www.myspeechlab.com (access code required).

*B*rief Contents

$\mathcal{D}$etailed Contents

6 Using Supporting Materials and Presentation Aids   113

7 Organizing Your Speech   142

8 Wording Your Speech   182

Specialized Contents

Research Links

The Research Links spread throughout the text explain the principles of effective and efficient research and identify lots of resource materials that you'll find useful in researching your speeches as well as throughout your college and professional career. Each of these sections ends with a reference to the next Research Link so your can read them in sequence as you would a chapter.

Test Yourself

Throughout this text are self-tests that ask you to pause and reflect on your thoughts and behaviors. In working with these tests, focus on the statements in the test, on the issues they raise, and on the thoughts they help generate. The number you get "right" or "wrong" or the score you get (some tests yield scores for comparison purposes) are far less important. These self-assessment instruments will help you to personalize the material in the text and apply it to your own public speaking, listening, and criticizing.

A Case of Ethics

These ethics boxes explain the principles of ethics and present you with an ethical dilemma that asks what you would do in this situation.

Public Speaking Sample Assistant

A variety of speeches are presented to help you see what a poor speech looks like (the speeches in Chapters 3 and 4 are purposely poor examples) and what excellent speeches look like (all the remaining speeches in the text are models of effectiveness) and the principles that make the difference.

Public Speaking Exercises

These exercises, presented at the end of each chapter, are designed to stimulate you to think more actively about the concepts and skills covered in the chapter and to help you practice your developing public speaking skills.

Welcome to *The Essential Elements of Public Speaking*

The Essential Elements of Public Speaking will guide you through one of the most important courses you'll take in your entire college career. Public speaking is a course that will prove exciting, challenging, and immensely practical. It is also a course that is likely to create some anxiety and apprehension; this is normal. Fortunately, the anxiety and apprehension can be managed, and we'll deal with that challenge right from the beginning (in Chapter 1).

This text and this course will help you master the skills you'll need to give effective informative, persuasive, and special occasion speeches as well as to listen more critically to the speeches of others. It will also help you increase your personal and professional communication abilities and will enhance a wide variety of academic and career skills such as organization, research, and language usage.

This book is purposely short but not simplified or "dumbed down." An "essentials" book is not an elementary book; it's an *efficient* book. And that's what this edition aims to be—an efficient tool that will enable you to learn the essential elements of public speaking. More specifically, this text will give you the skills to prepare and present effective informative, persuasive, and special occasion speeches to an audience.

Main Features of *The Essential Elements of Public Speaking*

Among the main features of this text are:

1. An early, brief overview of the steps in public speaking.
2. Research links.
3. Ethics cases.
4. Self-appraisal tests.
5. Frequent examples of speeches and outlines.
6. An emphasis on the cultural dimensions of public speaking.

In addition, each chapter concludes with a summary, a list of essential terms, public speaking exercises, and an invitation to visit MySpeechLab (www.myspeechlab.com) for additional materials to help you master the skills of public speaking.

Brief Overview of the Steps in Public Speaking

The second chapter, "Preparing and Presenting a Public Speech (in Brief)," presents **10 steps for preparing a public speech**. Here you'll learn to accomplish everything from selecting a topic to organizing your materials, rehearsing, and presenting your speech. This chapter is purposely short so that you can read it in one sitting, get a picture of the entire process of public speaking, and start giving speeches almost immediately. The remaining chapters elaborate on these steps and will help you gradually refine and perfect your public speaking skills.

Research Links

Research is essential to an effective public speech—as it is, of course, to your entire college and professional career. Knowing how to conduct research and how to evaluate it are crucial skills that are essential to, but not limited to, public speaking. Rather than appearing in a traditional dense chapter, discussions of research appear throughout the text in 14 **Research Link** boxes. These Research Links are presented in a progression, from general research principles in early chapters to more specialized topics in later chapters. In this way, you'll be better able to digest the information and gradually practice the research strategies. By the end of the course, you'll have mastered a detailed arsenal of research techniques that will help you throughout your college courses and into your professional life. Each Research Link ends with a note identifying and locating the next Link so that, if you wish, you can read them as an entire chapter. A complete list of the Research Links is presented in the Specialized Contents.

A Case of Ethics

Because public speaking is a powerful medium that can have enormous consequences, it has important moral implications. In this book each chapter contains an **A Case of Ethics** box describing a situation that raises an ethical issue and asking how you would respond. By the end of the text, you should have formulated a clear and defensible ethical standard to govern your own public speaking. A list of these ethics boxes appears in the Specialized Contents.

Test Yourself

Fourteen self-tests, called **Test Yourself**, are interspersed throughout the text. These tests will promote active learning and personalize the material. They'll help you assess those qualities that you need to master speaking in public. For example, in these tests you'll be encouraged to explore your own level of communication apprehension (Chapter 1), your openness to intercultural communication (Chapter 7), the power of your presentation style (Chapter 9), and your credibility (Chapter 11).

Public Speaking Sample Assistant

Throughout the text **Public Speaking Sample Assistant** boxes contain speeches and outlines along with annotations. With the exceptions of the speeches in

Chapters 3 and 4, which were purposely written to illustrate what *not* to do, all of the other speeches are models of effectiveness and will show you what excellent speeches look like. The annotations will help guide you through the essential elements of public speaking.

Culture

The effectiveness of public speaking principles will vary from one culture to another. Depending on cultural factors, different audiences may respond to speakers in different ways. For example, in some cultures an audience will respond positively to a speaker who appears modest and unassuming; in other cultures the audience may see this speaker as weak and lacking in confidence. A direct style will prove clear and persuasive in some cultures but may appear invasive and inappropriate in others. As a result of the tremendous cultural variations in the ways in which people respond to public speeches and speakers, **cultural insights** are integrated in each of the 12 chapters. Among the issues discussed are how members of different cultures give and respond to public criticism (Chapter 3), the cultural factors a speaker should consider in analyzing different audiences (Chapter 5), and the cultural differences in audience responses to emotional and credibility appeals (Chapter 11).

Summary/Essential Concepts and Skills

Each chapter ends with a series of summary statements, called **Essentials**, designed to help you review the key concepts of the chapter. You may find it helpful to look at these summary statements before reading the chapter to get a relatively complete overview of what's covered.

Essential Terms

Because knowing the specialized vocabulary of a discipline will help you think about and talk about the material more effectively, a list of key terms and the pages on which they are introduced is presented at the end of each chapter. These **Essential Terms** lists replace the Vocabulary Quiz that appeared in earlier editions.

Public Speaking Exercises

Each chapter ends with a variety of **Public Speaking Exercises** to help you work actively with the concepts and skills discussed in the text. The last exercise in each chapter, **What Do You Say?**, consists of a series of scenarios, each posing a situation requiring a public speaking decision. These exercises raise questions and issues that are best considered in an interactive format—with small groups, with the class as a whole, or even intrapersonally.

MySpeechLab

One of the most exciting developments in textbooks is the integration of the textbook with technology. *The Essential Elements of Public Speaking* comes with extensive technology support that complements the material presented in this text and in the typical introductory public speaking course. Most important in this connection is **MySpeechLab**, which may be accessed at www.myspeechlab.com (access code required). This website provides robust content, learning experiences, and guides to additional resources. Suggested experiences are offered at the end of each chapter in LogOn! MySpeechLab notes.

In addition, a wide variety of other supplements are available and are described in detail under "Ancillaries/Supplementary Materials."

What's New in This Third Edition?

This revised edition makes a major effort to focus more clearly than ever on the *essentials* of public speaking. Revisions designed to achieve that end

include a variety of both general and chapter-by-chapter specific changes.

General Changes

Among the general changes are changes in (1) chapter structure, (2) research links, (3) coverage of critical thinking/listening, (4) marginal notes, (5) key terms, and (6) speeches.

Chapter Structure Changes

Two major chapter changes have been made. First, "Preparing and Presenting a Public Speech (in Brief)" is now its own chapter (Chapter 2). Second, the chapter "Speaking in Small Groups" has been deleted and the material most essential to public speaking, under the heading of "Presenting the Group's Thinking," moved to Chapter 12, "Speaking on Special Occasions."

For those who want to cover small group communication as a unit in public speaking, two chapters from the sixth edition of my *Essentials of Human Communication* (2008) are available on the Web at www.myspeechlab.com (access code required).

Research Links

The Research Link boxes have been updated and consolidated so that there are now fewer but, in some cases, more extensive boxes (reduced from 24 in the previous edition to 14 in this edition). As already noted, each Research Link contains a note on the location of the next box to facilitate reading these as one complete chapter.

Critical Thinking/Listening

Critical thinking remains an essential feature of this text; in this edition, however, the material formerly discussed in Critical Thinking/Listening boxes has been integrated into the basal text.

Marginal Notes on Developing Strategies and Using Technology

The Developing Strategies and Using Technology marginal notes of earlier editions have been removed from the margins. The Strategy notes from the previous edition (and new ones) have been grouped together as the last public speaking exercise—called "What Do You Say?"—at the end of each chapter. The best of the Technology notes (as well as new ones) have been integrated into the basal text.

Essential Terms

The vocabulary quizzes have been replaced by a more comprehensive list of key terms along with the pages on which they are introduced and defined. In addition, and new to this edition, a glossary is included at the end of the text.

Speeches

New speeches and speech excerpts have been integrated into this edition. Among these new speeches are a student informative speech on social entrepreneurship (Chapter 8), a student persuasive speech on false confessions (Chapter 9), and a professor/poet's inspirational speech (Chapter 12). In addition, a variety of new speech excerpts appear throughout the text to illustrate the varied principles of public speaking.

Public Speaking Sample Assistants

The major speeches and outlines included in this text now appear throughout the chapters (rather than at the ends of chapters) in Public Speaking Sample Assistant boxes. These sample speeches are essential parts of the text and provide further illustration of effective (and in two cases ineffective) public speaking.

Chapter-by-Chapter Changes

Each of the chapters has been revised to achieve greater clarity, to include materials instructors using the text requested, and to incorporate new research and updated examples. Here are some of the major changes.

Chapter 1

"Introducing Public Speaking" is now devoted entirely to introducing public speaking and managing apprehension. Changes include:

- Streamlined discussion of the benefits of public speaking.
- New diagram of the public speaking process.
- Clarification of immediate and secondary audiences.
- Consideration of both trait and state apprehension and a discussion of cognitive reappraisal as a method for reducing apprehension.
- More thorough introduction of research and ethics.
- Discussion of plagiarism, giving it added importance right at the start.

Chapter 2

"Preparing and Presenting a Public Speech (in Brief)" is now devoted entirely to the presentation of the 10 steps in public speaking (in brief) so that students can begin speaking early in the semester and so that they can see the entire public speaking process

as a whole. This helps students to see how the individual pieces fit together when they're presented in more detail later in the text. Among the changes in this chapter are:

- A new self-test on public speaking to help identify some popular myths about speaking in public.
- A variety of new speech excerpts.

Chapter 3

"Listening and Criticism": Changes include:

- A new self-test on listening.
- More extensive discussion of empathy and of the distinction between thinking and feeling empathy.

Chapter 4

"Selecting Your Topic, Purpose, and Thesis" has been totally revised and now includes:

- Thorough discussion of what makes a good topic.
- New sections on "yourself" and on the online topic generator as sources of speech topics.
- Clarification of the specific purpose and how it should be constructed as well as a more extended discussion of the thesis and how these two concepts differ.

Chapter 5

"Analyzing and Adapting to Your Audience" now includes:

- Clarification of how audience age influences topic appropriateness.
- A new section on polling websites.
- A new self-test on how well you know your audience.
- Clarification of the roles played by attitudes, beliefs, and values.
- Expanded discussion of the psychology of the audience to include homogeneity and heterogeneity.

Chapter 6

"Using Supporting Materials and Presentation Aids" changes include:

- Discussion of analogies as supporting material.
- Use of a series of definitions as forms of supporting material.
- A new slide-show (PowerPoint) speech.

Chapter 7

"Organizing Your Speech" now includes:

- A new preparation outline.
- A new delivery outline.
- New and contemporary speech excerpts to illustrate ways to introduce and conclude a speech.

Chapter 8

"Wording Your Speech": Changes include:

- A new and excellent informative speech.
- Discussions of fallacies of language and figures of speech integrated into the text.
- A self-test on distinguishing facts and inferences.

Chapter 9

"Presenting Your Speech": Changes include:

- A new and excellent persuasive speech.
- New sections on speaking impromptu and speaking from manuscript.
- A new exercise on checking your pronunciation.
- A new self-test, "How Powerful Is Your Presentation Style?"

Chapter 10

"Informing Your Audience": Changes include:

- A new section on the goals of informative speaking.
- Discussion of speeches of description, definition, and demonstration in terms of their theses, main points, supporting materials, and organization.
- An extensive table on oral source citation, presented in conjunction with the Research Link on integrating and citing sources.

Chapter 11

"Persuading Your Audience" now includes:

- A new section on cultural sensitivity as a principle of persuasion (covering the five major cultural dimensions).
- Discussions of fallacies of pseudo-argument and personal attacks, now integrated into the text.

Chapter 12

"Speaking on Special Occasions": Changes include:

- A revised section on presenting the group's thinking.
- A new inspirational speech given by Nikki Giovanni after the mass killings at Virginia Tech University.

Ancillaries/Supplementary Materials

To learn more about our supplements and view sample materials, please visit www.mycoursetoolbox.com. Contact your Pearson representative for an access code to download instructor print supplements and for ordering information about all of these supplements.

Instructor Supplements

Print Supplements

- **Classroom Kit, Volumes I and II**, by Jim Benjamin, University of Toledo, Jacqueline Layng, University of Toledo, and Paul Porter, Indiana University–Purdue University Indianapolis. Our unparalleled Classroom Kit includes every instruction aid a public speaking professor needs to manage the classroom. We have made our resources even easier to use by placing all of our book-specific print supplements in two convenient volumes and electronic copies of many key resources on one CD-ROM, available separately. Organized by chapter, each volume contains an Instructor's Manual, Test Bank, and slides from *The Essential Elements of Public Speaking* PowerPoint Presentation. Electronic versions of the Instructor's Manual, Test Bank, PowerPoint, images from the text, and select video clips—all searchable by key terms—are made easily accessible to instructors on the accompanying Classroom Kit CD-ROM. The Instructor's Manual provides suggestions for constructing the course syllabus as well as chapter-by-chapter summaries, objectives, detailed outlines, discussion questions, and sample exercises and activities. The Test Bank includes more than 1,500 test questions including multiple choice, true/false, short answer, and in-depth essay formats. Each question's difficulty is rated on a scale of 1 to 3, making question selection easy. Answers for each question are given along with the page number where they can be found within the book.

- **A Guide for New Public Speaking Teachers: Building toward Success, 3/e**, by Calvin L. Troup, Duquesne University. This guide is designed to help new teachers prepare their introductory public speaking course effectively by covering such topics as preparation for the term, planning and structuring the course, evaluating speeches, using the textbook, and integrating technology into the classroom. The third edition includes a brief guide on teaching students for whom English is a second language.

- **Allyn & Bacon Public Speaking Transparency Package** This set of transparencies, produced using PowerPoint, includes 100 full-color transparencies that provide visual support for classroom lectures and discussions.
- **Great Ideas for Teaching Speech (GIFTS), 3/e,** by Raymond Zeuschner, California Polytechnic State University. This instructional booklet provides descriptions of and guidelines for assignments successfully used by experienced public speaking instructors in their classrooms.

Electronic Supplements

- **MySpeechLab** Where students learn to speak with confidence! MySpeechLab is an interactive and instructive online solution for introductory public speaking. Designed to be used as a supplement to a traditional lecture course, or completely administer an online course, MySpeechLab combines multimedia, video, speech preparation activities, research support, tests, and quizzes to make teaching and learning fun! Students benefit from a wealth of video clips that include student and professional speeches with running commentary, questions to consider, and helpful tips—all geared to help students learn to speak with confidence. Visit www.myspeechlab.com (access code required).
- **Classroom Kit CD-ROM** This exciting new supplement for instructors brings together electronic copies of the Instructor's Manual, the Test Bank, the PowerPoint presentation, images from the text, and select video clips for easy instructor access. This CD-ROM is organized by chapter and is searchable by key term.
- **VideoWorkshop for Public Speaking Version 2.0,** by Tasha Van Horn of Citrus College and Marilyn Reineck of Concordia University, St. Paul. *VideoWorkshop for Public Speaking* is more than just video footage you can watch. It's a total learning system. Our complete program includes quality video footage on an easy-to-use dual platform CD-ROM plus a Student Learning Guide. The result? A program that brings textbook concepts to life with ease that helps your students understand, analyze, and apply the objectives of the course.
- **Communication Digital Media Archive, Version 3.0** The Digital Media Archive CD-ROM contains electronic images of charts, graphs, maps, tables, and figures, along with media elements such as video, audio clips, and related Web links. These media assets are fully customizable to use with our pre-formatted PowerPoint outlines or to import into an instructor's own lectures. Available in Windows and Mac formats.
- **TestGen EQ: Computerized Test Bank** The user-friendly interface enables instructors to view, edit, and add questions, transfer questions into tests, and print tests in a variety of fonts. Search and sort features allow instructors to locate questions quickly and arrange them in preferred order. Available on the Web at www.ablongman.com/irc (access code required).
- **PowerPoint Presentation Package for *The Essential Elements of Public Speaking*, 3/e** by Paul Porter, Indiana University–Purdue University Indianapolis. This text-specific package consists of a collection of lecture outlines and graphic images keyed to every chapter in the text. Available on the Web at www.ablongman.com/irc.
- **Allyn & Bacon PowerPoint Presentation for Public Speaking** This course-specific PowerPoint outline adds visual punch to public speaking lectures with colorful screen designs and clip art. Our expanded Public Speaking PowerPoint package includes 125 slides and a brief User's Guide. Available on the Web at www.ablongman.com/irc.
- **A&B Classic and Contemporary Speeches DVD** This exciting supplement includes over 120 minutes of video footage in an easy-to-use DVD format. Each speech is accompanied by a biographical and historical summary that helps students understand the context and motivation behind each speech. Speakers featured include Martin Luther King Jr., John F. Kennedy, Richard Nixon, the Dalai Lama, Barbara Jordan, and Christopher Reeve.
- **A&B Public Speaking Video Library** Allyn & Bacon's Public Speaking Video Library contains a range of videos from which adopters can choose. The videos feature different types of speeches delivered on a multitude of topics, allowing you to choose the speeches best suited for your students. Please contact your Pearson representative for details and a complete list of videos and their contents to choose which would be most useful to you in your class. You can also go to www.mycoursetoolbox.com to view descriptions and tables of contents of all of our available public speaking videos.

- **Lecture Questions for Clickers,** by William Keith, University of Wisconsin-Milwaukee. An assortment of questions and activities covering a multitude of public speaking topics are presented in PowerPoint. These slides will help liven up your lectures and can be used along with the Personal Response System to get students more involved in the material. Available on the Web at www.ablongman.com/irc.

Student Supplements
Print Supplements

- **The Interviewing Guidebook**, by Joseph A. DeVito, focuses on the skills needed for the information-gathering and the employment interview (along with the job résumé and the letters that are a part of the interview process). Preparation worksheets, exercises, guides to online help, and scenarios for applying these skills make this brief and user-friendly text an extremely practical supplement to any communication course.

- **Preparing Visual Aids for Presentations, 4/e,** by Dan Cavanaugh. This visual booklet provides ideas to improve presentations, including suggestions for planning a presentation, guidelines for designing visual aids, storyboarding, and a PowerPoint presentation walk-through.

- **ResearchNavigator.com Guide: Speech Communication** This updated booklet, by Steven L. Epstein of Suffolk County Community College, includes tips, resources, and URLs to aid students conducting research on Pearson Education's research website, www.researchnavigator.com. The guide contains a student access code for the Research Navigator database, offering students unlimited access to a collection of more than 25,000 discipline-specific articles from top-tier academic publications and peer-reviewed journals, as well as the *New York Times* and popular news publications. The guide introduces students to the basics of the Internet and the World Wide Web, and includes tips for searching for articles on the site, and a list of journals useful for research in their discipline. Also included are hundreds of Web resources for the discipline, as well as information on how to correctly cite research.

- **Public Speaking in the Multicultural Environment, 2/e,** by Devorah A. Lieberman, Portland State University. This booklet helps students learn to analyze cultural diversity within their audiences and adapt their presentations accordingly.

- **Multicultural Activities Workbook,** by Marlene C. Cohen and Susan L. Richardson, both of Prince George's Community College, Maryland. This workbook is filled with hands-on activities that help broaden the content of speech classes to reflect the diverse cultural backgrounds of the class and society. The book includes checklists, surveys, and writing assignments that all help students succeed in speech communication by offering experiences that address a variety of learning styles.

- **Speech Preparation Workbook,** by Jennifer Dreyer and Gregory H. Patton, San Diego State University. This workbook takes students through the various stages of speech creation—from audience analysis to writing the speech—and provides supplementary assignments and tear-out forms.

- **The Speech Outline: Outlining to Plan, Organize, and Deliver a Speech: Activities and Exercises,** by Reeze L. Hanson and Sharon Condon of Haskell Indian Nations University. This brief workbook includes activities, exercises, and answers to help students develop and master the critical skill of outlining.

- **The Speech Preparation Workbook,** by Suzanne Osborn of the University of Memphis contains forms to help students prepare a self-introductory speech, analyze the audience, select a topic, conduct research, organize supporting materials, and outline speeches.

- **Brainstorms,** by Joseph A. DeVito. This is a guide to thinking more creatively about communication, or anything else. Students will find 19 practical, easy-to-use creative thinking techniques along with insights into the creative thinking process.

- **Study Card for Public Speaking** Colorful, affordable, and packed with useful information, Allyn & Bacon's Study Cards make studying easier, more efficient, and more enjoyable. Course information is distilled down to the basics, helping you quickly master the fundamentals, review a subject for understanding, or prepare for an exam. Because they're laminated for durability, you can keep these Study Cards for years to come and pull them out whenever you need a quick review.

Electronic Supplements

◆ **MySpeechLab** Where students learn to speak with confidence! MySpeechLab is an interactive and instructive online solution for introductory public speaking. Designed to be used as a supplement to a traditional lecture course, or completely administer an online course, MySpeechLab combines multimedia, video, speech preparation activities, research support, tests, and quizzes to make teaching and learning fun! Students benefit from a wealth of video clips that include student and professional speeches with running commentary, questions to consider, and helpful tips—all geared to help students learn to speak with confidence. Visit www.myspeechlab.com (access code required).

◆ **VideoWorkshop for Public Speaking Version 2.0** by Tasha Van Horn of Citrus College and Marilyn Reineck of Concordia University, St. Paul. VideoWorkshop for Public Speaking is more than just video footage you can watch. It's a total learning system. Our complete program includes quality video footage on an easy-to-use dual platform CD-ROM plus a Student Learning Guide. The result? A program that brings textbook concepts to life with ease that helps your students understand, analyze, and apply the objectives of the course.

◆ **News Resources for Speech Communication Access Code Card** News Resources for Speech Communication with Research Navigator is one-stop access to keep you abreast of the latest news events and for all of your research needs. Highlighted by an hourly feed of the latest news in the discipline from the *New York Times*, students will stay on the forefront of currency throughout the semester. In addition, Pearson's Research Navigator is the easiest way for students to start a research assignment or research paper. Complete with extensive help on the research process and four exclusive databases of credible and reliable source material including the EBSCO Academic Journal and Abstract Database, *New York Times* Search by Subject Archive, and *Financial Times* Article Archive and Company Financials, Research Navigator helps students quickly and efficiently make the most of their research time.

◆ **Speech Writer's Workshop CD-ROM, Version 2.0** This speechwriting software includes a Speech Handbook with tips for researching and preparing speeches, a Speech Workshop which guides students step-by-step through the speech writing-process, a Topics Dictionary which gives students hundreds of ideas for speeches, and the Documentor citation database that helps them to format bibliographic entries in either MLA or APA style.

◆ **Public Speaking Website** This open access website contains six modules students can use along with their public speaking text to learn about the process of public speaking and help prepare for speeches. Features focus on the five steps of speech preparation: (1) Assess Your Speechmaking Situation, (2) Analyze Your Audience, (3) Research Your Topic, (4) Organize and Write Your Speech, and (5) Deliver Your Presentation, as well as Discern Other Talks. Interactive activities aid in speech preparation. Notes from the Instructor provide additional details on selected topics. Visit www.ablongman.com/pubspeak.

◆ **Public Speaking Study Site** This course-specific website features public speaking study materials for students, including flashcards and a complete set of practice tests for all major topics. Students also will find Web links to sites with speeches in texts, audio, and video formats, as well as links to other valuable sites. Visit www.abpublicspeaking.com.

◆ **ResearchNavigator.com Guide: Speech Communication** This updated booklet, by Steven L. Epstein of Suffolk County Community College, includes tips, resources, and URLs to aid students conducting research on Pearson Education's research website, www.researchnavigator.com. The guide contains a student access code for the Research Navigator database, offering students unlimited access to a collection of more than 25,000 discipline-specific articles from top-tier academic publications and peer-reviewed journals, as well as the *New York Times* and popular news publications. The guide introduces students to the basics of the Internet and the World Wide Web, and includes tips for searching for articles on the site, and a list of journals useful for research in their discipline. Also included are hundreds of Web resources for the discipline, as well as information on how to correctly cite research. The guide is available packaged with new copies of the text.

◆ **VideoLab CD-ROM** This interactive study tool for students can be used independently or in class. It provides digital video of student speeches that can be viewed in conjunction with corresponding outlines, manuscripts, notecards, and instructor critiques. A series of drills to help students analyze content and delivery follows each speech.

Acknowledgments

I want to thank the many people who contributed to the development of the text you now hold. Thank you Karon Bowers, editor; Hilary Jackson, developmental editor; Jessica Cabana, editorial assistant; Suzan Czajkowski, marketing manager; Poyee Oster, photo researcher; Jay Howland, copy editor; and Tom Conville, project manager. All helped tremendously at all stages of the development and production of this book.

I also want to thank the reviewers of the previous editions who shared their experiences and insights with me. Their suggestions were most helpful and most appreciated. Thank you, Bruce Ardinger, Columbus State Community College; Robert Arend, Miramer College; Valerie Belew, Nashville State; Ellen R. Cohn, University of Pittsburgh; John R. Foster, Northwestern State University; Fred Garbowitz, Grand Rapids Community College; Victoria Leonard, College of the Canyons; Ken Sherwood, Los Angeles City College; Anita Tate, Weatherford College; Chérie C. White, Muskingum Area Technical College; Emma Gray, Portland State University; Audra L. McMullen, Towson University; Kimberly Kilpatrick, University of Texas, El Paso; Amanda Brown, University of Wisconsin, Stout; and Robert W. Wawee, The University of Houston–Downtown.

Introducing Public Speaking

Why Read This Chapter?

Because it introduces one of the most practical and empowering subjects you will study in your entire college career and will help you to:

- understand some of the personal, social, academic, and career benefits you'll get from studying public speaking

- understand the elements involved in this unique kind of communication

- manage your stage fright by mastering techniques to help you feel more comfortable giving a speech in front of an audience

There are only two types of speakers in the world: 1. the nervous and 2. liars.

—Samuel Langhorne Clemens (1835–1910)
Better known as Mark Twain, American humorist and lecturer, most famous for his *Huckleberry Finn* **and** *Tom Sawyer*

Public speaking is one of the essential skills you'll need to function effectively in today's society. The higher up you go in the world's hierarchy—say, from intern, to junior analyst, to manager, to CEO—the more important public speaking becomes. This text explains these essential skills, the skills you'll need to prepare and present effective public speeches. And, as you'll see throughout this text, these skills will also prove useful to you in a variety of other situations as well.

Although public speaking principles were probably developed soon after our species began to talk, it was in ancient Greece and Rome that our Western tradition of public speaking got its start. This Greco-Roman tradition has been enriched by the experiments, surveys, field studies, and historical studies that have been done since classical times and that continue to be done today.

Aristotle's *Rhetoric*, written some 2,300 years ago in ancient Greece, was one of the earliest systematic studies of public speaking. It was in this work that the three kinds of persuasive appeals—logos (or logical proof), pathos (emotional appeals), and ethos (appeals based on the character of the speaker)—were introduced. This three-part division of **rhetoric** is still followed today; Chapter 11 discusses these in more detail.

Roman rhetoricians added to the work of the Greeks. Quintilian, who taught in Rome during the first century, built an entire educational system—from the schooling of children through study in adulthood—based on the development of the effective and responsible orator. Over the following 2,000 years, the study of public speaking continued to grow and develop.

Contemporary public speaking—the kind discussed in this text—builds on this classical heritage but also incorporates insights from the humanities, the social and behavioral sciences, and computer science and information technology. Likewise, perspectives from different cultures are being integrated into our present study of public speaking. Table 1.1 shows some of the fields that contribute to contemporary public speaking and illustrates the wide research and theory base from which the principles of this discipline are drawn.

This brief introductory chapter discusses the benefits you'll derive from studying public speaking; the essential elements of every speech; and, what is probably your number one concern, how to manage the very normal fear of speaking in public.

THE BENEFITS OF PUBLIC SPEAKING

Fair questions to ask of any course or textbook are "What will I get out of this?" and "How will the effort and time I put into this class and this textbook benefit me?" Here are just a few of the benefits you'll derive from this text and from your course work in public speaking.

IMPROVE YOUR PERSONAL AND SOCIAL ABILITIES

Public speaking provides training in a variety of personal and social competencies. For example, in this text and in this course you'll learn to manage your fear of communication situations, develop greater self-confidence and self-presentation skills, enhance your own personal and interpersonal power and influence, and regulate and adapt your listening to the specific situation.

TABLE 1.1 Growth and Development of Public Speaking

Here are just a few of the academic roots of public speaking and some of the contributions made by these disciplines.

ACADEMIC ROOTS	CONTRIBUTIONS TO CONTEMPORARY PUBLIC SPEAKING
Classical rhetoric	Emphasis on substance; ethical responsibilities of the speaker; use of a combination of logical, ethical, and emotional appeals; the strategies of organization
Literary and rhetorical criticism	Approaches to and standards for evaluation; insights into style and language
Philosophy	Emphasis on the logical validity of arguments; continuing contribution to ethics
Public address	Insights into how famous speakers dealt with varied purposes and audiences to achieve desired effects
Psychology	Knowledge of how language is made easier to understand and remember; principles of attitude and behavior change; emphasis on speech effects
General Semantics	Emphasis on using language to describe reality accurately; techniques for avoiding common thinking errors that faulty language usage creates
Communication theory	Insights on information transmission; the importance of viewing the whole of the communication act; the understanding of such concepts as feedback, noise, channel, and message
Computer science and information technology	Creation of the virtual audience; design, outlining, and presentation software; search tools for research; easily accessed databases
Interpersonal communication	Transactionalism; emphasis on mutual influence of speaker and audience
Sociology	Data on audiences' attitudes, values, opinions, and beliefs and how these influence exposure to and responses to messages
Anthropology	Insights into the attitudes, beliefs, and values of different cultures and how these influence communication in general and public speaking in particular

IMPROVE YOUR ACADEMIC AND CAREER SKILLS

As you learn public speaking, you'll also learn a wide variety of academic and career skills, many of which are largely communication skills (as you can tell from reading the employment ads, especially for middle management positions in just about every field you can name). For example, you will learn to:

- conduct research efficiently and effectively, using the latest and the best techniques available
- critically analyze and evaluate arguments and evidence from any and all sources
- understand human motivation and make effective use of your insights in persuasive encounters and at the same time
- develop an effective communication style (whether for conversation or for that important job interview) that you feel comfortable with
- give criticism—and respond appropriately to criticism, to increase your insight into your own strengths and weaknesses
- communicate your competence, character, and charisma so as to make yourself believable

IMPROVE YOUR PUBLIC SPEAKING ABILITIES

Speakers aren't born; they're made. Through instruction, exposure to different speeches, experience with diverse audiences, feedback on your own speeches, and individual learning experiences, you can become an effective speaker. Regardless of your present level of competence, you can improve through proper training—hence this course and this book.

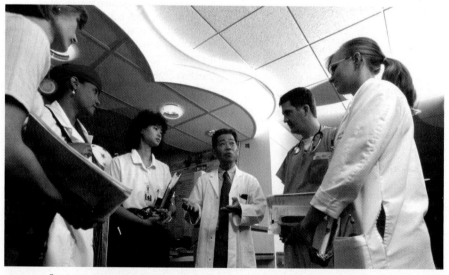

Consider the benefits of public speaking to someone in the profession you're preparing to enter. What types of public speeches are you most likely to give during your professional career (formal, informal, informative, persuasive, special occasion)?

At the end of this course, you'll be a more competent, confident, and effective public speaker. You'll also be a more effective listener—more open yet more critical, more empathic yet more discriminating. And you'll emerge a more competent and discerning critic of public communication. You'll learn to organize and explain complex concepts and processes clearly and effectively to a wide variety of listeners. You'll learn to support an argument with all the available means of persuasion and to present a persuasive appeal to audiences of varied types.

As a leader (and in many ways you can look at this course as training in leadership skills) you'll need the skills of effective communication to help preserve a free and open society. As a speaker who wants your message understood and accepted, as a listener who needs to evaluate and critically analyze ideas and arguments before making decisions, and as a critic who needs to evaluate and judge the thousands of public communications you hear every day, you will draw on the skills you'll learn in this course.

THE ESSENTIAL ELEMENTS OF PUBLIC SPEAKING

In **public speaking** a *speaker presents a relatively continuous message to a relatively large audience in a unique context* (see Figure 1.1). Like all communication, public speaking is a transactional process, a process whose elements are *inter*dependent (Watzlawick, 1978; Watzlawick, Beavin, & Jackson, 1967). In other words, each element in the public speaking process depends on and interacts with all other

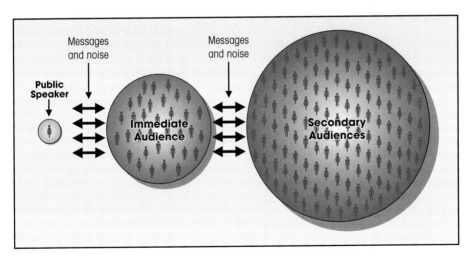

Figure 1.1

The Basic Elements of Public Speaking

This diagram is designed to illustrate the interplay of elements in the public speaking process and to emphasize that there are a variety of audiences of public speaking: (1) the immediate audience that hears the speaker as he or she is speaking, whether in person, on television, via the Internet, or even via cell phone, and (2) the additional audiences that get the material secondhand; for example, they read the speech, read about the speech, or hear from those who heard the speech or from those who heard about the speech from immediate audience members or from those who heard about the speech from those who heard about the speech.

elements. For example, the way in which you organize a speech will depend on such factors as your speech topic, your audience, the purpose you hope to achieve, and a host of other variables—all of which are explained in the remainder of this chapter and in the chapters to follow.

Especially important to appreciate is the mutual interaction and influence between speaker and audience. True, when you give a public speech you do most of the speaking and the audience does most of the listening. The audience, however, also sends messages in the form of feedback—such as applause, bored looks, nods of agreement or disagreement, or attentive glances. The audience also influences how you'll prepare and present your speech. It influences your arguments, language, method of organization, and every other choice you make. You would not, for example, present the same speech on saving money to high school students as you would to senior citizens.

Let's now consider the eight essential elements of public speaking: speaker, message, channels, noise, audience, context, presentation, and ethics.

SPEAKER

In conversation the speaker's role occurs in short spurts; Pat says something to which Chris replies to which Pat responds and so on. In public speaking you deliver a relatively long speech and usually are not interrupted. As the public **speaker** you're the center of the transaction; you and your speech are the reason for the gathering.

MESSAGE

Messages conveyed in public speaking include both verbal and nonverbal signals. In both conversation and public speaking, your message has a **purpose**. For example, in conversation you might want to tell a friend about what happened at a recent basketball game. In this case your purpose would be to inform. Or you might want to convince a coworker to switch vacation schedules with you. Here your purpose would be to persuade. And in public speaking, too, you communicate with a purpose.

Generally in conversation you don't give any real thought to how you're going to organize your message. In public speaking, however, organization is crucial, because it adds clarity to your message and therefore makes it easier for listeners to understand and to remember what you're saying.

In conversation you vary your language on the basis of the person with whom you're speaking, the topic you're talking about, and where you are. When talking with children, for example, you might use easier words and shorter sentences than you would with classmates. In public speaking you also adjust your language to your audience, the topic, and the situation.

In conversation the messages you send are essentially composed at the moment of utterance; you don't research them. In public speaking it's very different. Research is essential to the public speech and to any subject you might study. Because of this, Research Link boxes appear throughout the text and cover different aspects of conducting research. If you prefer, you can read all these boxes in sequence. Whether you read these boxes all at once or as they appear in the text, by the time you finish this text, you should know how to

Research Link

RESEARCH TIME MANAGEMENT

Because a great deal of your time—in this course and in numerous others—will be spent on research, learn to use your research time efficiently. Here are a few suggestions:

Multitask. Combine your research tasks and do them simultaneously. For example, when going to the library or logging on to the Internet, have more than one task in mind. If you know the topics of your next few speeches, or if you're writing a sociology paper on a related topic, do the research for both at the same time.

Watch detours. When you are searching the Net, it's easy to get lured into taking long detours. These are often excellent learning experiences and are not necessarily detrimental. For purposes of time management, however, it will help if you keep your purpose clearly in mind—even to the point of writing it down—as you surf the Net or lurk among chat groups.

Access your library from home. If possible, access your college library's online catalog of books from home; it will save you time if you can go to the library with your searches already completed. If your library subscribes to full text databases that can be accessed from your home computer (ProQuest and Lexis-Nexis are popular examples), you may be able to do all your research from the comfort of your home.

Consult your librarian. One useful but often overlooked suggestion is to consult your librarian. Librarians are experts in the very researching issues that may be giving you trouble. They'll be able to help you access biographical material, indexes of current articles, materials in specialized collections at other libraries, and a wide variety of computerized databases.

Take accurate research notes. The more accurate your notes are, the less time you'll waste going back to sources to check on a date or a spelling. Be sure to record the source of the material in detail—so that you can find that reference again should you need it and so that you can reference it in your speech outline. When you use material from the Web, be sure to print out or save the Web page, noting the URL and the date you accessed this site. In this way, you'll be able to cite a source even if the Web page disappears, a not unlikely possibility.

Organize your materials. Because you can access and print so much information so easily, you profit from organizing your materials as you collect them. If you want to collect your material on paper, loose-leaf notebooks or simple manila folders work well to keep everything relating to a speech or article in the same place and yet conveniently subdivided. If you want to file your material electronically, create a general folder (for the general topic) and subfolders (for specific topics) as you need them. This will work especially well if you can scan into your folder material you find in hard copy.

The next Research Link, "Libraries and Bookstores," appears on page 28.

research a wide variety of topics, locate reliable and current information, and evaluate the accuracy of a variety of sources. The first of these boxes appears above and provides some hints for researching efficiently. Research is a lot more enjoyable when it's done easily and without wasted time.

CHANNELS

The **channel** is the medium that carries message signals from sender to receiver. Both auditory and visual channels are significant in public speaking. Through the auditory channel you send spoken messages—your words and your sentences. Through the visual channel—eye contact (or the lack of it), body movement, hand and facial gestures, and clothing—you send visual messages. Increasingly, public speaking is mediated; public speeches are frequently delivered in a television studio and heard by millions in their own living rooms. Similarly, speeches may be digitally recorded and made available day and night to millions of Internet users. Politicians and business leaders currently post their speeches on websites, blogs, and newsgroups, and as video and sound capabilities become more universal, such speeches are likely to increase in frequency.

Noise

Noise is anything that distorts the message and prevents the listeners from receiving your message as you intended it to be received. It's revealing to distinguish noise from "signal." In this context the term *signal* refers to information that is useful to you, information that you want. Noise, on the other hand, is what you find useless; it's what you do not want. So, for example, an e-mail list or electronic newsgroup that contained lots of useful information would be high on signal and low on noise; if it contained lots of useless information, it would be high on noise and low on signal. Spam is high on noise and low on signal, as is static on the radio, television, or telephone. Noise may be physical (others talking loudly, cars honking, illegible handwriting, "garbage" on your computer screen), physiological (hearing or visual impairment, articulation disorders), psychological (preconceived ideas, wandering thoughts), or semantic (misunderstood meanings).

Public speaking involves visual as well as spoken messages, so it's important to realize that noise also may be visual. Sunglasses that concealed the nonverbal messages from your eyes would be considered noise, as would dark print on a dark background in your slides.

All public speaking situations involve noise. You won't be able to totally eliminate noise, but you can try to reduce its effects. Making your language more precise, organizing your thoughts more logically, and reinforcing your ideas with visual aids are some ways to combat the influence of noise.

Audience

In conversation the "audience" is often one listener or perhaps a few. The **audience** in public speaking is relatively "large," ranging from groups of perhaps 10 or 12 to hundreds of thousands, even millions.

As illustrated in Figure 1.1 and its caption, there is more than one audience. Recognizing that both immediate and secondary audiences exist is crucial to understanding the influence of public speaking throughout history as well as in any specific public speaking situation you might name. Abraham Lincoln's Gettysburg Address was presented to a relatively small audience, but it had influence far beyond that audience and that specific time. The same is true of many speeches; for example, Martin Luther King Jr.'s "I have a dream" speech, presented to thousands, has now influenced millions. The same is true, though on a smaller scale, with all speeches, including those you'll present in this class. When you address 20 or 30 students in class, that's 20 or 30 people who might relay your message or arguments to others and these people may continue the process. As you grow in influence and in public speaking competence, so will your influence on both immediate and secondary audiences.

In some public speaking situations—say, when you're addressing work colleagues—you may know your audience quite well. In other situations, however, you will not know your audience quite so well and will have to analyze them: to discover what they already know (so you don't repeat old news), to learn what their attitudes are (so you don't waste time persuading them of something they already believe), and so on.

But public speaking isn't just the art of adjusting messages to listeners; it also incorporates active involvement by the listeners. The listener plays a role in encouraging or discouraging the speaker, in offering constructive criticism, in evaluating public messages, and in performing a wide variety of other functions. Because listening and criticism are so important (and so often neglected), they are covered in some detail in Chapter 3.

CONTEXT

Speaker and listeners operate in a physical, sociopsychological, temporal, and cultural **context.** The context influences you as the speaker, the audience, the speech, and the effects of the speech. The *physical context* is the actual place in which you give your speech (the room, hallway, park, or auditorium). A presentation in a small intimate room needs to be very different from an address in a sports arena.

The *sociopsychological context* includes, for example, the relationship between speaker and audience: Is a supervisor speaking to workers or a worker speaking to supervisors? A principal addressing teachers or a parent addressing principals? This sociopsychological context also includes the audience's attitudes toward and knowledge of you and your subject. A speech endeavoring to influence a supportive audience will employ very different strategies than would a speech delivered to a hostile audience.

The *temporal context* includes factors such as the time of day and, more importantly, where your speech fits into the sequence of events. For example, does your speech follow another presentation that has taken an opposing position? Is your speech the sixth in a series exploring the same topic?

The *cultural context* has to do with the beliefs, lifestyles, values, and behaviors that the speaker and the audience bring with them and that bear on the topic and purpose of the speech. Appealing to "competitive spirit" and "financial gain" may prove effective with Wall Street executives but ineffective with people who are more comfortable with socialist or communist economic systems and beliefs.

PRESENTATION

In conversation you normally don't think of how you'd deliver or present your message; you don't concern yourself with how to stand or gesture or how to raise or lower your vocal volume. In public speaking, however, the situation is different. Because public speaking is a relatively new experience and you'll probably feel uncomfortable and self-conscious at first, you may wonder what to do with your hands or whether you should move about. With time and

Consider the attributes or qualities of the ethical speaker. How you would define the ethical speaker? How would you define the unethical speaker?

experience, you'll find that your **presentation** will follow naturally from what you're saying, just as it does in conversation. Perhaps the best advice at this point is to view public speaking as "enlarged conversation" and not to worry about delivery just yet. In your early efforts it's better to concentrate on content; as you gain confidence, you can direct your attention to refining and polishing your presentation skills.

ETHICS

Because your speech will have an effect on your audience, you have an obligation to consider **ethics**—issues of right and wrong, or the moral implication of your message. When you develop your topic, present your research, create persuasive appeals, and do any of the other tasks related to public speaking there are ethical issues to be considered (Bok, 1978; Jaksa & Pritchard, 1994; Johannesen, 1996; Thompson, 2000). You also have ethical obligations in your roles as listener and as critic.

Because ethics is so interwoven with your personal philosophy of life and the culture in which you were raised, it's difficult to propose general guidelines for specific individuals. Nevertheless, ethical responsibilities need to be considered as integral to any communication act. The decisions you make concerning communication must be guided by what you consider right as well as by what you consider effective.

In thinking about the ethics of communication and about the many ethical issues raised throughout this text, you can take the position that ethics is objective or that it's subjective. In an *objective view* you'd claim that the morality of an act—say, a communication message—is absolute and exists apart from the values or beliefs of any individual or culture. This objective view holds that there are standards that apply to all people in all situations at all times. If lying, advertising falsely, using illegally obtained evidence, and revealing secrets, for example, are considered unethical, then they'll be considered unethical regardless of the circumstances surrounding them or of the values and beliefs of the culture in which they occur.

In a *subjective view* you'd claim that the morality of an act depends on the culture's values and beliefs as well as on the particular circumstances. Thus, from a subjective position you would claim that the end might justify the means—a good result can justify the use of unethical means to achieve that result. For example, you might argue that lying is wrong to win votes or sell cigarettes, but that lying can be ethical if the end result is positive (such as trying to make someone who is unattractive feel better by telling them they look great, or telling a critically ill person that they'll feel better soon).

Because of the central importance of ethics in public speaking, each chapter contains an A Case of Ethics box. This first box, longer than the others, deals with the issue of plagiarism and explains in some detail the nature of plagiarism, why it's unacceptable, and how you can avoid even the suspicion of plagiarism.

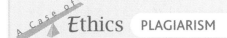
A Case of **Ethics**   PLAGIARISM

WHAT IS PLAGIARISM?

The word *plagiarism* refers to the process of passing off the work (ideas, words, illustrations) of others as your own. Understand that plagiarism is not the act of using another's ideas—we all do that. It is using another's ideas without acknowledging that they are the ideas of this other person; it is passing off the ideas as if they were yours.

Plagiarism exists on a continuum, ranging from representing as your own an entire term paper or speech written by someone else to using a quotation or research finding without citing the author. Plagiarism also can include getting help from a friend without acknowledging this assistance.

In some cultures—especially collectivist cultures (cultures that emphasize the group and mutual cooperation, such as Korea, Japan, and China)—teamwork is strongly encouraged. Students are encouraged to help other students with their work. In the United States and in many other individualist cultures (cultures that emphasize individuality and competitiveness), teamwork without acknowledgment is considered plagiarism.

In U.S. colleges and universities, plagiarism is a serious violation of the rules of academic honesty and can bring serious penalties, sometimes even expulsion. And it's interesting to note that instructors are mobilizing and are educating themselves in techniques for detecting plagiarism. Further, as with all crimes, ignorance of the law is not an acceptable defense against charges of plagiarism. This last point is especially important, because many people plagiarize through a lack of information as to what does and what does not constitute plagiarism.

WHY IS PLAGIARISM UNACCEPTABLE?

Here are just a few reasons why plagiarism is wrong.

- *Plagiarism is a violation of another's intellectual property rights. Much as it would be unfair to take another person's watch without permission, it's unfair to take another person's ideas without acknowledging that you did it.*

(continued)

- *You're in college to develop your own ideas and your own ways of expressing them; plagiarism defeats this fundamental purpose.*
- *Evaluations (everything from grades in school to promotions in the workplace) assume that what you present as your work is in fact your work.*

HOW YOU CAN AVOID PLAGIARISM

A few guidelines will help you avoid plagiarism.

Let's start with the easy part. You do not have to, and should not, cite sources for common knowledge—information that is readily available in numerous sources and is not likely to be disputed. For example, the population of Thailand, the amendments to the U.S. Constitution, the actions of the United Nations, or the way the heart pumps blood all are widely available knowledge, and you would not cite the almanac or the political science text from which you got this information. On the other hand, if you were talking about the attitudes of people from Thailand or the reasons the constitutional amendments were adopted, then you would need to cite your sources, because this information is not common knowledge and may well be disputed.

For information that is not common knowledge, you need to acknowledge your source. Three simple rules will help you avoid even the suggestion of plagiarism:

1. *Acknowledge the source of any ideas you present that are not your own.* If you learned of an idea in your history course, then cite the history instructor or the textbook. If you read an idea in an article, then cite the article.
2. *Acknowledge the words of another.* It's obvious what to do when you're quoting another person exactly; then of course, you need to cite the person you're quoting. You also should cite the person even when you paraphrase his or her words, because you are still using the other person's ideas. When paraphrases need to be credited may not always be clear, so some of the plagiarism websites established by different universities include exercises and extended examples; see, for example, Indiana University's site at www.indiana.edu/~istd/examples .html or Purdue University's at http://owl.english.purdue.edu/owl/ resource/589/04/. The same is true when you use the organizational structure of another person; just say, for example, "I'm following the line of reasoning proposed by James McCroskey in his discussion of apprehension."
3. *Acknowledge help from others.* If your roommate gave you examples or ideas or helped you style your speech, acknowledge the help. For example, notice how some of the award-winning speeches that are reprinted as models in this book give credit to the speakers' speech coaches.

Ethical Choice Point *For a speech on the causes and effects of illegal immigration, you come across an obscure blog that discusses this very topic. You can easily adapt this discussion to your speech assignment and present it as your own. Would this be plagiarism? How might you use this material ethically (without even the suggestion of plagiarism)?*

CULTURE AND GENDER

As we've seen, the cultural context is an essential element of public speaking. Let's look a little more closely at culture's impact. A walk through any large city, many small towns, or just about any college campus will convince you that the United States is largely a collection of different cultures, coexisting somewhat separately but also influencing one another. As demonstrated throughout this text, cultural differences span the entire public speaking spectrum—from the way you use eye contact to the way you develop an argument or present criticism (Chang & Holt, 1996).

Culture is the collection of beliefs, attitudes, values, and ways of behaving that are shared by a group of people and passed down from one generation to the next through communication rather than through genes. Thus, the term *culture* does not refer to genetic traits such as color of skin or shape of eyes. Culture does include beliefs in a supreme being, attitudes toward family, and the values people place on friendship or money.

Even though culture is not synonymous with race or nationality, members of a particular race are often enculturated into a similar set of beliefs, attitudes, and values. Similarly, members living in the same country are often taught similar beliefs, attitudes, and values. Thus, we often speak of "Hispanic culture" or "African American culture." But lest we be guilty of stereotyping, we need to recognize that within any large culture—especially a culture based on race or nationality—there will be enormous differences. The Kansas farmer may in some ways be closer to the Chinese farmer than to the Wall Street executive. Further, as an individual born into a particular race and nationality, you don't necessarily have to adopt the attitudes, beliefs, and values that may be dominant among the people of that race and nationality.

In a similar way, **gender** can be considered a cultural variable—largely because cultures teach boys and girls different attitudes, beliefs, values, and ways of communicating and relating to one another. In other words, you act like a man or a woman in part because of what your culture has taught you about how men and women should act. This does not, of course, deny that biological differences also play a role in the differences between male and female behavior. In fact, research continues to uncover biological roots of behavior once thought entirely learned, such as happiness and shyness.

There are lots of reasons for the cultural emphasis you'll find in this book (and probably in all your textbooks). Most prevalent, perhaps, are the vast demographic changes taking place throughout the United States. Whereas at one time the United States was largely a country populated by Europeans, it's now a country greatly influenced by enormous numbers of new citizens from South and Central America, Africa, and Asia. And the same is true on college and university campuses throughout the nation. With these changes come different communication customs and the need to understand and adapt to these new ways of looking at communication generally and public speaking specifically.

The principles for communicating information and for persuasion differ from one culture to another. If you're to understand public speaking, then you need to know how its principles vary on the basis of culture. Success in public speaking—at your job and in your social life—will depend in great part on your ability to communicate effectively with persons who may have different cultural perspectives.

Now that we've considered the essential elements of public speaking, especially culture, let's turn to what is probably your major concern: fear, or what's called "communication apprehension."

MANAGING YOUR APPREHENSION

"According to most studies," says comedian Jerry Seinfeld, "people's number one fear is public speaking. Death is number two. Does that sound right? This means to the average person, if you go to a funeral, you're better off in the casket than doing the eulogy" (http://thinkexist.com/quotes, accessed February 19, 2007). Apprehension in public speaking is normal. As Mark Twain made clear in the chapter-opening quotation, everyone experiences some degree of fear in the relatively formal public speaking situation. After all, in public speaking you're the sole focus of attention and are usually being evaluated for your performance. Experiencing nervousness or anxiety is a natural reaction. You are definitely not alone in these feelings.

Some people have a general **communication apprehension** that shows itself in all communication situations. These people suffer from **trait apprehension**—a general fear of communication, regardless of the specific situation. Their fear appears in conversations, small group settings, and public speaking situations. Not surprisingly, if you have high trait apprehension, you're also more likely to experience embarrassment in a variety of social situations (Withers & Vernon, 2006). Similarly, high apprehensives are likely to have problems in the work environment; for example, they may perform badly in employment interviews and may contribute few ideas on the job (Butler, 2005).

Other people experience communication apprehension in only certain communication situations. These people suffer from **state apprehension**—a fear that is specific to a given communication situation. For example, a speaker may fear public speaking but have no difficulty in talking with two or three other people. Or a speaker may fear job interviews but have no fear of public speaking. State apprehension is extremely common. Most people experience it for some situations; not surprisingly, it is public speaking that most people fear.

Communication apprehension exists on a continuum. Some people are so apprehensive that they're unable to function effectively in any communication situation and will try to avoid communication as much as possible. Other people are so mildly apprehensive that they appear to experience no fear at all; they're the ones who actively seek out communication opportunities. Most of us are between these extremes.

Although you may at first view communication apprehension as harmful, it's not necessarily so. In fact, apprehension can work for you. Fear can energize you. It

Consider the factors that cause apprehension. What two, three, or four factors seem to contribute most to your own apprehension? What specific actions can you take to reduce the influence of these factors?

may motivate you to work a little harder—to produce a speech that will be better than it might have been had you not been fearful. Further, the audience cannot see the apprehension that you may be experiencing. Even though you may think that the audience can hear your heart beat faster, they can't. They can't see your knees tremble. They can't sense your dry throat—at least not most of the time.

You may wish to pause here and take the self-test "How Apprehensive Are You in Public Speaking?" to measure your own level of fear of public speaking.

$\mathcal{T}$EST YOURSELF

How Apprehensive Are You in Public Speaking?

This questionnaire consists of six statements concerning your feelings about public speaking. Indicate the degree to which each statement applies to you by marking whether you (1) strongly agree, (2) agree, (3) are undecided, (4) disagree, or (5) strongly disagree with each statement. There are no right or wrong answers. Don't be concerned that some of the statements are similar to others. Work quickly; just record your first impression.

_____ **1.** I have no fear of giving a speech.

_____ **2.** Certain parts of my body feel very tense and rigid while giving a speech.

_____ **3.** I feel relaxed while giving a speech.

_____ **4.** My thoughts become confused and jumbled when I am giving a speech.

_____ **5.** I face the prospect of giving a speech with confidence.

_____ **6.** While giving a speech, I get so nervous that I forget facts I really know.

HOW DID YOU DO? To obtain your public speaking apprehension score, begin with the number 18 (selected so that you won't wind up with negative numbers) and add to it the scores for items 1, 3, and 5. Then, from this total, subtract the scores from items 2, 4, and 6. A score above 18 shows some degree of apprehension. Most people score above 18, so if you scored relatively high, you're among the vast majority of people.

WHAT WILL YOU DO? As you read the suggestions for reducing apprehension in the text, consider what you can do to incorporate these into your own public speaking experiences. Consider how these suggestions might be useful in reducing apprehension more generally—for example, in social situations and in small groups and meetings. An extremely thorough discussion of communication apprehension may be found in Richmond and McCroskey (1998), _Communication Apprehension_. Briefer discussions may be found at www.ablongman.com/devito; look for "general and specific apprehension," "degrees of apprehension," "positive and normal apprehension," and "culture and communication apprehension."

If you wish to test yourself on a variety of other factors, take a look at _Psychology Today_'s website, which offers a variety of self-tests: (www.psychologytoday.com/HTDocs/prod/ptoselftest/self_test.asp). Other websites containing self-tests include All the Tests (www.allthetests.com) and Queendom.com (www.queendom.com).

Source: McCroskey, J. C. (2001). _An introduction to rhetorical communication_ (8th ed.). Boston: Allyn & Bacon. Reprinted by permission of the author.

Here are several ways you can deal with and manage your own public speaking apprehension: (1) reverse the factors that cause apprehension, (2) restructure your thinking, (3) practice performance visualization, and (4) desensitize yourself (Richmond & McCroskey, 1998). And although these are the most widely reported strategies, they are not the only ones possible; for example, one study has found that group counseling significantly reduced apprehension and that apprehension remained reduced when again tested five months later (Young-Hong, 2004). The various techniques for reducing public speaking apprehension will also prove useful in helping you manage apprehensiveness in social and work situations. (If you continue to experience extremely high levels of apprehension, or if you're so fearful of the speaking situation that you simply cannot function, talk with your instructor.)

Let's look first at how you can reverse some of the factors that cause apprehension.

REVERSE THE FACTORS THAT CAUSE APPREHENSION

If you can reverse or at least lessen the factors that cause apprehension, you'll be able to reduce your apprehension significantly. Research has identified the following five factors as being especially important in contributing to your fear in public speaking (Beatty, 1988; Richmond & McCroskey, 1998):

- **Inexperience:** Having no experience in public speaking and seeing it as new and totally different from other situations you have been in
- **Subordinate status:** Seeing yourself as less important or lower in status than the members of your audience
- **Conspicuousness:** Seeing yourself as the center of attention
- **Lack of similarity:** Seeing yourself as very different from your audience
- **Prior history:** Having memories of previous times when you were apprehensive

Reducing the impact of these factors will help you manage and reduce your fear of public speaking. Here are some specific suggestions that derive from this research.

- **Gain experience.** New and different situations such as public speaking are likely to make anyone anxious, so try to reduce their newness and differentness. The best way to do this is to get as much public speaking experience as you can. With experience your initial fears and anxieties will give way to feelings of control, comfort, and pleasure. Experience will show you that the feelings of accomplishment you gain from public speaking are rewarding and will outweigh any initial anxiety. Try also to familiarize yourself with the public speaking context. For example, try to rehearse in the room in which you will give your speech.
- **See public speaking as conversation.** When you're the center of attention, as you are in public speaking, you feel especially conspicuous, and this often increases anxiety. It may help, therefore, to think of public speaking as another type of conversation (some theorists call it "enlarged conversation"). Or, if you're comfortable talking in small groups, visualize your

audience as an enlarged small group; it may dispel some of the anxiety you feel.

- **Stress similarity.** When you feel similar to (rather than different from) your audience, your anxiety should lessen. Therefore, try to emphasize the similarities between yourself and your audience. This is especially important when your audience consists of people from cultures different from your own (Stephan & Stephan, 1992): In such cases you're likely to feel fewer similarities with your listeners and therefore to experience greater anxiety (Gudykunst & Nishida, 1984; Gudykunst, Yang, & Nishida, 1985). So with all audiences, but especially with multicultural groups, stress similarities such as shared attitudes, values, or beliefs. This tactic will make you feel more at one with your listeners and therefore more confident as a speaker.

- **Prepare and practice thoroughly.** Much of the fear you experience is a fear of failure. Adequate and even extra preparation will lessen the possibility of failure and the accompanying apprehension (Smith & Frymier, 2006). Because apprehension is greatest during the beginning of the speech, try memorizing the first few sentences of your speech. If there are complicated facts or figures, be sure to write them out and plan to read them. This way you won't have to worry about forgetting them completely.

- **Move about and breathe deeply.** Physical activity—including movements of the whole body as well as small movements of the hands, face, and head—lessens apprehension. Using a visual aid, for example, will temporarily divert attention from you and will allow you to get rid of your excess energy as you move to display it. Also, try breathing deeply a few times before getting up to speak. You'll feel your body relax, and this will help you overcome your initial fear of walking to the front of the room.

- **Avoid chemicals as tension relievers.** Unless prescribed by a physician, avoid any chemical means for reducing apprehension. Tranquilizers, marijuana, or artificial stimulants are likely to create problems rather than reduce them. And, of course, alcohol does nothing to reduce public speaking apprehension (Himle, Abelson, & Haghightgou, 1999). These chemicals can impair your ability to remember the parts of your speech, to accurately read audience feedback, and to regulate the timing of your speech.

RESTRUCTURE YOUR THINKING

The suggestion to restructure your thinking might at first seem a strange idea. Yet **cognitive restructuring** or cognitive reappraisal—as the technique is technically known—is a proven technique for reducing a great number of fears and stresses (Ellis, 1988; Beck, 1988; Westbrook, Kennerley, & Kirk, 2007; Nordahl & Wells, 2007). The general idea behind this technique is that the way you think about a situation influences the way you react to the situation. If you can change the way you think about a situation (reframe it, restructure it, reappraise it) you'll be able to change your reactions to the situation. So, if you think that public speaking will produce stress (fear, apprehension, anxiety), then reappraising it as less threatening will reduce the stress, fear, apprehension, and anxiety.

Much public speaking apprehension is based on unrealistic thinking, on thinking that is self-defeating. For example, you may think that you're a poor speaker or that you're boring or that the audience won't like you or that you have to be perfect. If you maintain such self-defeating beliefs, consider restructuring your thinking by following these three steps:

1. Recognize that you may have internalized such beliefs. Bring them to consciousness; become mindful of the beliefs and of how they might influence your communication. Try to identify them in as specific terms as you can; for example, "The audience won't like me because I have an accent."

2. Recognize that these beliefs are, in fact, self-defeating and unrealistic. For example, to assume that you must be perfect is unrealistic simply because no one can be perfect. Thus, to assume that you must be perfect can only lead to failure. Aside from this, you're now in a learning environment and you're expected to make mistakes and to learn from them.

3. Substitute more realistic beliefs for the unrealistic ones. For example, try replacing the unrealistic belief that audiences won't like you with the more realistic belief that most listeners are much like yourself and are supportive of other speakers. Similarly, if you have an accent, it's likely that others in your audience have accents or have interacted with people with accents and have no negative feelings about people with accents. (Actually, everyone speaks with an accent.) Further, even if you're the only one with a different speech pattern, it's likely that you have a great many things in common with your listeners; focus on these. If you believe that you have to be perfect, substitute the belief that you can fail and fumble and that the entire world won't blow up as a result.

Positive and supportive thoughts will help you restructure your thinking. Remind yourself of your successes, strengths, and virtues. Concentrate on your potential, not on your limitations. Use **self-affirmations** such as "I'm friendly and can communicate this in my speeches," "I can learn the techniques for controlling my fear," "I'm a competent person and have the potential to be an effective speaker," "I can make mistakes and can learn from them," "I'm flexible and can adjust to different communication situations."

Maintain realistic expectations for yourself. Fear increases when you feel that you can't meet your own expectations or the expectations of your audience, especially when these are unrealistic to begin with (Ayres, 1986). Your second speech does not have to be perfect, or even better than that of the previous speaker. Just try to make it better than your own first speech.

Recognize, too, that even if you give six 10-minute speeches in this class, you will only have spoken for 60 minutes . . . one hour . . . 1/24 of a day . . . 1/35,064 of your four-year college life. Let your apprehension motivate you to produce a more thoroughly prepared and rehearsed speech. Don't let it, however, upset you to the point where it hampers your other activities.

PRACTICE PERFORMANCE VISUALIZATION

A variation of cognitive restructuring is **performance visualization**, a technique designed specifically to reduce the outward signs of apprehension and also to reduce the negative thinking that often creates anxiety (Ayres & Hopf, 1992, 1993; Ayres, Hopf, & Ayres, 1994; Ayres, 2005).

First, develop a positive attitude and a positive self-perception. Visualize yourself in the role of the effective public speaker. Visualize yourself walking to the front of the room—fully and totally confident, fully in control of the situation. The audience is in rapt attention and, as you finish, bursts into wild applause. Throughout this visualization, avoid all negative thoughts. As you visualize yourself as this effective speaker, take note of how you walk, look at your listeners, handle your notes, and respond to questions; also, think about how you feel about the public speaking experience.

Second, model your performance on that of an especially effective speaker. View a particularly competent public speaker on video, for example, and make a mental movie of it. As you review the actual and mental movie, shift yourself into the role of speaker; become this speaker.

DESENSITIZE YOURSELF

Systematic desensitization is a technique for dealing with a variety of fears, including those involved in public speaking (Goss, Thompson, & Olds, 1978; Richmond & McCroskey, 1998; Wolpe, 1957; Dwyer, 2005). The general idea is to create a hierarchy of behaviors leading up to the desired but feared behavior (say, speaking before an audience). One specific hierarchy might look like this:

5. Giving a speech in class
4. Introducing another speaker to the class
3. Speaking in a group in front of the class
2. Answering a question in class
1. Asking a question in class

The main objective of this experience is to learn to relax, beginning with relatively easy tasks and progressing to the behavior you're apprehensive about—in this case giving a speech in class. You begin at the bottom of the hierarchy and rehearse the first behavior mentally over a period of days until you can clearly visualize asking a question in class without any uncomfortable anxiety. Once you can accomplish this, move to the second level. Here you visualize a somewhat more threatening behavior; say, answering a question. Once you can do this, move to the third level, and so on until you get to the desired behavior.

In creating your hierarchy, use small steps to help you get from one step to the next more easily. Each success will make the next step easier. You might then go on to engage in the actual behaviors after you have comfortably visualized them: ask a question, answer a question, and so on.

Essentials of Introducing Public Speaking

This first chapter has looked at the nature of public speaking and at probably the most important obstacle to public speaking—namely, communication apprehension.

1. Public speaking is a **transactional process** in which (a) a speaker (b) addresses (c) a relatively large audience with (d) a relatively continuous message.

2. Among the **benefits of studying public speaking** are:
   - Increased personal and social abilities.
   - Improved academic and career skills in organization, research, style, and the like.
   - Improved public speaking abilities—as speaker, as listener, and as critic—which results in personal benefits as well as benefits to society.

3. The **essential elements of public speaking** are:
   - Speaker, the one who presents the speech.
   - Messages, the verbal and nonverbal signals.
   - Channels, the medium through which the signals pass from speaker to listener.
   - Noise, the interference that distorts messages.
   - Audience, the intended receivers of the speech.

- Context, the physical, sociopsychological, temporal, and cultural space in which the speech is presented.
- Presentation, the actual sending of the message, the delivery of the speech.
- Ethics, the moral dimension of communication.
- Culture, an especially important factor in public speaking.
  - Because of demographic changes and economic interdependence, cultural differences have become more significant.
  - Increased understanding of the role of culture in public speaking will help you improve your skills in a context that is becoming increasingly intercultural.

4. **Communication apprehension** is fear of speaking and is often especially high in public speaking. In managing your fear of public speaking, try to
   - Reverse the factors that contribute to apprehension (inexperience, subordinate status, conspicuousness, dissimilarity, and prior history).
   - Restructure your thinking.
   - Practice performance visualization.
   - Desensitize yourself.

Essential Terms: Introducing Public Speaking

Here are the essential terms used in this chapter and the pages on which they are introduced.

audience **(p. 8)**
channel **(p. 7)**
cognitive restructuring **(p. 17)**
communication apprehension
(p. 14)
context **(p. 9)**
culture **(p. 13)**

ethics **(p. 10)**
gender **(p. 13)**
message **(p. 6)**
noise **(p. 8)**
performance visualization **(p. 18)**
plagiarism **(p. 11)**
presentation **(p. 9)**

public speaking **(p. 5)**
rhetoric **(p. 2)**
self-affirmation **(p. 18)**
speaker **(p. 6)**
state apprehension **(p. 14)**
systematic desensitization **(p. 19)**
trait apprehension **(p. 14)**

Public Speaking Exercises

These exercises, presented at the end of each chapter, are designed to stimulate you to think more actively about the concepts and skills covered in the chapter and to help you practice your developing public speaking skills.

1.1 A Model of Public Speaking
Construct your own model of public speaking and indicate how it differs from various other forms of communication, such as face-to-face conversation, e-mail, blogging, interviewing, and small group communication.

1.2 Cultural Beliefs and Your Audience
Evaluate each of the cultural beliefs listed below in terms of how effective each would be if used as a basic assumption by a speaker addressing your public speaking class. Use the following scale: A = the audience would accept this assumption and welcome a speaker with this point of view; B = some members would listen open-mindedly and others wouldn't; or C = the audience would reject this assumption and would not welcome a speaker with this point of view. What guidelines for speeches to be given to this class audience does this analysis suggest?

_____ 1. A return to religious values is the best hope for the world.

_____ 2. Embryonic stem cell research should be encouraged.

_____ 3. The invasion of Iraq was morally unjustified.

_____ 4. Winning is all important; it's not how you play the game, it's whether or not you win that matters.

_____ 5. Keeping the United States militarily superior is the best way to preserve world peace.

_____ 6. Immigration to the United States should be significantly reduced.

____ 7. Gay and lesbian relationships are equal in all ways to heterosexual relationships.

____ 8. The strong and the rich are responsible for taking care of the weak and the poor.

____ 9. Getting to heaven should be life's major goal.

____ 10. Money is a positive good; the quest for financial success is a perfectly respectable (even a noble) goal.

1.3 What Do You Say?

Here are several situations that may come up in a public speaking class. Responding to these brief *What do you say?* scenarios will help you think critically about the material presented here and will suggest ways in which you might apply the principles and skills discussed in this chapter. Because it's so important to apply the skills and experiences you learn here to other public speaking situations, this *What do you say?* feature appears in all 12 chapters.

◆ **Apprehension.** This is Robin's first experience with public speaking, and she's very nervous. She's afraid she'll forget her speech or stumble somehow, so she's wondering if it would be a good idea to alert the audience to her nervousness. What would you advise Robin to do if her audience were your public speaking class?

◆ **Apprehension Management.** Lily has put off the required course in public speaking for as long as she could. She feels she's just too scared to ever get in front of a class and give a speech. What might you say to Lily to help her?

◆ **Cultural Insensitivity.** Ted is listening to Barney giving a speech critical of the cultural beliefs of many in the audience. Ted wonders if he should continue to listen attentively and thus encourage Barney to cause further damage to cultural understanding, or if he should give Barney negative feedback and perhaps wake him up. What would you advise Ted to do?

Log*On!* MySpeechLab

Introducing Public Speaking

Visit MySpeechLab (MSL) at www.myspeechlab.com. Here you'll find a wealth of material to help you master the principles of public speaking under the following hearings: (1) Explore (added explanations of concepts discussed in the text, some of which are interactive—asking you to respond to a series of prompts); (2) Outline (an outlining wizard to help you organize and outline your speeches); (3) Practice (tests for assessing your understanding of the concepts discussed in the text); (4) Visualize (diagrams or tables illustrating various concepts from this textbook and other communication texts, which are especially helpful since they offer the same material but present and organize it in different ways); and (5) Watch (videos of actual speeches, mainly by college students much like yourself but also some professional speakers).

For this chapter, two self-tests and further discussions of communication apprehension are offered here: "How Apprehensive Are You in Conversations?" (self-test), "How Shy Are You?" (self-test), "Positive and Normal Apprehension," "Culture and Communication Apprehension," and "Developing Confidence."

For added insight on a student's fear of public speaking, take a look at the video of the "Fear of Public Speaking" speech. "Bloopers" provides a useful and humorous look at mistakes in public speaking, which are never as serious as they seem when we worry about them.

Research Navigator (available through MSL or at www.researchnavigator.com) offers an extensive treatment of research. If you're new to this website, take the tour. Introductory essays on research, including plagiarism, are available from the "Research Process" tab.

Also visit the Allyn & Bacon public speaking website maintained by the publisher of this book at www.ablongman.com/pubspeak. Here you'll find insight into assessing your speech options, analyzing your audience, researching your topic, organizing your ideas, and delivering your speech. In addition, a number of commercial and educational websites contain speeches (for example, the History Channel at www.historychannel.com, Northwestern University's Douglass site at http://douglassarchives.org/, American Rhetoric at www.americanrhetoric.com, or the Great Speeches site at www.pbs.org/greatspeeches) for emotional appeals.

Preparing and Presenting a Public Speech (in Brief)

Why Read This Chapter?

Because it explains the steps you go through in preparing a public speech and will help you to:

- take the mystery out of the public speaking process and enable you to see the entire process as a whole, as a manageable undertaking

- start giving speeches early in the semester after learning the 10 steps for public speaking preparation and presentation

If all my possessions were taken from me with one exception, I would choose to keep the power of speech, for by it I would soon regain all the rest.

**—Daniel Webster (1782–1852)
American statesman and one
of the great speakers of the
antebellum period**

Before examining the steps in preparing a public speech, take the following self-test on popular beliefs about public speaking.

What Do You Believe about Public Speaking?

Respond to each of the following statements with T (true) if you believe the statement is usually or generally true and F (false) if you believe the statement is usually or generally false.

_____ **1.** Good public speakers are born, not made.

_____ **2.** The more speeches you give, the better you'll become at it.

_____ **3.** It's best to memorize your speech, especially if you're fearful or apprehensive about speaking before an audience.

_____ **4.** If you're a good writer, you'll be a good public speaker; a poor writer, a poor speaker.

_____ **5.** The First Amendment allows the public speaker total freedom of expression.

_____ **6.** Like a good novel, play, or essay, a good speech is relevant to all people at all times.

HOW DID YOU DO? All six of these statements are (generally) false and were written to highlight some of the myths about public speaking. As you'll see throughout this book, these assumptions can get in the way of your learning the skills of public speaking. Briefly, here are the reasons each of these statements is more false than true: (1) Effective public speaking is a learned skill. To be sure, some people are born brighter or more extroverted—characteristics that do help in public speaking. But, all people can improve their abilities and become effective public speakers. (2) This is true only if you practice effective skills. If you practice bad habits, you're likely to grow less effective rather than more effective; consequently, it's crucial to learn and follow the principles of effectiveness. (3) This belief, if acted on, is likely to be detrimental. Memorizing your speech is one of the worst things you can do; there are easier and more effective ways to deal with fear. (4) Although some communication skills apply to both writing and speaking, the two forms are more different than similar—in their focus on the audience, in their responsiveness to immediate feedback, and in their language. (5) Actually, freedom of speech does not legalize slander, libel, defamation, or plagiarism. In addition, as the frequent examples of cultural incorrectness highlighted by the media illustrate, even when speech is not illegal, it can have serious negative consequences when used in culturally insensitive ways. (6) Although there are exceptions (Lincoln's Gettysburg Address, Martin Luther King Jr.'s "I have a dream" speech), the most effective public speeches are those that are constructed for a specific time, for a specific audience, for a specific occasion.

WHAT WILL YOU DO? As you progress through the 10 steps of public speaking, focus on the uniqueness of public speaking and on how mistaken beliefs might get in the way of your learning the skills of this important form of communication.

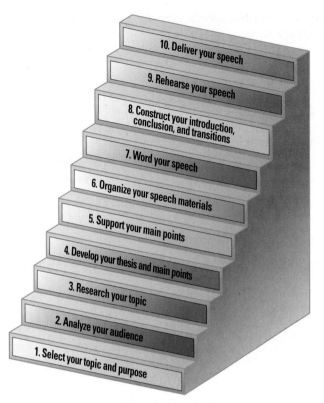

Figure 2.1

The Steps in Preparing and Presenting a Public Speech

As you can see, this figure presents the 10 steps in a linear fashion. The process of constructing a public speech, however, doesn't always follow such a logical sequence. So you'll probably not progress simply from Step 1, to 2, to 3, through to 10. Instead, after selecting your topic and purpose (Step 1) you may progress to Step 2 and analyze your audience. On the basis of this analysis, however, you may wish to go back and modify your topic, your purpose, or both. Similarly, after you research the topic (Step 3), you may want more information about your audience. You may, therefore, return to Step 2.

From Joseph A. DeVito, *The Elements of Public Speaking, 7e*. Published by Allyn & Bacon, Boston, MA. Copyright © 2000 by Pearson Education. Reprinted by permission of the publisher.

This chapter answers the FAQs you're likely to be wondering about by providing a brief overview of the public speaking process. By following the 10 steps outlined in this chapter and diagrammed in Figure 2.1, you'll be able to prepare and present an effective first speech almost immediately. The remainder of the text elaborates on these steps and will help you fine-tune your public speaking skills.

STEP 1: SELECT YOUR TOPIC AND PURPOSE

The first step in preparing a speech is to select the **topic** (or subject) and the purpose you hope to achieve. Let's look first at the topic. For your classroom speeches—where the objective is to learn the skills of public speaking—there are thousands of suitable topics. Suggestions may be found everywhere and anywhere. Take a look at the "Dictionary of Topics" on the text's Companion Website; it lists hundreds of suitable topics from abortion, academic freedom, and acupuncture to women, words, youth, and zodiac.

What makes a topic "suitable"? First, the topic of a public speech should be *worthwhile*; it should address an issue that has significant implications for the audience.

A topic should also be *appropriate* both to you as the speaker and to your audience. Try not to select a topic just because it will fulfill the requirements of an assignment. Instead, select a topic about which you know something and would like to learn more.

Topics should also be *culturally sensitive*. Culture plays an extremely important role in determining what people consider appropriate or worthwhile. For example, it would be considered inappropriate for an American businessperson in Pakistan to speak about politics or in Nigeria about religion or in Mexico about illegal aliens (Axtell, 1993). Because you're a college student, you can assume, to some extent, that the topics you're interested in will also prove interesting to your classmates.

Topics must also be *limited in scope*. Probably the major problem for beginning speakers is that they attempt to cover a huge topic in five minutes: the history of Egypt, why our tax structure should be changed, or the sociology of film. Such topics are too broad and cause the speaker to try to cover too much. In these cases, all the speaker succeeds in doing is telling the audience what it already knows.

Once you have your general topic, consider your **general purpose.** Generally, public speeches are designed to inform, to persuade, or to serve some ceremonial or special occasion function.

> The *informative speech* seeks to create understanding: to clarify, enlighten, correct misunderstandings, or demonstrate how something works.

> The *persuasive speech* seeks to influence attitudes or behaviors: to strengthen or change audience attitudes or to inspire hearers to take some specific action.

> The *special occasion speech*, containing elements of both information and persuasion, serves to introduce another speaker or a group of speakers, present a tribute, secure the goodwill of the listeners, or entertain the audience.

Your speech also will have a **specific purpose.** For example, specific informative purposes might be to inform the audience about a proposed education

Consider the topics on which you might give speeches. Do you have an expertise or a hobby about which you might speak? What topics, if any, would you prefer that speakers avoid?

budget or to describe the way a television pilot is audience tested. Specific persuasive purposes might be to persuade an audience to support a proposed budget or to influence them to vote for Smith. Specific purposes for special occasion speeches might include introducing a Nobel Prize winner in nuclear physics, celebrating Veterans Day, or giving a toast at a ceremony.

STEP 2: ANALYZE YOUR AUDIENCE

In public speaking your audience is central to your topic and purpose. In most cases, and especially in a public speaking class, you'll be thinking of both your audience and your topic at the same time; in fact, it's difficult to focus on one without also focusing on the other. Your success in informing or persuading an audience rests largely on **audience analysis**—the extent to which you know your listeners and the extent to which you've adapted your speech to them. Ask yourself, Who are they? What do they already know? What would they want to know more about? What special interests do they have? What opinions, attitudes, and beliefs do they have? Where do they stand on the issues you wish to address? What needs do they have?

For example, if you're going to speak on social security and health care for the elderly or on the importance of the job interview, it's obvious that the age of your listeners will influence how you develop your speech. Similarly, men and women often view topics differently. For example, if you planned to speak on caring for a newborn baby, you'd approach an audience of men very differently from an audience of women. With an audience of women, you could probably assume a much greater knowledge of the subject and a greater degree of comfort in dealing with it. With an audience of men, you might have to cover such elementary topics as the type of powder to use, how to test the temperature of a bottle, and the way to prepare a bottle of formula.

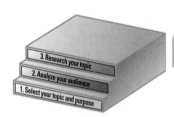

STEP 3: RESEARCH YOUR TOPIC

If your speech is to be worthwhile and if both you and your audience are to profit from it, you'll need to research your topic. **Research** will help you find the information to use as source material in your speech. Through research you'll find examples, illustrations, and definitions to help you inform your listeners; testimony, statistics, and arguments to support your major ideas; personal anecdotes, quotations, and stories to help you bring your topics to life.

Research, however, also serves another important function: It helps you persuade your listeners and makes you appear more believable. For example, if your listeners feel you've examined lots of research, they'll be more apt to see you as competent and knowledgeable and therefore will be more apt to believe what you say. And, of course, the content of the research itself can be convincing. When you present solid research to your listeners, you give them the very reasons they need to draw conclusions or to decide on a course of action.

Because of these dual roles that research plays in public speaking, it's crucial to conduct and critically evaluate research on your speech topic and to integrate this research into your speeches. Here are a few research principles to help you get started researching your speeches.

A Case of Ethics   ⚖ **Ethics**   USING RESEARCH

You recently read an excellent summary of research on aging and memory in a magazine article. The magazine is a particularly respectable publication, and so it's reasonable to assume that this research is reliable. But you feel that citing the original research studies will give your speech greater persuasive appeal and will make you look more thorough in your research.

Ethical Choice Point *Would it be ethical to cite the original research studies but not to mention that you're relying on a magazine summary? If not, how might you ethically use this material?*

- **Examine what you know.** Begin your search by examining what you already know. Write down what you know, for example, about books, articles, or websites on the topic that you're familiar with; jot down names of people who might know something about the topic. Also consider what you know from your own personal experiences and observations. Once you know what you know, you can start searching for what you don't know, attacking the problem systematically and efficiently.

- **Begin with a general overview.** Continue your search by getting an authoritative but general overview of the topic. An encyclopedia article, book chapter, or magazine article in print or online will serve this purpose well. This general overview will help you see the topic as a whole and understand how its various parts fit together.

- **Consult increasingly specific sources.** Follow up the general overview with increasingly more detailed and specialized sources. Fortunately, many general articles contain references or links to direct this next stage of your search for more specific information.

STEP 4: DEVELOP YOUR THESIS AND MAIN POINTS

In developing your **thesis** or **central idea**, identify the one idea that you want your audience to remember after you've concluded your speech. This one central idea is your thesis. It's the essence of what you want your audience to get out of your speech. If your speech is informative, then your thesis is the main idea that you want your audience to understand; for example, "A newspaper company has three divisions." If your speech is persuasive, then your thesis is the central idea that you want your audience to accept or believe; for example, "We should adopt the new e-mail system."

Once you have worded your thesis, identify its component ideas—the main ideas you want to use to clarify or support your thesis. We'll call these the **main points** of the speech. You can identify these main points by asking strategic questions of your thesis. These questions that you ask of your thesis are used to help

Research Link

LIBRARIES AND BOOKSTORES

Libraries are the major depositories of stored information and have evolved from a concentration on print sources to their current focus on computerized databases. Starting your research at the library (and with the librarian's assistance) is probably a wise move.

Increasingly you'll go to one virtual or online library to access other virtual libraries or databases maintained by local and national governments, cultural institutions, and various corporations and organizations. Here are a few online libraries that you'll find especially helpful.

- Quick Study, the University of Minnesota's Library Research Guide (http://tutorial.lib .umn.edu), will help you learn how to find the materials you need and will answer lots of questions you probably have about research.
- For a list of library catalogs that will help you find the location of the material you need, try www.libdex.com/. By clicking on "library-type index" you'll get a list of categories of libraries; for example, government or medical or religious.
- The largest library in the United States is the Library of Congress, which houses millions of books, maps, multimedia, and manuscripts. Time spent at this library (begin with www.loc.gov) will be well invested. The home page will guide you to a wealth of information.
- Maintained by the National Archives and Records Administration, the presidential libraries may be accessed at www.archives.gov/.

- The Virtual Library is a collection of links to 14 subject areas; for example, agriculture, business and economics, computing, communication and media, and education. Visit this at www.vlib.org.
- If you're not satisfied with your own college library, visit the libraries of some of the large state universities, such as the University of Pennsylvania (www.library.upenn .edu/ egi-bin/res/sr.egi) or the University of Illinois (http://gateway.library.uiuc .edu).
- The Internet Public Library (www.ipl.org) is actually not a library; it's a collection of links to a wide variety of materials. But it will function much like the reference desk at any of the world's best libraries.

Also visit some of the online bookstores, such as Amazon (www.amazon.com), Barnes & Noble (www.bn .com), or Borders (www.borders.com) and their brick-and-mortar counterparts. Another useful source is http: //aaupnet.org/ (the Association of American University Presses). Some online bookstores now enable you to search some of their books for specific topics and read a paragraph or so on each topic reference.

Of course, you'll also go to a brick-and-mortar library, because it houses materials that are not on the Net or that you want to access in print. Because each library functions somewhat differently, your best bet in learning about a specific library—such as your own college library—is to talk with the librarian about what the library has available, what kinds of training or tours it offers, and how materials are most easily accessed.

The next Research Link, "Interviewing for Information," appears on p. 46.

you generate your main points and would not normally appear in your outline or in the actual oral speech. For informative speeches the most helpful questions are "What?" and "How?" For example, for the thesis "A newspaper company has three divisions", you'd ask, "What are the divisions?" The answer to this question will yield your main points. Following one mass communication theorist (Rodman, 2001), we can list these main points in the form of a brief outline like this:

Thesis: "A newspaper company has three divisions." (What are the divisions?)

I. The publishing division makes major decisions on the entire paper.

II. The editorial division produces news and features.

III. The business division sells advertising and prints the paper.

For a persuasive speech, the question you'd ask of your thesis is often "Why?" For example, if your thesis is "We should adopt the new e-mail system," then the inevitable question is "Why should we adopt the new system?" Your answers to this question will identify the major parts of the speech, which might look like this:

Thesis: "We should adopt the new e-mail system." (Why should we adopt the new e-mail system?)

I. The new system is easier to operate.

II. The new system enables you to check your spelling.

III. The new system provides more options for organizing messages.

STEP 5: SUPPORT YOUR MAIN POINTS

Once you've identified your thesis and main points, turn your attention to supporting each point. Tell the audience what it needs to know about the newspaper divisions. Convince the audience that the new e-mail system is easier to use, has a spell-checker feature, and provides useful options for organizing e-mails.

In the informative speech your **supporting materials** primarily amplify—describe, illustrate, define, exemplify—the various concepts you discuss. For example, you want the causes of inflation to come alive for the audience. You want your listeners to see and feel the drug problem, the crime rate, or the economic hardships of the people you're talking about. Supporting materials accomplish this. Presenting definitions, for example, helps the audience to understand specialized terms; definitions breathe life into concepts that may otherwise be too abstract or vague. Statistics (summary figures that explain various trends) are essential for certain topics. Presentation aids—charts, maps, actual objects, slides, films, and so on—enliven normally vague concepts. Because presentation aids have become so important in public speaking, you may want to include these in each of your speeches—they're easy to use and inexpensive to produce, help you maintain attention, and communicate information more efficiently and more effectively. If you start using them with your first speeches, you'll develop considerable facility by the end of the semester. The best way to do this is to read Chapter 6's section on presentation aids (pages 113–141) immediately after you complete this chapter and to begin incorporating such aids into all your speeches.

In a persuasive speech your support is proof—material that offers evidence, argument, and motivational appeal and establishes your credibility. Proof helps you convince the audience to agree with you. Let's say, for example, that you want to persuade the audience to believe that the new e-mail system is easier to operate (your first main point, as noted above). To do this you need to give your audience good reasons for believing in its greater ease of operation. Your point might be supported this way:

I. The new e-mail system is easier to operate.

   A. It's easier to install.

   B. It's easier to configure to your personal preferences.

   C. It makes it easier to save and delete messages.

STEP 6: ORGANIZE YOUR SPEECH MATERIALS

The appropriate **organization** of your materials will help your audience understand and retain what you say. You might, for example, select a simple topical organization. This pattern involves dividing your topic into its logical subdivisions or subtopics. Each subtopic becomes a main point of your speech, and each is treated about equally. You'd then organize the supporting materials under each of the appropriate points. The body of the speech, then, might look like this:

I. Main point I
    A. Supporting material for I
    B. Supporting material for I
II. Main point II
    A. Supporting material for II
    B. Supporting material for II
    C. Supporting material for II
III. Main point III
    A. Supporting material for III
    B. Supporting material for III

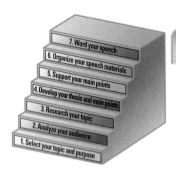

STEP 7: WORD YOUR SPEECH

Because your audience will hear your speech only once, make what you say instantly intelligible. Don't talk down to your audience; but do make your ideas, even complex ones, easy to understand at one hearing.

Use words that are simple rather than complex, concrete rather than abstract. Use personal and informal rather than impersonal and formal language. For example, use lots of pronouns (*I, me, you, our*) and contractions (*can't* rather than *cannot; I'll* rather than *I will*). Use simple and direct rather than complex and indirect sentences. Say "Vote in the next election" instead of "It is important that everyone vote in the next election."

Perhaps the most important advice at this point is that you should not write out your speech word for word. This will only make you sound as if you're reading to your audience. You'll lose the conversational quality that is so important in public speaking. Instead, outline your speech and speak with your audience, using the outline to remind yourself of your main ideas and the order in which you want to present them.

Title your speech. Create a title that's relatively short (so it's easy to remember)—two, three, or four words are often best. Choose a title that will attract the attention and arouse the interest of the listeners and that has a clear relationship to the major purpose of your speech.

Consider the types of supporting materials that your audience would enjoy hearing. How might you use such support in your own speeches?

STEP 8: CONSTRUCT YOUR INTRODUCTION, CONCLUSION, AND TRANSITIONS

The last items to consider are the introduction, conclusion, and transitions for your speech.

INTRODUCTION

In your **introduction,** try to accomplish three goals. First, gain your listeners' attention. A provocative statistic, a little-known fact, an interesting story, or a statement explaining the topic's significance will help secure this initial attention.

Here, for example, is how one student, Elizabeth Hobbs from Truman State University, used a dramatic example to gain and focus the audience's attention on her and her speech (Schnoor, 2006, p. 45):

> He was kidnapped in January 2004 while making a business trip to Macedonia. To be transported to a secret prison in Afghanistan, he was beaten, his underwear was forcibly removed and he was put into a diaper and chained spread eagle inside the plane. In Afghanistan, he was beaten, interrogated, and put into solitary confinement. To get out, he started a hunger strike, but after 37 days without food, a feeding tube was forced through his nose and into his stomach. Nearly five months later, he was released, with no explanation for his imprisonment. Does this sound like Chile under the Pinochet regime? Prisoner abuse in Uzbekistan? A Russian gulag? It wasn't. This is the story told by the *Houston Chronicle* on December 24, 2005 of a victim of America's War on Terror.

Second, establish connections among yourself, the topic, and the audience. Tell audience members why you're speaking on this topic. Tell them why you're

Consider how you feel now that you've completed all or most of the steps in preparing your speech. What one or two issues do you feel you need more information to more fully understand?

concerned with the topic and why you're competent to address them. These are questions that most audiences will automatically ask themselves. Here's one example of how this might be done.

You may be wondering why a twenty-five-year-old woman with no background in medicine or education is talking to you about AIDS education. I'm addressing you today as a mother of a child with AIDS, and I want to talk with you about my child's experience in school—and about every child's experience in school—your own children as well as mine.

Third, orient your audience; tell them what you're going to talk about.

I'm going to explain the ways in which war movies have changed through the years. I'm going to discuss examples of movies depicting World War II, the Korean War, Vietnam, and Iraq.

At times, orientations are connected with the thesis of the speech. For example, here's how one student, Sarah Collins of Cameron University, oriented the audience by identifying the three points (problems, causes, and solutions) she would cover in her speech on fraudulent charities: (Schnoor, 2006, p. 60):

By discussing the problems, causes, and solutions to fraudulent charities, we will provide a safe way to donate funds and ensure that our money isn't going to aid in the spread of hate messages.

Conclusion

In your **conclusion,** do at least two things. First, summarize your ideas. For example, you might restate your main points, summing up what you've told the audience.

Let's all support Grace Moore. She's our most effective negotiator. She's honest, and she knows what negotiation and our union are all about.

Here is how one student, Kristen K. Gunderson from Murray State University, summarized her speech on tax reform, reiterating the three points she covered in her speech (Schnoor, 2006, p. 28):

After analyzing the current U.S. tax system [first point], the flat tax trend that is working in Europe [second point] and finally, how Europe's trends could work for America [third point], it is certain that the U.S. can learn plenty from its neighbors across the Atlantic.

Second wrap up your speech. Develop a crisp ending that makes it clear to your audience that your speech is at an end.

I hope then that when you vote on Tuesday, you'll vote for Moore. She's our only real choice.

*T*RANSITIONS

After you've completed the introduction and conclusion, review the entire speech for **transitions:** Make sure that the parts flow into one another and that the movement from one part to another (say, from the introduction to the first major proposition) will be clear to the audience. Transitional words, phrases, and sentences will help you achieve this smoothness of movement.

- Connect your introduction's orientation to your first major proposition: *"Let's now look at the first of these three elements*, the central processing unit, in detail. The CPU is the heart of the computer. It consists of. . . ."
- Connect each main point to the next: *"But not only is* cigarette smoking dangerous to the smoker, *it's also* dangerous to the nonsmoker. Passive smoking is harmful to everyone. . . ."
- Connect your last main point to your conclusion: *"As we saw*, there were three sources of evidence against the butler. He had a motive; he had no alibi; he had the opportunity."

STEP 9: REHEARSE YOUR SPEECH

You've prepared your speech to deliver it to an audience, so your next step is **rehearsal,** or practice. Rehearse your speech, from start to finish, out loud, at least four times before presenting it in class. During these rehearsals, time your speech to make sure that you stay within the specified time limits. Practice any words or phrases you have difficulty with; consult a dictionary to clarify any doubts about pronunciation. Include in your outline any notes that you want to remember during the actual speech—notes to remind you to use a presentation aid or to read a quotation.

STEP 10: PRESENT YOUR SPEECH

In your actual presentation, use your voice and bodily action to reinforce your message. Make it easy for your listeners to understand your speech. Any vocal or body movements that draw attention to themselves (and away from what you're saying) obviously should be avoided. Here are a few guidelines that will prove helpful.

1. When called on to speak, approach the front of the room with enthusiasm; even if, like most speakers, you feel nervous, show your desire to speak with your listeners.
2. When at the front of the room, don't begin immediately; instead, pause, engage your audience eye to eye for a few brief moments, and then begin to talk directly to the audience. Talk at a volume that people can hear easily without straining.
3. Throughout your speech, maintain eye contact with your entire audience; avoid concentrating on only a few members or looking out of the window or at the floor.

A SPEECH OF INTRODUCTION

Public Speaking   *Sample Assistant*

Throughout this text you'll find Public Speaking Sample Assistant boxes, which are designed to help you visualize the public speech as a whole. The annotations will help you explore aspects of the speech designed to illustrate important principles that you're likely to find helpful in your own speeches. With the exceptions of the two speeches in Chapters 3 and 4, which are purposely designed to illustrate *in*effective speeches, all of these speeches are models of effective public speeches.

The relatively brief speech of introduction illustrated here is a commonly used first assignment in public speaking classes. Its purpose is to give each person in the class an early and nonthreatening public speaking experience and at the same time to give class members a chance to get to know each other. (A different type of speech of introduction is discussed in Chapter 12, "Speaking on Special Occasions."). In the speech presented here, one student introduces another student to the class. The speech, although fairly complete and detailed, would take only about three minutes to present.

[Introduction]

It's a real pleasure to introduce Joe Robinson to you. I want to tell you a little about Joe's background, his present situation, and his plans for the future.

In this introduction, the speaker accomplishes several interrelated purposes: to place the speech in a positive context, to explain the purpose of the speech and orient the audience, to tell them what the speech will cover, and to indicate that it will follow a time pattern—beginning with the past, moving to the present, and then ending with the proposed future. What other types of opening statements might be appropriate? In what other ways might you organize a speech of introduction?

[Transition]

Let's look first at Joe's past.

This transitional statement alerts listeners that the speaker is moving from the introduction to the first major part of what is called the "body" of the speech.

[Body, first main point (the past)]

Joe comes to us from Arizona, where he lived and worked on a small ranch with his father and grandparents—mostly working with dairy cows. Working on a farm gave Joe a deep love and appreciation for animals, which he carries with him today and into his future plans.

Joe's mother died when he was three years old, so he lived with his father most of his life. When his father, an Air Force lieutenant, was transferred to Stewart Air Force Base here in the Hudson Valley, Joe thought it would be a great opportunity to join his father and continue his education.

Joe also wanted to stay with his father to make sure he eats right, doesn't get involved with the wrong crowd, and meets the right woman to settle down with.

The speaker here gives us information about Joe's past that makes us see him as a unique individual. We also learn something pretty significant about Joe: the fact that his mother died when he was very young. The speaker continues here to answer one of the questions that audience members probably have; namely, why this somewhat older person is in this class and in this college. If this were a longer speech, what else might the speaker cover here? What else would you want to know about Joe's past?

Here the speaker shows that Joe has a sense of humor in his identifying why he wanted to stay with his father, the very same things that a father would say about a son. Can you make this more humorous?

[Transition]

So Joe and his father journeyed from the dairy farm of Arizona to the Hudson Valley.

Here's a simple transition, alerting the audience that the speaker is moving from the first main point (the past) to the second (the present). In what other ways might you state such a transition?

[Second main point (the present)]

Right now, with the money he saved while working on the ranch and with the help of a part-time job, Joe's here with us at Hudson Valley Community College.

Like many of us, Joe is a little apprehensive about college and worries that it's going to be a difficult and very different experience, especially at 28. Although an avid reader—mysteries and biographies are his favorites—Joe hasn't really studied, taken an exam, or written a term paper since high school, some 10 years ago. So he's a bit anxious but at the same time looking forward to the changes and the challenges of college life.

And again, like many of us, Joe's a bit apprehensive about taking a public speaking course.

Joe is currently working for a local animal shelter. He was especially drawn to this particular shelter because of their no- kill policy; lots of shelters will kill the animals they can't find adopted homes for, but this one sticks by its firm no-kill policy.

Here the speaker goes into the present and gives Joe a very human dimension by identifying his fears and concerns about being in college and taking this course and by emphasizing his concern for animals. The speaker also explains some commonalities between Joe and the rest of the audience (for example, feeling apprehension in a public speaking class is shared by nearly everyone). Some textbooks suggest that telling an audience that a speaker has apprehension about speaking is a bad idea. What do you think of this disclosure in this context?

[Transition]

But it's not the past or the present that Joe focuses on, it's the future.

This transition tells listeners that the speaker has finished talking about the past and present and is now moving on to the future.

[Third main point (the future)]

Joe is planning to complete his AB degree here at Hudson Valley Community and then move on to the State University at New Paltz, where he intends to major in communication with a focus on public relations.

His ideal job would be to work for an animal rights organization. He wants to help make people aware of the ways in which they can advance animal rights and stop so much of the cruelty to animals common throughout the world.

The speaker moves to the future and identifies Joe's educational plans. Having a plan is one thing that everyone has in common, and Joe's plan is something that most in the class would want to know about. The speaker also covers Joe's career goals—again, something the audience is likely to be interested in. In this the speaker also reveals important aspects of Joe's interests and belief system—his concern for animals and his dedication to building his career around this abiding interest. What kinds of information might this speech of introduction give you about the attitudes and beliefs of its intended audience?

[Transition, Internal Summary]

Joe's traveled an interesting road from a dairy farm in Arizona to the Hudson Valley, and the path to New Paltz and public relations should be just as interesting.

This transition (a kind of internal summary) tells you that the speaker has completed the three-part discussion (past, present, and future) and offers a basic summary of what has been discussed.

[Conclusion]

Having talked with Joe over the last few days, I'm sure he'll do well—he has lots of ideas, is determined to succeed, is open to new experiences, and enjoys interacting with people. I'd say that gives this interesting dairy farmer from Arizona a pretty good start as a student in this class, as a student at Hudson Valley Community, and as a soon-to-be public relations specialist.

In this concluding comment the speaker appropriately expresses a positive attitude toward Joe and summarizes some of Joe's positive qualities. These qualities are then tied to the past–present–future organization of the speech. Although the speaker doesn't say "thank you"—which can get trite when 20 speakers in succession say this—it's clear that this is the end of the speech from the last sentence, which brings Joe into his future profession. How effective do you think this conclusion is? What other types of conclusions might the speaker have used in this speech?

Essentials of Preparing and Presenting a Public Speech

This chapter identified and explained in brief the 10 steps to preparing and presenting a public speech.

1. **Select your topic** and general and specific purposes.

2. **Analyze your audience:** Seek to discover what is unique about your listeners and how you might adapt your speech to them.

3. **Research your topic** so that you know as much as you possibly can (within your time limits, of course).

4. **Develop your thesis** (your central idea) and the main points (or parts) that support your thesis.

5. **Support your main points** with a variety of supporting materials.

6. **Organize your speech** materials into an easily comprehended pattern.

7. **Word your speech**, focusing on being as clear as possible.

8. **Construct your introduction** (to gain attention, establish a speaker–audience–topic connection, and orient the audience), **conclusion** (to summarize, motivate, and close), **and transitions** (to hold the parts together and make going from one part to another clear to your audience).

9. **Rehearse your speech** until you feel confident and comfortable with the material and with your audience interaction.

10. **Present your speech** to your intended audience.

Essential Terms: Preparing and Presenting a Public Speech

audience analysis **(p. 26)**
conclusion **(p. 32)**
general purpose **(p. 25)**
introduction **(p. 31)**
main points **(p. 27)**

organization **(p. 30)**
rehearsal **(p. 33)**
research **(p. 26)**
specific purpose **(p. 25)**
supporting materials **(p. 29)**

thesis **(p. 27)**
topic **(p. 24)**
transition **(p. 33)**

Public Speaking Exercises

2.1 Preparing and Presenting a Speech

Apply the 10 steps to preparing and presenting a speech.

1. Select a topic, general purpose, and specific purpose. If you need help with selecting a topic, see the "Dictionary of Topics" at www.myspeechlab.com for suggestions.
2. Analyze this class as your potential audience and identify ways that you can relate your topic to the interests and needs of your audience.
3. Research your topic.
4. Develop your thesis and identify your main points.
5. Support these points with examples, illustrations, definitions, and so on.
6. Organize the speech materials you have collected.
7. Word your speech for maximum clarity.
8. Construct your introduction and conclusion and insert transitions at appropriate places.
9. Rehearse your speech.
10. Present your speech to your class.

Try to secure some feedback on your speech, and think about what you might do differently in your next speech—how you might improve your speech and its presentation.

2.2 Theses and Main Points

Here are five theses. For each, identify the inherent question to ask for generating the main points and generate at least two or three such main points that would be appropriate for a public speech given in your class.

◆ Take a course in cultural anthropology [or in any subject you want].

◆ The war in Iraq is similar to Vietnam [or is not similar].

◆ Religion is too influential [or not influential enough] in the U.S. government.

◆ Current drug laws that mandate life imprisonment for persons convicted three times for drug violations are excessive [or reasonable].

◆ Adoption by gay men and lesbians should be legal [or illegal] in all states.

2.3 What Do You Say?

◆ **Topic Appropriateness.** Mac, a student in his 20s who is on the college basketball team, wants to give a speech on his hobby, flower arranging. But he wonders if this topic is going to seem inappropriate to him as a speaker; he also wonders, if he does decide to speak on this topic, whether he should say anything about the topic's appearing inappropriate. What would you advise Mac to do?

◆ **Audience Analysis.** Stella is planning to give a speech on the need for a needle exchange program in her state. But she knows nothing of the audience other than that the occasion will be a high school PTA meeting. She has no information about the audience's cultural background, gender, social attitudes, or religious beliefs. What can Stella do to learn about her audience and to prepare for this potentially difficult situation?

◆ **Speaking Style.** Danny is planning to enter the ministry and wants to give his speeches to the class as if they were members of his congregation—for example, to speak on religious topics, assuming the listeners are of his faith—a kind of early preparation for his profession. If you were the public speaking instructor, what would you advise Danny to do?

LogOn! MySpeechLab

Preparing and Presenting a Public Speech (in Brief)

Log on to MySpeechLab (www.myspeechlab.com) for a complete annotated speech, "Adverse Drug Effects." The annotations will highlight some of the major features on which you'll want to focus. To explore a wide variety of topics suitable for public speaking, take a look at the "Dictionary of Topics" (listed with Chapter 4 materials). You'll also find some useful videos of speeches of self-introduction; see "Self-Introduction Speech" as well as the effective and ineffective versions of the same speech (Introduction Speech No. 1 and Introduction Speech No. 2).

Also see "The speech is a systematic process" (under *Visualize*) and "Choosing a Speech Topic" (*Watch*). And take a look at the Outlining Wizard (*Outline*) which will help you start organize your speeches.

While at MSL and in connection with the Research Link on libraries (p. 28), examine Using the Library on Research Navigator (accessible through MSL or at www.researchnavigator.com). Also take a look at the Link Library for communication for a variety of sources on hundreds of communication topics.

3 Listening and Criticism

Why Read This Chapter?

Because it will enable you to become a more effective listener and critic of public speeches by helping you to:

- improve your listening effectiveness in public speaking (or in any oral communication situation)

- analyze public speaking effectiveness and apply the insights to your own speeches

- express your evaluations in ways that will help speakers improve their skills

It takes two to speak the truth—one to speak, and another to listen.

—Henry David Thoreau (1817–1862),
Author, lecturer, and philosopher best known for *Walden* **and an emphasis on simplicity**

The first three sections of this chapter examine listening, which, according to the International Listening Association, is "the process of receiving, constructing meaning from, and responding to spoken and/or nonverbal messages" (Emmert, 1994, cited in Brownell, 2006). Here we look at the nature of listening as it occurs in the context of public speaking, the influence of culture on listening, and some principles for listening more effectively.

Listening skills yield numerous benefits. Effective listening will help you increase the amount of information you learn and will decrease the time you need to learn it. It will help you distinguish logical from illogical appeals and thus decrease your chances of getting duped. And, not surprisingly, effective listening will help you become a better public speaker. When you listen effectively to other speakers, you'll see more clearly what works and what doesn't work (and why); this will help you identify the principles of public speaking to follow, along with the pitfalls to avoid.

Before reading about listening, focus on your own listening tendencies by taking the accompanying self-test, "How Do You Listen?"

*T*EST YOURSELF

How Do You Listen?

Respond to each question using the following scale: 1 = always; 2 = frequently; 3 = sometimes; 4 = seldom; and 5 = never.

_____ **1.** I listen to what the speaker is saying and feeling; I try to feel what the speaker feels.

_____ **2.** I listen objectively; I focus on the logic of the ideas rather than on the emotional meaning of the speech.

_____ **3.** I listen without judging the speaker.

_____ **4.** I listen critically; I rarely suspend my critical, evaluative faculties.

_____ **5.** I listen to the literal meaning, to what the speaker says, rather than playing psychiatrist and focusing on hidden or deeper meanings.

_____ **6.** I listen for the speaker's hidden meanings, to what the speaker means but isn't verbalizing.

HOW DID YOU DO? These statements focus on the ways of listening discussed in this chapter. All of these ways are appropriate at some times but not at others; it depends. So the only responses that are really inappropriate are "always" and "never." Effective listening is listening that is tailored to the specific communication situation.

WHAT WILL YOU DO? Consider how you might use your responses on this self-test to begin to improve your listening effectiveness. A good way to begin doing this is to review the statements and try to identify situations in which each statement would be appropriate and situations in which each would be inappropriate.

LISTENING STAGES AND TECHNIQUES

Listening can be described as a series of five steps: receiving, understanding, remembering, evaluating, and responding. The process is represented in Figure 3.1.

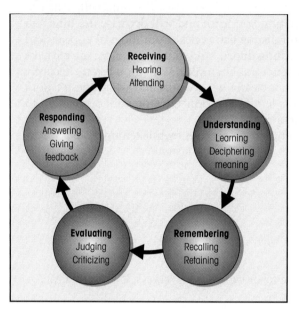

Figure 3.1

The Process of Listening

This five-step model draws on a variety of models that listening researchers have developed (Alessandra, 1986; Barker, 1990; Brownell, 2006).

From Joseph A. DeVito, *The Elements of Public Speaking*, 7e. Published by Allyn & Bacon, Boston, MA. Copyright © 2000 by Pearson Education. Reprinted by permission of the publisher.

RECEIVING

Unlike listening, hearing begins and ends with the first stage: **receiving.** Hearing is something that just happens when you get within earshot of some auditory stimulus. Listening is quite different; it begins (but does not end) with receiving a speaker's messages. The messages a listener receives are both verbal and nonverbal; they consist of words as well as gestures, facial expressions, variations in volume and rate, and lots more, as we will see throughout this book.

At this stage of listening you recognize not only what is said but also what is not said. For example, you receive both the politician's summary of accomplishments in education as well as his or her omission of failed promises to improve health care programs.

Receiving messages is a highly selective process. You don't listen to all the available auditory stimuli. Rather, you selectively tune in to certain messages and tune out others. Generally, you listen most carefully to messages that you feel will prove of value to you or that you find particularly interesting. At the same time, you give less attention to messages that have less value or interest. Thus, you may listen carefully when your instructor tells you what will appear on the examination but may listen less carefully to an extended story or to routine announcements. To improve your receiving skills:

- Look at the speaker; make your mind follow your body and focus attention on the person speaking.

- Focus your attention on the speaker's verbal and nonverbal messages, on what is said and on what isn't said.

- Avoid attending to distractions in the environment.
- Focus your attention on what the speaker is saying rather than on any questions or objections you may have to what the speaker is saying.

UNDERSTANDING

Understanding a speaker means grasping not only the thoughts that are expressed but also the emotional tone that accompanies these thoughts; for example, the urgency or the joy or sorrow expressed in the message. To enhance understanding:

- Relate the new information the speaker is giving to what you already know.
- See the speaker's messages from the speaker's point of view; avoid judging the message until you fully understand it as the speaker intended it.
- Rephrase (paraphrase) the speaker's ideas into your own words as you continue to listen.

REMEMBERING

Messages that you receive and understand need to be retained at least for some period of time. In public speaking situations you can enhance the process of **remembering** by taking notes or by taping the messages.

What you remember is actually not what was said, but what you think (or remember) was said. Memory for speech isn't reproductive; you don't simply reproduce in your memory what the speaker said. Rather, memory is reconstructive; you actually reconstruct the messages you hear into a system that seems to make sense to you. This is well illustrated in the exercise "Do You Really Remember What You Hear?" at the end of this chapter. In remembering:

- Identify the thesis or central idea and the main points.
- Summarize the message in a more easily retained form, being careful not to ignore crucial details or important qualifications.
- Repeat names and key concepts to yourself.
- Identify the organizational pattern and use it (visualize it) to organize what the speaker is saying.

EVALUATING

Evaluating consists of judging the message and the speaker's credibility, truthfulness, or usefulness in some way. At this stage your own biases and prejudices become especially influential. These will affect what you single out for evaluation and what you'll just let pass. They will influence what you judge good and what you judge bad. In some situations evaluation is more in the nature of critical analysis, a topic explored in detail later in this chapter. When evaluating:

- Resist evaluation until you feel you understand (at least reasonably well) the speaker's point of view.
- Distinguish facts from inferences (see Chapter 8), opinions, and personal interpretations that you're making as well as those made by the speaker.

Consider the kinds of listening obstacles that the average instructor faces in the classroom. Assuming that you'll experience similar listening obstacles as you give your speeches, what can you do to overcome such obstacles?

- Identify any biases, self-interests, or prejudices that may lead the speaker to slant unfairly what he or she is presenting.

- Identify any biases that may lead you to remember what supports your attitudes and beliefs and to forget what contradicts them.

RESPONDING

Responding occurs in two phases: (1) nonverbal (and occasionally verbal) responses you make while the speaker is talking and (2) responses you make after the speaker has stopped talking. Responses made while the speaker is talking should support the speaker and show that you're listening. These include what nonverbal researchers call backchanneling cues—gestures that let the speaker know that you're listening, such as nodding your head, smiling, and leaning forward (Burgoon & Bacue, 2003).

Responses you make to the speaker after he or she has stopped talking are generally more elaborate and might include questions of clarification ("I wasn't sure what you meant by reclassification"); expressions of agreement ("You're absolutely right on this, and I'll support your proposal when it comes up for a vote"); and expressions of disagreement ("I disagree that Japanese products are superior to those produced in the United States").

- Use a variety of backchanneling cues to support the speaker; using only one cue—for example, nodding constantly—will make it appear that you're not listening but are on automatic pilot.

- Support the speaker in your final responses by saying something positive.

- Own your own responses: State your thoughts and feelings as your own, and use I-messages. For example, say, "I think the new proposal will entail greater expense than you outlined" rather than "Everyone will object to the plan because it will cost too much."

CULTURE AND LISTENING

Listening is difficult, partly because of the inevitable differences between the communication systems of speaker and listener. Because each person has had a unique set of experiences, each person's communication and meaning system is going to be different from the next person's system. When speaker and listener come from different cultures, the differences and their effects are naturally much greater. Here are just a few areas where misunderstandings can occur.

LANGUAGE AND SPEECH

Even when speaker and listener speak the same language, they speak it with different meanings and different accents. No two speakers speak exactly the same language. Every speaker speaks an idiolect—a unique variation of the language. Speakers of the same language will sometimes have different meanings for the same terms because they have had different experiences.

Speakers and listeners who have different native languages and who may have learned English as a second language will have even greater differences in meaning. Translations are never precise and never fully capture the meaning in the other language. If your meaning for *house* was learned in a culture in which everyone lived in their own house with lots of land around it, then communicating your meaning for *house* with someone whose meaning was learned in a neighborhood of high-rise tenements is going to be difficult. Although you'll each hear the same word, the meanings you'll each develop will be drastically different. In adjusting your listening—especially when in an intercultural setting—understand that the speaker's meanings may be very different from yours even though you each know and speak the same language.

Another aspect of speech is the speaker's accent. In many classrooms throughout the United States, there will be a wide range of accents, both regional and foreign. People whose native language is tonal such as Chinese (in which differences in pitch signal important meaning differences), may speak English with variations in pitch that may seem unnatural to others. Those whose native language is Japanese may have trouble distinguishing *l* from *r*, as Japanese does not make this distinction. Regional accent differences may make it difficult for people from Mississippi and Maine, for example, to understand each other; words even may have different meanings in different regions, and this may make communication more difficult than if the speakers were from the same area.

NONVERBAL DIFFERENCES

As you listen to other people, you also "listen" to their **nonverbal communication.** If their nonverbal messages are drastically different from what you expect on the basis of the verbal message, the nonverbals may be seen as a kind of noise or interference or they may be seen as contradictory messages.

Additionally, speakers from different cultures have different display rules, cultural rules that govern which nonverbal behaviors are appropriate and which are inappropriate in a public setting. Also, different cultures may give very different meanings to the same nonverbal gesture. For example, Americans consider direct eye contact an expression of honesty and forthrightness, but the Japanese often view this as a lack of respect. The Japanese will glance at the other person's face rarely and then only for very short periods (Axtell, 1990; Matsumoto, 2006). Among some Latin Americans and Native Americans, direct eye contact between, say, a teacher and a student is considered inappropriate, perhaps aggressive; appropriate student behavior is to avoid eye contact with the teacher.

ETHNOCENTRISM

How do you feel about your own culture versus those of others? For example, do you believe that other cultures are backward when compared to yours? Do you believe that other cultures would do well to become more like your culture? Do you believe that people would be happier if they lived in your culture than they would in another? Do you believe that people from other cultures are less trustworthy than people from your own (Neuliep, Chaudoir, & McCroskey, 2001)?

If you answer yes to these and similar questions, it's likely that you're ethnocentric in your thinking. **Ethnocentrism** is a "nearly universal syndrome of attitudes and behaviors" (Hammond & Axelrod, 2006). It is the tendency to evaluate the values, beliefs, and behaviors of your own culture as being more positive, logical, and natural than those of other cultures. The nonethnocentric, on the other hand, would see himself or herself and others as different but equal, with neither being inferior nor superior.

Ethnocentric listening occurs when you listen to members of other cultures and consider them to be lacking in knowledge or expertise because they are from another culture, or when you acknowledge members of your own culture as knowledgeable and expert simply because they are from your own culture. Similarly, you're listening ethnocentrically when you listen to ideas about other cultures and view these as inferior simply because they differ from those of your own culture, or when you view ideas of your own culture as superior simply because they are from your own culture.

Ethnocentrism exists on a continuum. People are not either ethnocentric or nonethnocentric; most are somewhere between these polar opposites. And, of course, your degree of ethnocentrism varies depending on the group on which you focus. For example, if you're Greek American, you may have a low degree of ethnocentrism when dealing with Italian Americans (because of the similarities in the cultures of Greeks and Italians) but a high degree when dealing with Japanese Americans (because of the greater differences between the Greek and Japanese cultures). Most important for our purposes is that your degree of ethnocentrism—and we're all ethnocentric to some degree—will influence your listening effectiveness.

Recognizing the tendency toward ethnocentrism is the first step in combating any excesses. In addition, try following the suggestions for effective listening offered in this chapter, especially when you're in an intercultural public speaking situation. Also, expose yourself to culturally different experiences, but resist the temptation to evaluate these through your own cultural filters. For many this will not be an easy experience; however, in light of the tremendous advantages to be gained through increased intercultural experiences, the effort seems well worth it.

GENDER AND LISTENING

According to Deborah Tannen (1990) in her best-selling *You Just Don't Understand: Women and Men in Conversation*, women seek to build rapport and establish a closer relationship and so use listening to achieve these ends. Men, on the other hand, tend to play up their expertise, emphasize it, and use it to dominate the interaction. Women are apt to play down their expertise and are more interested in communicating supportiveness. Tannen argues that the goal of a man in conversation is to be accorded respect, so he seeks to show his knowledge and expertise. A woman, on the other hand, seeks to be liked, so she expresses agreement.

Men and women also show that they're listening in different ways (Hall, 2006). Women are more apt to give lots of listening cues, such as interjecting *yeah* or *uh-huh*, nodding in agreement, and smiling. A man is more likely to listen quietly, without giving a lot of listening cues as feedback. Tannen (1990) argues, however, that men do listen less to women than women listen to men. The reason, says Tannen, is that listening places a person in an inferior position, whereas speaking places the speaker in a superior role.

As a result of these differences, men may seem to assume a more combative posture while listening, as if getting ready to argue. They also may appear to ask questions that are more argumentative or that are designed to puncture holes in your position as a way to play up their own expertise. Women are more likely to ask supportive questions and perhaps to offer more positive criticism than men. Women also use more cues in listening in a public speaking context. They let the speaker see that they're listening. Men, on the other hand, seem to use fewer listening cues in a public speaking situation.

Men and women act this way to both men and women; their customary ways of communicating don't seem to change depending on whether the speaker is male or female. There's no evidence to show that these differences represent any negative motives—any conscious aim on the part of men to prove themselves superior or of women to ingratiate themselves. Rather, these differences in listening are largely the result of the ways in which men and women have been socialized.

Consider the techniques this librarian might use as she explains the new and complex online services. What might she do—and what might you do in your speeches—to encourage active listening?

GUIDELINES FOR LISTENING MORE EFFECTIVELY

Effective listening is extremely important, because you spend so much time listening. In fact, if you measured importance by the time you spend on an activity, listening would be your most important communication activity. Studies conducted from 1929 to 1980 showed that listening was the most often used form of communication (occupying about 45 to 53 percent of communication time), followed by speaking (about 16 to 30 percent), reading (about 16 to 17 percent), and writing (about 9 to 14 percent) (Barker, Edwards, Gaines, Gladney, & Holley, 1980; Rankin, 1929; Steil, Barker, & Watson, 1983; Werner, 1975; Wolvin & Coakley, 1996). This was true of high school and college students as well as of adults from a wide variety of fields. With the widespread use of the Internet, these studies have become dated, and today their findings are of limited value. However, anecdotal evidence (certainly not conclusive in any way) suggests that listening is probably still the most used communication activity. Just think of how you spend your day; listening probably occupies a considerable amount of time. Listening is also important in your professional life; regardless of what profession you enter, you'll always need the skills of effective listening (Allen, 1997; Salopek, 1999; Brownell, 2006).

LISTEN ACTIVELY

The first step in listening improvement is to recognize that it isn't a passive activity. You cannot listen without effort. Listening is a difficult process. In many ways it's more demanding than speaking. In speaking you control the situation; you can talk about what you like in the way you like. In listening, however, you have to follow the pace, the content, and the language of the speaker.

The best preparation for **active listening** is to act like an active listener: to focus your complete attention on the speaker (Perkins & Fogarty, 2006). Recall, for example, how your body almost automatically reacts to important news. Almost immediately you sit up straighter, cock your head toward the speaker, and remain relatively still and quiet. You do this almost reflexively, because this is how you listen

Research Link

INTERVIEWING FOR INFORMATION

One research activity that you'll often find helpful is to interview people who have special information that you might use in your speech. For example, you might want to interview a veterinarian for information on proper nutrition for household pets; an eyewitness for information on living through a hurricane; or average people for information on their opinions on politics, religion, or any of a wide variety of topics. In these information interviews, a great part of your effectiveness will hinge on your ability to listen actively, for total meaning, with empathy, with an open mind, and ethically, all of which are covered in this chapter. Here are a few additional suggestions to help you use interviewing to find needed information.

Select the person you wish to interview. You might, for example, look through your college catalog for an instructor teaching a course that involves your topic. Or visit newsgroups and look for people who have posted articles on your topic. If you want to contact a book author, you can always write to the author in care of the publisher or editor (listed on the copyright page), though many authors are now including their e-mail address. You often can find the address and phone number of a professional person in the Encyclopedia of Associations, or you can write to the person via the association's website. Newsgroup and listserv writers are of course the easiest to contact, as their e-mail addresses are included with their posts. To find an expert, try *The Yearbook of Experts, Authorities, and Spokespersons* or any of a variety of websites, such as www .experts.com or http://uscnews3.usc.edu/experts/.

Secure an appointment. Phone the person or send an e-mail requesting an interview. State the purpose of your request and say that you hope to conduct a brief interview by phone or that you'd like to send this person a series of questions by e-mail.

Develop your questions. Generally, ask questions that provide the interviewee with room to discuss the issues you want to raise. Thus, asking, "Do you have formal training in the area of family therapy?" may elicit a simple yes or no, which will not be very informative. On the other hand, asking, "Can you tell me something of your background in this field?" is open-ended, allowing the interviewee to talk in some detail. Phrase questions in a neutral manner. Try not to lead the interviewee to give the answers you want.

Establish rapport with the interviewee. Open the in-person, telephone, e-mail, or chat-group interview by thanking the person for making the time available and again stating your purpose. You might say something like: "I really appreciate your making time for this interview. As I mentioned, I'm preparing a speech on XYZ, and your experience in this area will help a great deal."

Ask for permission to tape or print the interview. It's a good idea to keep an accurate record of the interview, so ask permission to tape the interview if it's in person or by telephone. Taping will eliminate your worry about taking notes and having to ask the interviewee to slow down or repeat. It will also provide you with a much more accurate record of the interview than will handwritten notes. But always ask permission first. Similarly, if the interview is by e-mail or via chat group and you want to quote the interviewee's responses, ask permission first. An agreement to be interviewed does not include permission to print or distribute the interview or even parts of it.

Close with an expression of appreciation, and follow up with a thank-you note. Thank the person for making the time available for the interview and for being informative, cooperative, helpful, or whatever. Or perhaps you might send the person you interviewed a copy of your speech (e-mail would work well here), again with a note of thanks.

The next Research Link, "Primary and Secondary Sources," appears on page 72.

most effectively. This isn't to say that you should be tense and uncomfortable, but only that your body should reflect your active mind. In listening actively:

- Use your listening time to think about what the speaker is saying, summarizing the speaker's thoughts, formulating questions, drawing connections between what the speaker says and what you already know.

- Work at listening. Listening is hard, so be prepared to participate actively. Avoid "the entertainment syndrome," the expectation that you'll be amused and entertained by a speaker (Floyd, 1985). Set aside distractions (newspapers, magazines, headphones) so that your listening task will have less competition.

- Assume there's value in what the speaker is saying. Resist assuming that what you have to say is more valuable than the speaker's remarks.

- Take notes if appropriate. In some instances you'll want to take notes while the speaker is speaking. Taking notes may be helpful if you want to ask a question about a specific item of information or if you want to include a specific statement in your critical evaluation.

- Avoid becoming preoccupied with yourself. If you focus on yourself, you'll invariably miss much of what the speaker is saying. Similarly, avoid becoming preoccupied with external issues, with what you did last Saturday, or with your plans for the evening. The more you entertain thoughts of external matters, the less effectively you listen.

LISTEN FOR TOTAL MEANING

The meaning of a message isn't only in the words; it's also in the speaker's nonverbal behavior.

The meanings communicated in a speech will also depend on what the speaker does not say. The speaker on contemporary social problems who omits references to homeless people or to drug abuse communicates important messages by these very omissions. For example, listeners may infer that the speaker is poorly prepared, that the speaker's research was inadequate, or that the speaker is trying to fool the audience by not mentioning these issues. As a listener, therefore, be particularly sensitive to the meanings that significant omissions may communicate. As a speaker, recognize that most inferences that audiences draw from omissions are negative and will reflect negatively on your credibility and on the total impact of your speech. In listening for total meaning:

- Focus on both verbal and nonverbal messages. Recognize both consistent and inconsistent "packages" of messages and take these cues as guides for drawing inferences about the meaning the speaker is trying to communicate. Ask questions when in doubt.

- See the forest, then the trees. Connect the specifics to the speaker's general theme rather than merely remembering isolated facts and figures.

- Balance your attention between the surface and the underlying meanings. Don't disregard the literal (surface) meaning of the speech in your attempt to uncover the more hidden (deeper) meanings.

- Resist the temptation to filter out difficult or unpleasant messages. You don't want to hear that something you believe is untrue or to be told that people you respect are doing bad things, and yet these are the very messages you need to listen to with great care. These are the messages that will lead you to examine and reexamine your implicit and unconscious assumptions. If you filter out this kind of information, you risk failing to correct misinformation. You risk losing new and important insights.

LISTEN WITH EMPATHY

The word **empathy** refers to the process by which you are able to feel what others are feeling, to see the world as they see it, to walk in their shoes (Eisenberg & Strayer, 1987). Of course, you can never feel exactly what the speaker is feeling, but you can try to feel something of what he or she is feeling, to listen to the feelings as well as the thoughts.

Consider the potential problems of listening empathically? What might be the downside of empathic listening?

As you can imagine, empathy is a crucial part of listening. Empathic listening is best viewed in two stages. First, there is the empathy that you feel for the speaker, which enables you to understand better the speaker's thoughts and feelings. Second, there are the empathic responses that you communicate back to the speaker to let the speaker know that you do indeed understand what he or she means and feels. Let's start with a few suggestions for feeling empathy for the speaker.

■ See the speaker's point of view. Before you can understand what the speaker is saying, you have to see the message from the speaker's vantage point. Try putting yourself in the role of the speaker and looking at the topic from the speaker's perspective.

■ Understand the speaker's thoughts and feelings. Don't consider your listening task complete until you've understood what the speaker is feeling as well as thinking.

■ Avoid "offensive listening." Offensive listening is the tendency to listen to bits and pieces of information that will enable you to attack the speaker or to find fault with something the speaker has said.

■ Don't distort messages because of the "friend-or-foe" factor; in other words, avoid listening for positive statements about friends and negative statements about enemies. For example, if you dislike Fred, make the added effort to listen objectively to Fred's speeches or to comments that might reflect positively on Fred.

The second part of empathy—expressing your empathy back to the speaker—can best be accomplished in two steps corresponding to the two parts in true empathy: thinking empathy and feeling empathy (Bellafiore, 2005). In *thinking empathy* you express an understanding of what the person means. For example, when you paraphrase someone's comment, showing that you understand the meaning the person is trying to communicate, you're communicating *thinking empathy*. When you nod your head in approval of a speaker's argument, you're communicating *thinking empathy*. In communicating your *feeling empathy*, you express your feeling of what the other person is feeling. You demonstrate a similarity between what you're feeling and what the other person is feeling. When your facial expressions are appropriate to the tone of the speaker's talk, you're communicating *feeling empathy*. Often you'll respond with both thinking and feeling empathy in the same brief response; for example, when you preface a question you might ask the speaker with a comment such as *I couldn't imagine what it would be like to live through a hurricane but now I do; it must have been horrendous.*

LISTEN WITH AN OPEN MIND

Listening with an open mind is difficult. It isn't easy to listen to arguments attacking your cherished beliefs. Listening often stops when such remarks are made. Yet in these situations it's particularly important to continue listening openly and fairly. To listen with an open mind, try these suggestions.

Avoid prejudging. Delay both positive and negative evaluation until you've fully understood the intention and the content of the message being communicated.

Avoid filtering out difficult, unpleasant, or undesirable messages. Avoid distorting messages through oversimplification or leveling, the tendency to eliminate details and to simplify complex messages to make them easier to remember.

Recognize your own **biases.** They may interfere with accurate listening and cause you to distort message reception to fit your own prejudices and expectations. Biases may also lead to sharpening—an effect in which an item of information takes on increased importance because it seems to confirm your stereotypes or prejudices.

Avoid **assimilation**—the tendency to reconstruct messages so they reflect your own attitudes, prejudices, needs, and values. Assimilation is the tendency to hear relatively neutral messages ("Management plans to institute drastic changes in scheduling") as supporting your own attitudes and beliefs ("Management is going to screw up our schedules again").

Whether in a lecture auditorium or in a small group, avoid prejudging some speeches as uninteresting or irrelevant. All speeches are, at least potentially, interesting and useful. If you prejudge them and then tune them out, you may not be proved wrong; however, you will close yourself off from potentially useful information. Most important, perhaps, is that you're not giving the other person a fair hearing.

LISTEN ETHICALLY

As a listener you share not only in the success or failure of any communication but also in the moral implications of the communication exchange. Consequently, bear ethical issues in mind when listening as well as when speaking. Two major principles govern ethical listening:

Give the speaker an honest hearing. To repeat: Avoid prejudging the speaker before hearing her or him out. Try to put aside prejudices and preconceptions and to evaluate the speaker's message fairly. At the same time, try to empathize with the speaker. You don't have to agree with the speaker, but try to understand emotionally as well as intellectually what he or she means. Then accept or reject the speaker's ideas on the basis of the information offered, not on the basis of some bias or prejudice or incomplete understanding.

Give the speaker honest responses and feedback. In a learning environment such as a public speaking class, listening ethically means giving frank and constructive criticism to help the speaker improve. It also means reflecting honestly on the questions speakers raise. Much as the listener has a right to expect an active speaker, the speaker has the right to expect a listener who will actively deal with, rather than just passively hear, the message of a speech.

In learning the art of public speaking, you can gain much insight from the criticism offered by others as well as from your own efforts to critique others' speeches. The following sections consider the nature of criticism in a learning environment, the influence of culture on criticism, and the standards and principles for evaluating a speech and for making criticism easier and more effective.

A POORLY CONSTRUCTED INFORMATIVE SPEECH

Public Speaking *Sample Assistant*

Here is an especially poor speech, constructed to illustrate clearly and briefly some of the major faults that can occur in flawed informative speeches. You may find it useful to return to this speech at different points in the course; as the course progresses, your analysis will become more complete, more insightful, and more effective. After you have reviewed the speech and the comments on the right, offer a one- or two-minute criticism of the speech.

Three Jobs

Well, I mean, hello. Er . . . I'm new at public speaking, so I'm a little nervous. I've always been shy. So don't watch my knees shake.

This nervous reaction is understandable but is probably best not shared with the listeners. After all, you don't want the audience to be uncomfortable for you.

Ehm, let me see my notes here. [Mumbles to self while shuffling notes: "One, two, three, four, five—oh, they're all here."] Okay, here goes.

Going through your notes makes the audience feel that you didn't prepare adequately and may just be wasting their time.

Three jobs. That's my title, and I'm going to talk about three jobs.

This is the speaker's orientation. Is this sufficient? What else might the speaker have done in the introduction? The title seems adequate but is not terribly exciting. After reading the speech, try to give it a more appealing title. In general, don't use your title as your opening words.

The Health Care Field. This is the fastest growing job in the country; one of the fastest, I guess I mean. I know that you're not interested in this topic and that you're all studying accounting. But there are a lot of new jobs in the health care field. The *Star* had an article on health care and said that health care will be needed more in the future than it is now. And now, you know, like they need a lot of health care people. In the hospital where I work—on the west side, uptown—they never have enough health aides and they always tell me to become a health aide, like you know, to enter the health care field. To become a nurse. Or maybe a dental technician. But I hate going to the dentist. Maybe I will.

Here the speaker shows such uncertainty that we question his or her competence.

And we begin to wonder, why is the speaker talking about this to us?

A report in the Star may be entertaining, but it doesn't constitute evidence. What does this reference do to the credibility you ascribe to the speaker?

I don't know what's going to happen with the president's health plan, but whatever happens, it won't change the need for health aides. I mean, people will still get sick, so it really doesn't matter what happens with health care.

Everything in the speech must have a definite purpose. Asides such as this comment about not liking to go to the dentist are probably best omitted.

Here the speaker had an opportunity to connect the topic with important current political events but failed to say anything that was not obvious.

The Robotics Field. This includes things like artificial intelligence. I don't really know what that is, but it's like growing real fast. They use this in making automobiles and planes and I think in computers. Japan is a leading country in this field. A lot of people in India go into this field, but I'm not sure why.

Introducing these topics like this is clear but is probably not very interesting. How might each of the three main topics have been introduced more effectively?

Notice how vague the speaker is—"includes things like," "and I think in computers," "I'm not sure why." Language like this communicates very little information to listeners and leaves them with little confidence that the speaker knows what he or she is talking about.

The Computer Graphics Field. This field has a lot to do with designing and making lots of different products, like CAD and CAM. This field also includes computer-aided imagery—CAI. And in movies, I think. Like *Star Wars* and *Terminator* 2. I saw *Terminator* 2 four times. I didn't see *Star Wars* but I'm gonna rent the video. I don't know if you have to know a lot about computers or if you can just like be a designer and someone else will tell the computer what to do.

Again, there is little that is specific. CAD and CAM are not defined and CAI is explained as "computer-aided imagery" but unless we already knew what these were, we would still not know even after hearing the speaker. Again, the speaker inserts personal notes (for example, seeing Terminator 2 four times) that have no meaningful connection to the topic.

I got my information from a book that Carol Kleiman wrote, *The 100 Best Jobs for the 1990s and Beyond*. It was summarized in last Sunday's *News*.

The speaker uses only one source and, to make matters worse, doesn't even go to the original source but relies on a summary in the local newspaper. Especially with a topic like this, listeners are likely to want a variety of viewpoints and additional reliable sources.

Note too that the speech lacked any statistics. This is a subject that demands facts and figures. Listeners will want to know how many jobs will be available in these fields, what these fields will look like in 5 or 10 years, how much these fields pay, and so on.

My conclusion. These are three of the fastest growing fields in the U.S. and in the world I think—but not in Third World countries, I don't think, China and India and Africa. More like Europe and Germany. And the U.S.—the U.S. is the big one. I hope you enjoyed my speech. Thank you.

Using the word conclusion to signal that you're concluding is not a bad idea, but work it into the text instead of using it like a heading in a book chapter.

Again, the speaker makes us question his or her competence and preparation by expressing uncertainty.

I wasn't as nervous as I thought I'd be. Are there any questions?

Again, personal comments are best left out.

SPEECH CRITICISM

Critics and criticism are essential parts of any art. The word *criticism* comes into English from the Latin *criticus*, which means "able to discern," "able to judge." Speech **criticism**, therefore, is the process of evaluating a speech, of rendering a judgment of its value. Note that there is nothing inherently negative about criticism; criticism may be negative, but it also may be positive.

Perhaps the major value of criticism in the classroom is that it helps you improve your public speaking skills. Through the constructive criticism of others, you'll learn the principles of public speaking more effectively. You'll be shown what you do well; what you could improve; and, ideally, how to improve. As a listener-critic you'll also learn the principles of public speaking through assessing the speeches of others. Just as you learn when you teach, you also learn when you criticize.

When you give criticism—as you do in a public speaking class—you're telling the speaker that you've listened carefully and that you care enough about the speech and the speaker to offer suggestions for improvement.

Of course, criticism can be difficult—for the critic (whether student or instructor) as well as for the person criticized. As a critic, you may feel embarrassed or uncomfortable about offering evaluation. After all, you may think, "Who am I to criticize another person's speech; my own speech won't be any better." Or you may be reluctant to offend, fearing that your criticism may make the speaker feel uncomfortable. Or you may view criticism as a confrontation that will do more harm than good.

But reconsider this view. By offering criticism you're helping the speaker; you're giving the speaker another perspective that should prove useful in future speeches. When you offer criticism, you're not claiming to be a better speaker; you're simply offering another point of view. It's true that by offering criticism, you're stating a position with which others may disagree. That's one of the things that will make this class and the study of public speaking exciting and challenging.

Criticism is also difficult to receive. After working on a speech for a week or two and dealing with the normal anxiety that comes with giving a speech, the last thing you want is to stand in front of the class and hear others say what you did wrong. Public speaking is ego-involving, and it's normal to take criticism personally. But if you learn how to give and how to receive criticism, it will help you improve your public speaking skills. Constructive criticism also can serve as an important support mechanism for the developing public speaker, a way of patting the speaker on the back for all the positive effort.

CULTURE AND CRITICISM

There are vast cultural differences in what is considered proper when it comes to criticism. For example, criticism will be viewed very differently depending on whether members come from an **individualist culture** (which emphasizes the individual and places primary value on the individual's goals) or a **collectivist culture** (which emphasizes the group and places primary value on the group's goals).

Individual and collective tendencies are not mutually exclusive; this isn't an all-or-none cultural orientation but rather a matter of emphasis. For example, in basketball, you may follow an individualist orientation and compete with other members of your team for most baskets or most valuable player award. However, in a game you will act with a collective orientation to benefit the entire group—in this case, to enable your team to win the game. In actual practice both individual and collective tendencies will help you and your team achieve your goals. At times, however, these tendencies may conflict; for example, do you shoot for the basket and try to raise your own individual score, or do you pass the ball to another player who is better positioned to score the basket and thus benefit your team?

Those who come from cultures that are highly individualist and competitive (the United States, Germany, and Sweden are examples) may find public criticism a normal part of the learning process. Those who come from cultures that are more collectivist and therefore emphasize the group rather than the individual (Japan, Mexico, and Korea are examples) are likely to find giving and receiving public criticism uncomfortable. Thus, people from individualist cultures may readily criticize speakers and are likely to expect the same "courtesy" from listeners. "After all" such a person might reason, "if I'm going to criticize your skills to help you improve, I expect you to help me in the same way." Persons from collectivist cultures, on the other hand, may feel that it's more important to be polite and courteous than to help someone learn a skill. Cultural rules that maintain peaceful relations among the Japanese (Midooka, 1990; Hendry, 1995; Watts, 2004) and norms of politeness among many Asian cultures (Fraser, 1990) may conflict with the classroom cultural norm calling for listeners to express honest criticism. In some cultures being kind to the person is more important than telling the truth, and so class members may say things that are complimentary but untrue in a strict literal sense.

Collectivist cultures place a heavy emphasis on face-saving—on allowing people always to appear in a positive light (James, 1995). In these cultures people may prefer not to say anything negative in public. In fact they may even be reluctant to say anything positive, lest any omission be construed as negative. Japanese executives, for instance, are reluctant to say no in a business meeting for fear of offending the other person. But their yes, properly interpreted in light of the context and the general discussion, may mean no. In cultures in which face-saving is especially important, communication rules such as the following tend to prevail:

- Don't express negative evaluation in public; instead, compliment the person.
- Don't prove someone wrong, especially in public; express agreement even if you know the person is wrong.
- Don't correct someone's errors; don't even acknowledge them.
- Don't ask difficult questions, lest the person not know the answer and lose face or be embarrassed; generally, avoid asking questions.

The difficulties that these differences may cause may be lessened if they're discussed openly. Some people may become comfortable with public criticism once it's explained that the cultural norms of most public speaking classrooms include public criticism just as they incorporate informative and persuasive speaking and written outlines. Others may feel more comfortable offering written criticism as a substitute for oral and public criticism. Or perhaps private consultations can be arranged.

PRINCIPLES FOR MORE EFFECTIVE CRITICISM

A useful standard to use in evaluating a classroom speech is the speech's degree of conformity to the principles of the art. Using this standard, you'll evaluate a speech positively when it follows the principles of public speaking established by the critics, theorists, and practitioners of public speaking (as described throughout this text) and evaluate it negatively if it deviates from these principles. These principles include speaking on a subject that is worthwhile, relevant, and interesting to listeners; designing a speech for a specific audience; and constructing a speech that is based on sound research. A critical checklist for analyzing public speeches that is based on these principles is presented on the inside front cover of this book.

Before reading the specific suggestions for making critical evaluations a more effective part of the total learning process and avoiding some of the potentially negative aspects of criticism, take the following self-test, which asks you to identify what's wrong with selected critical comments.

*T*EST YOURSELF

What's Wrong with These Critical Comments?

For the purposes of this exercise, assume that each of the following 10 comments represents the critic's complete criticism. What's wrong with each?

_____ **1.** I loved the speech. It was great. Really great.

_____ **2.** The introduction didn't gain my attention.

_____ **3.** You weren't interested in your own topic. How do you expect us to be interested?

_____ **4.** Nobody was able to understand you.

_____ **5.** The speech was weak.

_____ **6.** The speech didn't do anything for me.

_____ **7.** Your position was unfair to those of us on athletic scholarships; we earned those scholarships.

_____ **8.** I found four things wrong with your speech. First,...

_____ **9.** You needed better research.

_____ **10.** I liked the speech; we need more police on campus.

HOW DID YOU DO? Before reading the following discussion, try to explain why each of these statements is ineffective. Visualize yourself as the speaker receiving such comments and ask yourself if these comments would help you in any way. If not, then they are probably not very effective critical evaluations.

WHAT WILL YOU DO? To help you improve your criticism, try to restate the basic meaning of each of these comments but in a more constructive manner.

Consider the possible negative reactions to speech criticism. What might the critic do to lessen any negative reactions people might have to criticism of their speech? What might the speaker do to lessen any of his or her own negative reactions?

STRESS THE POSITIVE

Egos are fragile, and public speaking is extremely personal. Speakers understand what Noel Coward meant when he said, "I love criticism just as long as it's unqualified praise." Part of your function as a critic is to strengthen the already positive aspects of someone's public speaking performance. Positive criticism is particularly important in itself, but it's almost essential as a preface to negative comments. There are always positive characteristics about any speech, and it's more productive to concentrate on these first. Thus, instead of saying (as in the self-test), "The speech didn't do anything for me," tell the speaker what you liked first, then bring up a weak point and suggest how it might be improved.

When criticizing a person's second or third speech, it's especially helpful if you can point out specific improvements ("You really held my attention in this speech," "I felt you were much more in control of the topic today than in your first speech").

Remember, too, that communication is irreversible. Once you say something, you can't take it back. Remember this when offering criticism, especially criticism that may be negative. If in doubt, err on the side of gentleness.

BE SPECIFIC

Criticism is most effective when it's specific. General statements such as "I thought your delivery was bad," "I thought your examples were good," or, as in the self-test, "I loved the speech. . . . Really great" and "The speech was weak" are poorly expressed criticisms. These statements don't specify what the speaker might do to improve delivery or to capitalize on the examples used. In commenting on delivery, refer to such specifics as eye contact, vocal volume, or whatever else is of consequence. In commenting on the examples, tell the speaker why they were good. Were they realistic? Were they especially interesting? Were they presented dramatically?

In giving negative criticism, specify and justify—to the extent that you can—positive alternatives. Here's an example.

> I thought the way you introduced your statistics was vague. I wasn't sure where the statistics came from or how recent or reliable they were. It might have been better to say something like "The U.S. Census figures for 2000 show. . . ." That way we would know that the statistics were as recent as possible and the most reliable available.

BE OBJECTIVE

In criticizing a speech, transcend your own biases as best you can, unlike the self-test's example ("Your position was unfair . . .; we earned those scholarships"). See the speech as objectively as possible. Assume, for example, that you're strongly for a woman's right to an abortion and you encounter a speech diametrically opposed to your position. In this situation you'll need to take special care not to dismiss the speech because of your own biases. Examine the speech from the point of view of a detached critic; evaluate, for example, the validity of the arguments and their suitability to the audience, the language, and the supporting materials. Conversely, take special care not to evaluate a speech positively because it presents a position with which you agree, as in "I liked the speech; we need more police on campus."

BE CONSTRUCTIVE

Your primary goal should be to provide the speaker with insight that will prove useful in future public speaking transactions. For example, to say that "The introduction didn't gain my attention" doesn't tell the speaker how he or she might have gained your attention. Instead, you might say, "The example about the computer crash would have more effectively gained my attention in the introduction."

Another way you can be constructive is to limit your criticism. Cataloging a speaker's weak points, as in "I found four things wrong with your speech," will overwhelm, not help, the speaker. If you're the sole critic, your criticism naturally will need to be more extensive. If you're one of many critics, limit your criticism to one or perhaps two points. In all cases, your guide should be the value your comments will have for the speaker.

FOCUS ON BEHAVIOR

Focus criticism on what the speaker said and did during the actual speech. Try to avoid the very natural tendency to read the mind of the speaker—to assume that you know why the speaker did one thing rather than another. Compare the critical comments presented in Table 3.1. Note that those in the first column, "Criticism as Attack," try to identify the reasons the speaker did as he or she did; they try to read the speaker's mind. At the same time, they blame the speaker for what happened. Those in the second column, "Criticism as Support," focus on the specific behavior. Note, too, that those in the first column are likely to encourage defensiveness; you can almost hear the speaker saying, "I was so interested in the topic." Those in the second column are less likely to create defensiveness and are more likely to be appreciated as honest reflections of how the critic perceived the speech.

TABLE 3.1 **Criticism as Attack and as Support**

Can you develop additional examples to illustrate criticism as attack and as support?

CRITICISM AS ATTACK	CRITICISM AS SUPPORT
"You weren't interested in your topic."	"I would have liked to see greater variety in your delivery. It would have made me feel that you were more interested."
"You should have put more time into the speech."	"I think it would have been more effective if you had looked at your notes less."
"You didn't care about your audience."	"I would have liked it if you had looked more directly at me while speaking."

OWN YOUR CRITICISM

In giving criticism, own your comments; take responsibility for them. The best way to express this ownership is to use **I-messages** rather than **you-messages.** That is, instead of saying, "You needed better research," say, "I would have been more persuaded if you had used more recent research."

Owning criticism also means avoiding attributing what you found wrong to others. Instead of saying, "Nobody was able to understand you," say, "I had difficulty understanding you. It would have helped me if you had spoken more slowly." Remember that your criticism is important precisely because it's your perception of what the speaker did and what the speaker could have done more effectively. Speaking for the entire audience ("We couldn't hear you clearly" or "No one was convinced by your arguments") will not help the speaker, and it's likely to prove demoralizing.

Employing I-messages also will prevent you from using "should messages," a type of expression that almost invariably creates defensiveness and resentment. When you say "You should have done this" or "You shouldn't have done that," you assume a superior position and imply that what you're saying is correct and that what the speaker did was incorrect. On the other hand, when you own your evaluations and use I-messages, you're giving your perceptions; it's then up to the speaker to accept or reject them.

RECOGNIZE YOUR ETHICAL OBLIGATIONS

Just as the speaker and listener have ethical obligations, so does the critic. Here are a few guidelines. First, the ethical critic *separates personal feelings about the speaker* from his or her evaluation of the speech. A liking for the speaker shouldn't lead you to give positive evaluations of the speech, nor should disliking the speaker lead you to give negative evaluations of the speech.

A Case of **Ethics**   CRITICIZING A SPEECH

You and a person you're dating fairly steadily are taking a public speaking course together, and your dating partner just gave a pretty terrible speech. Unfortunately, the instructor has asked you to offer a critique of the speech. The wrinkle here is that you've noticed that the grades your instructor gives for speeches seem heavily influenced by what student critics say. So, in effect, your critique will largely determine your date's grade—and perhaps your future relationship. You'd like to give your dating partner a positive critique. Besides, you figure, you can always tell the truth later and even help your partner improve.

Ethical Choice Point *How might you give an honest critique and still preserve the relationship? More generally, what ethical obligations does a critic have when evaluating the work of friends or romantic partners?*

Second, the ethical critic *separates personal feelings about the issues* from an evaluation of the validity of the arguments. The ethical critic recognizes the validity of an argument even if it contradicts a deeply held belief; similarly, he or she recognizes the fallaciousness of an argument even if it supports a deeply held belief.

Third, the ethical critic *is culturally sensitive*, is aware of his or her own ethnocentrism, and doesn't negatively evaluate customs and forms of speech simply because they deviate from her or his own. Similarly, the ethical critic does not positively evaluate a speech just because it supports her or his own cultural beliefs and values. The ethical critic does not discriminate against or favor speakers simply because they're of a particular sex, race, nationality, religion, age group, or affectional orientation.

LISTENING TO CRITICISM

At the same time that you need to express your criticism effectively, you'll also want to listen to criticism effectively. Here are some suggestions for making listening to criticism a less difficult and more productive experience. These suggestions, it needs to be added, are appropriate in a learning environment such as a public speaking class, where criticism is used as a learning tool. In business and professional public speaking, in contrast, listeners don't offer suggestions for improvement; rather, they focus on the issues you raised.

ACCEPT THE CRITIC'S VIEWPOINT

Criticism reflects the listener's perception. Because of this, the critic is always right. If the critic says that he or she wasn't convinced by your evidence, it doesn't help to identify the 10 or 12 research sources that you used in your speech; this critic was simply not convinced. Instead, consider why your evidence was not convincing. Perhaps you didn't make clear how the evidence was connected to your thesis or perhaps you raced through it too quickly. If you hear yourself saying, "But, I did . . . ," then consider the possibility that you're not accepting the critic's point of view.

LISTEN WITH AN OPEN MIND

If you've already given your first speech, you know that public speaking is highly ego-involving. Because of this it may be tempting to block out criticism. After all, it's not easy to listen to criticism, especially in a fairly public place like a classroom filled with your peers. But if you do block out such criticism, you'll likely lose out on some useful suggestions for improvement. Realize too that you're in a learning environment—a kind of public speaking laboratory—and you're expected to make mistakes. And if this is your first exposure to public speaking, there's likely to be much room for improvement. So listen to criticism with an open mind, and let the critics know that you're really paying attention to what they have to say. In this way you'll encourage critics to share their perceptions more freely; in the process you'll gain greater insight into how you come across to an audience.

SEPARATE SPEECH CRITICISM FROM PERSONAL CRITICISM

Because public speaking is so ego-involving, some speakers personalize the criticism to the point where they experience a suggestion for improvement as a personal attack. Even when this perception is not conscious, it seems to influence the way in which criticism is taken. So recognize that when some aspect of your speech is criticized, your personality or your worth as an individual isn't being criticized or attacked. Listen to speech criticism with the same detachment that you'd use in listening to a biology instructor help you adjust the lens on the microscope or a computer expert tell you how to import photos into your blog.

SEEK CLARIFICATION

If you don't understand the criticism, ask for clarification. For example, if you're told that your specific purpose was too broad but it's unclear to you how you might narrow it, ask the critic to explain—being careful not to appear defensive or confrontational. Even when the criticism is favorable, if you don't understand it or it's not specific enough, ask for clarification. If a critic says, "Your introduction was great," you might want to say something like "Did it grab your attention?" or "Was it clear what I was going to cover in the speech?" In this way you encourage the critic to elaborate.

EVALUATE THE CRITICISM

The suggestion to listen open-mindedly to criticism does not necessarily mean that you should do as critics say. Instead, evaluate what the critics suggest; perhaps even try out the suggestions (in your next rehearsal or in the actual speech); but then make your own decisions as to what criticisms you'll follow totally, what you'll modify and adapt, and what you'll reject.

Essentials of Listening and Criticism

This chapter looked at listening and criticism and offered suggestions for making your listening and your criticism more effective.

1. **Listening** is a five-stage process: (1) receiving the speaker's verbal and nonverbal messages, (2) understanding the speaker's thoughts and emotions, (3) remembering and retaining the messages, (4) evaluating or judging the messages, and (5) responding or reacting to the messages.

2. **Cultural differences** in language and speech, nonverbal behavioral differences, ethnocentrism, and gender differences can create listening difficulties.

3. Among the **principles for effective listening** are these:
   - Listen actively (use listening time; work hard; assume value; and, if appropriate, take notes).
   - Listen for total meaning (focus on both verbal and nonverbal messages, connect specifics to the general thesis, attend to both surface and deep meanings).
   - Listen with empathy (see the speaker's point of view, understand the speaker's feelings and thoughts, avoid offensive listening).
   - Listen with an open mind (avoid prejudging and filtering out difficult messages, recognize your own biases).
   - Listen ethically (give the speaker an honest hearing and honest feedback).

4. **Criticism** is a process of judging and evaluating a work. Criticism can (1) identify strengths and weaknesses and thereby help you improve as a public speaker, (2) identify standards for evaluating all sorts of public speeches, and (3) show that the audience is listening and is concerned about the speaker's progress.

5. **Cultural differences** in criticism need to be considered. Cultures differ in their views of criticism and in the rules considered appropriate. For example, members of individualist cultures may find public criticism easier and more acceptable than people from collectivist cultures.

6. Among the **principles for effective criticism** are these:
   - Stress the positive.
   - Be specific.
   - Be objective.
   - Be constructive.
   - Focus on behavior.
   - Own your criticism.
   - Recognize your ethical obligations.

7. In **listening to criticism**:
   - Accept the critic's viewpoint.
   - Listen with an open mind.
   - Separate speech criticism from personal criticism.
   - Seek clarification.
   - Evaluate the criticism.

Essential Terms: Listening and Criticism

active listening **(p. 45)**
assimilation **(p. 49)**
biases **(p. 49)**
collectivist culture **(p. 52)**
criticism **(p. 52)**
empathy **(p. 47)**
ethnocentrism **(p. 44)**

evaluating **(p. 41)**
I-messages **(p. 57)**
individualist culture **(p. 52)**
listening **(p. 39)**
nonverbal communication **(p. 43)**
owning criticism **(p. 57)**

receiving **(p. 40)**
remembering **(p. 41)**
responding **(p. 42)**
understanding **(p. 41)**
you-messages **(p. 57)**

Public Speaking Exercises

3.1 Do You Really Remember What You Hear?

When you remember a message, do you remember what was said, or do you remember what you think you heard? The commonsense response, of course, would be that you remember what was said. But before accepting this simple explanation, try to memorize the list of 12 words presented below, modeled on an idea from a research study (Glucksberg & Danks, 1975). Don't worry about the order of the words; only the number of words remembered counts. Take about 20 seconds to memorize as many words as possible. Then close the book and write down as many words as you can remember.

dining	table	milk
cafeteria	shopping	hungry
green beans	steak	having lunch
satisfied	knife	menu

Don't read any farther until you've tried to memorize and reproduce the list of words.

If you're like most people, you not only remembered a good number of the words on the list but also "remembered" at least one word that was not on the list: *eating*. Most people would recall the word as being on the list (whether they read the list as you've done here or hear it spoken)—but, as you can see, it wasn't. What happens is that in remembering you don't simply reproduce the list; you reconstruct it. In this case you gave the list meaning, and part of that meaning included the word *eating*. In remembering speech, then, you reconstruct the messages you hear into a system that makes sense to you—but, in the process, often remember distorted versions of what was said.

3.2 Understanding Your Own Listening Barriers

Most of us put on blinders when we encounter particular topics or particular spokespersons. Sometimes these blinders prevent us from listening fairly and objectively. For example, you may avoid listening to certain people or reading certain newspapers because they frequently contradict your beliefs. Sometimes these blinders color the information you take in, influencing you to take a positive view of some information (because it may support one of your deeply held beliefs) and a negative view of other information (because it may contradict such beliefs).

Read over the following speech situations and identify at least one barrier that you (or someone else) might set up for each situation.

1. Bill Cosby on educating children
2. Bill Gates on financial mistakes the government must avoid
3. A representative from General Motors urging greater restrictions on foreign imports
4. A homeless person petitioning to be allowed to sleep in the local public library
5. An Iranian couple talking about the need to return to fundamentalist Islamic values
6. A person with AIDS speaking in favor of lower drug prices

3.3 Listening to New Ideas

Ideally, speeches communicate information that is new and potentially useful to you as a listener. A useful technique in listening to new ideas is PIP'N, a technique that derives from the insights of Carl Rogers (1970) on paraphrase as a means for ensuring understanding and from Edward deBono's (1976) PMI (plus, minus, interesting) technique for critical thinking. In analyzing new ideas with the PIP'N technique, you follow four steps:

P = Paraphrase. State in your own words what you think the other person is saying. Paraphrasing will help you understand and remember the idea.

I = Interesting. Consider why the idea is interesting.

P = Positive. Think about what's good about the idea; for example, might it solve a problem or improve a situation?

N = Negative. Think about any negatives that the idea might entail; for example, might it be expensive or difficult to implement?

Consider how you might use PIP'N to gain insight—into, say, the cultural emphasis you find in your college textbooks or in a particular required course, or into the PIP'N technique itself.

3.4 What Do You Say?

◆ **Self-Identification.** Claire is planning to give a speech in favor of gay marriage. Claire herself is heterosexual, and she wonders if she should identify her affectional orientation in the speech. If Claire were giving her speech to your class, what would you see as the advantages and disadvantages of including reference to her own affectional orientation? Would the advantages and disadvantages you identified be different if Claire were a lesbian? What would you advise Claire to do?

◆ **Ethical Listening.** Simone is teaching a class in public speaking, and one of her students, a sincere and devout Iranian Muslim, gives a speech on "why women should be subservient to men." After the first two minutes of the speech, half the class walks out, returning 10 minutes later, after the speech is over. Simone decides to address this incident. What would you advise Simone to say?

◆ **Giving Criticism.** Hiro has been asked to serve as a guest judge for students in a sixth-grade class who are giving their first public speeches. The audience will consist of students, a few teachers, and the parents of the students. What advice would you give Hiro for presenting critiques? How might your advice differ if Hiro were critiquing the speeches of potential political candidates?

◆ **Criticizing a Speech.** Isaac has just given a speech on the glory of bullfighting. Peter sees bullfighting as cruelty to animals; to Isaac, however, this traditional spectacle is an important part of his culture.

As Peter bristles inside, the instructor asks him to critique the speech. How would you advise Peter to proceed?

Log*On!* MySpeechLab

Listening and Criticism

Visit MySpeechLab (www.myspeechlab.com) to explore further the topic of listening and criticism. See, for example, "Active Listening, Effective Listening, and Steps in Listening" (*Explore*). Also see "How to Listen with Questions," "Obstacles to Effective Listening," and "Standards for Criticism." Exercises relevant to this chapter include "Sequential Communication," 'Listening Actively," and "Typical Man, Typical Woman." A great way to begin focusing on speech criticism is to view two versions of the same speech. See for example, the effective and ineffective versions of the speeches "Untreated Depression" and "Brain Research." Also view the speech "Van Gogh's Incredible Life" and the critique of it (*Watch*).

In connection with the Research Link in this chapter (p. 46), take a look at the interviewing video on MSL.

The Allyn & Bacon public speaking website (www .ablongman.com/pubspeak) contains a wide variety of hot links to websites containing text, audio, and/or video files of speeches on which you can practice the skills of listening and criticism.

Selecting Your Topic, Purpose, and Thesis

4

Why Read This Chapter?

Because it will enable you to develop a more effective speech by helping you to:

- find a topic that is interesting to you and to your audience
- phrase a purpose statement that crystallizes what you hope to achieve in your speech and that will guide you as you prepare the speech
- formulate a thesis sentence, a statement of your central idea

There is no such thing as an uninteresting subject; there are only uninteresting people.

**—Gilbert Keith Chesterton (1874–1936)
English journalist and novelist, best known for his Father Brown mysteries**

Now that the basic steps in public speaking preparation have been established along with the fundamentals of controlling apprehension and the basics of listening and criticizing, you can focus on the first step in public speaking, selecting a topic (and narrowing it down so that you can cover it in the allotted time), selecting a purpose, and framing your central idea or thesis.

YOUR TOPIC

As you begin to think about public speaking and especially about your own speech, perhaps the first question you have is "What do I speak about?" "What topic would be appropriate?" The answer to this question will change as your life situation changes; in the years ahead you'll most likely speak on topics that grow out of your job or your social or political activities. In the classroom, however, where your objective is to learn the skills of public speaking, there are literally thousands of subjects to talk about. Nevertheless, the question remains: "What do I speak about?" To answer this question, focus on three related questions: What makes a good topic? How do I find such a topic? and How do I focus or limit my topic?

A GOOD PUBLIC SPEAKING TOPIC

A good public speaking topic is one that deals with matters of substance, is appropriate to you and the audience, and is culturally sensitive. Let's consider each briefly. These three characteristics suggest some guidelines for selecting a good topic.

Substantive

The most important criterion of a good topic is that it *deal with matters of substance*. So select a topic that is important enough to merit the time and attention of a group of intelligent people. Ask yourself: Would this topic engage the attention of my classmates? Would a reputable newspaper cover such a topic? Would students find this topic relevant to their social or professional lives?

Appropriate

Select a topic that is *appropriate to you as the speaker*. For example, if you're male, it probably isn't a good idea to give a speech on the stages of childbirth. On the other hand, if you're female and have just given birth, this might be a good topic. If you've never been incarcerated, then a speech on what life is like in prison is probably not going to ring true to your audience. If you're known as someone with lots of money who is always spending, then giving a speech on how to scrape by on $3 a day is not likely to be well received. The best way to look at this criterion is to ask if—given what the audience already knows about you and what you'll tell them during your speech—your listeners will see you as a knowledgeable and believable spokesperson on this topic. If the answer is yes, then you have a topic appropriate to you as a speaker. If the answer is no, then it will probably be useful to continue your search for an appropriate topic. The next section focuses on this search.

Also, select a topic that is *appropriate to your audience in terms of their interests and needs*. Giving a speech on the usefulness of a computer to students in your class will be inappropriate simply because they already know about that. But that same topic may be quite appropriate if given at a senior center where most of the members do not own computers. Giving a speech advocating a specific religious belief may well prove insulting to members of the audience who don't share your religious beliefs. Yet that same speech may be very well received by members of a particular religious congregation. So always look to your audience when thinking about a topic, and try to gauge their reaction to it. After all, your audience is giving you their time and attention; selecting a topic that is responsive to their needs and interests seems only fair.

Culturally Sensitive

A good topic is *culturally sensitive*. So select a topic that will not offend members of other cultures (who may even be in your audience). But also recognize that we live in a time when a person's degree of **cultural sensitivity** is taken as a sign of education and sophistication, attainments that can only help a speaker.

In many Arab, Asian, and African cultures, for example, discussing sex in an audience of both men and women would be considered obscene and offensive. In Scandinavian cultures, on the other hand, sex is expected to be discussed openly and without embarrassment or discomfort. Listed below are some topics that intercultural experts recommend that Americans avoid when traveling abroad. These **taboo topics** change with the times, however, so what is true today may not be true tomorrow (Axtell, 1993; Allan & Burridge, 2007):

- In the Caribbean avoid discussions of race, local politics, and religion.
- In Colombia avoid politics and criticism of bullfighting.
- In Egypt avoid Middle Eastern politics.
- In Japan avoid discussion of World War II.
- In Mexico avoid talking about the Mexican-American War and illegal aliens.
- In the Philippines avoid discussing politics, religion, corruption, or foreign aid.
- In South Korea don't talk about internal politics or voice criticism of the government, socialism, or communism.
- In Spain avoid discussions of family, religion, or jobs, and refrain from negative comments on bullfighting.

*F*INDING TOPICS

Here are five ways to find topics: yourself, brainstorming, surveys, news items, and topic generators.

Yourself

Perhaps your first step in thinking about appropriate speech topics is to look at yourself. What are you interested in? What engages your time and interest? If you were in a bookstore, what book topics would encourage you to flip through the books? What titles of magazine articles would interest you enough so that you would thumb through the magazine? What topics would encourage you actually to buy the magazine? In short, think about your own interests; they may be similar to your audience's.

At the same time that you consider your interests, consider your own unique experiences. Have you been a part of well-known events or lived in different places? Do you have special talents? Are you knowledgeable about odd or different topics? What are your hobbies? If you're a philatelist, a speech on unique stamps or the value of some stamps or the way in which stamps are printed might prove interesting. If you're a spelunker, perhaps a speech on caves, how they form, and what they mean to the ecology might prove interesting.

If you plan a speech on a topic that you're interested in and want to learn more about, you'll enjoy and profit from the entire experience a great deal more. The research that you do for your speech, for example, will be more meaningful; the facts you uncover will be more interesting. At the same time, your enthusiasm for your topic is likely to make your delivery more exciting, less anxiety-provoking, and more engaging to the audience. All around, you win by selecting a topic in which you're especially interested or to which you have a special connection.

Brainstorming

Another useful method for finding a topic is **brainstorming**, a technique designed to enable you to generate lots of topics in a relatively short time (DeVito, 1996; Osborn, 1957). You begin with your "problem," which in this case is "What will I talk about?" You then record any and all ideas that occur to you. Allow your mind to free-associate. Don't censor yourself; instead, allow your ideas to flow as freely as possible. Record all your thoughts, regardless of how silly or inappropriate they may seem. Write them down or record them on tape. Try to generate as many ideas as possible. The more ideas you think of, the better your chances of finding a suitable topic in your list. After you've generated a sizable list—it should take you no longer than five minutes—read over the list or replay the tape. Do any of the topics on your list suggest other topics? If so, write these down as well. Can you combine or extend your ideas? Which ideas seem workable?

Surveys

Look at some of the national and regional polls concerning what people consider important—polls that identify the significant issues, the urgent problems. For example, Medical News Today (www.medicalnewstoday.com, accessed February 11, 2007) identifies such health topics as bird flu, cervical cancer vaccination, the increase in autism, the need for interpersonal skills training within the health care professions, AIDS, DNA patenting, and genetic modification. The Rand Corporation (www.rand.org/pubs, accessed February 11, 2007) identified such technological issues as eugenics, cloning, stem cells, privacy of genetic profiles, biological weapons, smart materials (clothing, vehicles, identification systems), integrated microsystems, the pace of technological change, class disparities, and reduced privacy. And in the workplace, Deacons (www.deacons.com, accessed February 11, 2007), an international law firm in Asia and Australia, identifies such issues as fatigue management, hazardous substance management, workplace stress, ergonomics, and risk management.

Survey data are now easier than ever to get, because many of the larger poll results are available on the Internet. For example, the Gallup Organization maintains a website at www.gallup.com that includes national and international surveys on political, social, consumer, and other issues speakers often talk about. The Polling Report website also will prove useful; it provides a wealth of polling data on issues in fields such as political science, business, journalism, health, and social science (www.pollingreport.com). Other sources are search directories such as Hotbot or Yahoo!, where you can examine the major directory topics and any subdivisions of those you'd care to pursue—a process that's explained later in this chapter. Many search engines and browsers provide lists of "hot topics," which are often useful starting points. These topics are exactly the topics that people are talking about and therefore often make excellent speech topics.

Or you can conduct a survey yourself. Roam through the nonfiction section of your bookstore (online, if you prefer—for example, at Amazon, www.amazon.com, Barnes and Noble, www.bn.com, or Borders, www.borders.com) and you'll quickly develop a list of the topics book buyers consider important. A glance at your newspaper's best-seller list will give you an even quicker overview.

News Items

Other useful starting points are newspapers and newsmagazines. Here you'll find the important international and domestic issues, the financial issues, and the social issues all conveniently packaged in one place. The editorial page and the letters to the editor also are useful indicators of what people are concerned about.

Newsmagazines such as *Time* and *Newsweek* and financial magazines such as *Forbes*, *Money*, and *Fortune* (in print or online) will provide a wealth of suggestions. Similarly, news shows such as *20/20*, *60 Minutes*, and *Meet the Press*

Consider the topics that television news programs select. How might you use these topics as starting points for developing informative or persuasive speeches? Focusing on just this week, what topics are the national media highlighting?

and even the ubiquitous talk shows (and their corresponding websites) often identify the very issues that people are concerned with and on which there are conflicting points of view.

Topic Lists

One of the easiest ways of examining and selecting a potential topic is to look at some of the topic lists that are available. For example, "The Dictionary of Topics" (available at www.myspeechlab.com) lists hundreds of appropriate topics for informative and persuasive speeches. It's simply a dictionary-like listing of subjects within which each topic is broken down into several subtopics. These subtopics should begin to suggest potential subjects for your informative and persuasive speeches. A small sample of this dictionary is presented in Table 4.1.

There are also useful topic lists that have been compiled by various communication and English instructors. For example, the University of Hawaii maintains a website, Topic Selection Helper, which lists hundreds of topics (www.hawaii.edu/mauispeech/html/infotopichelp.html), accessed February 11, 2007). Similarly, Cincinnati State Technical and Community College has lists for informative and persuasive speeches at http://faculty.cinstate.cc.oh.us/gesellsc/publicspeaking/topics.html.

Some websites contain **topic generators** where you can repeatedly press a button and view a wide variety of topics. For example, WritingFix (www.writingfix.com, accessed February 11, 2007) helps you with topics for writing (which can often, though not always, be adapted for public speaking). And McMaster eBusiness Research Center (http://merc.mcmaster.ca/mclaren/ebiztopics.html, accessed February 11, 2007) maintains a topic generator for business topics.

There is another class of websites that will sell you speeches and term papers for a fee, and in searching for topics you're likely to run across these sites. Avoid these websites. Many colleges now have software to identify plagiarism, so it's easy to get caught; considering that the consequences are often severe, it's not worth going that route. Another reason for not using these sites and services is that by letting others do your work for you, you'll never learn the very skills that you'll need in your life.

LIMITING TOPICS

Probably the major error beginning speakers make is to try to cover a huge topic in too short a time. The inevitable result is that such speakers cannot cover anything in depth; they touch on everything superficially. To be suitable for a public speech, a topic must be limited in scope; it must be narrowed down to fit the time restrictions and yet permit some depth of coverage.

Another reason to narrow your topic is that it will help you focus your collecting of research materials. If your topic is too broad, you'll be forced to review a lot more research material than you're going to need. On the other hand, if you narrow your topic, you can search for information more efficiently. Here are three methods for narrowing and limiting your topic: topoi, tree diagrams, and search directories.

Topoi, the System of Topics

Topoi, the system of topics is a technique that comes from the classical rhetorics of ancient Greece and Rome but today is used more widely as a stimulus to creative thinking (DeVito, 1996). Using this method of **topoi**, you ask yourself a

TABLE 4.1 The Dictionary of Topics

This table presents just a few general topics to illustrate how you can use existing lists as ideas for speech topics. Lists like these will stimulate you to think of subjects dealing with topics you're interested in but may not have thought of as appropriate to a public speech. Each topic is broken down into several subtopics that should stimulate you to see these as potential ideas for your informative and persuasive speeches. Just a small sampling of topics is presented here; a much more extensive "dictionary of topics" may be found at www.myspeechlab.com.

Abortion arguments for and against; techniques of; religious dimension; legal views; differing views of

Academic freedom nature of; censorship; teachers' role in curriculum development; and government; and research; restrictions on

Acupuncture nature of; development of; current practices in; effectiveness of; dangers of

Adoption agencies for; procedures; difficulties in; illegal; concealment of biological parents; search for birth parents

Advertising techniques; expenditures; ethical; unethical; subliminal; leading agencies; history of; slogans

Age ageism; aging processes; aid to the aged; discrimination against the aged; treatment of the aged; different cultural views of aging; sex differences

Aggression aggressive behavior in animals; in humans; as innate; as learned; and territoriality

Agriculture science of; history of; in ancient societies; technology of; theories of

Air pollution travel; embolism; law; navigation; power; raids

Alcoholism nature of; Alcoholics Anonymous; Al Anon; abstinence; among the young; treatment of

Amnesty in draft evasion; in criminal law; and pardons; in Civil War; in Vietnam War; conditions of

Animals experimentation; intelligence of; aggression in; ethology; and communication

series of questions about your general subject. The process will help you see divisions of your general topic on which you might want to focus. Table 4.2 provides an example; the column on the left contains seven general questions (Who? What? Why? When? Where? How? and So?) and a series of subquestions (which will vary depending on your topic). The right column illustrates how some of the questions on the left might suggest specific aspects of the general subject of "homelessness."

Tree Diagrams

Tree diagrams help you to divide your topic repeatedly into its significant parts. Starting with the general topic, you divide it into its parts. Then you take one of these parts and divide it into its parts. You continue with this dividing process until the topic seems manageable—until you believe you can reasonably cover it in some depth in the time allotted.

TABLE 4.2 Topoi, the System of Topics

These questions should enable you to use general topics to generate more specific ideas for your speeches. Try this system on any one of the topics listed in the Dictionary of Topics at www.myspeechlab.com. You'll be amazed at how many topics you'll be able to find. Your problem will quickly change from "What can I speak on?" to "Which one of these should I speak on?" Here's an example on the topic of homelessness.

GENERAL QUESTIONS	SUBJECT-SPECIFIC QUESTIONS
Who? Who is he or she, or who are they? Who is responsible? To whom was it done?	Who are the homeless? Who is the typical homeless person? Who is responsible for the increase in homelessness? Who cares for the homeless?
What? What is it? What effects does it have? What is it like? What is it different from? What are some examples?	What does it mean to be homeless? What does homelessness do to the people themselves? What does homelessness do to the society in general? What does homelessness mean to you and me?
Why? Why does it happen? Why does it not happen?	Why is there homelessness? Why are there so many homeless people? Why did this happen? Why does it happen in the larger cities more than in smaller towns? Why is it more prevalent in some countries than in others?
When? When did it happen? When will it occur? When will it end?	When did homelessness become so prevalent? When does it occur in the life of a person?
Where? Where did it come from? Where is it going? Where is it now?	Where is homelessness most prevalent? Where is there an absence of homelessness?
How? How does it work? How is it used? How do you do it? How do you operate it? How is it organized?	How does someone become homeless? How can we help the homeless? How can we prevent others from becoming homeless?
So? What does it mean? What is important about it? Why should I be concerned with this? Who cares?	Why is homelessness such an important social problem? Why must we be concerned with homelessness? How does all this affect me?

Figure 4.1 illustrates a tree diagram that begins with the topic of mass communication. Take the topic of television programs as the first general topic area. Television programs, without some limitation, would take a lifetime to cover adequately. So you might divide this topic into such subtopics as comedy, children's programs, educational programs, news, movies, reality programs, soap operas, game shows, and sports. You might then take one of these topics, say comedy, and divide it into subtopics. Perhaps you might consider it on a time basis and divide television comedy into its significant time periods: pre-1960, 1961–1999, 2000 to the present. Or you might focus on situation comedies. Here you might examine a topic such as women in situation comedies,

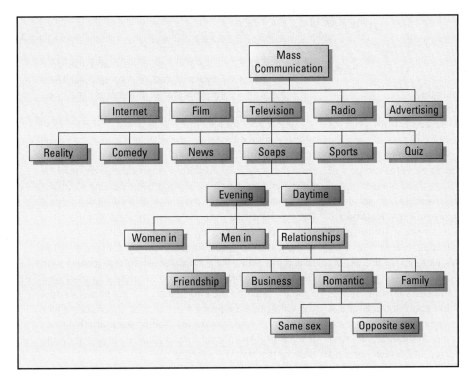

Figure 4.1
A Tree Diagram for Limiting Speech Topics
How would you draw a tree diagram for limiting topics beginning with such general subjects as immigration, education, sports, transportation, or politics? An alternative method for limiting topics with the "Fishbone Diagram" may be found at www.myspeechlab.com.

From Joseph A. DeVito, *The Elements of Public Speaking, 7e.* Published by Allyn & Bacon, Boston, MA. Copyright © 2000 by Pearson Education. Reprinted by permission of the publisher.

race relations in situation comedies, or family relationships in situation comedies. The resultant topics are at least beginning to look manageable.

Search Directories

A more technologically sophisticated way of both selecting and limiting your topic is to let a search directory do some of the work for you. A **search directory** is a nested list of topics. You go from the general to the specific by selecting a topic, and then a subdivision of that topic, and then a subdivision of that subdivision. Eventually you'll find your way to relatively specific areas and websites that will suggest topics that may be suitable for a classroom speech.

YOUR PURPOSE

The purpose of your speech is the goal you want to achieve; it identifies the effect that you want your speech to have on your audience. In constructing your speech you'll first identify your general purpose and then your **specific purpose**.

GENERAL PURPOSE

Since you're now in a course in learning public speaking skills, your **general purpose** will likely be chosen for you. And in this the classroom is very like the real world. The situation, the audience you'll address, and the nature of your job will dictate whether your speech is to be informative or persuasive. If you're a lawyer giving a closing at a trial, your speech must be persuasive. If you're an engineer explaining new blueprints, your speech must be informative. If you're

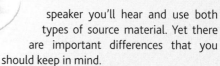

Research Link

PRIMARY AND SECONDARY SOURCES

As a researcher, be sure to distinguish between primary and secondary source material whether your materials come from print or online. *Primary sources* include, for example, an original research study reported in an academic journal, a corporation's annual report, and an eyewitness report of an accident. With primary sources there is nothing (or very little) standing between the event (say, an accident) and the reporting of it (the eyewitness testimony). *Secondary sources* include, for example, a summary of research appearing in a popular magazine, a television news report on a corporation's earnings, and a report by someone who talked to someone who witnessed an accident. With secondary sources someone stands between the actual event and the report; for example, a science reporter reads the scientist's monograph (primary source), then writes up a summary for the popular press (secondary source). As a listener and speaker you'll hear and use both types of source material. Yet there are important differences that you should keep in mind.

Secondary source material is less reliable than primary source material, because it is a step removed from the actual facts or events. The writer of secondary material may have forgotten important parts, may be biased and so may have slanted the reporting to reflect his or her attitudes, or may have distorted the material because he or she misunderstood the data. On the other hand, the writer may have been able to express complicated scientific data in simple language—often making it easier for a nonscientist to understand than the original report. When using or listening to secondary sources, examine the information for any particular spin the writer may be giving the material. If possible, check the primary source material itself to see if anything was left out or if the conclusions are really warranted on the basis of the primary evidence.

The next Research Link, "General Reference Works," appears on page 91

a college professor, your speeches will be largely informative; if a politician, mostly persuasive.

As discussed in Chapter 2, *to inform* and *to persuade* are the two major types of general purposes of public speeches. Another type of general purpose is to serve some specific occasion function—to toast, to bid farewell, to present an award. *Special occasion speeches* in many ways combine informative and persuasive purposes.

In the **informative speech** you seek to create understanding: to clarify, to enlighten, to correct misunderstandings, to demonstrate how something works. In this type of speech you'll rely most heavily on materials that amplify—examples, illustrations, definitions, testimony, visual aids, and the like.

In the **persuasive speech** you try to influence attitudes or behaviors; you seek to strengthen or change existing attitudes or get the audience to take some action. In this type of speech you'll rely heavily on materials that offer proof—on evidence, argument, and psychological appeals, for example.

In the **special occasion speech**, which contains elements of information and persuasion, you might, for example, introduce another speaker or a group of speakers, present a tribute, try to secure the goodwill of the listeners, toast your friends' anniversary, or "just" entertain your listeners.

SPECIFIC PURPOSE

Once you have chosen your general purpose, develop your specific purpose by identifying more precisely what you aim to accomplish. For example, in an informative speech, your specific purpose will identify the information you want to convey to your audience. Here are a few possible specific purposes for a speech on the topic of stem cell research:

General purpose: To inform.

Specific purposes: To inform my audience of the differences between embryonic and adult stem cell research.

To inform my audience of two areas of stem cell research progress.

To inform my audience of the current federal regulations on funding stem cell research.

You may find it helpful to view your specific informative purpose in behavioral terms, identifying how you want the audience to demonstrate what they've learned from your speech. Here are a few examples:

- After listening to my speech, listeners should be able to describe the procedures for systematic desensitization.

- After listening to my speech, listeners should be able to define the three major differences between communism and capitalism.

- After listening to my speech, listeners should be able to demonstrate the five steps of active listening.

In a persuasive speech, your specific purpose identifies what you want your audience to believe, to think, or perhaps to do. Here are a few examples:

General purpose: To persuade.

Specific purposes: To persuade listeners to use systematic desensitization to reduce their apprehension.

To persuade listeners to believe that capitalism is superior to communism.

To persuade listeners to use active listening more often.

As you formulate your specific purpose, follow these five guidelines: Use an infinitive phrase; focus the purpose in terms of its impact on your audience; limit it to one idea; limit it to what you can reasonably expect to achieve; and use specific terms.

Use an Infinitive Phrase

Begin the statement of each specific purpose with your general purpose (to inform, to persuade) and elaborate on your general purpose. For example: *To inform my audience of the new registration procedures* or *To persuade my audience to contribute a book for the library fund-raiser* or *To introduce the main speaker of the day to my audience.*

Focus on the Audience

Right now your audience is your public speaking class, and it may at first seem unnecessary to include reference to them in each specific purpose, as was done in the examples in the previous paragraph. Actually, however, referring to the audience is crucial, because it keeps you focused on the people you want to inform or persuade; it's a reminder that everything you do in your speech needs to be directed by the purpose you want to achieve with this specific audience. Your speech purpose must be relevant to your audience. In your life and career, you'll probably address a variety of different audiences, and you need to keep each unique and distinct audience clearly in focus.

Limit Your Specific Purpose to One Idea

Avoid the common pitfall of trying to accomplish too much in too short a time. For example, *To persuade my audience of the prevalence of date rape in our community and that they should attend the dating seminars offered on campus* contains two specific purposes, not one. Select one or the other. Beware of any specific purpose that contains the word *and*; it's often a sign that you have more than one purpose.

Limit Your Specific Purpose to What Is Reasonable

Limit your specific purpose to what you can reasonably develop and achieve in the allotted time. Specific purposes that are too broad are useless. Note how broad and overly general are such purposes as *To inform my audience about clothing design* or *To persuade my audience to improve their health.* You couldn't hope to cover such topics in one speech. It would be much more reasonable to have such purposes as *To inform my audience of the importance of color in clothing design* or *To persuade my audience to exercise three times a week.*

Use Specific Terms

Phrase your specific purpose with specific terms. The more precise your specific purpose, the more effectively it will guide you in the remaining steps of preparing your speech. Notice that the purposes used as examples of covering too much are also overly general and very unspecific ("clothing design" can mean hundreds of things as can "improve your health"). Instead of the overly general *To persuade my audience to help the homeless,* consider the more specific *To persuade my audience to donate a few hours a month to make phone calls for the Homeless Coalition.*

YOUR THESIS

Like your specific purpose, your **thesis** needs to be given special attention. This section defines the thesis and explains how you should word and use it in your preparation and in your actual speech.

WHAT IS A THESIS?

As you'll recall from Chapter 2, your thesis is your central idea; it's the theme, the essence of your speech. It's your point of view; it's what you want the audience to get out of your speech. The thesis of Lincoln's Second Inaugural Address was that Northerners and Southerners should work together for the entire nation's welfare; the thesis of Martin Luther King Jr.'s "I have a dream" speech was that true equality is a right of African Americans and all people; and the thesis of political campaign speeches is generally something like: "Vote for me," or "I'm the better candidate," or "My opponent is the wrong choice."

In an informative speech your thesis states what you want your audience to learn. For example, a suitable thesis for an informative speech on jealousy might be "There are two main theories of jealousy." Notice that here, as in all informative speeches, the thesis is relatively neutral and objective.

In a persuasive speech your thesis states what you want your audience to believe or accept; it summarizes the claim you're making, the position you're taking. For example, let's say that you're planning to present a speech against using animals for experimentation. Your thesis statement might be something like "Animal experimentation should be banned." Here are a few additional examples of persuasive speech theses:

- We should all contribute to the Homeless Shelter Project.
- Everyone over 40 should get tested for colon cancer.
- Condoms should be distributed free of charge.

A POORLY CONSTRUCTED PERSUASIVE SPEECH

Public Speaking   *Sample Assistant*

This speech was written to illustrate some really broad as well as some rather subtle errors that a beginning speaker might make in consticting a persuasive speech. First, read the entire speech without reading any of the questions in the right-hand column. Then, after you've read the entire speech, reread each paragraph and respond to the critical thinking questions. What other questions and issues might prove productive to explore?

XXX Has Got to Go

You probably didn't read the papers this weekend, but there's a XXX movie, I mean video, store that moved in on Broad and Fifth Streets. My parents, who are retired teachers, are protesting it, and so am I. My parents are organizing a protest for the next weekend.

What do you think of the title of the speech? Visualizing yourself as a listener, how would the opening comment make you feel? Does the speaker gain your attention? What thesis do you think the speaker will support? Does mentioning "my parents" help or hurt the speaker's credibility?

There must be hundreds of XXX video stores in the country and they all need to be closed down. I have a lot of reasons.

What is the speaker's thesis? What impression are you beginning to get of the speaker?

First, my parents think it should be closed down. My parents are retired teachers and have organized protests over the proposed new homeless shelter and to prevent the city from making that park on Elm Street. So they know what they're doing.

How do the speaker's parents sound to you? Do they sound like credible leaders with a consistent cause? Professional protesters (with perhaps a negative agenda)? What evidence is offered to support the assertion that we should believe the speaker's parents? Is this adequate? What would you need to know about people before believing them?

The XXX video place is immoral. No good religious people would ever go there.

What does this statement assume about the audience? How would this statement be responded to by your public speaking class? What are some reasons why the speaker might not have explained how XXX video stores are immoral?

These stores bring crime into the neighborhood. I have proof of that. Morristown's crime increased after the XXX video store opened. And in Martinsville, where they got rid of the video store, crime did not increase. If we allow the video store in our own town, then we're going to be like Morristown and our crime is going to increase.

What do you think of the reasoning used here? Are there other factors that could have influenced Morristown's crime increase? Is there any evidence that getting rid of the video store resulted in the stable crime rate in Martinsville? What assumption about the audience does the speaker make in using Martinsville and Morristown as analogies?

These stores make lots of garbage. The plastic wrappings from the videos will add to our already overextended and overutilized landfill. And a lot of them are going to wind up as litter on the streets.

Do you agree with this argument about the garbage? Is this argument in any way unique to the video store? Is it likely that people will open the wrappers and drop them on the street?

The XXX Video House stays open seven days a week, 24 hours a day. People will be forced to work at all hours and on Sunday, and that's not fair. And the store will increase the noise level at night, with cars pulling up and all.

What validity do you give to each of these arguments? Given the 24-hour policy, how might you construct an argument against the video store? Are there advantages of a neighborhood store's 24-hour policy that the audience may be thinking of, thus countering the speaker's argument? If there are, how should the speaker deal with them?

The XXX Video House—that's it's name, by the way—doesn't carry regular videos that most people want. So why do we want them?

On hearing this, would you be likely to extend this argument and start asking yourself "Do we now close up all stores that most people don't want?"

The XXX Video House got a lease from an owner who doesn't even live in the community, someone by the name of, well, it's an organization called XYX Management. And their address is Carlson Place in Jeffersonville. So they don't even live here.

Is there a connection between who the owner is and whether the video store should or shouldn't be closed? Could the speaker have effectively used this information in support of the thesis to close the video store?

A neighboring store owner says he thinks the store is in violation of several fire laws. He says they have no sprinkler system and no metal doors to prevent the spread of a fire. So he thinks they should be closed down, too.

What credibility do you ascribe to the "neighboring store owner"? Do you begin to wonder if the speaker would simply agree to have the store brought up to the fire code laws?

Last week on *Oprah* three women were on and they were in the XXX movie business, and they were all on drugs, and had been in jail, and they said it all started when they went into the porno business. One woman wanted to be a teacher, another wanted to be a nurse, and the other wanted to be a beautician. If there weren't any XXX video stores then there wouldn't be a porn business; and, you know, pornography is part of organized crime and so if you stop pornography you take a bite out of crime.

What is the cause and what is the effect that the speaker is asserting? How likely is it that the proposed cause actually produced the effect? Might there have been causes other than the pornography that might have led these women into drugs? What credibility do you give to people you see on talk shows? Does it vary with the specific talk show? Do you accept the argument that there would be no pornography business without video stores? What would have to be proved to you before you accepted this connection? How do you respond to the expression "Take a bite out of crime"?

One of the reasons I think it should be closed is that the legitimate video stores—the ones that have only a small selection of XXX movies somewhere in the back—will lose business. And if they continue to lose business, they'll leave the neighborhood and we'll have no video stores.

Is the speaker implying that this is the real reason against XXX video stores? Do you start wondering if the speaker is against XXX video stores—as seemed in the last argument—or just against stores that sell these exclusively? What effect does this impression have on your evaluation of the speaker's credibility and the speaker's thesis?

That's a lot of reasons against XXX movie houses. I have a quote here: Reason is "a portion of the divine spirit set in a human body." Seneca.

How do you feel about the number of "reasons"? Would you have preferred fewer reasons more fully developed or more reasons? What purpose does this quotation serve?

In conclusion and to wrap it up and close my speech, I want to repeat and say again that the XXX video stores should all be closed down. They corrupt minors. And they're offensive to men and women and especially women. I hope you'll all protest with the Marshalls—my mother and father—and there'll be lots of others there too.

In light of this conclusion might the speaker have introduced the speech differently? What does the speaker's thesis seem to be now? What do you think of the argument that XXX video stores are offensive? What effect does this argument have, being stated here in the conclusion? Do you think you'd go to the protest? Why or why not?

As you can see, these thesis statements identify what you want your audience to believe or do as a result of your speech—you want them to contribute to the homeless shelter, to believe that everyone over 40 should be tested for colon cancer, and to be convinced that condoms should be distributed without charge. Notice that in persuasive speeches the thesis statement puts forth a point of view, an opinion. The thesis is arguable; it's debatable.

How DO THESIS AND SPECIFIC PURPOSE DIFFER?

The thesis and the specific purpose are similar in that they are both guides to help you select and organize your speech materials. Because they both serve these similar goals, they are often confused, so let's consider some of the ways in which they are different.

First, the thesis and purpose differ in their form of expression. The specific purpose is worded as an infinitive phrase; for example, "To inform my audience of the provisions of the new education budget" or "To persuade my audience to vote in favor of the new education budget." The thesis, on the other hand, is phrased as a complete declarative sentence; for example, "The education budget must be increased."

Second, they differ in their focus. The specific purpose is audience-focused; it identifies the change you hope to achieve in your audience. For example, your specific purpose may be for the audience to gain information, to believe something, or to act in a certain way. The thesis, on the other hand, is message-focused. It identifies the main idea of your speech; it summarizes—it epitomizes—the content of your speech. It's the one idea that you want your audience to remember even if they forget everything else.

A Case of Ethics   EVALUATING THESES

Visualize yourself as a public speaking instructor. Your students are getting ready to deliver their first round of speeches. You've asked them to submit their thesis statements to you so that you can make sure they're on the right track and can offer whatever help may be needed. Among the theses you receive are the following:

1. You can cheat on your income tax with two great strategies.
2. Help revitalize the KKK.
3. Growing marijuana can be fun and profitable.
4. The Holocaust has been exaggerated.
5. Employers should have the right to discriminate on the basis of religion, sex, affectional orientation, race, or nationality.

Ethical Choice Point *Would it be ethical to allow these speeches to be delivered in class? On the other hand, would it be ethical to censor your students' points of view? More generally, what ethical obligations does an instructor have in regulating (or not regulating) issues spoken on in a college classroom? What ethical responsibilities do students have in selecting and developing classroom speeches?*

Third, the specific purpose and thesis differ in their concern for practical limitations. No matter how sweeping or ambitious the thesis, the specific purpose must take into consideration the time you have to speak and the attitudes of the audience toward you and your topic. The specific purpose, therefore, needs to be phrased with these practical limitations in mind. For example, the thesis might be that "Colleges are not educating students for today's world." The speech, however, might have any one of several different specific purposes; for example, (1) To persuade my audience that colleges must change to keep pace with today's world, (2) To persuade my audience to adapt the Illinois Educational Proposal, or (3) To persuade my audience to quit college. The thesis epitomizes the speech without regard to practical limitations of, say, time or current audience attitudes.

The following examples may clarify further the difference between purpose and thesis:

General purpose:	To inform.
Specific purpose:	To inform my audience of three ways to save on their phone bills.
Thesis:	You can reduce your phone bills.

General purpose:	To persuade.
Specific purpose:	To persuade my audience to take a computer science course.
Thesis:	Computer science knowledge is essential.

Especially in your early stages of mastering public speaking, formulate both the specific purpose and the thesis statement. With both of these as guides, you'll be able to construct a more coherent and more understandable speech.

WORDING AND USING YOUR THESIS

Here are a few suggestions on how to word and use your thesis.

Limit Your Thesis to One Central Idea

Be sure to limit your thesis statement to one and only one central idea. A statement such as "Animal experimentation should be banned, and companies engaging in it should be prosecuted" contains not one but two basic ideas. Whenever you see an *and* or a semicolon (;) in a thesis statement, it probably contains more than one idea.

State Your Thesis as a Complete Declarative Sentence

In phrasing your thesis, word it as a complete declarative sentence; for example, "Hate speech corrupts" or "Speak out against hate speech" or "Support the college's new hate speech code." This will help you focus your thinking, your collecting of materials, and your organizational pattern. Avoid stating your thesis as a question or a sentence fragment; these will not provide the clear and specific focus you need to use the thesis effectively.

Use Your Thesis Statement to Generate Main Points

Within each thesis there is an essential question that allows you to explore and subdivide the thesis. Your objective here is to find this question and use it

Consider the last few college lectures you've heard. What were their general purposes? Their specific purposes? Their theses? Were these clear? If not, what might the lecturer have done to make them clearer to the students?

to help you discover the major ideas or assertions or propositions that will support this thesis. For example, let's take a hypothetical proposed bill—call it the Hart Bill—and let's say your thesis is "The Hart Bill provides needed services for senior citizens." When the thesis is stated in this form, the obvious question suggested is "What are the needed services?" The answer to this question suggests the main parts of your speech; let's say, health, food, shelter, and recreational services. These four areas then become the four main points of your speech.

Some public speaking instructors and trainers advise speakers to include their main points in the statement of the thesis. If you did this, your thesis for the above speech would be "The Hart Bill provides needed health, food, shelter, and recreational services for senior citizens." You may find it helpful to use the briefer thesis statement for some speech topics and purposes and the more expanded thesis statement for others.

Regardless of whether you use the brief or the expanded thesis, an outline of the main points would look like this:

General purpose: To inform.
Specific purpose: To inform my audience of the provisions of the Hart Bill.
Thesis: The Hart Bill provides needed services for senior citizens.

(Or, if you were using an expanded thesis, it might be stated like this: "The Hart Bill provides needed health, food, shelter, and recreational services for senior citizens.")

I. The Hart Bill provides needed health services.
II. The Hart Bill provides needed food services.
III. The Hart Bill provides needed shelter services.
IV. The Hart Bill provides needed recreational services.

Consider how the culture of an audience might influence what is considered appropriate and what is considered inappropriate. How might the cultural composition of your class influence the topics, specific purposes, or theses of your speeches?

The remainder of the speech would then be filled in with supporting materials. Under main point I, for example, you might identify several health services and explain how the Hart Bill would provide them. This first main point of your speech might, in outline, look something like this:

I. The Hart Bill provides needed health services.

   A. Neighborhood clinics will be established.

   B. Medical hotlines will be established.

In the completed speech, this first main point and its two subordinate statements might be spoken like this:

> The Hart Bill provides senior citizens with the health services they need so badly. Let me give you some examples of these necessary health services. One of the most important services will be the establishment of neighborhood health clinics. These clinics will help senior citizens get needed health advice and medical care right in their own neighborhoods.
>
> A second important health service will be the health hotlines. These phone numbers will be for the exclusive use of senior citizens. These hotlines will connect seniors with trained medical personnel who will be able to give advice and send emergency medical services to seniors as needed.

Use Your Thesis to Suggest Organizational Patterns

Your thesis will provide you with useful guidelines in selecting the organization for your main points. For example, let's suppose your thesis is "We can improve our own college education." Your answer to the inherent question "What can we do?" will suggest a possible organizational pattern. If, for example, you identify the remedies in the order in which they should be taken, then a time-order pattern will be appropriate. If you itemize a number of possible solutions, all of which are of about equal importance, then a topical pattern will be appropriate. If your thesis is "The proposed fringe benefits package has both advantages and disadvantages," then your speech might logically be organized into two parts: advantages and disadvantages. These and other patterns are explained in detail in Chapter 7, "Organizing Your Speech."

Use Your Thesis to Focus Audience Attention

Because the thesis sentence focuses the audience's attention on your central idea and reveals what you hope to achieve in your speech, you'll want to consider the options you have for stating your thesis. Various options include, for example:

- Stating your thesis early in the speech, perhaps in the introduction.
- Stating your thesis late in the speech.
- Stating your thesis explicitly and directly.
- Indirectly stating your thesis; allowing the audience to infer it.

Here are a few guidelines that will help you make a strategically effective decision about how and when to present your thesis to your audience.

- In an informative speech, state your thesis early, clearly, and directly: "Immigration patterns are predicted to change drastically over the next 50 years"; "Carpal tunnel syndrome can be corrected with surgery"; or "An iPhone can organize your life."

- In a persuasive speech addressed to an audience already in agreement with you, state your thesis explicitly and early in your speech: "Immigration laws should be changed"; "You can avoid carpal tunnel syndrome with rest and exercise"; or "You should get a PDA today."

- In a persuasive speech addressed to an audience opposed to your position, give your evidence and arguments first and gradually move the audience into a more positive frame of mind before stating your thesis explicitly.

- When you are speaking to a relatively uneducated or uninformed audience, it is probably best to state your thesis explicitly. If the thesis is not explicit, the listeners may fail to grasp what your thesis is and therefore may be less likely to change their attitudes or behaviors.

- Recognize, too, that there are cultural differences in the way a thesis should be stated. In some Asian cultures, for example, making a point too directly or asking directly for audience compliance may be considered rude or insulting.

Essentials of Selecting Your Topic, Purpose, and Thesis

In this chapter we considered the speech topic and ways to find and limit it, general and specific speech purposes and how to phrase them, and speech theses and how to word and use them to best effect.

1. **Suitable speech topics** are topics that are substantive, appropriate to you and your audience, and culturally sensitive.

2. Topics may be found through:
   - Yourself.
   - Brainstorming.
   - Surveys.
   - News items.
   - Topic lists.

3. **Speech topics may be limited** by:
   - Topoi, the system of topics.
   - Tree diagrams.
   - Search directories.

4. **Speech purposes** are both general (for example, to inform or to persuade) and specific (for example, to inform an audience of new health plan options). A specific purpose should be:
   - Worded as an infinitive phrase.
   - Focused on the audience.
   - Limited to one idea.
   - Limited to what you can reasonably accomplish.
   - Phrased with precise terms.

5. The **speech thesis** is your central idea; the theme, the essence of your speech.

6. In **wording and using your thesis**:
   - Limit your thesis to one central idea
   - State your thesis as a complete declarative sentence
   - Use your thesis statement to generate main ideas
   - Use your thesis to suggest organizational patterns
   - Use your thesis to focus audience attention

Essential Terms: Selecting Your Topic, Purpose, and Thesis

brainstorming **(p. 66)**
cultural sensitivity **(p. 65)**
general purpose **(p. 71)**
informative speech **(p. 72)**
persuasive speech **(p. 72)**

search directory **(p. 71)**
special occasion speech **(p. 72)**
specific purpose **(p. 71)**
taboo topics **(p. 65)**
thesis **(p. 74)**

topic **(p. 64)**
topic generators **(p. 68)**
topoi **(p. 68)**
tree diagrams **(p. 69)**

Public Speaking Exercises

4.1 Brainstorming for Topics

With a small group of students or with the class as a whole sitting in a circle, brainstorm for suitable speech topics. Be sure to appoint someone to write down all the contributions or use a recorder.

After this brainstorming session, consider:

1. Did any members give negative criticism (even nonverbally)?

2. Did any members hesitate to contribute really wild ideas? Why?

3. Was it necessary to restimulate the group members at any point? Did this help?

4. Did some useful speech topics emerge in the brainstorming session?

4.2 Limiting Topics

Here are a few overly general topics. Using one of the methods discussed in this chapter (or any other method you're familiar with), limit each topic to a subject that would be reasonable for a 5- to 10-minute speech.

1. Dangerous sports
2. Race relationships
3. Parole
4. Censorship on the Internet
5. Ecological problems
6. Problems faced by college students
7. Morality
8. Health and fitness
9. Ethical issues in politics
10. Urban violence

4.3 What Do You Say?

◆ **Taboo Topics.** Derek, a student in your public speaking class, wonders if any topic would be considered taboo for class presentation. What topics, if any, would you consider taboo and advise Derek not to address in his speeches in this class? Why?

◆ **Limiting a Topic.** Richard wants to give a speech on women's rights, but he can't seem to narrow the topic down to manageable proportions. Everything he comes across seems important and cries out for inclusion. What advice would you give to Richard to help him limit and focus his general topic?

◆ **Defining Purpose.** Izzie is considering developing her 10-minute persuasive speech around one of the following purposes: to persuade her listeners (1) to vote for the pro-life candidate in the upcoming election, (2) to contribute $250 to the college's scholarship fund, or (3) to attend a religious ceremony of a religion other than the listeners' own. If the audience were your public speaking class, how would you suggest that Izzie rephrase or redefine any one of these purposes?

◆ **Statement of Thesis.** George and Miranda want to give their speeches on opposite sides of Megan's Law—the law requiring that community residents be notified if a convicted sex offender is living in the neighborhood. George is against the law and Miranda is for it. If George and Miranda were giving their speeches to your class, what would you advise each of them to do concerning his or her thesis statement?

◆ **Unpopular Thesis.** Meredith has decided to tackle the hypocrisy she sees in her classmates—most of whom publicly support the value of racial equality but privately express racist attitudes. She's afraid, however, that the audience will walk out on her as soon as she states her thesis. What would you advise Meredith to do?

Log*On!* MySpeechLab

Selecting Your Topic, Purpose, and Thesis

Visit MySpeechLab (www.myspeechlab.com) for Chapter 4. Here you'll find an extensive list of potential public speaking topics in "The Dictionary of Topics" and another way of limiting topics in the "Fishbone Diagram." Also see "Sample Speech Topics" for a brief but useful list of topics (*Visualize*) and "Visual Brainstorming" (*Explore*). In addition, an exercise providing insight into "Generating Main Points from Thesis Statements" is provided. Also take a look at "Finding Sources" in Research Navigator (accessed through MSL). If you have the opportunity, view one or two of the speech videos on MSL (especially useful are "Choosing a Speech Topic" and its critique [*Watch*]) and discuss these in small groups in terms of how the viewers perceived the specific purpose and the thesis of each speech.

5 Analyzing and Adapting to Your Audience

Why Read This Chapter?

Because it will enable you to tailor your speech to your specific audience by helping you to:

- discover the demographics or sociology of your listeners (age, culture, gender, religion, for example) and their psychology (willingness to listen, attitudes toward your thesis, for example)

- adapt your speech to these specific listeners

- adapt to your audience during the actual speech

Your audience gives you everything you need. They tell you. There is no director who can direct you like an audience.

—Fanny Brice (1891–1951)
Singer, actor, comedian, and the real "Funny Girl"

You can inform or persuade an audience only if you know who they are, what they know, and what they believe. Once you have this information, you can begin to tailor your speech to these specific listeners. In this chapter we look at the nature of today's audiences, ways to analyze the sociology and psychology of the audience, and some suggestions for adapting to the audience during the actual speech.

AUDIENCES AND AUDIENCE ANALYSIS

The public speaking *audience* is best defined as a group of people with the common purpose of listening and responding to a speech. An audience can be of almost any size—5 people listening to a street orator, 20 students in a classroom, thousands at a stadium listening to a political or religious speaker. *Audience analysis* is the process of discovering useful information about these listeners so as to tailor a speech to them.

THE AUDIENCE: TWO BASIC CHARACTERISTICS

Among all the qualities that might be said to characterize today's audiences, two stand out: uniqueness (no audience is like any other audience) and diversity (audiences are never truly homogeneous). Let's look at each of these briefly.

All Audiences Are Unique

Each public speaking audience you address is unique. Audiences are unique because people are different and unique as individuals; but even when you address the same persons repeatedly (as you will in this course and in various business and other situations), the individuals are not necessarily the same as they were the last time you addressed them. For example, audiences on September 10 and on September 12, 2001, may have been composed of the same people, but probably very few audience members were the same in attitudes and beliefs on those two different dates. Not only world events but also personal experiences change us all—even if in less dramatic ways—to some extent and in some way.

All Audiences Are Diverse

As important as uniqueness is the contemporary audience's diversity—in age, race, gender, religion, affectional orientation, nationality, economic situation, relationship status, occupation, political affiliation, attitudes, values, and beliefs, and in hundreds of other ways. If you're in a typical college classroom in the United States, your classroom audience represents a diverse group of people. Further, each subgroup within this diverse group is itself diverse. People of the same age will differ in race, gender, religion, and so on. And those of the same religion will differ from one another in age, nationality, politics, and so on. As you prepare to learn about your audience, keep this notion of diversity in mind. It will help you focus on your audience as a mix of unique individuals rather than a blend.

In addition to being sensitive to cultural differences, develop sensitivity to those in your audience who may have one or more disabilities. Scan your audience for any listeners who may have difficulty in hearing or seeing you. Don't identify them or in any way call attention to them, but keep their needs in mind as you present your speech. Here are just a few suggestions for such a situation; these hints would be helpful with any audience but are especially significant when your listeners have sight or hearing disabilities.

1. If there are people in the audience who are blind or partially sighted, explain your visual aids in a bit more detail. For example, instead of saying, "As you can see from the graph, we're in good shape," consider saying, "As you can see from this graph, which shows a 40 percent increase in sales, we're in good shape." If you're using handouts, be especially sure to explain fully what their purpose is, and make it a point to reiterate the information on them. If you're writing on the chalkboard, say aloud what you're writing.

2. If you notice persons with hearing deficits, be sure to maintain an adequate volume (loudness) and to speak distinctly. Be especially careful not to drop your voice at the ends of sentences. If you see your audience leaning forward or struggling to hear you, increase your volume.

3. Use normal vocabulary, and don't avoid topics that you would speak on to (for example) an audience of all sighted people with good hearing. Don't avoid terms such as *see, hear, look, listen,* or even *blind* or *deaf.* Don't avoid illustrating your speech with an example from a television show or a song.

4. Try to eliminate as much "noise" as you can. For example, audible noise might include the sounds of voices in nearby hallways or other classrooms; visual noise might take the form of sun washing out the colors on your slides. Sometimes something as simple as closing the door or pulling the shades is all that's necessary to make your speech more understandable.

5. In talking about people with disabilities, use language that emphasizes the person rather than the disability. Refer to "persons with disabilities" rather than "disabled persons." If your speech topic requires you to discuss people with a specific disability, be sure you have done adequate research on the terms preferred by that population. For example, many people born with *achondroplastic dwarfism* prefer to be referred to as "little people." In general, people with disabilities are able in most respects; in only some situations does the specific disability come into play.

A Case of Ethics RESPECTING AUDIENCE INTERESTS

You've just been hired by an advertising agency to design a campaign to promote a cereal that's extremely high in sugar and trans fat—both of which you know are not healthy. The job, however, is a particularly good one, and should you succeed on this account, your future in advertising would be assured. Yet you wonder if you can ethically give persuasive force to selling this product, which is not in the best interests of your audience of consumers.

Ethical Choice Point *What would you do in this situation? More generally, what ethical guidelines should a speaker follow in balancing self- and audience interests?*

And, of course, persons with disabilities have responsibilities too. So, if you have hearing problems, take a seat close to the front of the room. If you hear better in one ear than the other, be sure to position yourself on the proper side of the room. If you have vision problems, be sure to bring your glasses and to sit as close to the front as is comfortable.

LEARNING ABOUT YOUR AUDIENCE

You can seek out audience information in four general ways: observation, data collection, interviewing, and inference (Sprague & Stuart, 2008). Let's explore each.

Observe

Think about your audience based on the way they present themselves physically. What can you infer about their economic status from their clothing and jewelry, for example? Might their clothing reveal any conservative or liberal leanings? Might clothing provide clues to attitudes on economics or politics? What do they do in their free time? Where do they live? What do they talk about? Are different cultures represented? Do your observations give you any clue as to what audience members' interests or concerns might be? Be careful that this analysis doesn't turn into stereotyping based on appearance; rather, use visual cues to give you hints as to the nature of the audience.

Collect Data Systematically

Two major ways to collect data immediately suggest themselves: polling sites, which can enable you to discover what a wide range of people are thinking about varied topics, and questionnaires, which can reveal what your specific audience (in this case, your class) thinks.

Polling Sites.   A good place to start with understanding what people think is to visit some of the numerous polling sites on the Internet. Here you'll find a variety of information on all sorts of attitudes and opinions on economics, business, politics, lifestyles, buying habits, and more; search for "opinion poll" or, if you have access, visit Research Navigator at www.researchnavigator.com for lots of suggestions. One of the most extensive polling websites is the Gallup Organization's at www.gallup.com. Many newspapers maintain polls, one of the best of which is maintained by the *Washington Post* (www.washingtonpost.com). Another useful source is the Polling Report (www.pollingreport.com), which tracks trends in American public opinion.

Many universities conduct polls and make the results available on their websites. Some of the best include the Cornell Institute for Social and Economic Research's website, with hot links to a wide variety of polls and surveys, at www.ciser.cornell.edu/info/polls.shtml; Marist College's Institute for Public Opinion (www.maristpoll.marist.edu); Quinnipiac University's Polling Institute (www.quinnipiac.edu); and Fairleigh Dickenson University's Public Opinion Research Center (http://publicmind.fdu.edu).

Audience Questionnaires.   Another useful way to secure information about your audience is to use a questionnaire. Let's say you've taken a course in website design and are thinking about giving an informative speech on

Consider the topics comedians joke about. What two or three topics would you avoid joking about in your class speeches? What two or three topics would you assume would be safe?

ways to design effective Web pages. One thing you'll need to know is how much your audience already knows about Web design. A questionnaire asking them about their experience with Web design can help you judge the level at which to approach the topic, the information that you can assume the audience already has, the terms you need to define, and so on. You might also want to find out how much experience the audience members have had with Web pages, either as users or as designers.

To help you answer these and other relevant questions, you might compose a questionnaire. If your class is set up as a listserv, or if members can communicate through some Web group (like BlackBoard or WebCT), these questionnaires will be extremely easy to distribute: You can do it with one e-mail questionnaire sent to the listserv. Other members of the class can then respond to the questionnaire, and you can tabulate the results and use the information you discover as you prepare your speech. Do caution other members of the listserv that they should send back questionnaires directly and only to you. If classmates return questionnaires to the listserv, then everyone in the class will get everyone else's responses; in a class of 25 students, each person would receive 625 responses. If your class is not established as a listserv, you can still distribute printed questionnaires before class begins or as students are leaving.

Audience questionnaires are even more useful as background for persuasive speeches. Let's say you plan to give a speech in favor of allowing single people to adopt children. To develop an effective speech, you need to know your audience's attitudes toward single-parent adoption. Are they in favor of this idea? Opposed to it? Do they have reservations? If so, what are they? Are audience members undecided? To answer such questions, you might use a questionnaire such as that presented in Figure 5.1.

In constructing your questionnaire, keep it brief, express thanks to responders for filling it out, and include whatever background information the responders will need to fill out the form. Generally, it's best not to reveal your thesis in the questionnaire—after all, you're going to use this information to help formulate your thesis; besides, you may not want the audience to know your thesis before you give them some evidence and specific examples that support your position.

Interview Members of Your Audience

In a classroom situation you can easily take the time to interview members of your audience in order to find out more about them. But if you're to speak to an audience you'll not meet prior to your speech, you might interview those who know the audience members better than you do. For example, you might talk with the person who invited you to speak and inquire about the audi-

AUDIENCE QUESTIONNAIRE

I'm planning to give my persuasive speech on adoption. I'd like to know your attitudes on a few issues relating to this topic. I'd appreciate it if you'd complete this questionnaire and return it to jdevito@hunter.cuny.edu.

1. How do you feel about single people's adopting children?
  _____ strongly in favor of it
  _____ in favor of it
  _____ neutral
  _____ opposed to it
  _____ strongly opposed to it

2. Is your attitude the same for interracial adoption? For gays and lesbians who adopt? Please explain.

3. What are your main reasons for your current attitudes?

4. What underlying values and beliefs do you think contribute to your current attitudes?

Thanks,
Joe

Figure 5.1
Audience Questionnaire for a Persuasive Speech
What are the disadvantages of stating your position on the issue in your questionnaire? Can you identify any possible advantages?

ence's culture, age, gender, knowledge and educational levels, religious background, and so forth.

Use Inference and Empathy

Use your knowledge of human behavior and human motivation and try to adopt the perspective of the audience. Intelligent inference and empathy will help you estimate your listeners' **attitudes, beliefs,** and **values,** and even their thoughts and emotions on your topic (Sprague & Stuart, 2008). For example, let's say you're addressing your class on the need to eliminate (or expand) affirmative action. What might you infer about your audience—are they likely to be in favor of affirmative action or opposed to it? Can they be easily classified in terms of their liberal or conservative leanings? How informed are they likely to be about the topic and about the advantages and disadvantages of affirmative action? What feelings might they have about affirmative action?

Now that the strategies for learning about your audience are clear, consider how well you know your current audience, your public speaking class, by taking the accompanying self-test, "How Well Do You Know Your Audience?"

TEST YOURSELF

How Well Do You Know Your Audience?

Here are some statements of beliefs that members of your class may agree or disagree with—and which you might want to use as basic theses (propositions) in your in-class speeches. Try predicting how favorable or unfavorable you think your class members would be to each of these beliefs. Use a 10-point scale ranging from 1 (extremely unfavorable) through 5 (relatively neutral) to 10 (extremely favorable).

_____ **1.** The welfare of the family must come first, even before your own.

_____ **2.** Sex outside of marriage is wrong and sinful.

_____ **3.** In a heterosexual relationship, a wife should submit graciously to the leadership of her husband.

_____ **4.** Individual states should be allowed to fly the Confederate flag if they wish.

_____ **5.** Intercultural relationships are OK in business but should be discouraged when it comes to intimate or romantic relationships; generally, the races should be kept "pure."

_____ **6.** Money is good; the quest for financial success is a perfectly respectable (even noble) one.

_____ **7.** Immigration into the United States should be curtailed, at least until current immigrants are assimilated.

_____ **8.** Parents who prevent their children from receiving the latest scientific cures because of a belief in faith healing should be prosecuted.

_____ **9.** Same-sex marriage should be legalized.

_____ **10.** Medicinal marijuana should be readily available.

_____ **11.** Physician-assisted suicide should be legalized.

_____ **12.** Male and female prostitution should be legalized and taxed like any other income producing occupation.

HOW DID YOU DO? After you've indicated your predictions, discuss these with the class as a whole to measure how accurate you were in guessing your audience's beliefs.

WHAT WILL YOU DO? As you can tell from just these 12 theses, misestimating the audience's position can create serious problems for the speaker. To assume, for example, that your audience believes that prostitution should be legalized, when they're really strongly against it, will prevent you from refuting their current attitudes and beliefs and will lead your listeners to see you as out of touch with them. Resolve to learn as much as you possibly can about any audience you address.

Let's turn now to some of the ways in which audiences differ—sociologically and psychologically—and consider how you might analyze and adapt to the unique and diverse audiences you'll face.

Research Link

GENERAL REFERENCE WORKS

General reference works are excellent starting points for researching your topic.

One of the best general reference works is the standard encyclopedia. Any good encyclopedia will give you a general overview of your subject and suggestions for additional reading. The most comprehensive and the most prestigious is the *Encyclopaedia Britannica*, available in print, on CD-ROM, and online. A variety of other encyclopedias also are available in print, on CD-ROM, or online. The best way to search for these is to visit Freeality.com (www.freeality.com/encyclop.htm) and search through the available general and specific encyclopedias.

Perhaps the most widely known online encyclopedia, and one that you'll find extremely useful, is Wikipedia (www.wikipedia.com). This encyclopedia is a bit different from those mentioned above. The articles in Wikipedia— some brief and some extremely long and detailed—are written by people who are not necessarily experts. Many of the articles are reviewed, updated, and corrected periodically. But, because this work doesn't have the authority of the more traditional encyclopedias, you'll need to check the facts and statistics—most of which you'll find easy to do because of the extensive hot links written into each article and the list of additional sources provided for most articles.

Another excellent general reference work is the almanac. Like encyclopedias, almanacs are available in print (usually inexpensively) and online. Start with InfoPlease (www.infoplease.com) which contains a wide variety of hot links to similar works covering such categories as the World, U.S. History and Government, Biography, Sports, Business, Society and Culture, Health and Science, and Arts and Entertainment. Another useful source is the Internet Public Library's list of almanac resources at www.ipl.org/ref/RR/static/ref05.00.00.html.

The next Research Link, "News Sources," appears on page 92.

ANALYZE AUDIENCE SOCIOLOGY

Sociological audience analysis includes consideration of six major sociological or demographic variables of audiences: (1) age, (2) gender, (3) affectional orientation, (4) educational and intellectual levels, (5) religion and religiousness, and (6) cultural factors.

AGE

Different age groups have different attitudes and beliefs largely because they have had different experiences in different contexts. Take these differences into consideration in preparing your speeches.

In examining the following questions, recognize that culture will greatly influence attitudes toward age. Among some Native Americans and Chinese, for example, there is great respect for the aged, and the elders are frequently asked for advice and guidance by the young. Among some groups in the United States—though certainly not all or even necessarily a majority—the aged are often ignored and devalued. Programs for the aged, scholarships for students, or parental and child responsibilities are likely to be regarded very differently by members of these different cultures.

1. Do the age groups in your audience differ in the goals, interests, and day-to-day concerns that may be related to your topic and purpose? Would your class audience be interested in such topics as (1) achieving corporate success, (2) raising a family, or (3) successful job interviewing? If your class is

Research Link

NEWS SOURCES

Often you'll want to read reports on scientific breakthroughs, political speeches, congressional actions, obituaries, financial news, international developments, United Nations actions, or any of a host of other topics. Or you may wish to select the time of a particular event and learn something about what else was going on in the world at that particular time. For this type of information you may want to consult one or more of the many news sources. Especially relevant are newspaper indexes, newspaper and newsmagazine websites, news wire services, and broadcast news networks.

- *Newspaper indexes.* One way to start a newspaper search is to consult a newspaper index, such as www.all-links.com/newscentral, www.newspapers.com, www.newslink.org/menu .html, and www.newspaperlinks.com. At sites like these you'll find hot links to thousands of national and local newspapers.
- *Newspaper and newsmagazine websites.* Most newspapers and magazines maintain their own websites from which you can access current and past issues. Here are a few to get you started: www.latimes.com/ (*Los Angeles Times*), www .usatoday.com/ (*USA Today*), www.wsj.com (*Wall Street Journal*), www.nytimes.com (the *New York Times*), and www.washingtonpost.com (the *Washington Post*).

- *News wire services.* Four wire services should prove helpful. The Associated Press can be accessed at www.ap.org/, Reuters at www.reuters .com/, United Press International at www.upi .com, and PR Newswire at www.prnewswire .com/. The advantage of getting your information from a news wire service is that it's more complete than you'd find in a newspaper; newspapers often must cut copy to fit space requirements and in some cases may put a politically or socially motivated spin on the news.
- *News networks online.* All of the television news stations maintain extremely useful websites. Here are some of the most useful: Access CNN at www.cnn.com/, ESPN at http://espn .sportszone.com/, ABC News at www.abcnews .com/newsflash, CBS News at www.cbs.com/ news/, or MSNBC News at www.msnbc.com/ news.

As you read these news sources, you'll find it helpful to compare the news available on one of the major newspapers' websites (for example, the *Washington Post* site or the *New York Times* site) with the news presented by a wire service such as the Associated Press (www.ap.org) or Reuters (www.reuters.com). Which seems the more reliable? The more complete? The more impartial?

The next Research Link, "Biographical Material," appears on page 120.

typical (say, with most members from 18 to 24 or so) they are likely to react somewhat like this:

1. Irrelevant. I'm not there yet; I need to know how to get my foot in the door.
2. Uninteresting. I'm not thinking about raising a family just yet.
3. Relevant and interesting. Here is something that might help me achieve my immediate goals, like getting a job.

At the same time, recognize that topic (1) might be highly relevant to middle-management people; topic (2) might be interesting to new mothers and fathers; and topic (3) might be irrelevant and uninteresting to a group of people in their 80s.

Very often, the age of your audience will give you clues as to what they may and may not be interested in, what their goals are, what they feel they need and want. Show your audience how they can more effectively achieve their goals, and you'll have an interested and attentive group of listeners in front of you.

2. Do the groups differ in their ability to absorb and process information? With a young audience, it may be best to keep up a steady, even swift

Consider the influence that the culture, age, gender, affectional orientation, educational level, or religion of the speaker might have on you as a listener. Are you more influenced by speakers who are similar to you and less influenced by speakers who are different from you? If so, what might the speaker do to counteract this very common ethnocentric attitude?

pace. If possible, use visuals. Make sure their attention doesn't wander. With older persons, you may wish to maintain a more moderate pace.

3. Do the groups differ in their respect for tradition and the past? Is one age group (traditionally the young) more likely to view innovation and change positively? Might appeals to tradition be more appropriate for an older audience? Might appeals to discovery, exploration, newness, and change find a more receptive hearing among the young?

GENDER

Gender is one of the most difficult audience variables to analyze. The rapid social changes taking place today make it difficult to pin down the effects of gender. At one time researchers focused primarily on biological sex differences. Now, however, many researchers are focusing on psychological sex roles. When we focus on a psychological sex role, we consider a person feminine if that person has internalized those traits (attitudes and behaviors) that society considers feminine and rejected those traits society considers masculine. We consider a person masculine if that person has internalized those traits society considers masculine and rejected those traits society considers feminine. Thus, a biological woman may display masculine sex-role traits and behaviors, and a biological man may display feminine sex-role traits and behaviors (Pearson, West, & Turner, 1995).

Because of society's training, biological males generally internalize masculine traits and biological females generally internalize feminine traits. So there's probably great overlap between biological sex roles and psychological sex roles, even though they're not equivalent.

Although it's not possible to make generalizations about all men or all women, you may be able to make some assumptions about the men and women in your *specific audience*. Here are some questions to guide your analysis of this very difficult audience characteristic.

1. Do men and women differ in the values they consider important and that are related to your topic and purpose? Traditionally, men have been found to place greater importance on theoretical, economic, and political values. Traditionally, women have been found to place greater importance on aesthetic, social, and religious values. Of course, you're unlikely ever to find yourself speaking to an audience of all "traditional" men and "traditional" women. Rather, your audience is likely to be composed of men and women whose values overlap. Be careful not to assume that the women in your audience are religious simply because they're women and that the men, because they're men, are not; or that the men are interested in sports and the stock market but that the women are not.

2. Will your topic be seen differently by men and by women? Although both men and women may find the topic important, they may nevertheless view it from different perspectives. For example, men and women don't view such topics as abortion, date rape, performance anxiety, anorexia, equal pay for equal work, or exercise in the same way. So if you're giving a speech on date rape on campus, you need to make a special effort to relate the topic and your purpose to the attitudes, knowledge, and feelings that the men and the women in your audience bring with them.

3. Will men or women respond differently to the language and style of your speech? Research shows that men and women differ in language usage a lot less than the stereotypes might have us believe. And yet research does support at least two differences: Women are more polite than men in their speech and are more indirect, especially when stating something that is unpleasant or negative (Holmes 1995; Pearson, West, & Turner, 1995). Depending on your specific audience, you may want to make the inference—based on this research—that women have less favorable reactions to slang or to expressions you might label vulgar. Your best bet, of course, is to avoid slang or any expression that may be interpreted as vulgar and to avoid this especially when your audience is mixed. You also may want to infer that women will prefer a more indirect form of criticism or argument, a less confrontational style of speaking, than will men.

At the same time that you might want to adapt your speech to gender differences, realize the danger of stereotyping. For example, imagine that you're listening to a variety of speakers who evidence the following behaviors. Which ones do you imagine as men and which do you imagine as women? Can you group the behaviors into two categories: "communication behaviors characteristic of men" and "communication behaviors characteristic of women"? Are some behaviors equally characteristic of both men and women?

1. This speaker is emotional rather than logical.
2. This speaker is vague rather than precise.
3. This speaker jumps from one idea to another.
4. This speaker is more social and personal than businesslike.
5. This speaker lacks force and power.

Although popular stereotypes would portray all these behaviors as being more characteristic of women, careful research on gender differences (for example, Kramarae, 1981; Coates & Cameron, 1989; Burgoon & Bacue, 2003; Pearson, West, & Turner, 1995; Gamble & Gamble, 2003) finds that none of the behaviors are more characteristic of one gender than another. So look for gender differences, but be careful to avoid stereotypes.

AFFECTIONAL ORIENTATION

The issue of affectional orientation—a term preferred to *sexual orientation*, which implies that a same-sex orientation is primarily or exclusively sexual, whereas *affectional orientation* is broader and more relationally focused—has received enormous media attention within the last decade or so, especially when you compare today's coverage to the way the subject was treated 40 or 50 years ago. The *New York Times*, for example, now regularly features same-sex unions along with those of opposite-sex couples in their Sunday Styles section, and gay and lesbian celebrities and fictional characters are common in the media. Despite these changes, because of the social climate, much of the gay and lesbian experience remains unreported and unknown. Yet you can be reasonably sure that in all your public speaking experiences, you will never address an audience that is totally heterosexual.

If it's difficult to generalize about culture or gender, it's even more difficult to generalize about affectional orientation. Again, however, you may find a few general questions helpful.

1. Will the affectional orientation of the audience members influence the way they see your topic? If your topic is politics, the military's current policies on gay men and lesbians, taxes, marriage, or any of a host of other topics, the answer is probably yes. Polls and frequent news items consistently report on attitudes among gay men and lesbians that differ from those of heterosexuals in significant ways. But don't assume that heterosexuals and homosexuals necessarily see things differently on every topic. There are differences but there are also many similarities.

2. Will the attitudes and behaviors of the audience conform to popular stereotypes of gay men, lesbians, and heterosexual men and women? Here the answer is a clear no. The differences within any large group are always great; be sure not to assume sameness among members of any large group. You're going to find that heterosexual women vary greatly in their attitudes toward most issues, just as do gay men.

3. Should the affectional orientation of audience members influence your language and style? Although clearly the answer is that it should not, you might want to be on the lookout for stereotypical portrayals in your examples or for using language that is not as inclusive as it might be. As you consider this issue, try to assume the perspective of the audience member who is most unlike you and to ask yourself if your examples or language might prove offensive. Be very careful in your examples and illustrations that you don't use stereotypes (the heterosexual male as boorish, the gay male as compulsively neat). Especially with an educated audience, stereotypes are likely to destroy your credibility.

EDUCATIONAL AND INTELLECTUAL LEVELS

An educated person may not be very intelligent; conversely, an intelligent person may not be well educated. In most cases, however, education and intelligence do seem to go together. Further, they seem to influence the reception of a speech in similar ways. So we'll consider these factors together, using the shorthand "educated" to refer to both qualities.

In looking at the education and intelligence of your audience, consider asking questions such as the following:

1. Is the educational level of audience members related to their level of social or political activism? Generally, educated people are more responsive to the needs of others. They more actively engage in causes of a social and political nature. Appeals to humanitarianism and broad social motives should work well with an educated audience; for example, speeches on raising the minimum wage, reducing homelessness, securing equal rights for gay men and lesbians, or making health care available for those who can't afford it. When speaking to less-educated groups, concentrate on the value your speech has to their immediate needs and to the satisfaction of their immediate goals.

2. Will the interests and concerns of audience members differ on the basis of their educational level? Generally, educated people are more concerned with issues outside their immediate field of operation. They're concerned with international affairs, economic issues, and the broader philosophical and sociological issues confronting the nation and the world. Educated groups recognize that these issues affect them in many ways. Often uneducated people don't see the connection. Therefore, when speaking to a less-educated audience, draw connections explicitly to relate such topics to their more immediate concerns.

3. Will educational levels influence how critical the audience will be of your evidence and argument? More educated audiences will probably be less swayed by appeals to emotion and to authority (see Chapter 11). They'll be more skeptical of generalizations (as you should be of my generalizations in this chapter). They'll question the validity of statistics and frequently will demand better substantiation of your propositions. Therefore, pay special attention to the logic of your evidence and arguments in addressing an educated audience.

RELIGION AND RELIGIOUSNESS

Today there's great diversity among the religious backgrounds of audiences. And the attitudes of religions vary widely on numerous issues: abortion, same-sex marriage, women's rights, and divorce (Bates & Fratkin, 1999). Attitudes also vary within religions; almost invariably there are conservative, liberal, and middle-of-the-road groups within each (Henslin, 2000). In some Christian communities, for example, gay men and lesbians may be ordained ministers and same-sex marriages may be performed. In other Christian communities the attitudes are vastly different. According to a 2006 Pew Research Center study, the clergy have addressed such issues as the following from the pulpit: hunger and poverty, abortion, the situation in Iraq, laws regarding homosexuals, the environment, evolution, the death penalty, stem cell research, and immigration. There seem few topics that religion does not address—despite the fact that almost half the population (46 percent) believe that religion should stay out of politics (http://people-press.org/reports/pdf/287.pdf, accessed February 18, 2007). In short, generalizations regarding religion, as with gender, are changing rapidly.

1. Will religious audience members see your topic or purpose from the point of view of religion? Religion permeates all topics and all issues. On a most obvious level, we know that views on such issues as birth control, abortion, and divorce are closely connected to religious affiliation. Similarly, attitudes about premarital sex, marriage, child rearing, money, cohabitation, responsibilities toward parents, and thousands of other issues are clearly influenced by religion. Religion also is important, however, in areas where its connection isn't so obvious. For example, religion influences people's ideas concerning such topics as obedience to authority; responsibility to government; and the usefulness of such qualities as honesty, guilt, and happiness.

2. Does your topic or purpose attack the religious beliefs of any segment of your audience? Even people who claim total alienation from the religion in which they were raised may still have strong emotional (though perhaps unconscious) ties to that religion. These ties may continue to influence such individuals' attitudes and beliefs. When dealing with any religious beliefs (and particularly when disagreeing with them), recognize that you're likely to meet stiff opposition. Proceed slowly and inductively. Present your evidence and argument before expressing your disagreement.

3. Do the religious beliefs of your audience differ in any significant ways from the official teachings of their religion? Don't assume that the rank-and-file members of a faith necessarily accept religious leaders' opinions or pronouncements. Official statements by religious leaders often take more conservative positions than those of laypeople.

CULTURAL FACTORS

Nationality, race, and cultural identity are crucial in audience analysis. Largely because of different training and experiences, various cultural groups will have different interests, values, and goals. Further, cultural factors also will influence each of the remaining factors; for example, attitudes toward age and gender will differ greatly from one culture to another (Harris & Johnson, 2000).

The use of cultural information about your audience to help you select the right motivational appeals may be effective only in certain situations. For example, researchers have found that appeals to self-interest have greater influence on audiences from individualist cultures than on audiences from collectivist cultures. And appeals to other-interests are relatively more influential on audiences of collectivist cultures than on people from individualist cultures (Han & Shavitt, 1994; Dillard & Marshall, 2003). Thus, using an audience's cultural information to select appeals works best when you speak to audiences that are almost exclusively from one cultural orientation and when all or almost all members of that audience subscribe to the specific values you are addressing (Dillard & Marshall, 2003).

You can use cultural information to avoid offending members of the audience, however. Consider some general questions you might ask yourself:

1. Are the attitudes and beliefs held by different cultures relevant to your topic and purpose? Find out what these are. For example, the degree to which listeners are loyal to family members, feel responsibility for the aged, and believe in the value of education will vary from one culture to another. Build your appeals around your audience's attitudes and beliefs.

2. Will the cultures differ in their expectations of the speaker? Members of some cultures—for example, many Asian cultures—expect speakers to be humble and to avoid self-praise and self-commendation. With these groups, if you appear too confident or mention your accomplishments and credits too directly or too often, you run the risk of appearing forward, pushy, or superior. On the other hand, if you are addressing an American audience, the humbleness and avoidance of self-praise that will work for you in some other cultures may work against you, and you'll be perceived as less competent than you otherwise might be. Try to discover the kind of presentation style your audience expects. Then, if you wish, adjust your style—your directness, the ways you mention your qualifications and establish your own believability, the way you address the audience members, and even the way you dress for the occasion.

3. Are the differences within cultures relevant to your topic and purpose? Speakers who fail to demonstrate an understanding of cultural differences will be distrusted. For example, speakers, especially those who are seen to be outsiders, who imply that all African Americans are athletic and all lesbians are masculine will quickly lose credibility. Many African Americans are poor athletes, and many lesbians are extremely feminine. Once again, avoid any implication that you're stereotyping audience members (or the groups to which they belong). It's sure to work against achieving your purpose.

OTHER AUDIENCE FACTORS

No list of audience characteristics can possibly be complete, and the list presented here is no exception. You'll need another category—"other factors"— to identify any additional characteristics that might be significant to your particular audience. For example:

- **Are the audience's occupation and income relevant to your speech?** Is your audience's level of job security and occupational pride related to your topic, purpose, or examples? Will people from different economic levels have different preferences for immediate or long-range goals? Will different groups have different demands on their time that will influence their ability to comply with suggestions to, say, participate in social or political causes?

- **Is the audience's relational status relevant?** Will the relational status of your audience members influence the way they view your topic or purpose? Will singles be interested in hearing about the problems of selecting preschools? Will those already in long-term relationships be interested in the depression many people who are not in close relationships experience during the holidays?

- **Are the special interests of the audience relevant?** Do the special interests of your audience members relate to your topic or purpose? What special interests do the audience members have? What occupies their leisure time? How can you integrate these interests into your examples and illustrations or use them as you select quotations?

- **Are the audience's political beliefs relevant?** Will audience members' political affiliations influence how they view your topic or purpose? Are they politically liberal? Conservative? Might this influence how you develop your speech?

- **Are organizational relationships relevant?** Might audience members' affiliations give you cues as to their other beliefs and values? Might you use references to these organizations in your speech, perhaps as examples or illustrations?

Context Characteristics

In addition to analyzing specific listeners, think about **context factors**—aspects of the specific context in which you'll speak. Here are a few questions you might ask as you prepare your speech:

- **How many listeners will you address?** Generally, the larger the audience, the more formal the speech presentation should be. With a small audience, you may be more casual and informal. In a large audience you'll have a wider variety of religions, a greater range of occupations and income levels, and so on. All the variables noted earlier will be intensified in a large audience. Therefore, you'll need supporting materials that will appeal to all members.

- **Where will you speak?** The physical environment—indoors or outdoors, room or auditorium, sitting or standing audience—will obviously influence your speech presentation. Also, consider the equipment that is available. Is there a chalkboard, flip chart, or transparency projector? Is there a slide projector and screen? Is there a computer with the projector for showing computer slides? Are chalk and markers available? As Chapter 6 will emphasize, it's vital that you check on the compatibility of the equipment in the room with the equipment on which you prepared your materials. If at all possible, rehearse in the room you'll be speaking in with the same equipment that you'll have when you deliver your speech.

- **Why are you speaking?** What's the occasion? When you give a speech as a class assignment, for example, you'll probably be operating under a number of restrictions—time limitations, the type of general purpose you can use, the types of supporting materials, and various other matters. When you are invited to speak because of who you are, you'll have greater freedom to talk about what interests you—which, by virtue of the fact that you were invited, will also interest the audience.

- **When will you speak?** If your speech is to be given in an early morning class, say around 8 a.m., then take into consideration that some of your listeners will still be half asleep. Express your appreciation for their attendance; compliment their attention. If necessary, wake them up with your voice, gestures, attention-gaining materials, visual aids, and the like. If your speech is in the evening, when most of your listeners are anxious to get home, recognize this fact as well.

Analyze Audience Psychology

Psychological audience analysis considers audience members along such dimensions as willing-to-unwilling, favorable-to-unfavorable, and knowledgeable-to-unknowledgeable.

How Willing Is Your Audience?

Audiences gather with varying degrees of willingness to hear a speaker. Some are anxious to hear the speaker and may even have paid a substantial admission price. The "lecture circuit," for example, is a most lucrative aspect of public life.

But whereas some audiences are willing to pay to hear a speaker, others don't seem to care one way or the other. Other audiences need to be persuaded to listen (or at least to sit still during the speech). Still other audiences gather because they have to. For example, negotiations on a union contract may require members to attend meetings where officers give speeches.

Your immediate concern, of course, is with the willingness of your fellow students to listen to your speeches. How willing are they? Do they come to class because they have to, or do they come because they're interested in what you'll say? If they're a willing group, then you have few problems. If they're an unwilling group, all is not lost; you just have to work a little harder in adapting your speech. Here are a few suggestions to help change your listeners from unwilling to willing.

- **Get their interest and attention as early in your speech as possible.** Then maintain this attention throughout your speech by using little-known facts, humor, quotations, startling statistics, examples, narratives, audiovisual aids, and the like. For example, Judith Maxwell (1987), then chair of the Economic Council of Canada, used humor to gain the interest and attention of her audience. She then quickly connected this humor to the topic of her talk:

  Yogi Berra said something once that's relevant to a discussion of economic forecasting. "If you don't know where you're going, you could wind up somewhere else." Whether we are business economists or economists in the public sector, what society expects from us is advice on how to "know where we are going."

- **Reward the audience for their attendance and attention.** Do this in advance of your main arguments. Let the audience know you're aware they're making a sacrifice in coming to hear you speak. Tell them you appreciate it. One student, giving a speech close to midterm time, said simply:

  I know how easy it is to cut classes during midterm time to finish the unread chapters and do everything else you have to do. So I especially appreciate your being here this morning. What I have to say, however, will interest you and will be of direct benefit to all of you.

- **Relate your topic and supporting materials directly to your audience's needs and wants.** Show the audience how they can save time, make more money, solve their problems, or become more popular. If you fail to do this, then your audience has good reason for not listening.

HOW FAVORABLE IS YOUR AUDIENCE?

Audiences vary in the degree to which they're favorable or unfavorable toward your thesis or point of view. And even within the same audience, of course, you're likely to have some who agree with you and others who disagree and perhaps still others who are undecided. If you hope to change an audience's attitudes, beliefs, or values and ultimately their behaviors, you must understand their current attitudes, beliefs, and values and how these might influence the way they view your speech and especially your thesis. In estimating this possible influence, you'll find it helpful to ask some of the following questions about their attitudes, beliefs, and values.

An **attitude** is a tendency to respond for or against an object, person, or position.

- What attitudes do your listeners have that might influence their response to your thesis? If your audience has a favorable attitude toward conservation, then they'll likely be more favorable toward speeches on the need to reduce pollution, to drive smaller cars, and to recycle. On the other hand, they might not favor proposals for reducing fines for companies guilty of pollution or for larger SUVs.

- How might you use the listeners' current attitudes to adapt your speech to them? For example, if you know their attitudes and your thesis is consistent with them, you might mention your attitudinal similarity.

A **belief** is a conviction in the existence or truth of something.

- What beliefs do your listeners have that will impact on your speech? If they believe in God and in a specific religion, then they will likely respond well to religious examples, will respect testimony from religious leaders, and will likely believe what the religion teaches. At the same time, they're likely to resist ideas that go against their religious beliefs. Capital punishment, abortion, and same-sex marriage are just some of the topics about which the listeners' religious beliefs will influence their responses.

- How can you use the beliefs of the audience in adapting your speech to them?

A **value** is the worth a person puts on something or some action.

- What values does your audience have, and how might these impact on your topic? For example, if your listeners value equality and cultural diversity, they're likely to favor interracial adoption and fewer restrictions on immigration than would those who do not value cultural diversity.

- How can you use the values of your listeners to adapt your speech to them? For example, if people value financial success, they'll likely be interested in hearing speeches on the stock market, foreign currency, and the stories of successful entrepreneurs. Further, topics that promise financial rewards or that teach skills that will prove financially beneficial will be responded to favorably.

Of course, when you face an audience whose attitudes, beliefs, and values are consistent with your thesis, your adaptation task is going to be relatively easy. But when you face an audience whose attitudes, beliefs, and values are contrary to your thesis, adapting your speech becomes much more difficult. Here are a few suggestions for dealing with the unfavorably disposed audience.

- **Clear up any possible misapprehensions.** Often disagreement is caused by a lack of understanding. If you feel this is the case, then your first task is to clear this up. For example, if the audience is hostile to the new team approach you are advocating because they wrongly think it will result in a reduction in their autonomy, then explain to them very directly, saying something like:

  I realize that many people oppose this new team approach because they feel it will reduce their own autonomy and control. Well, it won't; as a matter of fact, with this approach, each person will actually gain greater control, greater power, greater autonomy.

Build on commonalities. Emphasize not the differences between you and your listeners but the similarities. Stress what you and the audience share as people, as interested citizens, as fellow students. Theorist and critic Kenneth Burke (1950) argued that we achieve persuasion through identification with the audience. Identification involves emphasizing similarities between speaker and audience. When audience members see common ground between themselves and you, they become more favorable both to you and to your speech.

Here, for example, Alan Nelson (1986) identified with the city of his audience in the introduction to a talk on the sanctuary movement:

> Returning to the Golden Gate, my home area, reminds me of another harbor and a beautiful statue . . . the Statue of Liberty, which has stood for 100 years in New York Harbor, is being rededicated this year and represents the heritage of America.

Organize your speech inductively. Try to build your speech from areas of agreement, through areas of slight disagreement, up to the point where major differences exist between the audience's attitudes and your own position. Let's say, for example, that you represent management and you wish to persuade employees to accept a particular wage offer. You might begin with such areas of agreement as the mutual desire for improved working conditions or for long-term economic growth. Once areas of agreement are established, it's easier to bring up differences such as, perhaps, the need to delay salary increases until next year. In any disagreement or conflict, there are still areas of agreement; emphasize these before considering areas of disagreement.

Strive for small gains. Don't use a five-minute speech to try to convince a pro-life group to contribute money for the new abortion clinic or a pro-choice group to vote against liberalizing abortion laws. Be content to get your listeners to see some validity in your position and to listen fairly. About-face changes take a long time to achieve. Attempting to exert too much persuasion or asking for too much change can result only in failure or resentment.

Acknowledge the differences explicitly. If it's clear to the audience that they and you are at opposite ends of the issue, it may be helpful to acknowledge this very directly. Show the audience that you understand and respect their position but that you'd like them to consider a different way of looking at things. Say something like:

> I know you don't all agree that elementary school teachers should have to take tests every several years to maintain their certification. Some teachers are going to lose their certification, and that isn't pleasant. And we all feel sorry that this will happen. What isn't widely known, however, is that the vast majority of teachers will actually benefit from this proposal. And I'd like an opportunity to sketch out the benefits that many of us will enjoy as a result of this new testing procedure.

AN INFORMATIVE SPEECH

Public Speaking   *Sample Assistant*

Here is an informative speech on "Plasti-Bone," a new procedure to handle bone injuries and diseases. This speech was given by Nicole Martin, University of Texas at Austin.

Just Press Print

The year is 2413, and once again Earth is being threatened by an evil force. This time the fate of mankind rests in the hands of Bruce Willis and the "Fifth Element." Unfortunately, the Fifth Element —Earth's savior—played with thespian excellence by Milla Jovavich, is attacked on her way to Earth, and all that is left of her is a single piece of bone. However, scientists of her time, using her remains, are able to literally print her back to life using a tissue reformulator. The Earth is saved, Bruce and Milla fall in love, and all is good in the universe again. Flashback to today, where *Business Week* of June 23, 2003, explains that doctors have invented a new method for replacing bone tissue destroyed by injury or disease, and our reality begins to look curiously like a science-fiction movie. The website for the Center for Orthopedics and Sports Medicine, last updated April 3, 2003, estimates that there are nearly half a million bone graft surgeries performed each year, and the bone printer, or "Plasti-Bone," is set to revolutionize the way doctors and patients handle physical injuries and bone diseases—simply by printing out new bone material.

So, to better understand the implications of a technique that the *Ventura County Star* of July 21, 2003, expects will reap $80 billion in sales by the year 2010, let's first examine what Plasti-Bone is; second, identify how the process works and its benefits; and, finally, explore the limitations and future prospects of the technology that the *Dallas Medical Journal* of August 2003 calls "another beneficial blurring of the line between computing and care."

In 1998 the U.S. Navy began funding an investigation into solutions to amputation for wounded naval troops. It took five years, but in 2003 Advanced Ceramics Research of Tucson, Arizona,

In this opener the speaker connects a popular movie with the rather complicated process that is the subject of the speech. How effectively would this opener gain the attention of members of your class?

If you were giving this speech to your class, what audience factors would be significant? How important would such factors as the following be: culture, age, gender, affectional orientation, educational and intellectual levels, or religion and religiousness?

Here the speaker provides a detailed orientation. The speech, we learn here, will be in three parts: (1) the nature of Plasti-Bone, (2) the way the process works and its benefits, and (3) the limitations and future of the technology. Is this about the right level of detail for an orientation if this audience were your class? If not, what would you do differently?

answered the call with Plasti-Bone, an artificial substance that can be used to fix or replace broken or damaged bones. For this next sequence, revisit your inner child and think of a really large and expensive Play-Doh Fun Factory where the outgoing material is inserted into the body rather than eaten by a five-year-old. According to *Navy News Week* of June 16, 2003, the idea is to gain a precise 3-D image of a bone before injury by using either a CAT scan or a magnetic resonance imaging system. For example, if the right forearm is broken, doctors use a mirror image of the left forearm to figure out how the implant should be shaped. With our Play-Doh machine, the various shape molds are included in the box. But the image for Plasti-Bone is created through "rapid prototyping"—basically, a 3-D printer. The machine prints a plastic or ceramic material—called a graft or template—into the shape specified by the 3-D image data sent by the computer. The *Plain Dealer* of July 3, 2003, reveals that rapid prototyping machines squeeze out complex shapes, extruding a thin thread from a nozzle that weaves back and forth under computer control; layers of the resulting mesh stack to make a model, or part, which is then used as a scaffold into which human bone can regenerate. Admittedly, a little more complicated than our Play-Doh Fun Factory—but immensely more fascinating as well.

Now what makes Plasti-Bone so unique is the material. The *Times-Picayune* of August 19, 2003, explains that the base material for the scaffold is a polymer called polybutalyne terephthalate, or PBT, a chemical cousin to the plastic used for milk jugs. The only difference is that PBT is coated with calcium phosphate, which attaches to bone cells, allowing the structure to be absorbed by the body. Within a matter of months inside the body, the PBT-based Plasti-Bone begins to function, amazingly, just like a real bone.

Now, the Fifth Element's medical miracle was a lot of special effects—but how the Plasti-Bone process works and its medical benefits are almost as divine. At the moment, reconstructing crushed or severely damaged bones is a painstaking process, states the *New Scientist* of June 20, 2003. To bridge gaps, surgeons use scaffolds made of biocompatible materials and bone grafts taken from elsewhere in the body, with strength provided by steel pins. Unfortunately, explains the *Deseret Morning News* of Salt Lake City on July 21, 2003, these metallic

Here the speaker begins the first main point, focusing on what Plasti-Bone is. As you can tell, the process is fairly complex, but the speaker helps the uninformed listener understand Plasti-Bone with a clever analogy to Play-Doh. It's a good example of how you can explain the unknown by relating it to something known.

Now that you know something about the speech topic, how would you evaluate your class on such psychological dimensions as willingness to listen, degree of favorableness to the topic, and knowledge? What two or three major adjustments to the speech as presented here would you make on the basis of your audience analysis?

Here the speaker continues with the explanation of Plasti-Bone by explaining what it consists of.

Here the speaker begins the second main point and explains the benefits and advantages of the Plasti-Bone process. The speaker succeeds in explaining the benefits of this process by neatly comparing it to the process that is currently widely used.

inserts can't be absorbed by the body and must eventually be replaced. In fact, the 2004 *Navy Opportunity Forum* explains that with current implant materials, loss of strength occurs before substantial bone growth has taken place, and 20 percent failure is the norm. Plasti-Bone, however, works in quite a different way. The *News Illustrated* of August 17, 2003, describes the surgical implantation process: The damaged bone pieces are surgically removed and the sterilized computer-generated graft is implanted; the graft is glued into place with a ceramic paste that is harmless to the body yet strong enough to eliminate the need for support pins; then a cast is placed over the limb to keep it immobile. The result is a bone implant that surrounding natural bone slowly will grow into over the next four to six months. Not bad for a bone that, according to the previously cited *New Scientist,* will take only an hour and a half to create.

But the speed of the Plasti-Bone process isn't all that's remarkable: The Scripps Howard News Service of July 21, 2003, states that the porous nature of the Plasti-Bone material allows blood flow through the healing area, while the material is tough enough to resist the corrosiveness of human blood. Eventually, the implant is "bioresorbed" and replaced with a completely natural bone. As University of Arizona orthopedics professor John Szivek states in the *Arizona Daily Star* of July 17, 2003, "Once it's dissolved, it's gone, and the body doesn't have to deal with it and the surgeon doesn't have to go back in to take it out." And, amazingly, Ranji Vaidyanathan, principal investigator at Advanced Ceramics Research, confirms in a personal interview on March 16, 2004, that the technology will cost patients an amount significantly less than current procedures, which range between $5,000 and $6,000.

The speaker continues here with another advantage of Plasti-Bone, namely that it's porous and resistant to corrosion and that ultimately it is replaced with natural bone.

Notice this brief qualification of the credentials of the person whose testimony is used here.

In order to save the world, Bruce Willis and the Supreme Being had to overcome a devious villain and a big ball of evil matter. Though not as threatening, Plasti-Bone's future has its own share of obstacles—but its ending promises to be equally supreme. Unfortunately, Plasti-Bone's arrival on the market could take a little time. *Biotech Week* of July 9, 2003, explains that only tissue cultures and animals have been used to test the new material. But as Vaidyanathan states in the previously cited *Dallas Medical Journal,* in tests rats with Plasti-Bone have been up and running just a few weeks after implantation. The product currently is awaiting

The speaker here begins the third main point of the speech—the limitations and problems associated with the process.

If you were giving this speech to your class, what kinds of audience responses might you expect? What might you do to deal effectively with these responses?

approval of safety from the U.S. Food and Drug Administration to begin human testing, and as a result, the product will probably not be seen on the market for a few years.

After approval, though, Plasti-Bone's potential makes it a possible fifth element in its own right. In addition to the half a million bone graft surgeries each year, the Dr. Joseph F. Smith Medical Library website, last accessed and updated on March 12, 2004, reveals that 65,000 amputations are performed annually in the United States, with a long rehabilitation process, and that the average infection rate is 15 percent. According to the *Engineer* of May 30, 2003, Plasti-Bone holds the promise to improve recovery time and minimize infection rates for patients. Consider American climber Aron Ralston, who—according to *People Yearbook* magazine of 2004—and just about every major magazine and newspaper in May of last year—amputated his own arm after a thousand-pound boulder fell on him during an expedition in Colorado. Even though the probability of being crushed by a huge boulder is low, had Plasti-Bone been available, Ralston might have had the opportunity to "grow" his natural arm back without resorting to the current prosthetic arm that he now uses. And in a press release from the Office of Naval Research on June 12, 2003, this medical innovation offers significant benefits to bones damaged by cancer. According to the American Cancer Society's publication *Cancer Facts and Figures 2004*, about 2,500 cases of cancer in the bones will be diagnosed this year, with about 1,300 deaths from these cancers expected. With Plasti-Bone, patients will be able to remove the cancerous bones—saving their bodies and their lives.

Thanks to Bruce Willis, Earth was once again saved from doom and destruction, and very soon damaged bones and limbs will offer the same thanks to Plasti-Bone. By examining what Plasti-Bone is, how it works and its benefits, and the limitations and future prospects of the process, while it is clear we are still a ways away from having cruise ships that take us to the depths of the universe or flying automobiles, the success of Plasti-Bone could soon have scientists of today actually living the life of the movies—and all they have to do is press "print."

Throughout this speech you'll find references to websites effectively woven into the fabric of the speech. You don't have to give the URLs of websites you cite in your speeches, but you probably should have them ready just in case someone asks a question or would like to access a site.

Here the speaker returns to the introductory example of Bruce Willis and signals that the conclusion is coming. The speaker summarizes the speech by reiterating the three main points that were covered and ends by again referring back to the movie talked about in the introduction.

How KNOWLEDGEABLE IS YOUR AUDIENCE?

Listeners differ greatly in the knowledge they have. Some listeners will be quite knowledgeable about your topic; others will be almost totally ignorant. Mixed audiences are the most difficult ones.

If you're unaware of the audience's knowledge level, you won't know what to assume and what to explain. You won't know how much information will overload the channels or how much will bore the audience to sleep. Perhaps you want to show that their previous knowledge is now inadequate. Perhaps you want to demonstrate a new slant to old issues. Or perhaps you want to show that what you have to say will not repeat but instead will build on the already extensive knowledge of the audience. However you accomplish this, you need to make the audience see that what you have to say is new. Make them realize that you won't simply repeat what they already know.

Treat audiences that lack knowledge of the topic very carefully. Never confuse a lack of knowledge with a lack of ability to understand.

- **Don't talk down to your audience.** This is perhaps the greatest communication error that teachers make. Having taught a subject for years, they face, semester after semester, students who have no knowledge of the topic. As a result, many teachers tend to talk down to the students and, in the process, lose their audience.

- **Don't confuse a lack of knowledge with a lack of intelligence.** An audience may have no knowledge of your topic but be quite capable of following a clearly presented, logically developed argument. Try especially hard to use concrete examples, audiovisual aids, and simple language. Fill in background details as required. Avoid jargon and specialized terms that may not be clear to someone new to the subject. In sum, never overestimate your audience's knowledge, but never underestimate their intelligence.

- **Let your listeners know that you're aware of their knowledge and expertise.** Try to do this as early in the speech as possible. Emphasize that what you have to say will not be redundant. Tell them that you'll be presenting recent developments or new approaches. In short, let them know that they'll not be wasting their time listening to your speech.

- **Emphasize your credibility, especially your competence in this general subject area** (see Chapter 11). Let your listeners know that you have earned the right to speak. Let them know that what you have to say is based on a firm grasp of the material.

Here, for example, Senator Christopher Dodd of Connecticut, addressing the Jesse Jackson Wall Street Summit (January 9, 2007), establishes his credibility (http://dodd.senate.gov, accessed February 27, 2007):

> When Dr. King and President Kennedy asked young Americans to serve the cause of freedom and justice, I was among those who answered in the affirmative. I joined the Peace Corps as a young man. I lived and worked in a small village in the Dominican Republic. I worked side by side with people who had a different ethnic heritage, a different nationality, and a different language than me. I was very much in the minority. Yet, I was accepted into the community. We all brought different abilities and experiences to our common work. And together, we achieved significant things. We built a road, a school, and several homes.

Consider the ways college instructors adapt their lectures to their students. For example, have instructors responded to puzzled looks, elaborated on an example that didn't seem to work as planned, or picked up the pace when there's more to cover than time allows? What one suggestion would you offer the typical college instructor to better adapt his or her speech to the classroom audience?

How Homogeneous Is Your Audience?

In analyzing your audience, consider their **homogeneity** or **heterogeneity**—the degree to which they do or do not share similar characteristics, values, attitudes, knowledge, and so on. *Homogeneous audiences* consist of individuals who are very much alike; *heterogeneous audiences* consist of widely different individuals. Obviously, it's easier to address a homogeneous group than a heterogeneous group. If your listeners are alike, your arguments will be as effective for one as for another. The language appropriate for one will be appropriate for another, and so on, through all the elements of the public speaking transaction. With a heterogeneous group, the situation is very different. Here are three general principles that will help you in this difficult but not impossible task.

The greater the heterogeneity of the audience, the more extensive your analysis should be. A heterogeneous audience requires a more complex analysis and a more careful plan of adaptation than a homogeneous audience. Consider, for example, a PTA audience composed of parents (differing widely in income, education, and cultural background) and teachers (differing widely in background, training, and age). Members of each of these groups will have different points of view, backgrounds, and expectations. Recognize these differences and take special care to relate your message to all listeners.

When the audience is too heterogeneous, it's sometimes helpful to subdivide it and appeal to each section separately. A common example is the audience consisting of men and women. Say the topic is abortion on demand. To limit yourself to arguments that would appeal equally to men and women might seriously damage your case. Consider, therefore, concentrating first on arguments that women relate to most positively and then on those to which men relate most positively. You thus avoid using supporting materials that fall in between the groups and that are effective with neither. Do be careful, however; in trying to appeal to each group, you risk spreading your arguments too thin and emerging with no real theme—as sometimes happens when politicians try to appeal to every constituent and wind up with virtually no position of their own.

Homogeneity does not equal attitudinal sameness. The audience that is similar in age, gender, educational background, and so on will probably also share similar attitudes and beliefs. However, this isn't always true. Heterogeneity increases with the size of the group. As any group expands in size, its characteristics become more diverse. Keep this in mind when you're analyzing your audiences.

ANALYZE AND ADAPT DURING THE SPEECH

In addition to analyzing your audience and making adaptations in your speech *before* delivering the speech, devote attention to analysis and adaptation *during* the speech. This during-the-speech analysis is especially important when you know little of your audience or find yourself facing an audience very different from the one you expected. Here are a few suggestions.

FOCUS ON LISTENERS AS MESSAGE SENDERS

As you're speaking, look at your audience. Remember that just as you're sending messages to your listeners, they're also sending messages to you. Pay attention to these messages; on the basis of what they tell you, make the necessary adjustments.

Remember that members of different cultures operate with different **display rules**, cultural rules that state what types of expressions are appropriate to reveal—and what expressions are inappropriate to reveal and should be kept hidden. Some display rules call for open and free expression of feelings and responses; these listeners will be easy to read. Other display rules call for little expression, and these listeners will be difficult to read.

You can make a wide variety of adjustments to each type of audience response. For example, if your audience shows signs of boredom, increase your volume, move closer to them, or tell them that what you're going to say will be of value to them. If your audience shows signs of disagreement or hostility, stress a similarity you have with them. If your audience looks puzzled or confused, pause a moment and rephrase your ideas, provide necessary definitions, or insert an internal summary. If your audience seems impatient, say, for example, "my last argument . . ." instead of your originally planned "my third argument. . . ."

ASK "WHAT IF" QUESTIONS

The more preparation you put into your speech, the better prepared you'll be to make on-the-spot adjustments and adaptations. For example, let's say you have been told that you're to explain the opportunities available to the nontraditional student at your college. You've been told that your audience will consist mainly of working women in their 30s and 40s who are just beginning college. As you prepare your speech with this audience in mind, ask yourself **"what if" questions**. For example:

- What if the audience has a large number of men?
- What if the audience consists of women much older than 40?
- What if the audience members also come with their spouses or their children?

Keeping such questions in mind will force you to consider alternatives as you prepare your speech. This way, you'll have extra options readily available if you face an audience that is not what you're used to or is different from what you expected.

ADDRESS AUDIENCE RESPONSES DIRECTLY

Another way of dealing with audience responses is to confront them directly. To people who are reacting negatively to your message, for example, you might say:

> Regardless of your present position, hear me out and see if this new way of doing things will not simplify your accounting procedures.

Or, to those who seem puzzled, you might say:

> This plan may seem confusing, but bear with me; it will become clear in a moment.

Or, to those who seem impatient, you might respond:

> I know this has been a long day, but give me just a few more minutes and you'll be able to save hours recording your accounts.

By responding to your listeners' reactions and feedback, you acknowledge their needs. You let them know that you hear them, that you're with them, and that you're responding to their very real concerns.

Essentials of Analyzing and Adapting to Your Audience

This chapter looked at the audience and particularly at how you can analyze your listeners and adapt your speeches to them.

1. In **seeking information about your audience**, consider the values of observation, collecting data (for example, with audience questionnaires), interviewing members, and using intelligent inference and empathy.

2. In analyzing **the sociology of your audience**, consider especially the following characteristics:
   - Age
   - Gender (biological sex role and psychological sex role)
   - Affectional orientation
   - Educational and intellectual levels
   - Religion and religiousness
   - Cultural factors

3. In addition, look into **other relevant audience factors** such as your audience's occupation and income status, relational status, special interests, and political attitudes and beliefs, and consider context factors.

4. In analyzing **audience psychology** consider your listeners' willingness, degree of favorableness toward your ideas, knowledge level, and degree of homogeneity.

5. In **adapting to an unwilling audience**:
   - Secure their attention as early as possible.
   - Reward the audience for their attendance and attention.
   - Relate your topic and supporting materials to the audience's needs and interests.

6. In **adapting to an unfavorable audience**:
   - Clear up any possible misunderstandings.
   - Build on the similarities you have with the audience.
   - Build your speech from areas of agreement up to the major areas of difference.
   - Strive for small gains.

7. In **adapting to an unknowledgeable audience**:
   - Avoid talking down to your listeners (or to any audience).
   - Avoid confusing a lack of knowledge with a lack of intelligence.

8. In **adapting to a knowledgeable audience**:
   - Let your listeners know that you're aware of their expertise.
   - Establish your credibility.

9. In **adapting to a heterogeneous audience**:
   - Give special attention to analyzing the differences among listeners.
   - Consider appealing to each of the major groups within the audience separately.

   - Don't assume that homogeneous listeners will all have the same attitudes and values.

10. To help you **adapt your speech during your presentation**:
    - Focus on audience members as message senders, not merely as message receivers.
    - Ask "what if" questions as you prepare your speech.
    - Address audience responses directly.

Essential Terms: Analyzing and Adapting to Your Audience

attitude **(p. 89)**
belief **(p. 89)**
context factors **(p. 99)**
display rules **(p. 109)**

heterogeneity **(p. 108)**
homogeneity **(p. 108)**
psychological audience analysis **(p. 99)**

sociological audience analysis **(p. 91)**
value **(p. 89)**
"what if" questions **(p. 109)**

Public Speaking Exercises

5.1 Analyzing an Unknown Audience

This experience should familiarize you with some of the essential steps in analyzing an audience on the basis of relatively little evidence and in predicting their attitudes on the basis of that analysis. The class should be broken up into small groups of five or six members. Each group will be given a different magazine; their task is to analyze the audience (i.e., the readers or subscribers) of that particular magazine in terms of the characteristics discussed in this chapter. The only information the groups will have about their audience is that they're avid and typical readers of the given magazine. Pay particular attention to the types of articles published in the magazine, the advertisements, the photographs or illustrations, the editorial statements, the price of the magazine, and so on. Magazines that differ widely from one another are most appropriate for this experience.

After the audiences have been analyzed, try to identify at least three favorable and three unfavorable attitudes that each audience probably holds on contemporary issues. On what basis do you make these predictions? If you had to address this audience and advocate a position with which it disagreed, what adaptations would you make? What strategies would you use to prepare and present this persuasive speech?

Each group should share with the rest of the class the results of their efforts, taking special care to point out not only their conclusions but also the evidence and reasoning they used in arriving at the conclusions.

5.2 Predicting Listeners' Attitudes

Analyze the audience in each of the five situations presented below in terms of their willingness, favorableness, and knowledge. On the basis of this analysis, what one suggestion would you give the speaker to help him or her better adapt the speech to this audience?

1. Film students listening to Woody Allen talk about how to break into films.
2. High school athletes listening to a college athletic director speaking against sports scholarships.
3. Pregnant women listening to an advertising executive speak on how advertisers try to protect consumers.
4. Office managers listening to an organizational communication consultant speaking on ways to increase employee morale and productivity.
5. Chicago high school seniors listening to a college recruiter speak on the advantages of a small rural college.

5.3 What Do You Say?

◆ **Audience Attitudes.** Denny is planning to give a persuasive speech to your class urging listeners to support the National Rifle Association in its efforts to fight gun control. He wonders, first, what attitudes the members of the class have on this topic, and second, how he can adjust his speech on the basis of these (predicted) attitudes. How would you advise Denny?

◆ **Unwilling Audience.** Shirley is scheduled to give a speech on careers in computer technology to a group of high school students who have been forced to attend this Saturday career day. The audience definitely qualifies as unwilling. What advice can you give Shirley to help her deal with this type of audience?

◆ **Inattentive Audience.** Alan is giving a speech on the problem of teenage drug abuse and notices that several entire back rows of the audience have totally tuned him out; they're reading, working on their laptops, or just daydreaming. What might Alan do to encourage these audience members to pay attention?

◆ **Negative Feedback.** While giving her speech, Denise notices from the expressions on the faces of her audience that they are totally against her thesis and are ready to tune her out. What would be the best thing Denise could do to induce the audience to continue listening and to give her a fair hearing?

Log*On!* MySpeechLab

Analyzing and Adapting to Your Audience

Visit MySpeechLab (www.myspeechlab.com) for additional insight into the public speaking audience and to learn how you can better adapt your speeches to specific audiences. See "How Active Is Your Audience?," "Predicting Listeners' Attitudes," and "Analyzing an Unknown Audience." An excellent speech on sexual harassment by Meleena Erikson, "See Jane, See Jane's Dilemma," is presented with annotations and questions for analysis. Also view one or two of the speech videos (for example, credit card crisis, Vietnamese culture, or voting) and respond to the prompts that help explain how the speaker analyzed and adapted to the audience. Look too at the Explore activities and respond to the questions to help you analyze your own audience. A variety of useful visuals are also offered here on audience questionnaires, dimensions of an audience, and levels of influence.

While at MSL and in connection with the Research Link on news sources (p. 91), take a look at the vast amount of information available in two world-class newspapers, the *New York Times* and the *Financial Times* of London, both of which are available through MSL.

Also visit the Allyn & Bacon public speaking website (www.ablongman.com/pubspeak); it contains lots of useful advice on analyzing your audience.

Using Supporting Materials and Presentation Aids

6

Why Read This Chapter?

Because it will contribute to your public speaking success by helping you to:

- select supporting materials (such as examples and statistics) to make your speech come alive in the minds of the audience

- develop interesting and appropriate presentation aids, including PowerPoint presentations, to further inform and persuade

He or she is greatest who contributes the greatest original practical example.

Walt Whitman (1819–1892) —American journalist, teacher, editor, and poet, most famous for his *Leaves of Grass*

This chapter begins by examining the various types of supporting materials and explaining how to use them most effectively: examples, analogies, definitions, narratives, testimony, and statistics. Next it focuses on presentation aids and how to use them effectively.

SUPPORTING MATERIALS

Supporting materials are a vital part of an effective public speech; they add concreteness, help maintain interest and attention, and provide vital information and persuasive appeal. In this section we cover examples, narration, testimony, and statistics. In the next section we consider a special kind of support, the presentation aid.

EXAMPLES

Examples are specific instances that are explained in varying degrees of detail. A relatively brief specific instance is referred to as an example; a longer and more detailed example is referred to as an **illustration**; and an example told in storylike form is referred to as a narrative, as discussed in a later section. In using examples, keep in mind that their function is to make your ideas vivid and easily understood; examples are not ends in themselves. Make them only as long as necessary to ensure that your purpose is achieved.

Use examples when you want to make an abstract idea concrete. Specific examples can make the audience see what you mean when you talk about such abstract concepts as "persecution," "denial of freedom," "love," or "friendship." Your examples also encourage listeners to see *your* mental pictures of these concepts rather than seeing their own. In a speech on free speech and song lyrics, Sam Brownback (1998, p. 454), a U.S. senator from Kansas, uses some pretty powerful examples to make his point:

> Women are objectified, often in the most obscene and degrading ways. Songs such as Prodigy's single "Smack My Bitch Up" or "Don't Trust a Bitch" by the group "Mo Thugs" encourage animosity and even violence towards women. The alternative group Nine Inch Nails enjoyed both critical and commercial success with their song "Big Man with a Gun" which describes forcing a woman into oral sex and shooting her in the head at pointblank range.
>
> Shock-rock bands such as "Marilyn Manson" or "Cannibal Corpse" go ever further, with lyrics describing violence, rape, and torture. Consider just a few song titles by the group "Cannibal Corpse," "Orgasm by Torture," or "Stripped, Raped and Strangled." As their titles indicate, the lyrics to these songs celebrate hideous crimes against women.

Use relevant examples. Make sure your example is directly relevant to the proposition you want it to support, and make its relationship with your assertion explicit. Remember that although this relationship is clear to you (because you've constructed the speech), the audience is going to hear your speech only once. Show the audience exactly how your example relates to the assertion or concept you're explaining. Here for example, New York's Mayor Rudolph Giuliani, in his address to the United Nations after the World Trade Center attack of September 11, 2001, gave relevant examples to support his proposition that we are a land of immigrants and must continue to be so (www.washingtonpost.com/wp-srv/nation/specials/attached/transcripts/giulianitext_100101.html):

> New York City was built by immigrants and it will remain the greatest city in the world so long as we continue to renew ourselves with and benefit from the energizing spirit from new people coming here to create a better future for themselves and their families. Come to Flushing, Queens, where immigrants from many lands have created a vibrant, vital commercial and residential community. Their children challenge and astonish us in our public school classrooms every day. Similarly, you can see growing and dynamic immigrant communities in every borough of our city: Russians in Brighton Beach, West Indians in Crown Heights, Dominicans in Washington Heights, the new wave of Irish in the Bronx, and Koreans in Willow Brook on Staten Island.

Distinguish between real and hypothetical examples. Don't try to foist a hypothetical example on the audience as a real one. If they recognize the deception, they'll resent your attempt to fool them. Use phraseology such as the following to let the audience know when you're using a hypothetical example:

- We could imagine a situation such as . . .
- I think an ideal friend would be someone who . . .
- A hypothetical example of this type of friendship would be like . . .

If the example is real, let the audience know this as well. Help the audience to see what you want them to see with such statements as "A situation such as this occurred recently; it involved . . ." or "I have a friend who . . ." or simply "An actual example of this was reported when . . . ."

Use a series of very brief examples to emphasize the widespread nature or significance of an issue or problem. Here, for example, U.S. Senator from California Dianne Feinstein (2006) uses a series of examples to make the point that law enforcement officers are in danger from gang violence (http://Feinstein.senate.com accessed January 14, 2007):

> Los Angeles Police Officer Ricardo Lizarraga. Killed while responding to a domestic violence call, by a man who drew a gun and shot him twice in the back. The suspect was a known member of the Rollin 20s Bloods.
> Merced Police Officer Stephan Gray. Officer Gray was shot and killed when a suspect (a gang member he had encountered before) fired two bullets into this chest.
> The list goes on:
> Los Angeles Sheriff's Deputy Jeffrey Ortiz.
> Burbank Police Officer Matthew Pavelka.
> California Highway Patrol Officer Thomas Steiner.
> And San Francisco Police Officer Isaac Espinoza.

ANALOGIES

Analogies are comparisons that are often extremely useful in making your ideas clear and vivid to your audience. Analogies may be of two types: figurative and literal.

Figurative analogies compare items from different classes—for example, the flexibility afforded by a car with the freedom of a bird, a college degree with a passport to success, playing baseball with running a corporation. Figurative analogies are useful for illustrating possible similarities; they provide vivid examples that are easily remembered. But they do not constitute evidence of the truth or falsity of an assertion. Speakers who present figurative analogies as proof may be doing so because there is no real evidence.

Literal analogies compare items from the same class, such as two cars or two cities. For example, in a literal analogy you might argue (1) that two companies are similar—both are multinational, multibillion-dollar pharmaceutical companies, both have advertising budgets in the hundreds of millions of dollars, and so on; and (2) that therefore the advertising techniques that worked for one company will work for the other.

In evaluating your literal analogies, ask yourself two questions:

- Are the cases compared (in this example, the two pharmaceutical companies) alike in essential respects? Or do the two cases differ from each other in ways that might negate the comparison? For example, do the two companies differ in the location of their headquarters? Do they differ in the types of drugs they manufacture? Do they differ in their pricing of drugs?

- Do the differences make a difference? Obviously, not all differences are significant. Very likely a difference between two companies' headquarters locations is not a difference that would bear on the type of advertising that would prove effective. On the other hand, differences in the types of drugs the companies sell or in their pricing might well prove significant. These differences might have an impact on the type of advertising that would prove most effective; advertising techniques used to sell over-the-counter painkillers like aspirin might not prove effective in selling drugs to treat cancer or diabetes.

DEFINITIONS

A **definition** is a statement of the meaning of a term or concept; it explains what something is. Use definitions when you wish to explain difficult or unfamiliar concepts or when you wish to make a concept more vivid or forceful.

As you can appreciate, definitions are often helpful when you are explaining a concept that the audience may not be familiar with or may have misconceptions about. If the purpose of the definition is to clarify, then it must do just that. This would be too obvious to mention except for the fact that so many speakers, perhaps for want of something to say, define terms that don't need extended definitions. Some speakers use definitions that don't clarify and that, in fact, complicate an already complex concept. Make sure your definitions define only what needs defining.

As you think of terms to define, or after you've selected a term, take a look at The OneLook Dictionary Search website at www.onelook.com. This website will enable you to search a wide variety of dictionaries at the same time. There are, of course, many other useful online dictionaries; search for "dictionary," "definitions," or "thesaurus" and you'll find a wealth of material for speeches of definition.

Here are some of the most important ways in which you can define a term.

Definition by Etymology

One way to define a term is to trace its historical or linguistic development. In defining the word communication, for example, you might note that it comes from the Latin *communis*, meaning "common"; in "communicating" you seek to establish a commonness, a sharing, a similarity with another individual. And *woman* comes from the Anglo-Saxon *wifman*, which meant literally a "wife man," where the word *man* was applied to both sexes. Through phonetic change *wifman* became *woman*. Most larger dictionaries and, of course, etymological dictionaries will help you find useful etymological definitions.

Or you might define a term by noting not its linguistic etymology, but how it came to mean what it now means. For example, you might note that *spam*, meaning unwanted e-mail, comes from a Monty Python television skit in which every item on the menu contained the product Spam. And much as the diner was forced to get Spam, so the e-mail user gets spam, even when he or she wants something else.

Definition by Authority

You can often clarify a term by explaining how a particular authority views it. You might, for example, define *lateral thinking* by authority and say that Edward deBono, who developed lateral thinking in 1966, has noted that "lateral thinking involves moving sideways to look at things in a different way. Instead of fixing on one particular approach and then working forward from that, the lateral thinker tries to find other approaches." Or you might use the authority of cynic and satirist Ambrose Bierce and define love as nothing but "a temporary insanity curable by marriage" and friendship as "a ship big enough to carry two in fair weather, but only one in foul."

Definition by Negation

You also might define a term by noting what the term is not; that is, define it by negation. "A wife," you might say, "isn't a cook, a cleaning person, a babysitter, a seamstress, a sex partner. A wife is . . ." or "A teacher isn't someone who tells you what you should know but rather one who . . . ."

Here Michael Marien (1992) defines futurists first negatively and then positively:

> Futurists do not use crystal balls. Indeed, they're generally loath to make firm predictions of what will happen. Rather, they make forecasts of what is probable, sketch scenarios of what is possible, and/or point to desirable futures—what is preferable and what strategies we should pursue to get there.

Definition by Specific Examples

An example is not a definition, but it can serve defining functions; it can help clarify terms or phrases. Here, for example, Ohio Congressman Dennis Kucinich uses a series of specific examples to clarify what he means by "human rights" in a speech presented to the Wall Street Project Conference on January 8, 2007 (www.politicalaffairs.net, accessed March 10, 2007):

> We have a right to a job.
>
> We have a right to a living wage.
>
> We have a right to an education.
>
> We have a right to health care.
>
> We have a right to decent and affordable housing.
>
> We have a right to a secure pension.

We have a right to air fit to breathe.

We have a right to water fit to drink.

We have a right to be free of the paralyzing fear of crime.

Definition by Direct Symbolization

You also might define a term by direct symbolization—by showing the actual thing or a picture or model of it. For example, a sales representative explaining a new computer keyboard would obviously use an actual keyboard in the speech. Similarly, a speech on magazine layout or types of fabrics would include actual layout pages and fabric samples.

NARRATION

Narratives, or stories, are often useful as supporting materials in a speech. **Narration** gives the audience what it wants: a good story. It helps you maintain attention, because listeners automatically seem to perk up when a story is told. If your narrative is a personal story, then it's likely that it will increase your credibility and show you as a real person. Listeners like to know about speakers, and the personal narrative meets this desire. Notice how you remember the little stories that celebrities tell during television interviews.

The main value of narration is that it allows you to bring an abstract concept down to specifics. For example, to illustrate the dangers of greed, you might retell the fable of the man and woman who killed the goose that laid the golden egg: Thinking that they'd get all the gold at once, they lost the very thing that could have made them rich. To illustrate determination, you might tell the story of any of numerous great people who rose to prominence against the odds.

Consider the speeches you've listened to recently. What types of supporting materials held your interest and attention? What kinds of support bored you?

Narratives may be of different types, and each type serves a somewhat different purpose. Following communication writer Clella Jaffe (2007), we distinguish three general types of narrative: explanatory, exemplary, and persuasive.

1. **Explanatory narratives** explain the way things are. The biblical book of Genesis, for example, explains the development of the world.
2. **Exemplary narratives** provide examples of excellence to follow or admire. The stories of the lives of saints and martyrs are exemplary narratives, as are success stories of the Horatio Alger type. Similarly, motivational speakers often include exemplary narratives in their speeches and will tell their own story of being out of shape or unenlightened.
3. **Persuasive narratives** try to strengthen or change beliefs and attitudes. When a celebrity tells us of the plight of starving children, he or she is using a persuasive narrative. The parables in religious writings are persuasive narratives that urge readers to lead life in a particular way.

Keep narratives short and few in number. In most cases, one or possibly two narratives are sufficient in a short five- to seven-minute speech. Be sure you don't get carried away and elaborate more than necessary, especially if the narrative is personal.

Maintain a reasonable chronological order. Events happen in time and are best recounted in a time sequence. Avoid shifting back and forth through time. Start at the beginning and end at the end.

Make explicit the connection between your story and the point you're making. Be sure that the audience will see the connection between the story and the purpose of your speech. If they don't, you risk not only losing the effectiveness of the story but also losing your listeners' attention as they try to figure out why you told that story.

TESTIMONY

The term **testimony** refers to the opinions of experts or to the accounts of witnesses. Testimony helps to amplify your speech by adding a note of authority to your arguments.

Testimony may, therefore, be used in either of two ways. First, you may cite the opinions, beliefs, predictions, or values of some authority or expert. For example, you might want to state an economist's predictions concerning inflation and depression, or you might want to support your analysis by citing an art critic's evaluation of a painting or art movement. The faculty of your college or university is one of the best, if rarely used, sources of expert information for almost any speech topic. Regardless of what your topic is, a faculty member of some department likely knows a great deal about the subject. At the very least, faculty members will be able to direct you to appropriate sources. Experts in the community can serve similar functions. Local politicians, religious leaders, doctors, lawyers, museum directors, and the like often are suitable sources of information.

Beyond your college or university lies a world of experts—religious and business leaders, politicians, educators at other colleges and research institutes, medical personnel, researchers in almost any field imaginable. Ask yourself if your speech and your audience could profit from the insights of experts. If your answer is yes—and few topics could not so profit—then consider the steps suggested in the Research Link in Chapter 3 (p. 46) for interviewing such experts. Interviews can take place in person; by telephone; or, as is becoming increasingly popular, over the Internet, especially in e-mail or chat groups.

Of course, if 500 public speaking students all descend on the faculty or on the community, chaos can easily result. So going to these experts is often discouraged as a class assignment. But it's often a useful practice for speeches you'll give later in life.

Second, you may want to use the testimony of an eyewitness to some event or situation. For example, you might cite the testimony of someone who saw an accident, of a person who spent two years in a maximum-security prison, or of a person who had a particular operation.

Whether you use the testimony of a world-famous authority or draw on an eyewitness account, you need to establish your source's credibility—to demonstrate to the audience that your expert is in fact an authority or that your eyewitness is believable.

Stress the competence of the person. Whether the person is an expert or a witness, make sure the audience sees this person as competent. To cite the predictions of a world-famous economist of whom your audience has never heard will mean little, so first explain the person's competence. To prepare the audience to accept what this person says, you might introduce the testimony by saying, for example:

> This prediction comes from the world's leading economist, who has successfully predicted all major finacial trends over the past 20 years.

Stress the unbiased nature of the testimony. If listeners perceive the testimony to be biased—whether or not it really is—it will have little effect. You want to

Research Link

BIOGRAPHICAL MATERIAL

As a speaker you'll often need information about particular individuals. For example, in using expert testimony, it's helpful to stress your experts' qualifications, which you can easily learn about from even brief biographies. Or you may want to look up authors of books or articles to find out something about their education, their training, or their other writings. Or you may wish to discover if there have been critical evaluations of authors' work such as book reviews or articles about them or their writings. Knowing something about your sources enables you to more effectively evaluate their competence, convey their credibility to the audience, and answer audience questions about them.

One of the most enjoyable and useful biography sites is maintained by The Biography Channel (www.biography.com), which contains biographies of some 25,000 individuals from all walks of life.

Another great source is the Biography and Genealogy Master Index, which indexes several hundred biographical sources. Online versions of this are maintained by a variety of colleges; one of the best is that of Arizona State University Libraries (www.asu.edu/lib/resources/db/biogr.htm). This master index will send you to numerous specialized works.

Other excellent general resources include the Biography Almanac available at Infoplease (www.infoplease.com), which lists some 30,000 biographies; the University of Michigan's Internet Public Library (http://ipl.sils.umich.edu), which contains a great list of biography websites; and the Biographical Dictionary (http://s9.com/biography), which covers some 28,000 men and women.

The next Research Link, "The Government," appears on page 157.

check out the biases of a witness so that you may present accurate information. But you also want to make the audience see that the testimony is in fact unbiased. You might say something like this:

> Researchers and testers at *Consumer Reports*, none of whom have any vested interest in the products examined, found wide differences in car safety. Let's look at some of these findings. In the October 2001 issue, for example, . . .

Stress the recency of the testimony. When you say, for example, "General Bailey, who was interviewed last week in the *Washington Post*, noted that the United States has twice the military power of any other world power," you show your audience that your information is recent and up to date.

STATISTICS

Let's say you want to show that the salaries for home health aides should be raised, that defendants' level of wealth influences their likelihood of criminal conviction, or that significant numbers of people get their news from the Internet. To support these types of propositions, you might use **statistics**—summary figures that help you communicate the important characteristic of a complex set of numbers. For most speeches and most audiences, simple statistics work best; for example, measures of **central tendency**, correlation, and percentages. Let's consider each of these types of simple statistics as they might be used in public speaking.

Measures of central tendency describe the general pattern in a group of numbers. Two useful measures are the **mean** (the arithmetic average of a set of numbers) and the **median** (the middle score; 50 percent of the cases fall above and 50 percent fall below it). When you use a mean or a median, make it clear why this figure is important. For example, if you wanted to show that home health aides should be paid higher salaries, you might compare the mean salaries of home health aides to the means for other health care workers or for workers who have similar education and responsibilities. Once this difference was clear to your audience, you could relate it to your thesis and demonstrate that this salary difference, this gap between the two means, was significant and needed to be redressed.

Measures of correlation describe how closely two or more things are related. For example, there's a high positive correlation between smoking and lung cancer; smokers have a much greater incidence of lung cancer than nonsmokers. Correlations also can be negative. For example, there's a negative correlation between the amount of money you have and the likelihood that you'll be convicted of a crime. As your money increases, the likelihood of criminal conviction decreases. When using correlations, make clear to your audience why the relationship between, say, money and criminal conviction is important and how this correlation relates to the proposition you want to support.

Percentages allow you to express a score as a portion of 100. That is, saying that 78 percent of people favor coffee over tea means that 78 out of every 100 people favor coffee over tea. Percentages are useful if you want to show, for example, the amount of a proposed tuition increase, the growth of cable television over the past 10 years, or various divorce rates in different parts of the world. In some cases you might want to compare percentages. For example, you might compare the percentage tuition increase at your school to the national average increase or to the increase for schools similar to yours. To illustrate

Consider the one person you would most like to interview for your next speech. What questions would you ask? What impact do you think this type of support would have on your audience?

the potential for future Internet growth, you might note that in Asia (with 56 percent of the world's population) only 11 percent of people use the Internet.

Excellent aids for using and interpreting statistics may be found at http://nilesonline.com/stats/. This site will assist you in understanding and evaluating research results and in using statistics in your own speeches. Generally, the following few suggestions will help you use statistics effectively in public speeches:

▪ Make sure the statistics are clear to your audience—remember, your listeners will hear these figures only once. Round off figures so they're easy to comprehend and retain. Instead of saying, "The median income of workers in this city is $49,347," consider saying "around $50,000" or "just under $50,000."

▪ Make the significance of the statistics explicit. For example, if you state that the average home health aide makes less than $30,000 a year, you need to relate that figure to the salaries of other workers and to your proposition that home health aide salaries need to be increased. Don't just rattle off statistics; use them to support a specific proposition.

▪ Reinforce your oral presentation of statistics with some type of presentation aid—perhaps a graph or a chart. Numbers are difficult to grasp and remember if they're presented without visual reinforcement. When possible, let your audience see *and* hear the numbers; they'll be better able to see their relevance and remember them.

▪ Use statistics in moderation. Most listeners' capacity for numerical data presented in a speech is limited, so use statistics sparingly.

Here is a good example of how U.S. Senator Barack Obama of Illinois used statistics in his speech to the 2006 Global Summit on AIDS and the Church (http://obama.senate.gov, accessed January 14, 2007):

> You know, AIDS is a story often told by numbers. Forty million infected with HIV. Nearly 4.5 million this year alone. Twelve million orphans in Africa. Eight thousand deaths and 6,000 new infections every single day. In some places, 90 percent of those with HIV do not know they have it. And we just learned that AIDS is set to become the third leading cause of death worldwide in the coming years. These are staggering, these numbers, and they help us understand the magnitude of this pandemic.

PRESENTATION AIDS

As you plan your speech, consider using some kind of **presentation aid**—a visual or auditory means for clarifying ideas. Ask yourself how you can visually present what you want your audience to remember. For example, if you want your audience to see the growing impact of the sales tax, consider showing them a chart of rising sales tax over the last 10 years. If you want them to see that Brand A is superior to Brand X, consider showing them a comparison chart identifying the superiority of Brand A. Presentation aids are not added frills—they are integral parts of your speech. They will help you gain your listeners' attention and maintain their interest; they can add clarity, reinforce your message, and contribute to your credibility and confidence (Sojourner & Wogalter, 1998).

- **Presentation aids help you gain attention and maintain interest.** Americans today have grown up on multimedia entertainment. We are used to it and we enjoy it. It's not surprising, then, that we as members of an audience appreciate it when a speaker makes use of visuals or audio aids. We perk up when the speaker says, "I want you to look at this chart showing the employment picture for the next five years" or "Listen to the vocal range in this voice." Presentation aids provide variety in what we see and hear, something audiences will appreciate and respond to favorably.

- **Presentation aids add clarity.** Let's say you want to illustrate the projected growth in broadband usage at home. You might note that in the United States in 2002, 18.9 million people had broadband access; in 2003 it was 26.2 million; in 2004, 33.5 million ... and in 2008 the projection is for broadband usage by 61.5 million Americans. But such recitals get boring pretty fast. Further, the numbers you want the audience to appreciate are difficult to retain in memory, so by the time you get to the current figures, your listeners have already forgotten the previous figures. As a result, the very growth that you want your audience to see is likely to get lost. It would be much easier to communicate this kind of information in a bar graph.

- **Presentation aids reinforce your message.** Presentation aids help ensure that your listeners understand and remember what you've said. Visual aids help you present the same information in two different ways: verbally, as audience members hear you explain the aid, and visually, as they see the chart, map, or model. The same is true with audio aids. For example, you might discuss the range of vocal variety and at the same time provide recorded samples. This kind of one-two punch helps the audience understand your ideas more clearly and remember them more accurately.

Presentation aids contribute to credibility and confidence. If you use appropriate and professional-looking presentation aids—and shortly we'll see how you can do this—your listeners are likely to see you as a hightly credible speaker, as someone who cares enough about both them and the topic to do this "extra" work. When listeners view you as credible and have confidence in you, they're more likely to listen carefully and to believe what you have to say.

Presentation aids help reduce apprehension. When you have to concentrate on coordinating your speech with your presentation aids, you're less likely to focus on yourself—and self-focus often increases apprehension. In addition, the movement involved in using presentation aids relaxes many speakers, and with greater relaxation comes greater confidence.

*T*YPES OF PRESENTATION AIDS

Among the presentation aids you have available are the object itself, models of the object, graphs, word charts, maps, people, photographs, and illustrations.

The Object Itself

As a general rule (to which there are many exceptions), the best presentation aid is the object itself. Bring it to your speech if you can. Notice that infomercials sell their products not only by talking about them but by showing them to potential buyers. You see what George Foreman's Lean Mean Grilling Machine looks like and how it works. You see the jewelry, the clothing, the new mop from a wide variety of angles and in varied settings.

Models

Models—replicas of the actual object—are useful for a variety of purposes. For example, if you wanted to explain complex structures such as the human auditory or vocal mechanism, the brain, or the structure of DNA, a model would prove useful. Models help to clarify the relative sizes and positions of parts and how each part interacts with each other part.

Graphs

Graphs are useful for showing differences over time, clarifying how a whole is divided into parts, and comparing different amounts or sizes. Figure 6.1 on page 125 shows a variety of graphs that can be drawn freehand or generated with the graphics capabilities of any word-processing or presentation software. Keep your graphs as simple as possible. In a **pie chart**, for example, don't have more than five segments. Similarly, in a bar graph limit the number of items to five or fewer. As in the graphs shown in Figure 6.1, be sure you add the legend, the labels, and the numerical values you wish to emphasize.

United States Population 2000

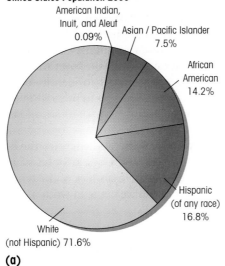

American Indian,
Inuit, and Aleut
0.09%

Asian / Pacific Islander
7.5%

African
American
14.2%

Hispanic
(of any race)
16.8%

White
(not Hispanic) 71.6%

(a)

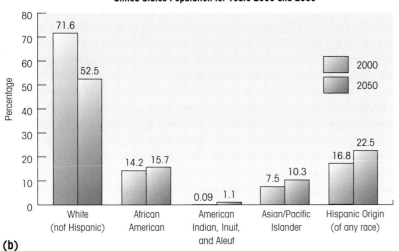

United States Population for Years 2000 and 2050

☐ 2000
☐ 2050

Percentage

71.6 · 52.5 · 14.2 · 15.7 · 0.09 · 1.1 · 7.5 · 10.3 · 16.8 · 22.5

White
(not Hispanic)

African
American

American
Indian, Inuit,
and Aleut

Asian/Pacific
Islander

Hispanic Origin
(of any race)

(b)

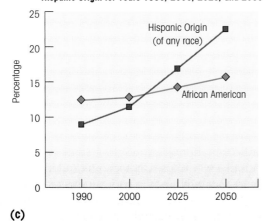

**United States Population of African Americans and People of
Hispanic Origin for Years 1990, 2000, 2025, and 2050**

Hispanic Origin
(of any race)

African American

Percentage

1990 · 2000 · 2025 · 2050

(c)

Figure 6.1
Assorted Graphs
A pie chart (a) shows the
cultural diversity in the
population of the United States
as recorded by the 2000 census.
The pie chart is particularly
helpful for showing relative
proportions. However, the pie
chart is useful only when the
total equals 100 percent. A bar
graph (b) illustrates the
population figures for 2000 (the
same figures that appear in the
pie chart) and projected figures
for the year 2050. This graph
enables you to see at a glance
demographic changes that are
predicted to occur by 2050. A
line graph (c) illustrates the
percentages of African Americans
and Hispanics for four different
periods: the actual percentages
as recorded in 1990 and 2000
and the projected percentages
for the years 2025 and 2050.
This graph not only enables you
to see the changes over the years
but also enables you to compare
the relative changes of the two
groups. Additional groups could
have been added, but the graph
would become increasingly
difficult to read. The figures for
all graphs are taken from the
Census Bureau website
(www.census.gov).

Consider the value of presentation aids. What types of presentation aids might you use to illustrate key points in your next speech?

Word Charts

Word charts (which also can contain numbers and even graphics) are useful for identifying the key points in one of your propositions or in your entire speech—in the order in which you cover them, of course. Or you could use a word chart to identify the steps in a process—for example, the steps in programming a VCR, in dealing with sexual harassment, or in downloading the latest version of Netscape. Another use of charts is to show information you want your audience to write down. Emergency phone numbers, addresses, or titles of recommended books or websites are examples of the type of information that listeners will welcome in written form.

Maps

If you want to illustrate the locations of geographic features such as cities, lakes, rivers, or mountain ranges, maps will obviously prove useful as presentation aids. But maps also can be used for illustrating population densities, immigration patterns, world literacy rates, varied economic conditions, the spread of diseases, and hundreds of other issues you may wish to examine in your speeches. A wide variety of maps may be downloaded from the Internet and then shown as slides or transparencies. Chances are you'll find a map on the Internet for exactly the purpose you need.

Two exceptional online map collections can be accessed at the Library of Congress (http://memory.LOC.gov/ammem/gmdhtml/gmdhtml.html) or the University of Texas (www.lib.utexas.edu/libs/pcl/map_collection/map_collection.html).

People

If you want to demonstrate the muscles of the body, or different voice patterns, skin complexions, or hairstyles, consider using people as your aids. Aside from the obvious assistance they provide in demonstrating their muscles or voice qualities, people help to secure and maintain the attention and interest of the audience.

Photographs and Illustrations

Types of trees, styles of art, kinds of exercise machines, or the horrors of war—all can be made more meaningful with photographs and illustrations. The best way to use these images is to convert them to slides. If you're using a computer presentation program (explained later) and you have a scanner, you can import your photos into your presentation with relative ease. Or you can have them converted to slides. Once they're converted to slides, you'll be able to project them in a format large enough for everyone to see clearly. You'll also be able to point to specific parts of the photo as you explain the devastation of war or the fine art of combining colors and textures. You can also convert the images to transparencies to use with a transparency projector, although you'll lose some of the detail that you would have in slides. Another way to use photographs and illustrations is to have them enlarged to a size large enough for the entire audience to see. Try to mount these on cardboard so they'll be easier to handle. Most copy shops provide this service—though the cost may be considerable, especially if you have several photos to convert and you need them in color. Nevertheless, this is an option that may prove useful in some situations. Passing pictures around the room is generally a bad idea. Listeners will wait for the pictures to circulate to them, will wonder what the pictures contain, and will miss a great deal of your speech in the interim.

THE MEDIA OF PRESENTATION AIDS

Once you've decided on the type of presentation aid you'll use, you need to decide on the medium you'll use to present it. Acquire skill in using both low-tech (the chalkboard or flip chart) and high-tech (the computerized slide show) resources. In this way you'll be able to select your presentation aids from the wide array available, choosing on the basis of the message you want to communicate and the audience to whom you'll be speaking.

Chalkboards

The easiest aid to use, though not necessarily the most effective, is the chalkboard. The chalkboard may be used effectively to record key terms or important definitions or even to outline the general structure of your speech. Don't use it when you can present the same information with a preplanned chart or model. It takes too long to write out anything substantial. If you do write on the board, be careful not to turn your back to the audience, even briefly. In just a few moments, you can easily lose the attention of your audience.

Chartboards

Chartboards are useful when you have one or two relatively simple graphs or charts that you want to display during your speech. If you want to display them for several minutes, be sure you have a way of holding them up. For example, bring masking tape if you intend to secure them to the chalkboard, or enlist the aid of an audience member to hold them up. Black lettering on a white board generally works best; it provides the best contrast and is the easiest for people to read.

Flip Charts

Flip charts, large pads of paper (usually about 24 × 24 inches) mounted on a stand or easel, can be used to record a variety of information that you reveal by flipping the pages as you deliver your speech. For example, if you were to discuss the various departments in an organization, you might have the key points relating to each department on a separate page of your flip chart. As you discussed the advertising department, you'd show the chart relevant to the advertising department. When you moved on to discuss the personnel department, you'd flip to the chart dealing with personnel.

Slides and Transparencies

Slides and transparencies are helpful in showing a series of visuals that may be of very different types; for example, photographs, illustrations, charts, or tables. The slides can easily be created with many of the popular computer programs (see "Computer-Assisted Presentations," p. 131). To produce actual 35mm slides, you'll need considerable lead time, so be sure to build this into your preparation time. If you don't have access to slide projectors or if you don't have the lead time needed to construct the slides, consider the somewhat less sophisticated transparencies. You can create your visual in any of the word processing or spreadsheet programs you normally use, then use a laser printer or copier to produce the transparencies.

Audios and Videos

Consider the value of using music or recorded speech to support your ideas—and also to add a note of variety that will set your speeches apart from most other speakers' presentations. A speech on advertising jingles, music styles, or dialects would be greatly helped, for example, by having actual samples for the audience to hear. Similarly, videos can serve a variety of purposes in public speaking. Basically, you have two options with videos. First, you can record a scene from a film or television show with your DVD recorder and show it at the appropriate time in your speech. Thus, for example, you might record examples of sexism in television sitcoms, violence on television talk shows, or types of families depicted in feature films and show these excerpts during your speech. Second, you can create your own video. Videos are best used in small doses; in many instances just 20- or 30-second excerpts will prove sufficient to illustrate your point. Avoid using long excerpts that will divert attention from your message; just use enough video to help your listeners understand the point you're making, not to rehash the plot of the entire movie.

Handouts

Handouts, printed materials that you distribute to the audience, are especially helpful in explaining complex material and also in providing listeners with a permanent record of some aspect of your speech. Handouts are also useful for presenting complex information that you want your audience to refer to throughout the speech. Handouts encourage listeners to take notes—especially if you leave enough white space or even provide a specific place for notes—which keeps them actively involved in your presentation. A variety of handouts can be easily prepared with many of the computer presentation packages that we'll consider in the last section of this chapter. Of course, if you distribute your handouts during your speech, you run the risk of your listeners reading the handout and not concentrating on your speech. On the other hand, if they're getting the information you want to communicate—even if it's primarily from the handout—that isn't too bad. You can encourage listeners to listen to you when you want them to and to look at the handout when you want them to by simply telling them "Look at the graph on the top of page 2 of the handout; it summarizes recent census figures on immigration" or "We'll get back to the handout in a minute; now, however, I want to direct your attention to this next slide" (or "to the second argument"). If you distribute your handouts at the end of the speech, they won't interfere with your presentation but may never get read. After all, listeners might reason, they heard the speech, so why bother going through the handout as well? To counteract this very natural tendency, you might include additional material on your handout and mention this to your audience when you distribute it.

Once you have the idea you want to present in an aid and you know the medium you want to use, direct your attention to preparing and using the aid so it best serves your purpose.

*P*REPARING PRESENTATION AIDS

In preparing presentation aids, make sure that they add clarity to your speech, that they're appealing to the listeners, and that they're culturally sensitive.

Clarity is the most important consideration. To achieve clarity, follow a few simple suggestions:

1. Use colors that will make your message instantly clear; light colors on dark backgrounds or dark colors on light backgrounds provide the best contrast and seem to work best for most purposes. Be careful of using yellow, which is often difficult to see, especially if there's glare from the sun.

2. Use direct phrases (not complete sentences); use **bullets** to highlight your points or your support (see Figure 6.2, p. 133). Just as you phrase your propositions in parallel style, phrase your bullets in parallel style; in many cases this involves using the same part of speech (for example, all nouns or all infinitive phrases). And make sure that any connection between a graphic and its meaning is immediately clear. If it isn't, explain it.

3. Use the aid to highlight a few essential points; don't clutter it with too much information. Four bullets on a slide or chart, for example, are as much information as you should include.

4. Use typefaces that can easily be read from all parts of the room.

5. Give the aid a title—a general heading for the slide, chart, or transparency—to further guide your listeners' attention and focus.

Presentation aids should be appealing to your audience. At the same time, although presentation aids should be attractive enough to engage the attention of the audience, they should not be so attractive that they're distracting. The almost nude body draped across a car may be effective in selling underwear, but would probably detract if your objective is to explain the profit-and-loss statement of General Motors.

Presentation aids should be culturally sensitive. Be sure, too, that they can easily be interpreted by people from other cultures. Just as what you say will be interpreted within a cultural framework, so too will the symbols and colors you use in your aid. For example, when speaking to international audiences, you need to use universal symbols or explain those that are not universal. Be careful that icons don't reveal an ethnocentric bias (see the following self-test). For example, using the American dollar sign to symbolize "wealth" might be quite logical in your public speaking class but might be interpreted as ethnocentric if used with an audience of international visitors.

TEST YOURSELF

Can You Distinguish Universal from Culture-Specific Icons?

Here are 10 icons and the meaning intended to be conveyed. Write U if you think the symbol is universal throughout all cultures and CS if you think the symbol is culture-specific. What reasons do you have for each of your choices?

_____ **1.** ♀ ♂ , female/male

_____ **2.** 🎓 , college/college graduation

_____ **3.** 🌎 , the world

____ 4. , good idea/creativity

____ 5. , wheelchair access

____ 6. , good luck

____ 7. , fire

____ 8. , atom/atomic/radioactive

____ 9. , no smoking

____ 10. , music

HOW DID YOU DO? Icons 1, 5, 7, 8, 9, and 10 would be considered universal; the others are specific to different cultures. Icon 3 is universal in depicting the world, although the positioning of the globe (with North America at the center, for example) would be considered culture-specific.

WHAT WILL YOU DO? Before selecting icons or any visual representations, ask yourself how your audience will interpret them. This will be especially important if you're from a culture very different from the majority of your audience. As always, when in doubt, find out; ask questions.

*U*SING PRESENTATION AIDS

Your presentation aids will be more effective if you follow a few simple guidelines.

- *Know your aids intimately.* Be sure you know in what order your aids are to be presented and how you plan to introduce them. Know exactly what goes where and when. Do all your rehearsal with your presentation aids so that you'll be able to introduce and use them smoothly and effectively.
- *Test the presentation aids before giving your speech.* Be certain that aids can be seen easily from all parts of the room. Don't underestimate, for example, how large lettering must be to be seen by those in the back of the room.
- *Rehearse your speech with the presentation aids incorporated into the presentation.* Practice your actual movements with the aids you'll use. If you're going to use a chart, how will you use it? Will it stand by itself? Will you ask another student to hold it for you?
- *Integrate presentation aids into your speech seamlessly.* Just as a verbal example should flow naturally into the text and seem an integral part of the speech, so should the presentation aid. It should appear not as an afterthought but as an essential part of the speech.

▪ *Avoid talking to your aid.* Talk to your audience at all times. Know your aids so well that you can point to what you want without breaking eye contact with your audience.

▪ *Use your aid only when it's relevant.* Show each aid when you want the audience to concentrate on it and then remove it. If you don't remove it, the audience's attention may remain focused on the visual when you want them to focus on what you'll be saying next.

COMPUTER-ASSISTED PRESENTATIONS

A variety of **presentation software** packages are available; Microsoft's Power-Point, Corel Presentations, and Lotus Freelance are among the most popular and are very similar in what they do and how they do it. The speech presented in the Public Speaking Sample Assistant box on pages 135–136 illustrates what a set of slides might look like; the slides are built around the speech outline discussed in Chapter 7 (pp. 170–172) and were constructed in PowerPoint. As you review this figure, try to visualize how you'd use a slide show to present your next speech.

Computer-assisted presentations possess all of the advantages of aids already noted (for example, maintaining interest and attention, adding clarity, and reinforcing your message). In addition, however, they have advantages all their own, so many in fact that you'll want to seriously consider using this technology in your speeches. They give your speech a professional, up-to-date look, and in the process add to your credibility. They show you're prepared and care about your topic and audience.

As you read the following material, which applies PowerPoint technology to public speaking, take one of the many PowerPoint tutorials available online. A tutorial may be on your own computer or may be available somewhere on your campus. If not, visit one of the excellent tutorials from different colleges that are available to everyone; for example, visit Florida Gulf Coast University at www.fgcu.edu/support/office2000/ppt/, the University of Rhode Island at http://einstein.cs.uri.edu/tutorials/csc101/powerpoint/pp.html, or Indiana–Purdue University at www.science.iupui.edu/SAC98/pp.htm. If you need more advanced training, try the University of Northern Iowa's advanced tutorial at www.uni.edu/plschool/index/profdev/briley/Advppt.html.

Ways of Using Presentation Software

Presentation software enables you to produce a variety of aids. For example, you can construct your slides on your computer and then have 35mm slides developed from disk. To do this you'd have to have a slide printer or send them out (you can do this via modem) to a lab specializing in converting electronic files into 35mm slides. You may have access to a slide printer at your school, so do check first. Similarly, your local office supply store or photocopy shop may have exactly the services you need.

Or you can create your slides and then show them on your computer screen. If you're speaking to a very small group, it may be possible to have your listeners gather around your computer as you speak. With larger audiences, however, you'll need a computer projector or LCD projection panel.

Assuming you have a properly equipped computer in the classroom, you can copy your entire presentation to a floppy, Zip, or CD-ROM disk and bring it with you the day of the speech.

Computer presentation software also enables you to print out a variety of materials: slides, slides with speaker's notes, slides with room for listener notes, and outlines of your speech. You can print out your complete set of slides to distribute to your listeners. Or you can print out a select portion of the slides, or even slides that you didn't have time to cover in your speech but which you'd like your audience to look at later. The most popular options are to print out two, three, or up to six slides per page. The two-slide option provides for easy readability and would be especially useful for slides of tables or graphs that you want to present to your listeners in an easy-to-read size. The three-slide option is probably the most widely used; it prints the three slides down the left side of the page with space for listeners to write notes on the right. This option is useful if you want to interact with your audience and you want them to take notes as you're speaking. Naturally, you'll distribute this handout before you begin your speech, during your introduction, or perhaps at that point when you want your listeners to begin taking notes. A sample three-slide printout with space for notes is provided in Figure 6.2 on page 133. If you want to provide listeners with a complete set of slides, then the six-slide option may be the most appropriate. You can, of course, also print out any selection of slides you wish—perhaps only those slides that contain graphs, or perhaps only those slides that summarize your talk.

Another useful option is to print out your slides with your speaker's notes. That way you'll have your slides and any notes you may find useful—examples you want to use, statistics that would be difficult to memorize, quotations that you want to read to your audience, delivery notes, or anything that you care to record. The audience will see the slides but not your speaker's notes. It's generally best to record these notes in outline form, with key words rather than complete sentences. This will prevent you from falling into the trap of reading your speech. A sample printout showing a slide plus speaker's notes is provided in Figure 6.3 on page 134.

Another useful printout is the speech outline. Two outline options are generally available: the collapsed outline and the full outline. The collapsed outline contains only the slide titles and is useful if you want to give your audience a general outline of your talk. If you want your listeners to fill in the outline with the information you'll talk about, then you can distribute this collapsed outline at the beginning of your speech. The full outline option (slide titles plus bullets) is useful for providing listeners with a relatively complete record of your speech and also can be helpful if you cover a lot of technical information that listeners will have to refer to later. You might hand out a full outline, for example, if you were giving a speech on company health care or pension plans and you wanted to provide your listeners with detailed information on each option, or if you wanted to provide listeners with addresses and phone numbers. You would normally distribute a full outline not at the beginning but after your speech, because such a complete outline could lead your audience to read and not to listen.

You also can create overhead transparencies from your computer slides. You can make these on many printers and most copiers simply by just substituting transparency paper for regular paper.

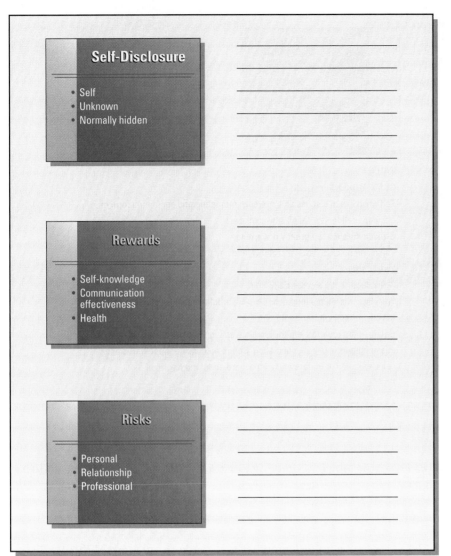

Figure 6.2

Slides with Space for Listeners' Notes

This is an especially popular handout because it's so easily prepared and because it provides a neat combination of what you said and what listeners might be thinking.

Suggestions for Designing Slides

Your slides will be more effective and easier to produce if you follow these few simple suggestions.

Use the templates provided by your software. Allow the design wizards to help you choose colors and typefaces. These are created by professional designers who are experts at blending colors, fonts, and designs into clear and appealing renderings.

Use consistent typeface, size, and color. Give each item in your outline that has the same level head (for example, all your main ponts) the same typeface, size, and color throughout your presentation. This will help your listeners follow the organization of your speech. If you're using one of the predesigned templates, this will be done for you.

Figure 6.3

Slide and Speaker's Notes

This example is from slide number 4, the orientation, in the Self-Disclosure PowerPoint slides on page 135.

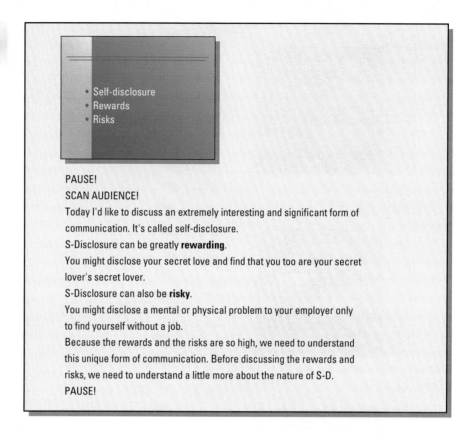

Be brief. Your objective in designing these slides is to provide the audience with key words and ideas that will reinforce what you're saying in your speech; you don't want your audience to spend their time reading rather than listening. Generally, put one complete thought on a slide, and don't try to put too many words on one slide.

Use colors for contrast. Remember that many people have difficulty distinguishing red from green; so if you want to distinguish ideas, it is probably best to avoid this color pairing. Similarly, if you're going to print out your slides in shades of gray, make sure the tones you choose provide clear contrasts. Also, be careful that you don't choose colors that recall holidays that have nothing to do with your speech—for example, red and green for Christmas or orange and black for Halloween. Remember, too, the cultural attitudes toward different colors; for example, among some Asian cultures, writing a person's name in red means that the person has died.

Use only the visuals that you really need. Presentation software packages make inserting visuals so easy that they sometimes encourage us to include too many visuals. Most presentation packages provide a variety of graphic pictures, animated graphics, photos, and videos that are useful for a wide variety of speeches. With the help of a scanner, you can add your own visuals. Use visuals when you have room on the slide and when the visual is directly related to your speech thesis and purpose. In deciding whether or not to include a visual, ask yourself if the inclusion of this graph or photo will

A SLIDE-SHOW SPEECH

Public Speaking *Sample Assistant*

This PowerPoint speech is intended to illustrate the general structure of a slide-show speech and is derived from the speech in the Public Speaking Sample Assistant on pages 170–172; you may find it helpful to look ahead to that speech to consider how you might improve this purposely sparse slide show. This PowerPoint presentation is available online at MySpeechLab (www.myspeechlab.com). Copy it to your computer and try altering this basic outline as you learn more about PowerPoint or similar presentation software.

Slide 1
Speech title

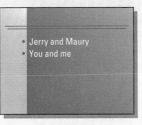

1. This first slide aims to gain attention with these provocative confessions. These three bullets would come up one at a time, with the speaker pausing for (hopefully) some laughter. After you review the entire list of slides, try inserting graphics where you think they'd be appropriate.

Slide 2
The thesis
of the speech

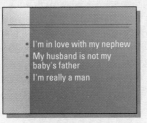

2. This slide recalls the popular confessions heard on the *Jerry Springer Show* and *Maury* but also relates the process of self-disclosure to the speaker and the audience, establishing a speaker–audience–topic connection.

Slide 3
Attention-getting device;
corresponds
to the
Introduction's
"I A"

3. This third slide introduces the topic of the speech, self-disclosure.

Slide 4
S-A-T
connection;
corresponds
to the
Introduction's
"II A–B"

4. This slide orients the audience by identifying the three main ideas to be discussed in the speech: the nature of self-disclosure, its rewards, and its risks. As with slide number 1, these three bullets should come up one at a time to give the speaker a chance to elaborate on each item and to give the audience a chance to digest the information. This slide show does not contain transitions. If you think they might help, insert transitions.

Slide 5

Orientation; corresponds to the Introduction's "III A–D"

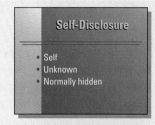

5. This fifth slide focuses on the first major idea: that self-disclosure is communication about the self, about something previously unknown, and about something that is normally kept hidden. Note here that very few words are used in the actual slide; the speaker will elaborate on each of these items in the actual speech. The words on slides are best thought of as tags you want the audience to hang on to as you explain each point.

Slide 6

First main point; corresponds to the Body's "I A"

6. This sixth slide focuses on the second main idea: that the rewards of self-disclosure include fuller self-knowledge, greater communication effectiveness, and improved health. The rewards should come up on the screen one at a time, rather than all together.

Slide 7

Second main point; corresponds to the Body's "II A–B"

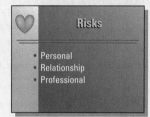

7. Slide 7 is the third main idea: that the risks of self-disclosure include possible personal, relationship, and professional problems. What types of graphics might make this slide more interesting and yet not take attention away from the main ideas?

Slide 8

Third main point; corresponds to the Body's "III A–B"

8. This slide begins the conclusion and summarizes the three main points of the speech: the nature of self-disclosure, the rewards, and the risks.

Slide 9

Fourth main point; corresponds to the Body's "IV A–B"

9. While this slide, which contains only the words *Self-Disclosure*, is on screen, the speaker would likely motivate the audience to learn more about self-disclosure. Take a look at the conclusion of the speech from which this slide show was derived (page 172) and create slides for the specific suggestions for learning more about self-disclosure.

Slide 10

Summary; corresponds to the Conclusion's "I A–D"

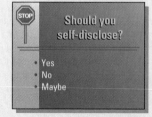

10. This final slide closes the speech by repeating the theme of the speech; namely, that self-disclosure is both rewarding and risky and that these rewards and risks need to be weighed in any decision to self-disclose.

advance the purpose of your speech. If it does, use it; if it doesn't, don't. In using video, remember that this takes up enormous amounts of disk space. If you're using floppy disks, a several-second video can take up a full third or even half of your disk; if you're using Zip disks or CDs, you'll have enough room for just about any speech you'd make.

Use transitions. As verbal transitions help you move from one part of your speech to another, presentational transitions help you move from one slide to the next with the desired effect—blinds folding from left or right or top or bottom or a quick fade. Don't try to use too many different transitions in the same talk; it will detract attention from what you're saying. Generally, it's best to use the same type of transition for all your slides in a single presentation. You might vary this a bit by, say, having the last slide introduced by a somewhat different transition, but any more variation is likely to work against the listeners' focusing on your message. In choosing transitions select one that is consistent with your speech purpose; don't use a perky black-and-yellow checkerboard transition in a speech on child abuse, for example.

Use sound effects. A wide variety of sound effects come with most presentation packages, ranging from individual sounds—foghorn, drumroll, or doorbell—to excerpts from musical compositions. Consider using sound effects in your speech, perhaps especially with your transitions. But, as with graphics, go easy; overdoing it is sure to make your speech seem carelessly put together.

Use build effects. Help focus your listeners' attention with "build effects," the ways in which your bulleted items come onto the screen. For example, you can have each bulleted phrase fly from the top of the screen into its position; with the next mouse click, the second bullet flies into position. Or you can have your bullets slide in from right to left or from left to right. And so on.

Use charts and tables when appropriate. Charts and tables are useful, as noted above, when you want to communicate complex information that would take too much text for one slide to explain. You have a tremendous variety of chart and graph types (for example, pie, bar, and cumulative charts) and tables to choose from. If you're using presentation software that's part of a suite, then you'll find it especially easy to import files from your word processor or spreadsheet. Also, consider the advantages of chart animation. Just as you can display bullets as you discuss each one, you can display the chart in parts so as to focus the audience's attention on exactly the part of the chart you want. You can achieve somewhat the same effect with transparencies by covering up the chart and gradually revealing the parts you want the audience to focus on.

Anticipate questions. If there's a question-and-answer period following your speech, consider preparing a few extra slides for your responses to questions you anticipate being asked. Then, when someone asks you a predicted question, you can say: "I anticipated that someone might ask that question; it raises an important issue. The data are presented in this chart." You can then show the slide and explain it more fully. This is surely going the extra mile, but it can help make your speech a real standout.

Use the spell-check. You don't want professional-looking slides with misspellings; it can ruin your credibility and seriously damage the impact of your speech.

Anticipate technical problems. If you're planning to use a slide show, for example, consider what you'd do if the slide projector didn't arrive on time or

Consider the common errors that speakers make when using visual aids. What two or three principles do you see violated most often? What major mistakes do speakers make when using PowerPoint?

the electricity didn't work. A useful backup procedure is to have transparencies and handouts ready just in case something goes wrong.

Rehearsing with Presentation Programs

Presentation packages are especially helpful for rehearsing your speech and timing it precisely. As you rehearse, the computer program records the time you spend on each slide and will display that time under each slide; it will also record the presentation's total time. You can see these times at the bottom of each slide in a variety of views, but they won't appear in the printed handout, such as appears in Figure 6.3. You can use these times to program each slide so you can set it to run automatically. Or you can use the times to see if you're devoting the amount of time to each of your ideas that you want to. If you find in your rehearsal that your speech is too long, these times can help you see which parts may be taking up too much time and perhaps could be shortened.

Presentation software allows you to rehearse individually selected slides as many times as you want. But make sure that you go through the speech from beginning to end toward the end of your rehearsal period. Rehearse with this system as long as improvements result; when you find that rehearsal no longer serves any useful purpose, then stop.

Another type of rehearsal is to check out the equipment available in the room you'll speak in and its compatibility with the presentation software you're using. If possible, rehearse with the very equipment you'll have available on the day you're speaking. In this way you can adjust to or remedy any incompatibilities or idiosyncrasies that are identified. Further, you'll discover how long it takes to warm up the slide projector or to load PowerPoint, so you won't have to use up your speaking time for these preparations.

The Actual Presentation

During your actual presentation you can control your slides with your mouse, advancing to the next one or going back to a previously shown slide. If you set the package to run automatically, programming each slide to be shown for its own particular amount of time, you won't be tied to the mouse—assuming you don't have a remote mouse. You can, of course, override the automatic programming by simply clicking your mouse either to advance or to go back to a slide that perhaps went by too quickly.

As with any presentation aid, make sure that you focus on the audience; don't allow the computer or the slides to get in the way of your immediate contact with the audience.

Consider using the pen—actually your mouse—to write on and highlight certain words or figures in the slides. But it's not very easy to write with a mouse, so don't plan on writing very much. Underlining or circling key terms and figures is probably the best use for the pen.

Essentials of Using Supporting Materials and Presentation Aids

This chapter focused on supporting materials, especially examples, analogies, definitions, narration, testimony, and statistics, and considered presentation aids at some length.

1. **Examples** are specific instances explained in varying degrees of detail and are most effective when:
   - They are used to explain a concept rather than as ends in themselves.
   - The relationship between the concept and the example is explicit.
   - The distinction between a real and a hypothetical example is clear.

2. **Analogies** are comparisons of items from different classes (figurative analogy) or from similar classes (literal analogy).

3. **Definitions** are statements of the meaning of a term or concept. Terms may be defined by etymology, authority, negation, specific examples, or direct symbolization.

4. **Narration**, the telling of stories to illustrate assertions, can be explanatory, exemplary, or persuasive. Narratives are most effective when they are relatively short, presented in chronological order, and clearly connected to the speech purpose.

5. **Testimony**, the opinion of an expert or an eyewitness account, can lend authority or otherwise amplify assertions. To make testimony effective, stress the competence of the authority, the unbiased nature of the testimony, and the recency of the observation or opinion.

6. **Statistics** are figures that summarize the important characteristics of an otherwise complex set of numbers. Statistics are especially effective when they are clear, meaningful to the audience, connected to the idea they support, visually and verbally reinforced, and used in moderation.

7. Common types of **presentation aids** are the actual object, models, graphs, word charts, maps, people, and photos and illustrations. Among the available media for presentation aids are the chalkboard, chartboards, flip charts, slide and transparency projections, audio and videotapes, and handouts.

8. In **using presentation aids** know your aids intimately, test your aids before using them, don't talk to your presentation aid, and use the aid when it's relevant.

9. **Computer-assisted presentations** offer a variety of advantages. Presentation software can provide great choice and flexibility; facilitate rehearsal and timing; facilitate the printing of handouts; and enable you to construct computer slide presentations, 35mm slides, handouts, and transparencies.

10. In **designing computer slides**, consider using the templates provided. Aim for consistency in typeface, size, and color; seek brevity; and consider using color contrasts to emphasize your ideas. Use only the visuals you need; use transitions, sound effects, and build effects; employ charts and tables effectively; consider preparing additional slides for anticipated questions; and use the spell-check.

11. **Rehearse** your speech with your presentation software, time your speech carefully, and make sure that you have all the needed equipment.

12. During **the actual presentation**, use your mouse to control the timing of slides, make sure that your slides don't interfere with your speaker–audience contact, and use the pen when appropriate.

Essential Terms: Using Supporting Materials and Presentation Aids

Public Speaking Exercises

6.1 Amplifying Statements

Select one the following overly broad statements and amplify it, using at least three different methods of amplification. Because the purpose of this exercise is to provide greater insight into amplification forms and methods, you may, for this exercise, invent facts, figures, illustrations, examples, and the like.

1. Significant social contributions have been made by persons over 65.
2. The writer of this article is an authority.
3. Attitudes toward women in the workplace have changed over the last 20 years.
4. The college sounds ideal.
5. September 11, 2001, was a world-changing, life-changing event.
6. The athlete enjoyed a lavish lifestyle.

6.2 Galileo and the Ghosts

Galileo and the Ghosts is a technique for seeing a topic or problem through the eyes of a particular group of people (von Oech, 1990; Higgins, 1994; DeVito, 1996). In "ghost-thinking" (analogous to ghostwriting), you select a team of four to eight "people"—for example, historical figures like Galileo or Aristotle, fictional figures like Wonder Woman or James Bond, or persons from other cultures or of a different gender or affectional orientation. Selecting people who are very different from you and from one another will increase the chances that different perspectives will be raised.

You then pose a question or problem and ask yourself how each of these ghost-thinkers would answer your question or solve your problem, allowing yourself to listen to what each has to say. Of course, you're really listening to yourself—but to yourself acting in the role of another person. The technique forces you to step outside of your normal role and to consider the perspective of someone totally different from you. Try selecting a ghost-thinking team and asking your "team" for suggestions for supporting materials for your next speech.

6.3 Critically Evaluating Testimony

If you were presenting testimony from one of the following "experts," how would you establish the person's qualifications so that your audience would accept what he or she said?

1. Nutritionist on the importance of a proper diet
2. Real estate agent advising to buy real estate now
3. Nurse on the nature of eating disorders
4. Pet store owner on how to feed your pet
5. Teacher on how to write a book

6.4 Analyzing Presentation Aids

Select a print advertisement and analyze the visuals. For purposes of this exercise, consider the text of the ad as the spoken speech and the visuals in the ad as the presentation aids for the speech.

1. What types of aids were used?
2. What functions did the presentation aids serve?
3. Were the aids clear?
4. Were they relevant?
5. Were the aids appealing?
6. Were the aids culturally sensitive?

6.5 What Do You Say?

◆ **Testimony.** Hank wants to present the testimony of a retired judge to explain the problems that probation causes, but he wonders what facts would most effectively establish this judge's credentials and credibility. What would you advise Hank to do?

◆ **Graphs.** Peggy has asked your advice on the kinds of graphs that would be most effective in illustrating each of the following theses: (1) The new school auditorium will result in higher taxes; (2) inflation is under control; (3) the divorce rate is increasing. What suggestions can you offer Peggy?

◆ **Slide-Show Speech.** Bobby is planning a slide show, but he worries that using slides for each topic might be too much repetition. And yet he wants to gain some experience in using this technique, as it's widely used in the field he hopes to enter. What advice would you give Bobby to help him make sure that his slides complement rather than repeat what he says?

◆ **Supporting Materials.** Luanne is planning to give a speech on road rage and wants to show that it's a real problem needing a real solution. What kinds of supporting materials would help Luanne to establish the severity of the problem for, say, an audience of students from your college? How about for an audience consisting of the parents of students in your class?

LogOn! MySpeechLab

Using Supporting Materials and Presentation Aids

Visit MySpeechLab (www.myspeechlab.com) for additional insight into presentation aids; "Some Typefaces" (table) will help you select appropriate fonts for your PowerPoint slides. In addition, see "Color and Culture" (table) and the exercises "Analyzing Presentation Aids" and "Coloring Meanings." An excellent video of a speech on "PowerPoint" illustrates the basic principles of PowerPoint presentations and at the same time gives useful techniques for public speaking. Also view the videos of the two versions of "Writing Position Papers," one of which uses visual aids and one of which doesn't. A variety of additional speeches dealing with immigration (with a useful critique), green slime, and tissue engineering will further illustrate how to use supporting materials and particularly presentation aids. Under Visualize take a look at the bar graph and the PowerPoint slides illustrating some common faults.

The Allyn & Bacon public speaking website (www.ablongman.com/pubspeak) contains useful tips on using PowerPoint and hot links to useful websites dealing with PowerPoint technology.

7

Organizing Your Speech

Why Read This Chapter?

Because it will enable you to organize your speech by helping you to:

- organize your ideas so that your audience can more easily follow, understand, and remember what you say
- appropriately develop and connect the parts of your speech
- select an organizing pattern that best fits your topic, purpose, thesis, and audience
- develop outlines that will help you rehearse and deliver your speech

If you're going to play the game properly, you'd better know every rule.

—**Barbara Jordan (1936–1996)**
Lawyer and Texas
congresswoman, one of the
first African American women
to be elected to the House
of Representatives

Organizing your speech will yield several significant benefits. One such benefit is that the organizing process will help guide your speech preparation; once you can see the speech as a whole (even in a preliminary and unfinished form), you'll be able to see what needs further developing and what needs paring down. Organizing your speech will also help you achieve your purpose: Whether your aim is to inform or to persuade, your audience will be better able to follow your thinking if you present it in an organized pattern. They'll also find an organized speech easier to remember. Lastly, when you present a clearly organized speech, you enhance your own credibility; your audience is more likely to see you as a competent person and as someone who is truly concerned with achieving your purpose.

In this chapter we first look at organizing the body of the speech, in which you set forth your main ideas. Once you've accomplished this, you can move on to develop your introduction, your conclusion, and the transitions that hold the pieces of the speech together. As you are developing these parts of the speech, you'll also be preparing outlines of your speech.

THE BODY OF THE SPEECH

Begin organizing your speech by selecting and wording your main points. Let's look first at how you can select and word your main points and then at how you can logically arrange them.

SELECT AND WORD YOUR MAIN POINTS

Chapter 4's discussion of the thesis showed how you can develop your main points or propositions by asking strategic questions. To see how this works in detail, imagine that you're giving a speech to a group of high school students on the values of a college education. Your thesis is: "A college education is valuable." You then ask, "Why is it valuable?" From this question you generate your main points. Your first step may be to brainstorm this question and generate as many answers as possible without evaluating them. You may come up with answers such as the following:

1. It helps you get a good job.
2. It increases your earning potential.
3. It gives you greater job mobility.
4. It helps you secure more creative work.
5. It helps you to appreciate the arts more fully.
6. It helps you to understand an extremely complex world.
7. It helps you understand different cultures.
8. It allows you to avoid taking a regular job for a few years.
9. It helps you meet lots of people and make new friends.
10. It helps you increase your personal effectiveness.

There are, of course, other possibilities, but for purposes of illustration, these 10 possible main points will suffice. But not all 10 are equally valuable or relevant to your audience, so you should look over the list to see how to make it shorter and more meaningful. Try these suggestions:

1. Eliminate those points that seem least important to your thesis. On this basis you might want to eliminate number 8, as this seems least consistent with your intended emphasis on the positive values of college.

2. Combine those points that have a common focus. Notice, for example, that the first four points all center on the values of college in terms of jobs. You might, therefore, consider grouping these four items into one proposition:

A college education helps you get a good job.

This point might become a main point, which you could develop by defining what you mean by a "good job." This main point or proposition and its elaboration might look like this:

I. A college education helps you get a good job.

   A. College graduates earn higher salaries.

   B. College graduates enter more creative jobs.

   C. College graduates have greater job mobility.

Note that A, B, and C are all aspects or subdivisions of a "good job."

3. Select those points that are most relevant or interesting to your audience. On this basis you might eliminate numbers 5 and 7, on the assumption that the audience will not see learning about the arts or different cultures as exciting or valuable at the present time. You also might decide that high school students would be more interested in increasing personal effectiveness, so you might select number 10 for inclusion as a second main point:

A college education increases your personal effectiveness.

Earlier you developed the subordinate points in your first proposition (the A, B, and C of I above) by defining more clearly what you meant by a "good job." Follow the same process here by defining what you mean by "personal effectiveness." It might look something like this:

II. A college education helps increase your personal effectiveness.

   A. A college education helps you improve your ability to communicate.

   B. A college education helps you acquire the skills for learning how to think.

   C. A college education helps you acquire coping skills.

Follow this same general procedure to develop the subheadings under A, B, and C. For example, point A might be divided into two major subheads:

A. A college education helps improve your ability to communicate.

   1. College improves your writing skills.

   2. College improves your speech skills.

Develop points B and C in essentially the same way, defining more clearly (in B) what you mean by "learning how to think" and (in C) what you mean by "coping skills."

4. Use two, three, or four main points. For your class speeches, which will generally range from 5 to 15 minutes, use two, three, or four main points. Too many main points will result in a speech that's confusing, contains too much information, and proves difficult to remember.

5. Word each of your main points in the same (parallel) style. Statements phrased in parallel style share the same grammatical structure and many of the same words. Julius Caesar's famous "I came, I saw, I conquered" is a good example of parallel style: Each statement is structured the same way, using the pronoun *I* plus a verb in the past tense. Phrase points labeled with roman numerals in parallel style. Likewise, phrase points labeled with capital letters and subordinate to the same roman numeral (for example, A, B, and C under point I or A, B, and C under point II) in a similar style. Parallel styling will help the audience follow and remember your speech. Notice in the following that the first outline is more difficult to understand than the second, which is phrased in parallel style.

Not This	**This**
The mass media serve four functions.	The mass media serve four functions.
I. The media entertain.	I. The media entertain.
II. The media function to inform their audiences.	II. The media inform.
III. Creating ties of union is a major media function.	III. The media create ties of union.
IV. The conferral of status is a function of all media.	IV. The media confer status.

6. Develop your main points so they're separate and discrete. Don't allow your main points to overlap each other. Each section labeled with a roman numeral should be a separate entity.

Not This	**This**
I. Color and style are important in clothing selection.	I. Color is important in clothing selection.
	II. Style is important in clothing selection.

 **Ethics**   GETTING HELP FROM OTHERS

You have a speech due next week, and you're having trouble constructing your outline. But your friend, who is great at developing outlines, offers to help you write it. You could really use the help; also, in the process you figure you'll learn something about outlining. And besides, you'll fill in the outline, type it up, and present the speech.

Ethical Choice Point *Would it be ethical to accept this help? If not, how might you ethically avail yourself of your friend's help? More generally, what ethical guidelines should a speaker follow in acknowledging help from other people?*

ORGANIZE YOUR MAIN POINTS

Once you've identified the main points you wish to include in your speech, organize them into a clearly identified organizational pattern. For online assistance with organizing your speech, see the organizing wizard at MySpeechLab (www.myspeechlab.com). Here we consider some of the more useful patterns.

Topical Pattern

When your topic conveniently divides itself into subdivisions, each of which is clear and approximately equal in importance, the **topical pattern** is useful. A speech on important cities of the world might be organized into a topical pattern, as might speeches on problems facing the college graduate, great works of literature, the world's major religions, and the like. For example, the topical pattern would be an obvious choice for organizing a speech on the powers of the government. The topic itself divides into three parts: legislative, executive, and judicial. Similarly, a talk on the major stock exchanges might follow a topical pattern; a sample outline might look like this:

The Stock Exchanges

I. The New York Stock Exchange focuses on the largest companies.

II. The Nasdaq focuses largely on technology companies.

III. The American Stock Exchange focuses on the smaller companies.

Here is another example: a speech on ways to help people who have disabilities, in which each subtopic is treated about equally. The speaker is seeking to persuade the audience to devote some of their leisure time to helping people with disabilities, using the thesis "Leisure time can be well used to help people." Asking a strategic question of this thesis—"How can leisure time be spent helping people with disabilities?" or "What can we do to help people with disabilities?"—lets the speaker easily identify the main points:

Helping Others

I. Read for people with visual impairments.

    A. Read to students with visual impairments.

    B. Record a textbook for students with visual impairments.

II. Run errands for students with limited mobility.

III. Type for students who have manual difficulties.

Temporal Pattern

With the **temporal pattern**, or time pattern, your speech is organized chronologically into two, three, or four major parts—beginning with the past and working up to the present or the future, or beginning with the present or the future and working back to the past. The temporal (sometimes called "chronological") pattern is especially appropriate for informative speeches in which you wish to describe events or processes that occur over time. It's also useful when you wish to tell a story, demonstrate how something works, or explain how to do something. Most historical topics lend themselves to organization by time. The events leading up to the Civil War, the steps toward a college education, or the history of writing would all be appropriate for temporal patterning. A speech on television scheduling might be organized in a temporal pattern, covering each of the four television periods in a time sequence beginning with the morning and ending with the evening—a pattern everyone would find easy to follow.

Television Scheduling

I. Morning television gets people ready for their day.

II. Daytime television keeps the homebound viewer company.

III. Prime-time television appeals to everyone.

IV. Late-night television appeals to adults.

Spatial Pattern

Organizing your main points on the basis of space is useful when you wish to describe objects or places—progressing from top to bottom, from left to right, from inside to outside, or from east to west, for example. The structure of a place, an object, or even an animal is easily placed into a **spatial pattern**. You might describe the layout of a hospital, school, or skyscraper, or perhaps even the skeletal structure of a dinosaur, with a spatial pattern of organization. Here's an example of an outline describing the structure of the traditional textbook using a spatial pattern:

The Textbook

I. The front matter contains the preface and the table of contents.

II. The text proper contains the chapters.

III. The back matter contains the glossary, bibliography, and index.

Problem–Solution Pattern

The **problem–solution pattern** is especially useful in persuasive speeches, in which you want to convince the audience that a problem exists and that your solution would solve or lessen the problem. Let's say that you want to persuade your audience that jury awards for damages should be limited. A problem–solution pattern might be appropriate here. In the first part of your speech, you'd identify the problem(s) created by these large awards; in the second part you'd present the solution. A sample outline for such a speech might look something like this:

Jury Awards

I. Jury awards for damages are out of control. [the general problem]

    A. These awards increase insurance rates. [a specific problem]

    B. These awards increase medical costs. [a second specific problem]

    C. These awards place unfair burdens on business. [a third specific problem]

II. Jury awards need to be limited. [the general solution]

A. Greater evidence should be required before a case can be brought to trial. [a specific solution]

B. Part of the award should be turned over to the state. [a second specific solution]

C. Realistic estimates of financial damage must be used. [a third specific solution]

Here's another example to clarify the problem–solution organizational pattern. In this speech the speaker seeks to persuade the audience that cigarette advertising should be banned from all media. The thesis is that "Cigarette advertising should be abolished." Asking the strategic question "Why should it be abolished?" suggests the main points:

Smoking

I. Cigarette smoking is a national problem.

  A. Cigarette smoking causes lung cancer.

  B. Cigarette smoking pollutes the air.

  C. Cigarette smoking raises the cost of health care.

II. Cigarette smoking would be lessened if advertisements were prohibited.

  A. Fewer people would start to smoke.

  B. Smokers would smoke less.

In delivering such a speech, a speaker might begin like this:

> I think we all realize that cigarette smoking is a national problem that affects each and every one of us. No one escapes the problems caused by cigarette smoking—not the smoker and not the nonsmoker. Cigarette smoking causes lung cancer. Cigarette smoking pollutes the air. And cigarette smoking raises the cost of health care for everyone.
>
> Let's look first at the most publicized of all smoking problems: lung cancer. There can be no doubt—the scientific evidence is overwhelming—that cigarette smoking is a direct cause of lung cancer. Research conducted by the American Cancer Institute and by research institutes throughout the world all come to the same conclusion: cigarette smoking causes lung cancer. Consider some of the specific evidence. A recent study—reported in the January, 2004, issue of the . . . .

Cause–Effect Pattern

The **cause–effect pattern** is useful in speeches in which you want to show your audience the causal connection existing between two events or elements. Your speech divides into two major sections—causes and effects. For example, a speech on the reasons for highway accidents or birth defects might lend itself to a cause–effect pattern. Here you might first consider, say, the causes of highway accidents or birth defects and then some of the effects; for example, the number of deaths, the number of accidents, and so on.

In some cases you might want to place the effects first and then discuss the causes. Let's say you want to demonstrate the causes for an increase in gang violence. You might want to use an effect-to-cause pattern that might look something like this:

I. Gang violence is increasing. [general effect]

   A. Gang violence is increasing among boys and girls. [a specific effect]

   B. Gang violence is increasing among younger people. [a second specific effect]

   C. Gang violence is increasing in the suburbs. [a third specific effect]

II. Three factors contribute to the increase in gang violence. [general causal statement]

   A. Young people lack family guidance and discipline. [a specific cause]

   B. Young people have poor role models. [a second specific cause]

   C. Young people have few opportunities for recreation. [a third specific cause]

The Motivated Sequence

The **motivated sequence** is another pattern for organizing a speech in such a way that your audience responds positively to your purpose (McKerrow, Gronbeck, Ehninger, & Monroe, 2007). This approach was developed by communication professor Alan H. Monroe in the 1930s, originally as a way to organize sales presentations. Now it's widely used in all sorts of oral and written communications. In fact, you'll probably find that you can analyze almost any persuasive message—from political speeches to television advertisements to Internet ribbon ads—in terms of the motivated sequence. The motivated sequence is especially appropriate for speeches designed to move listeners to action (to persuade the audience to do something). But you'll find it useful for informative speeches as well.

The organizational patterns we have considered so far divide speeches into three parts—introduction, body, and conclusion. The motivated sequence works a little differently; it organizes the speech into five parts or steps:

Step 1. Attention: Gain your listeners' attention.

Step 2. Need: Demonstrate that there's a problem, that your listeners have a need.

Step 3. Satisfaction: Show how your listeners can resolve their problem or satisfy their need.

Step 4. Visualization: Show your listeners what the situation would be like with this problem eliminated, with this need satisfied.

Step 5. Action: Tell your listeners what they must do to resolve their problem, to satisfy their need.

While walking down the street one day, a young boy with a shoe-shine box called out to a Wall Street–type executive:

> Hey, man. You look great. But your shoes are a mess. You don't want to walk into a meeting with mud on your shoes, do you? I can fix that for you. You'll look a lot better for that meeting if you have shined shoes. Sit right here and I'll polish them up.

Consider the movtivated sequence in the speeches of politicians. Read a political speech or advertisement and note how the speaker (1) gained attention, (2) established the need, (3) satisfied the need, (4) visualized the need satisfied, and (5) urged action.

In this brief "advertisement" the young boy executed all five steps of the motivated sequence:

Hey, man. You look great. [Step 1. Attention: Caught the attention of a passerby with a simple compliment.]

But your shoes are a mess. You don't want to walk into a meeting with mud on your shoes, do you? [Step 2. Need: Demonstrated that the man had a problem and a need for change existed.]

I can fix that for you. [Step 3. Satisfaction: Told the man that the problem could be corrected.]

You'll look a lot better for that meeting if you have shined shoes. [Step 4. Visualization: Showed how things would be better if the problem were resolved.]

Sit right here and I'll polish them up. [Step 5. Action: Told the man what he had to do to resolve the problem and satisfy the need.]

Let's look at each of these steps in more detail and see how you might use each of them in actual speeches.

Step 1: Gain Attention. In this step you gain the audience's undivided attention and get them to focus on you and your message. If you execute this step effectively, your audience should be anxious and ready to hear what you have to say. A variety of attention-getting devices are explained in the discussion of the introduction (pp. 158–162).

Regardless of what attention device you use, demonstrate your enthusiasm. Enthusiasm is highly contagious: If you show that you're enthusiastic, your attitude is likely to infect the audience, and they too will become involved and energized. Deliver your opening remarks with appropriate gestures, and vary bodily movement. Similarly, vary your voice so that it demonstrates your own involvement in the subject of your speech.

In phrasing your introductory remarks, involve the audience directly. Use *you* if appropriate, and use connecting pronouns—*us* and *we*—that show that you and your listeners are involved in this together.

For example, in a speech aiming to persuade your listeners to vote in favor of establishing a community youth center, you might gain attention by using a provocative question: *If you could reduce juvenile crime by some 20 percent by just flipping a lever, would you do it?* Or you might make reference to specific audience members: *I know that several of you here have been the victims of juvenile vandalism. Thom, your drug store was broken into last month by three teenagers who said they did it because they were bored. And Loraine, your video rental shop's windows were broken by teenagers who, in a drunken spree, decided to have a rock fight. And. . . .*

Step 2: Establish the Need.   In the second part of the motivated sequence, you demonstrate that there's a problem, that something is wrong, that a need exists. Your listeners should feel that they have something to learn (if you are making an informative speech) or that they have to change their attitudes or do something (if it's a persuasive speech). Here are some examples, first for informative speeches and second for persuasive speeches.

State the problem or need. If you're giving an informative speech, the problem or need might be lack of information. For example, in an informative speech on how to gain access to your credit history, you might establish the need for information by saying, "You need access to your credit history because it's the best way to prevent yourself from being a victim of fraud," or, "Millions of people become victims of credit fraud because they don't have access to their own credit history," or, "You're more likely to become a victim of fraud if you don't regularly check your credit history."

If you're giving a persuasive speech, you might focus on your listeners' need to change their attitudes or their behaviors. For example, in a speech aiming to persuade your listeners to participate actively in the political process, you might establish the need by saying something like this: "You need to participate actively in the politics of your city if you want elected officials to address your needs and the needs of people like you." Or, in a speech on the need to establish a community youth center as a way of reducing juvenile crime, you might say, "Juvenile crime has been increasing dramatically in our community over the last several years. We need to do something about it."

Show why this is really a problem. Make sure your audience understands that this problem affects them directly—that it is not simply some abstract problem that will not touch them personally. You also might support the existence of need with illustrations, statistics, testimony, and other forms of support we already explored in Chapter 6. Too, you might show your listeners how this need affects those values that motivate their behavior, such as their financial security, their career success, and their individual happiness (motivators that we'll examine in more detail in Chapter 11). In the speech on the youth center, you might say, "Federal crime statistics show that juvenile crime is likely to increase over the next several years, and it will happen in our community if we don't take a stand and do something about it *now*," or "Next year, your store, Jack, or yours, Shauna, may be broken into."

Step 3: Satisfy the Need.   In this step you present the "answer" or the "solution" that would eliminate the problem or satisfy the need that you demonstrated in Step 2. On the basis of this satisfaction step, your listeners should now believe that what you're informing them about or persuading them to do will effectively satisfy the need. So show here how the problem can be solved and why your solution will work.

Show your listeners that your plan will satisfy the need or solve the problem. Here you might say quite simply, "The best way to reduce credit card fraud is to check your credit history regularly," or, "Like our neighboring towns, we need to create a youth center for high school students to reduce juvenile crime and vandalism."

Show why your solution will work. You want your audience to understand that what you're asking them to believe or do will actually lead to resolving the problem or satisfying the need you identified in Step 2. So you might say something like: "Youth crime has been dramatically reduced in all of our neighboring towns since they established youth centers. The same will happen here."

This step is also a good place to answer any objections you anticipate from your listeners. For example, if you anticipate that audience members will object to the youth center for fear it would increase their taxes, you might answer this now. For example, you might say, "A major portion of the financing will be secured from New York State grants, and local merchants have already agreed to contribute whatever additional financing is needed. So this youth center will impose absolutely no financial burden on anyone."

Notice that in an informative speech you could have stopped after the satisfaction step, because you would have accomplished your goal of informing the audience about the youth centers and how they can effectively reduce juvenile crime. In a persuasive speech, on the other hand, you must continue at least as far as Step 4, visualization (if your purpose is limited to strengthening or changing attitudes or beliefs), or go on to Step 5, action (if your purpose is to get your listeners to do something).

Step 4: Visualize the Need Satisfied.

In this step of the motivated sequence, you take the audience beyond the present time and place and enable them to imagine, to visualize, the situation as it would be if the problem were eliminated, if the need were satisfied as you suggested in Step 3. Through this visualization you aim to intensify your listeners' feelings or beliefs. You can achieve this visualization with any one or combination of these basic strategies.

Demonstrate the benefits that your listeners will receive if your ideas are put into operation. You might, for example, point to the decrease in crime that accompanies the establishment of youth centers, or to the social and vocational skills that the students will learn there. Or you could visualize the need satisfied by returning to your introductory examples and say something like: "Wouldn't it have been great if Thom's drugstore had never been broken into and the time, energy, and expense that Thom had to go through could have been spent taking a well-deserved vacation? And Loraine, wouldn't it have been nice if your windows had never been broken? And. . . ."

Demonstrate the negative effects that will occur if your plan is not put into operation. Here you might argue, for example, that without such a youth center, juvenile crime will increase or students will fail to learn safe sex practices normally taught at these youth centers that are not currently taught at home or in the schools.

Demonstrate the combined positive and negative effects. You might combine both the demonstration of the positive effects that will result if your plan is put into operation and the negative effects that will result if your plan is denied.

You might then say something like this: "Without a youth center teen crime is likely to increase, as the statistics from similar towns that I'll show will illustrate. But with such a center juvenile crime is likely to decrease, and I'll also show you very recent and very dramatic statistics from towns just like ours that had the foresight to establish such centers."

Step 5: Ask for Action.   In this final step you tell the audience what they should do to ensure that the need (as demonstrated in Step 2) is satisfied (as described in Step 3). Here you want to move the audience in a particular direction; for example, to vote in favor of additional research funding for AIDS or against cigarette advertising, to attend the next student government meeting, or to contribute free time to for the blind. In completing this step consider two basic strategies.

Tell the audience exactly what they must do. Frequently, speakers use emotional appeals here (see Chapter 11). Or you might give your listeners guidelines for future action, saying something like this: "Proposition 14, establishing a youth center in the old post office building, is coming up for a vote next week. Vote *yes*, and urge your family members, your friends, and your work colleagues to also vote *yes*. It will make our town a better place for us all."

Remind your listeners of the connections you've established throughout your speech. Throughout your motivated sequence speech, you've established a series of important connections and relationships. Make sure your listeners remember them and see how the action you ask for here is related. Make sure they see that the action you ask for here will satisfy the need and enable them to live in a world (in a community, in our example of the youth center) that is a lot better than it would be otherwise.

Stress specific advantages. Stress the specific advantages of the desired behaviors to your specific audience. In other words, don't ask your audience to engage in behaviors solely for abstract reasons. Give them concrete, specific reasons why they will benefit from the actions you want them to engage in. Instead of telling your listeners that they should devote time to reading to blind students because it's the right thing to do, show them how much they will enjoy the experience and how much they will personally benefit from it.

Because your organizational pattern serves primarily to help your listeners follow your speech, you might want to tell your listeners (in your introduction or as a transition between the introduction and the body of your speech) what pattern you'll be following. Here are just a few examples:

- In explaining the goals of television scheduling, we'll start with morning TV and go through the day to late-night TV.
- I'll first explain the problems with jury awards and then propose three workable solutions.
- First we'll look at the increase in gang violence, and then we'll look at three of the causes.

Additional Organizational Patterns

The six patterns just considered are the most common and the most useful for organizing most public speeches. But there are other patterns that might be appropriate for different topics.

- The *structure–function pattern* is useful in informative speeches in which you want to discuss how something is constructed (its structural aspects) and what it does (its functional aspects). This pattern might be useful, for example, in a speech explaining what a business organization is and what it does, identifying the parts of a university and how they operate, or describing the sensory systems of the body and their various functions. This pattern also might be useful in a discussion of the nature of a living organism: its anatomy (that is, its structures) and its physiology (that is, its functions).

- Arranging your material in a *comparison-and-contrast pattern* is useful in informative speeches in which you want to analyze two different theories, proposals, departments, or products in terms of their similarities and differences. In this type of speech you would be concerned not only with explaining each theory or proposal but also with clarifying how they're similar and how they're different.

- The *pro-and-con pattern*, sometimes called the *advantages–disadvantages pattern*, is useful in informative speeches in which you want to explain objectively the advantages (the pros) and the disadvantages (the cons) of a plan, method, or product. Or you can use this pattern in a persuasive speech in which you want to show the superiority of one plan or position over another.

- The *claim-and-proof pattern* is especially useful in a persuasive speech in which you want to prove the truth or usefulness of a particular proposition. It's the pattern that you see frequently in trials, where the claim made by the prosecution is that the defendant is guilty and the proof is the varied evidence designed to show that the defendant had a motive, opportunity, and no alibi. In this pattern your speech would consist of two major parts. In the first part you'd explain your claim (tuition must not be raised, library hours must be expanded, courses in AIDS education must be instituted). In the second part you'd offer your evidence or proof; for example, evidence to show why tuition must not be raised.

- The *multiple-definition pattern* is useful for informative speeches in which you want to explain the nature of a concept. (What is a born-again Christian? What is a scholar? What is multiculturalism?) In this pattern each major heading would consist of a different type of definition or way of looking at the concept.

- The *Who? What? Why? Where? When? pattern* is used by journalists and is useful when you wish to report or explain an event; for example, a robbery, political coup, war, or trial. Here the major parts of your speech would deal with the answers to several or all of these five questions.

- The *fiction–fact pattern* may be useful when you wish to clarify certain misconceptions that people have about various things. For example, if you were giving a speech on fiction and fact about the flu, you might use this pattern. You would first give the fiction (for example, "you can get the flu from a flu shot," or "antibiotics can help the flu," or "older people spread the flu most often") and then follow it by the fact—you can't get the flu from a flu shot; antibiotics are useful only against bacteria, not against viruses such as the flu virus; and children, rather than older people, spread the flu most often and most easily.

How Open Are You Interculturally?

Select an adjective denoting a specific culture (national, racial, or religious) different from your own, and substitute this culture for the phrase *culturally different* in each statement below. Indicate how likely you are to do what the statement suggests, using the following scale: Very likely = 5, likely = 4, neither likely nor unlikely = 3, unlikely = 2, and very unlikely = 1.

_____ **1.** Listen open-mindedly and fairly to a speech by a *culturally different* person.

_____ **2.** Critique a speech by a *culturally different person* with the same degree of objectivity and supportiveness that you'd give to someone who was culturally similar to you.

_____ **3.** Evaluate evidence in a speech by a *culturally different* person according to exactly the same standards that you'd use in evaluating evidence presented by someone culturally similar to you.

_____ **4.** Attribute the same degree of credibility to the *culturally different* person that you'd attribute to those who were culturally similar to you.

_____ **5.** Participate in a work team with a *culturally different* person with the same degree of willingness and enthusiasm that you'd have working with someone culturally similar to you.

HOW DID YOU DO? This test was designed to raise questions rather than to provide answers about your degree of intercultural openness in public speaking. High scores for any question or group of questions indicate considerable intercultural openness; low scores indicate a lack of intercultural openness.

WHAT WILL YOU DO? Use these numbers for purposes of thinking critically about your intercultural openness rather than to indicate any absolute level of openness or closed-mindedness. Did you select the "culturally different" group on the basis of how positive or negative your attitudes were? What group would you be most open to interacting with? Least open?

Cultural Considerations in Organization

Before considering this brief discussion of culture and the organization of speeches, take the following self-test to examine your own **intercultural openness**.

Cultural considerations are as important in organization as they are in all other aspects of public speaking. One factor that's especially important is whether the audience's culture is high-context or low-context (Hall & Hall, 1987). **High-context cultures** (Japanese, Arabic, Latin American, Thai, Korean, Apache, and Mexican are examples) are those in which much of the information in communication is in the context or in the person rather than in the actual spoken message. Both speaker and listener already know the information from, say, previous interactions, assumptions each makes about the other, or shared experiences. **Low-context cultures** (German, Swedish, Norwegian, and American are examples) are those in which most information is explicitly stated in the verbal message. In formal communications, the information would be in written form as well, as it is with contracts, prenuptial agreements, or apartment leases.

To appreciate the distinction between high and low context, consider giving directions to the recycling center. Someone who knows the neighborhood (a high-context situation) probably knows the local landmarks. So you can give directions such as "next to the laundromat on Main Street" or "the corner of Albany and Elm." With a newcomer (a low-context situation), you can't assume that you have a common body of shared information; you have to use directions that even a stranger would understand—for example, "make a left at the next stop sign" or "go two blocks and then turn right."

Extending this distinction to speech organization, we can see that members of high-context cultures will probably prefer an organization in which the supporting materials are offered and the audience is allowed to infer the general principle or proposition themselves. Low-context culture members, on the other hand, will likely prefer an organization in which the proposition is clearly and directly stated and the supporting materials are clearly linked to the proposition.

Persons from the United States speaking in Japan, to take one well-researched example, need to be careful lest they make their point too obvious or too direct and thus inadvertently insult their audience. Speakers in Japan are expected to lead their listeners to the conclusion through example, illustration, and various other indirect means (Lustig & Koester, 2006). Persons from Japan speaking in the United States need to be careful lest their indirectness be perceived as unnecessarily vague, underhanded, or suggestive of an attempt to withhold information.

To give an example, you might organize a speech on the need for random drug testing in the workplace somewhat differently depending on whether you were addressing a high-context or a low-context audience.

High-Context Audience	**Low-Context Audience**
Implicitness and indirectness are preferred	Explicitness and directness are preferred
The main point is implicitly identified only after the evidence is presented	The main point is clearly stated at the outset, even before the evidence is presented
Drugs in the workplace cause accidents. Drugs in the workplace contribute to the national drug problem. Drugs in the workplace increase costs for employers and consumers. These are some factors we need to think about as we consider the proposal to establish random workplace drug testing.	*Random drug testing in the workplace is a must. It will reduce accidents. It will reduce the national drug problem. It will reduce costs. Let's examine each of these reasons why random drug testing in the workplace should become standard.*

Research Link

THE GOVERNMENT

The various governments throughout the United States (federal, state, and municipal) publish an enormous amount of information that you're sure to find useful in speeches on almost any topic. One excellent starting point is Google's government search (www.usgov.google.com). This engine covers all websites in the *.gov* domain. The amount of information you'll find, however, may at first be daunting. For example, if you searched for "publications," you'd find more than 4 million websites; more than 11 million for "education," and more than 24 million for "health." You'll definitely need to limit your search. One way to do this is of course to include additional terms (for example, health + drugs + teenagers) or use phrases in quotations ("teenage drug use").

Another way is to visit one or more of the 13 relevant departments of the federal government (these are the Departments of Agriculture, Commerce, Defense, Education, Energy, Health and Human Services, Housing and Urban Development, Interior, Justice, Labor, State, Treasury, and Transportation). All issue reports, pamphlets, books, and assorted documents dealing with their various concerns. Here are a few of the topics on which some of the departments have information that you'll find useful in researching your speeches.

- Department of the Treasury (www.ustreas.gov): taxes, property auctions, savings, economy, financial markets, international business, and money management.
- Department of Housing and Urban Development (www.hud.gov): home buying, selling, renting, and owning; fair housing, foreclosures, consumer information, FHA refunds, homelessness; and information for tenants, landlords, farm workers, senior citizens, and victims of discrimination.
- Department of Defense (www.defenselink.mil/): news releases, speech texts, military pay/benefits, casualty reports.
- Department of Justice (www.usdoj.gov): drugs and drug enforcement; Patriot Act information; trafficking in persons; inmate locator; Americans with Disabilities Act; sentencing statistics; and information from the Bureau of Alcohol, Tobacco, Firearms, and Explosives.
- Department of Health and Human Services (www.hhs.gov): aging, AIDS, disease, safety issues, food and drug information, disaster and emergency protection, families and children, disabilities, homelessness, and immigration.
- Department of Education (www.ed.gov): teaching resources in science, math, history, and language arts; innovations in education; reports on performance and accountability; "no child left behind" reports; at-risk and gifted students; Pell grant program; religious expression in schools.
- Department of Labor (www.dol.gov): pensions, unemployment, wages, insurance and just about any topic even remotely related to labor.

Other departments are equally prolific in their publishing of a wide range of information and are worth visiting. At each of these departments, you'll be able to find statistics appropriate to the topics covered; but an easier way is to log on to FedStats (www.fedstats.gov). Here you'll find statistics from more than 100 U.S. federal agencies, including statistical profiles of each state, country, and city as well as statistics on crime, population, economics, mortality, and energy, along with comparisons with other countries.

The next Research Link, "The Web," appears on page 186.

INTRODUCTIONS, CONCLUSIONS, AND TRANSITIONS

Now that you have the body of your speech organized, devote your attention to the introduction, conclusion, and transitions that will hold the parts of your speech together.

As you read about introductions, conclusions, and transitions, also visit some websites containing speeches and examine the ways the speakers introduced, concluded, and tied the parts of their speeches together. Especially good websites include: History and Politics Out Loud (www.hpol.org), the History Channel (www.historychannel.com/speeches), and C-Span (www.c-span.org/classroom/lang/speeches.asp). Also see the excellent collection of websites compiled by Allan Louden (www.wfu.edu/~louden/Political%20Communication/Class%20Information/SPEECH, accessed July 12, 2007). Many of these sites include audio and/or video material.

INTRODUCTIONS

Together with your general appearance and your nonverbal messages, your introduction gives your listeners their first impression of you and your speech. And, as you know, first impressions are very resistant to change. Because of this the introduction is an especially important part of the speech. It sets the tone for the rest of the speech; it tells your listeners what kind of a speech they'll hear.

Begin collecting suitable material for your introduction as you prepare the entire speech, but wait until all the other parts are completed before you put the pieces together. In this way you'll be better able to determine which elements should be included and which should be eliminated.

Your introduction should serve three functions: gain attention, establish a speaker–audience–topic connection, and orient the audience as to what is to follow. Let's look at how you can accomplish each of these functions.

Function 1. Gain Attention

Your introduction should gain the **attention** of your audience and focus it on your speech topic. (And, of course, it should help you maintain that attention throughout your speech.) You can secure attention in numerous ways; here are just a few.

Ask a Question.   Questions are effective because they're a change from the more common declarative statements, and listeners automatically pay attention to change. Rhetorical questions—questions to which you don't expect an answer—are especially helpful in focusing the audience's attention on your subject: "Do you want to live a happy life?" "Do you want to succeed in college?" "Do you want to meet the love of your life?" "Have you ever suffered from loneliness?" Also useful are polling-type questions, questions that ask the audience for a show of hands: "How many of you have suffered through a boring lecture?" "How many of you intend to continue school after graduating from college?"

Refer to Recent Happenings.   Referring to a previous speech, a recent event, or a prominent person currently making news helps gain attention, because the audience is familiar with this and will pay attention to see how you're going to connect it to your speech topic.

Use an Illustration or Dramatic Story.   Much as we are drawn to soap operas, so we are drawn to illustrations and stories about people. Here's a good example of using a dramatic illustration to gain attention; it comes from a speech on gang violence given by U.S. Senator from California Dianne Feinstein (2006) (http://Feinstein.senate.com, accessed January 14, 2007).

On September 24 of this year, Los Angeles experienced a new low. Three-year-old Kaitlyn Avila was shot point-blank by a gang member who mistakenly thought her father was a member of a rival gang. The gang member shot and

Consider the introductions you've heard recently—in speeches or in lectures. As a listener, what types of introductions do you find ineffective?

wounded her father, then intentionally fired into little Kaitlyn's chest. This is the first time law enforcement officials remember a young child being "targeted" in a gang shooting.

Use a Quotation.   Quotations are useful because the audience is likely to pay attention to the brief and clever remarks of someone they have heard of or read about. Make sure that the quotation is directly relevant to your topic; if you have to explain its relevance, it probably isn't worth using.

Quotations are easy to find; visit some of the quotations sites at www. bartleby.com, www.yahoo.com/Reference/Quotations/ or http://us.imdb.com/. You may find it helpful also to say something about the author of the quotation by consulting some of the biography sites mentioned in the Research Link on page 157.

Cite a Little-Known Fact or Statistic.   These help pique an audience's attention. Headlines on unemployment statistics, crime in the schools, and political corruption sell newspapers because they gain attention. In a speech on the need for more severe punishments for hate speech, the speaker might cite a specific hate speech incident that the audience hadn't heard of yet or the statistic that violence inspired by hate speech tripled over the last six months.

Use Humor.   Humor is useful because it relaxes the audience and establishes a quick connection between speaker and listeners. In using humor make sure it's relevant to your topic, brief, tasteful, seemingly spontaneous, and appropriate to you as a speaker and to the audience. A good example occurs in actor Tim Robbins's introduction to a speech he delivered to the National Press Club on April 15, 2003 (www.commondreams.org/cgi-bin/print.cgi?file=views03/0416-01.htm, accessed February 6, 2004):

> Thank you. And thanks for the invitation. I had originally been asked here to talk about the war and our current political situation, but I have instead chosen to hijack this opportunity and talk about baseball and show business. (Laughter.) Just kidding. Sort of.

Function 2. Establish a Speaker–Audience–Topic Relationship

In addition to gaining attention, use your introduction to establish a connection among yourself as the speaker, the audience members, and your topic. Try to answer your listeners' inevitable question of why they should listen to you speak on this topic. You can establish an effective speaker–audience–topic (or S–A–T) relationship in any of numerous ways.

Establish Your Credibility.   The introduction is a particularly important time to establish your competence, character, and charisma (see Chapter 11). Here, for example, Ohio congressman and 2008 presidential hopeful Dennis Kucinich establishes his credibility by telling the audience of his background and his own accomplishments in a speech at the Tenth Annual Wall Street Project Conference on January 15, 2007 (www.politicalaffairs.net, accessed February 27, 2007):

> I am a product of the city. My parents never owned a home. I grew up in 21 different places by the time I was 17, including a few cars. I've learned about opportunities. I've learned that if you believe it you can conceive it. I've learned about pulling oneself up by bootstraps. I've also seen the cynicism which comes when you tell people to pull themselves up by their bootstraps and then you steal their shoes. I've seen people dreaming the dreams and stuck singing "Sixteen Tons."

Refer to Others Present.   Referring to others present not only will help you to gain attention; it also will help you to establish an effective speaker–audience–topic relationship. This next example is taken from a the classic movie, *It's a Wonderful Life* (1946). Here the hero, George Bailey (played by James Stewart) appeals to the crowd not to draw their money out of the savings and loan, because a run on the bank would give the villain, Potter (Lionel Barrymore), control of the entire town (www.americanrhetoric.com/MovieSpeeches, accessed January 14, 2007):

> Joe, you had one of those Potter houses, didn't you? Well, have you forgotten? Have you forgotten what he charged you for that broken-down shack? Here, Ed. You know, you remember last year when things weren't going so well, and you couldn't make your payments. Well, you didn't lose your house, did you? You think Potter would have let you keep it?

In this example Harvey Mackay (1991) refers not only to the audience but also to their present thoughts and feelings:

> I'm flattered to be here today, but not so flattered that I'm going to let it go to my head. Yes, I was delighted to be asked to be your commencement speaker. But I also know the truth: By the time you're my age, 99 out of 100 will have completely forgotten who spoke at your graduation.
>
> And, I can accept that. Because I can't remember the name of my commencement speaker either. What I do remember from graduation day is the way I felt: excited, scared, and challenged. I was wondering what the world was like out there, and how I would manage to make an impact.

Express Your Pleasure or Interest in Speaking.   Here Senator Christopher Dodd (2007, January 9) expresses his pleasure at speaking at Reverend Jesse Jackson's Tenth Annual Wall Street Summit (www.politicalaffairs.net, accessed January 14, 2007).

> It's an honor for me to be invited to speak to you today at this, the 10th Anniversary of the Wall Street Economic Summit. Reverend Jackson, you should take

enormous pride in the success of this event, and the growth of the Rainbow Push Wall Street Project. Your efforts over the years have helped millions more Americans achieve their dreams and aspirations. These are my first formal remarks since becoming Chairman-elect of the Senate Committee on Banking, Housing, and Urban Affairs. I'm proud and pleased to be delivering them at this gathering.

Compliment the Audience.   Complimenting the audience is a commonly used technique to establish an S–A–T connection in much professional public speaking. In the classroom, however, this technique may seem awkward and obvious and so is probably best avoided. But it's important to realize that paying the audience an honest and sincere compliment (never overdoing it), not only will encourage your hearers to give you their attention but will help make them feel a part of your speech. In some cultures—Japan and Korea are good examples—the speaker is expected to compliment the audience, the beauty of the country, or its culture. It's one of the essential parts of the introduction. In this example musician Billy Joel compliments his audience, the graduating class of the Berklee College of Music, directly and honestly (www .berklee.edu/commencement/past/bjoel.html, accessed February 6, 2004):

> I am truly pleased that the road has twisted and turned its way up the East Coast to Boston. The Berklee College of Music represents the finest contemporary music school there is, and I am honored to be here with you this morning to celebrate.

Express Similarities with the Audience.   By stressing your own similarity with members of the audience, you create a bond with them and become an "insider" instead of an "outsider." Here Lester M. Crawford, Acting Commissioner of Food and Drugs, in a speech before the World Pharma IT Congress on June 6, 2005, established an S-A-T connection by expressing similarities (www .fda.gov, accessed January 14, 2007):

> I think most people would be surprised to find the Commissioner of Food and Drugs at an IT conference. And certainly, I was asking myself just this question during most of this morning's presentations. However, I think it's signficiant to stress the importance of IT in the health care industry and that's why I'm pleased to be here today.

Function 3. Orient the Audience

The introduction should orient the audience in some way as to what is to follow in the body of the speech. Preview for the audience what you're going to say. The **orientation** may be covered in a variety of ways.

Give a General Idea of Your Subject.   Orientation can consist simply of a statement of your topic. For example, you might say, "Tonight I'm going to discuss atomic waste" or "I want to talk with you about the problems our society has created for the aged." In a speech at the groundbreaking ceremony for the Dr. Martin Luther King Jr. National Memorial on November 13, 2006, U.S. Senator Barack Obama of Illinois gave a general idea of what he'd say in the main part of his speech (http://obama.senate.gov, accessed January 14, 2007):

> I have two daughters, ages five and eight. And when I see the plans for this memorial, I think about what it will [be] like when I first bring them here upon the memorial's completion. . . . And at some point, I know that one of my daughters will ask, perhaps my youngest, will ask, "Daddy, why is this monument here? What did this man do?" How might I answer them?

Identify the Main Points You'll Cover. In your orientation you may want to identify very briefly the main points you'll cover. Here Texas Governor Rick Perry, in a speech to the Border Governors' Conference on August 25, 2006 (www.governor.state.tx.us/divisions/press/speeches, accessed January 14, 2007), orients the audience by briefly identifying the three main points he will cover in this speech:

> In signing this declaration, we commit our resources and our resolve to making the border healthier, better educated, and more secure.

Give a Detailed Preview. Or you may wish to give a detailed preview of the main points of your speech, as in this example of an address by Microsoft founder Bill Gates at the United Nations Media Leaders Summit on January 15, 2004 (www.gatesfoundation.org/MediaCenter/Speeches/BillgSpeeches/BGSpeechMedia-04, accessed February 6, 2004):

> I hope to do three things today: explain why I believe the media's role in increasing visibility for HIV/AIDS is so important, why I'm optimistic about the opportunities ahead, and what I believe is needed to stop this epidemic.

Identify Your Goal. Here California Governor Arnold Schwarzenegger orients the audience by giving a general idea of the goal he hopes to achieve (http://gov.ca.gov, accessed January 14, 2007):

> Hello everybody. Thank you for being here. I believe that in Sacramento this year, we are going to make history. Using a comprehensive approach built on shared responsibility where everyone does their part we will fix California's broken health care system and create a model that the rest of the nation can follow. I know everyone has been eager to hear exactly what we are proposing.

Conclusions

Your conclusion is especially important because it's often the part of the speech that the audience remembers most clearly. Let your conclusion serve three major functions: to summarize, motivate, and provide closure.

Function 1. Summarize

You may summarize your speech in a variety of ways.

Restate Your Thesis or Purpose. In the restatement type of summary, you recap the essential thrust of your speech, repeating your thesis or perhaps the goals you hoped to achieve. Here is how Carrie Willis (Schnoor, 2000, p. 15), a student from Tallahassee Community College, restated the importance of her thesis on "drowsy driving" and also summarized the main points of her speech:

> While this problem is as old as cars, it's not disappearing. And it won't disappear until you choose to do something about it. Today, we have gained a better understanding of the problem of falling asleep at the wheel, and why it continues to exist, while finally suggesting several initiatives to help end this epidemic. Six innocent college students were killed, all because someone didn't take the precautionary steps to avoid the tragedy. So, next time you're on the road and you find yourself dozing off, pull over and take a nap, because those 30 minutes could save your life.

Here's another example, from a speech by President Jimmy Carter to the people of Cuba (www.americanrhetoric .com/speeches/jimmycartercubaspeech.htm, accessed February 6, 2004):

> After 43 years of animosity, we hope that someday soon, you can reach across the great divide that separates our two countries and say, "We are ready to join the community of democracies," and I hope that Americans will soon open our arms to you and say, "We welcome you as our friends."

Restate the Importance of the Topic.   Another method for concluding is to tell the audience again why your topic or thesis is so important. In this excerpt Commissioner of Internal Revenue Margaret Milner Richardson (1995, p. 203) concludes her speech by restating the importance of her topic:

> Thank you for taking this journey with me into the future. By sharing with you our vision of the future, I hope you will not only understand where we have been as an agency but where we will be in the future. You are an indispensable part of that future. I look forward to working with you to bring tax administration into the twenty-first century.

Restate Your Main Points.   In this type of summary you restate your thesis and the main points you used to support it. In his conclusion Carl Wayne Hensley (1994, p. 319) restates his main points as questions:

> Now, do you see why I assert that mediation provides a sensible approach for settling divorce-related issues? Do you see why I believe that mediation has to become a way of life in America when the divorce rate is so overwhelming? Do you understand that mediation helps the couple manage conflict, helps the couple engage in a win–win exchange, and helps the couple stabilize individually? Do you see more clearly that mediation does provide a sensible approach for settling divorce-related issues?

Consider the conclusions you've heard in recent speeches or lectures. What types of conclusions do you find most memorable? What are the major mistakes speakers make in concluding their speeches?

Function 2. Motivate

A second function of the conclusion—most appropriate in persuasive speeches—is to motivate your audience to do what you want them to do. In your conclusion you have the opportunity to give the audience one final push in the direction you wish them to take. Whether it's to buy stock, vote a particular way, or change an attitude, you can use the conclusion for a final motivation, a final appeal. Here are three excellent ways to motivate.

Ask for a Specific Response.   Specify what you want the audience to do after listening to your speech. Clarence Darrow (Peterson, 1965), in his summation speech in defense of Henry Sweet, an African American man charged with murder, directed his conclusion at motivating the jury to vote not guilty in a case that drew national and worldwide attention because of the racial issues involved. A vote of not guilty was in fact quickly returned by a jury of 12 white men.

> Gentlemen, what do you think of our duty in this case? I have watched day after day these black, tense faces that have crowded this court. These black faces that now are looking to you 12 whites, feeling that the hopes and fears of a race are in your keeping. This case is about to end, gentlemen. To them, it is life. Not one of

their color sits on this jury. Their fate is in the hands of 12 whites. Their eyes are fixed on you, their hearts go out to you, and their hopes hang on your verdict. This is all. I ask you, on behalf of this defendant, on behalf of these helpless ones who turn to you, and more than that—on behalf of this great state, and this great city, which must face this problem and face it fairly—I ask you, in the name of progress and of the human race, to return a verdict of not guilty in this case!

Reiterate the Importance of the Issue. In a speech designed to strengthen attitudes, it may prove of value to restate the importance of the issue to the audience and to the community at large. Here, for example, Alberto Mora, in accepting the 2006 John F. Kennedy Profile in Courage award on May 26, 2006 (www .jfklibrary.org/Education+and+Public+Programs/Profile+in+Courage+Award/, accessed July 12, 2007), restates why it's so important to address the issue of cruelty and torture:

> We should care because the issues raised by a policy of cruelty are too fundamental to be left unaddressed, unanswered, or ambiguous. We should care because a tolerance of cruelty will corrode our values and our rights and degrade the world in which we live. It will corrupt our heritage, cheapen the value of the soldiers upon whose past and present sacrifices our freedoms depend, and debase the legacy we will leave to our sons and daughters. We should care because it is intolerable to us that anyone should believe for a second that our nation is tolerant of cruelty. And we should care because each of us knows that this issue has not gone away.

Provide Directions for Future Action. Another type of motivational conclusion is to spell out the action you wish the audience to take. Here's an example from a speech on universal health care that California's Governor Arnold Schwarzenegger delivered on January 8, 2007 (http://gov.ca.gov/index, accessed February 27, 2007):

> I look forward to a vigorous and open debate. Everything will be on the table and I want to hear from everyone. But I know we can do this. Everyone in the legislature is focused on solving this problem. Several proposals have already been put forward. If we have the will, and I believe that we do, we can heal our broken system. We can make health care more affordable, accessible, and equitable for everyone.

Function 3. Provide Closure

The third function of your conclusion is to provide **closure**. Often your summary will accomplish this, but in some instances it will prove insufficient. End your speech with a conclusion that is crisp and definite. Make the audience know that you have definitely and clearly ended. Some kind of wrap-up, some sort of final statement, is helpful in providing this feeling of closure. Here are three ways you can achieve closure.

Refer to Subsequent Events. You can achieve closure by looking ahead to events that will take place either that day or soon afterwards. Notice how effectively U.S. Secretary of State Madeleine K. Albright (1998) uses this method in a speech on NATO:

> Our task is to make clear what our alliance will do and what our partnership will mean in a Europe truly whole and free, and in a world that looks to us for principles and purposeful leadership for peace, for prosperity, and for freedom. In this spirit, I look forward to our discussion today and to our work together in the months and years to come.

Refer Back to the Introduction.   It's sometimes useful to connect your conclusion with your introduction. Here, for example, Jill Reiss (Schnoor, 1994, p. 3), a student from George Mason University, after noting the hard work that Thomas Edison put into his inventions, concludes her speech by referring to Edison again:

> Today we've examined what ecofoam peanuts are, how they compare to other alternatives, and their problems as well as their promises as an environmentally conscious product. American Excelsior, like Thomas Edison, has been willing to invest the perspiration necessary to bring its inspirations to work.

Here's another example from one of the most famous of all farewell speeches, baseball great Lou Gehrig's farewell to baseball. In his introduction Gehrig, who was at the time dying of what has come to be called Lou Gehrig's disease, said: "Fans, for the past two weeks you have been reading about the bad break I got. Yet today I consider myself the luckiest man on the face of the earth." In the conclusion he refers back to this introductory statement, very simply:

> So, I close in saying that I might have been given a bad break, but I've got an awful lot to live for.

Thank the Audience.   Speakers frequently conclude their speeches by thanking the audience for their attention or for their invitation to the speaker to address them. Here, for example, John Dalton (1994, p. 298) expresses his appreciation to the audience:

> I am very grateful to you for the opportunity to share my concerns with you, and I hope that you will give me the benefit of your own knowledge and expertise as I continue to address these matters. If at the end of my tenure as Secretary of the Navy I am remembered for having encouraged the men and women of the Navy and Marine Corps to value and adhere to personal integrity and sacrificial service to others I will be *deeply satisfied* indeed.
>
> Thank you very much, and God bless you.

COMMON FAULTS OF INTRODUCTIONS AND CONCLUSIONS

The introduction and conclusion are crucial to the success of your speech. So be especially careful to avoid the most common faults.

Don't Apologize (Generally).   In much of the United States and western Europe, an apology is seen as an excuse for a lack of competence or effectiveness. To apologize in your speech is therefore to encourage your listeners to look for faults and to alert them that your speech could have and should have been better. So the general advice to avoid apologizing is reasonable in these cultures. However, in many other cultures—Japanese, Chinese, and Korean are good examples—the speaker is expected to begin with an apology. It's a way of complimenting the audience and placing them in a superior position. The speaker who doesn't apologize or act humbly may be seen as an arrogant individual who feels superior to the audience.

Don't Rely on Gimmicks.   Avoid gimmicks that gain attention but are irrelevant to the nature of the speech or inconsistent with your treatment of the topic. Thus, for example, slamming a book on the desk or telling a joke that bears no relation to the rest of your speech may accomplish the very limited goal of gaining attention, but it will not advance your purpose. Also, some listeners may resent such tactics, feeling that you fooled them into paying attention.

Don't Preface Your Introduction. Don't preface your speech with such common but ineffective statements as "I'm really nervous, but here goes," "Before I begin my talk, I want to say . . .," or "I hope I can remember everything I want to say."

Don't Introduce New Material in Your Conclusion. You may, of course, give new expression to ideas covered in the body of the speech, but don't introduce new material in your conclusion. Instead, use your conclusion to reinforce what you've already said in your discussion and to summarize your essential points.

TRANSITIONS

Remember that your audience will hear your speech just once. They must understand it as you speak it, or your message will be lost. As discussed in Chapter 2, transitions help listeners understand your speech more effectively and efficiently.

Transitions are words, phrases, or sentences that connect the various parts of your speech. They provide the audience with guideposts that help them follow the development of your thoughts and arguments. You can enhance your transitions by pausing for just a brief moment before and/or after your transition. This will help the audience see that you've completed one part of your speech and are leading into the next part. You might also take a step forward or to the side before or after your transition. This will also help to reinforce the movement from one part of your speech to another. Use transitions in at least the following places:

- between the introduction and the body of the speech
- between the body and the conclusion
- between the main points in the body of the speech

In addition, consider using transitions:

To announce the start of a major proposition or piece of evidence:

First, . . .

A second argument . . .

A closely related problem . . .

If you want further evidence, look at . . .

Next, consider . . .

My next point . . .

An even more compelling argument . . .

To signal that you're drawing a conclusion from previously given evidence and argument:

Thus, . . .

Therefore, . . .

So, as you can see . . .

It follows, then, that . . .

To alert the audience to the introduction of a qualification or exception:

But, . . .

However, also consider . . .

To remind listeners of what has just been said and that it's connected with another issue that will now be considered:

In contrast to . . . , consider also . . .

Not only . . . , but also . . .

In addition to . . . , we also need to look at . . .

Not only should we . . . , but we should also . . .

To signal the part of your speech you're approaching:

By way of introduction . . .

In conclusion . . .

Now, let's discuss why we are here today . . .

So, what's the solution? What should we do?

To summarize: A special type of transition is the internal summary, a statement that reviews what you've already discussed. It's a statement that usually recaps some major subdivision of your speech. Incorporate internal summaries into your speech—perhaps working them into the transitions connecting your main points. Notice how the internal summary presented below reminds listeners of what they've just heard *and previews what they'll hear next*:

> Inadequate recreational facilities, poor schooling, and a lack of adequate role models seem to be the major problems facing our youngsters. Each of these, however, can be remedied and even eliminated. Here's what we can do.

OUTLINING THE SPEECH

The **outline** is a blueprint for your speech; it lays out the elements of the speech and their relationship to one another. With this blueprint in front of you, you can see at a glance all the elements of organization considered here—the introduction and conclusion, the transitions, the main points and their relationship to the thesis and purpose, and the adequacy of the supporting materials. Like a blueprint for a building, the outline enables you to spot weaknesses that might otherwise go undetected.

Begin outlining at the time you begin constructing your speech. Don't wait until you've collected all your material, but begin outlining as you're collecting material, organizing it, and styling it. In this way you'll take the best advantage of one of the major functions of an outline—to tell you where change is needed.

CONSTRUCTING THE OUTLINE

After you've completed your research and have mapped out an organizational plan for your speech, put this plan (this blueprint) on paper. That is, construct what is called a **preparation outline** of your speech, using the following guidelines.

Preface the Outline with Identifying Data

Before you begin the outline proper, identify the general and specific purposes as well as your thesis. You also may want to include a working title—a title that you may change as you continue to polish and perfect your speech. This prefatory material should look something like this:

What Do Media Do?

General purpose: To inform.
Specific purpose: To inform my audience of four functions of the media.
Thesis: The media serve four functions.

These identifying notes are not part of your speech proper. They're not, for example, mentioned in your oral presentation. Rather, they're guides to the preparation of the speech and the outline. They're like road signs to keep you going in the right direction and to signal when you've gone off course.

Outline the Introduction, Body, and Conclusion as Separate Units

The introduction, body, and conclusion of the speech, although intimately connected, should be labeled separately and should be kept distinct in your outline. Like the identifying data above, these labels are not spoken to the audience but are further guides to your preparation.

By keeping the introduction, body, and conclusion as separate units, you'll be able to see at a glance if they do, in fact, serve the functions you want them to serve. You'll be able to see where there are problems and where repair is necessary. At the same time, make sure that you examine and see the speech as a whole—in which the introduction leads to the body and the conclusion summarizes your main points and brings your speech to a close.

Insert Transitions

Insert [using square brackets] transitions between the introduction and the body, between the body and the conclusion, among the main points of the body, and wherever else you think they might be useful.

Append a List of References

Some instructors require that you append a list of references to the written preparation outline of each of your speeches. If this is requested, then place the list at the end of the outline or on a separate page. Some instructors require that only sources cited in the speech be included in the list of references, whereas others require that the full list of sources consulted be provided (those mentioned in the speech as well as those not mentioned).

Whatever the specific requirements in your course, remember that source citations will prove most effective with your audience if you carefully integrate them into the speech. It will count for little if you consult the latest works by the greatest authorities but never mention this to your audience. So, when appropriate, weave into your speech the source material you've consulted. In your outline, refer to the source material by author's name, date, and page in parentheses; then provide the complete citation in your list of references.

In your actual speech it might prove more effective to include the source with your statement. It might be phrased something like this:

> According to John Naisbitt, author of the nationwide best seller *Megatrends*, the bellwether states are California, Florida, Washington, Colorado, and Connecticut.

Use a Consistent Set of Symbols

The following is the standard, accepted sequence of symbols for outlining.

   I.
      A.
         1.
            a.
               (1)
                  (a)

Begin the introduction, the body, and the conclusion with roman numeral I. Treat each of the three major parts as a complete unit.

Not This	This
Introduction	Introduction
I.	I.
II.	II.
Body	Body
III.	I.
IV.	II.
V.	III.
Conclusion	Conclusion
VI.	I.
VII	II.

Use Complete Declarative Sentences

Phrase your ideas in the outline in complete declarative sentences rather than as questions or as phrases. This will further assist you in examining the essential relationships. It's much easier, for example, to see if one item of information supports another if both are phrased in the declarative mode. If one is a question and one is a statement, this will be more difficult.

SAMPLE OUTLINES

Now that the principles of outlining and organization are clear, here are some specific examples to illustrate how these principles are used in specific outlines. The Public Speaking Sample Assistant boxes that follow present a variety of outlines.

Preparation Outlines

The preparation outline is the main outline that you construct and—in most learning environments—turn in to your instructor. It is a detailed blueprint for your speech. Two preparation outlines are presented in the accompanying

Public Speaking Sample Assistant boxes: a preparation outline following a topical organization appears here and a preparation outline following a motivated sequence pattern is on page 173.

A PREPARATION OUTLINE WITH ANNOTATIONS (TOPICAL ORGANIZATION)

Public Speaking *Sample Assistant*

Self-Disclosure

General purpose: To inform.

Specific purpose: To inform my audience of the advantages and disadvantages of self-disclosing.

Thesis: Self-disclosure has advantages and disadvantages.

Generally the title, thesis, and general and specific purposes of the speech are prefaced to the outline. When the outline is an assignment that is to be handed in, additional information may be requested.

Note the general format for the outline: the headings (introduction, body, and conclusion) are clearly labeled and the sections are separated visually.

INTRODUCTION

I. We've all heard them:

  A. I'm in love with my nephew.

  B. My husband is not my baby's father.

  C. I'm really a woman.

II. We've all disclosed.

  A. Sometimes it was positive, sometimes negative, but always significant.

  B. Knowing the potential consequences will help us make better decisions.

III. We look at this important form of communication in three parts:

  A. First, we look at the nature of self-disclosure.

  B. Second, we look at the potential rewards.

  C. Third, we look at the potential risks.

  [Let's look first at the nature of this type of communication.]

Notice that the introduction serves the three functions discussed in the text: it gains attention (by these extreme confessions); establishes an S–A–T connection (by noting that all of us, speaker and audience, have had this experience); and orients the audience (by identifying the three major ideas of the speech).

Note how the indenting helps you to see clearly the relationship that one item bears to another. For example, in Introduction I, the outline format helps you to see that A, B, and C are explanations (amplification and support) for I.

These brief statements are designed to get attention and perhaps a laugh or two, but also to introduce the nature of the topic.

Here the speaker seeks to establish a speaker–audience–topic connection.

Here the speaker orients the audience and explains the three parts of the speech. The use of guide phrases (first, second, third) helps the audience fix clearly in mind the major divisions of the speech.

This transition cues the audience that the speaker will consider the first of the major parts of the speech. Notice that transitions are inserted between all major parts of the speech. Athough they may seem too numerous in this abbreviated outline, they'll be appreciated by your audience because the transitions will help them follow and understand your speech.

BODY

I. Self-disclosure is a form of communication (Petronio, 2000).

  A. S-D is about the self.

    1. It can be about what you did.

    2. It can be about what you think.

  B. S-D is new information.

  C. S-D is normally about information usually kept hidden.

    1. It can be something about which you're ashamed.

    2. It can be something for which you'd be punished in some way.

    [Knowing what self-disclosure is, we can now look at its potential rewards.]

II. Self-disclosure has three potential rewards.

  A. It gives us self-knowledge.

  B. It increases communication effectiveness (Schmidt & Cornelius, 1987).

  C. It improves physiological health (Sheese, Brown, & Graziano, 2004).

  [Although these benefits are substantial, there are also risks.]

III. Self-disclosure has three potential risks.

  A. It can involve personal risks.

    1. This happened to a close friend.

    2. This also happened with well-known celebrities.

  B. It can involve relationship risks (Petronio, 2000).

    1. This happens on Jerry Springer five times a week.

    2. It also happened to me.

  C. It can involve professional risks (Korda, 1975; Fesko, 2001).

    1. This occurred recently at work.

    2. There are also lots of political examples.

    [Let me summarize this brief excursion into self-disclosure.]

Notice the parallel structure throughout the outline. For example, note that II and III in the body are phrased in similar style. Although this may seem unnecessarily redundant, it will help your audience follow your speech more closely and will also help you in logically structuring your thoughts.

Note that the references are integrated throughout the outline just as they would be in a term paper. In the actual speech, the speaker might say something like: "Communication theorist Sandra Petronio presents evidence to show that. . . ."

These examples would naturally be recounted in greater detail in the actual speech. One of the values of outlining these examples is that you'll be able to see at a glance how many you have and how much time you have available to devote to each example. Examples, especially personal ones, have a way of growing beyond their importance to the speech.

This transition helps the audience see that the speaker is finished discussing what self-disclosure is and will now consider the potential rewards.

Note that each statement in the outline is a complete sentence. You can easily convert this outline into a phrase or key-word outline for use in delivery (see Public Speaking Sample Assistant, page 173). The full sentences, however, will help you see more clearly relationships among items.

This transition connects what was just discussed to what will be discussed next.

As you see, transitions are inserted between all major parts of the speech. Although they may seem too numerous in this abbreviated outline, they'll be appreciated by your audience as useful aids that help them follow your speech.

CONCLUSION

I. Self-disclosure is a type of communication.

    A. It's about the self, concerns something new, and something that you usually keep hidden.

    B. Self-disclosure can lead to increased self-knowledge, better communication, and improved health.

    C. Self-disclosure can also create risks to your personal, relational, and professional lives.

II. Self-disclosure is not only an interesting type of communication; it's also vital.

    A. You may want to explore this further by simply typing "self-disclosure" in your favorite search engine.

    B. If you want a more scholarly presentation, take a look at Sandra Petronio's *Balancing the Secrets of Private Disclosures* in the library or online.

III. The bottom line, of course: should you self-disclose?

    A. Yes.

    B. No.

    C. Maybe.

This first part of the conclusion summarizes the major parts of the speech. The longer the speech, the more extensive the summary should be.

Notice that the Introduction's III A, B, and C correspond to the Body's I, II, and III, and to the Conclusion's I A, B, and C. This pattern will help you emphasize the major ideas in your speech—first in the orientation, second in the body of the speech, and third in the conclusion's summary.

This step, in which the speaker motivates the listeners to continue learning about self-disclosure, is optional in informative speeches. In persuasive speeches, you'd use this step to encourage listeners to act on your purpose—to vote, to donate time, to give blood, and so on.

This step provides closure; it makes it clear that the speech is finished. It also serves to encourage reflection on the part of the audience as to their own self-disclosing communication.

REFERENCES

This reference list includes only the sources cited in the speech.

Korda, M. (1975). *Power! How to get it, how to use it*. New York: Ballantine.

Fresko, S. L. (2001). Disclosure of HIV status in the workplace. *Health and Social Work 25*, 235–244.

Petronio, S. (Ed.). (2000). *Balancing the secrets of private disclosures*. Mahwah, NJ: Erlbaum.

Schmidt, T. O., & Cornelius, R. R. (1987). Self-disclosure in everyday life. *Journal of Social and Personal Relationships, 4*, 365–373.

Sheese, B. E., Brown, E. L, & Graziano, W. G. (2004). Emotional expression in cyberspace: Searching for moderators of the Pennebaker disclosure effect via e-mail. *Health Psychology, 23* (September), 457–464.

PREPARATION OUTLINE WITH ANNOTATIONS (MOTIVATED SEQUENCE ORGANIZATION)

Public Speaking   *Sample Assistant*

This outline illustrates how you might construct an outline and a speech using the motivated sequence. To model the five steps in the motivated sequence, we'll return to the example given earlier in the chapter—the establishment of a youth center as a means of combating juvenile crime. In a longer speech, if you wanted to persuade an audience to establish a youth center, you might want to select two or three general arguments rather than limiting yourself to the one argument about reducing juvenile crime.

The Youth Center

General purpose: To persuade.

Specific purpose: To persuade my listeners to vote in favor of Proposition 14 establishing a community youth center.

Thesis: A youth center will reduce juvenile crime.

I. If you could reduce juvenile crime by some 20 percent by just flipping a lever, would you do it?
   A. Thom's drug store was broken into by teenagers.
   B. Loraine's video store windows were broken by teenagers.

II. Juvenile crime is on the rise.
   A. The overall number of crimes has increased.
   B. In 2001 there were 32 juvenile crimes.
      1. In 2004 there were 47 such crimes.
      2. In 2006 there were 63 such crimes.
   C. The number of serious crimes also has increased.
      1. In 2001 there were 30 misdemeanors and 2 felonies.
      2. In 2006 there were 35 misdemeanors and 28 felonies.

III. A youth center will help reduce juvenile crime.
   A. Three of our neighboring towns reduced juvenile crime after establishing a youth center.
      1. In Marlboro there was a 20 percent decline in overall juvenile crime.

I. Attention step

The speaker asks a question to gain attention and follows it with specific examples of juvenile crime that audience members have experienced. The question and the specific examples focus on one single issue: the need to reduce juvenile crime. If the speech were a broader and longer one that included other reasons for the youth center, then it would have been appropriate to preview them here as well.

II. Need step

The speaker states the need directly and clearly and shows that a problem exists. The speaker then demonstrates that the rise in crime is significant both in absolute numbers and in the severity of the crimes. To increase the listeners' ability to understand these figures, it would help if these figures were written on a chalkboard, on a prepared chart, or on PowerPoint slides. In a longer speech, other needs might also be identified in this step; for example, the need to offer teenagers a place where they can learn useful vocational and social skills.

III. Satisfaction step

In this step the speaker shows the listeners that the proposal to establish a youth center has great benefits and no significant drawbacks.

2. In both Highland and Ellenville the number of serious crimes declined 25 percent.

B. The youth center will not increase our tax burden.

    1. New York State grants will pay for most of the expenses.

    2. Local merchants have agreed to pay any remaining expenses.

IV. Juvenile crime will decrease as a result of the youth center.

A. If we follow the example of our neighbors, our juvenile crime rates are likely to decrease by 20 to 25 percent.

B. Thom's store would not have been broken into.

C. Loraine's windows would not have been broken.

V. Vote *yes* on Proposition 14.

A. In next week's election, you'll be asked to vote on Proposition 14, establishing a youth center.

B. Vote *yes* if you want to help reduce juvenile crime.

C. Urge your family members, your friends, and your work colleagues also to vote *yes*.

The speaker argues that the youth center will satisfy the need to reduce juvenile crime by showing statistics from neighboring towns. The speaker also answers the objection and removes any doubts about increased taxes. If the speaker had reason to believe that listeners might have other possible objections, those objections, too, should be answered in this step.

IV. Visualization step

Here the speaker visualizes what the town would be like if the youth center were established, using both the statistics developed earlier and the personal examples introduced at the beginning of the speech.

V. Action step

In this step the speaker asks listeners to take specific actions—to vote in favor of the youth center and to urge others to do the same. The speaker also reiterates the main theme of the speech; namely, that the youth center will help reduce juvenile crime.

Template Outlines

A **template outline**, like the templates you use for writing letters or résumés or greeting or business cards, is a preestablished format into which you insert your specific information. A sample template outline for a speech using a topical oganization pattern is presented in the Public Speaking Sample Assistant box on page 170. Note that in this template outline there are three main points (I, II, and III in the body). These correspond to the III A, B, and C of the introduction (in which you'd orient the audience), and to the I A, B, and C of the conclusion (in which you'd summarize your main points). The transitions are signaled by square brackets. As you review this outline, the faintly printed watermarks will remind you of the functions of each outline item. A variety of other template outlines are provided at www.myspeechlab.com.

Delivery Outline

After you construct your preparation outline, you can begin to construct your **delivery outline**, an outline consisting of key words or phrases that will assist

TEMPLATE OUTLINE (TOPICAL ORGANIZATION)

Public Speaking *Sample Assistant*

Here's a template outline—a kind of template for structuring a speech. This particular outline would be appropriate for a speech using a topical organization pattern. Note that in this skeletal outline there are three main points (I, II, and III in the body). These correspond to the II A, B, and C in the introduction (where you'd summarize your main points). The transitions are signaled by square brackets. As you review this outline, the faintly printed watermarks will remind you of the functions of each outline item.

Template Outline

General purpose:
<u>your general aim (to inform, to persuade, to entertain)</u>

Specific purpose:
<u>what you hope to achieve from this speech</u>

Thesis:
<u>your main assertion; the core of your speech</u>

INTRODUCTION

I. <u>gain attention</u>

II. <u>establish speaker–audience–topic connection</u>

III. <u>orient audience</u>

    A. <u>first main point; same as I in body</u>

    B. <u>second main point; same as II in body</u>

    C. <u>third main point; same as III in body</u>

[Transition:
<u>connect the introduction to the body</u>]

BODY

I. <u>first main point</u>

    A. <u>support for I (the first main point)</u>

    B. <u>further support for I</u>

[Transition:
<u>connect the first main point to the second</u>]

II. <u>second main point</u>

    A. <u>support for II (the second main point)</u>

    B. <u>further support for II</u>

[Transition:
connect the second main point to the third
_____]

III. third main point _____

    A. support for III _____

    B. further support for III _____

[Transition:
connect the third main point (or all main points) to the conclusion
_____]

CONCLUSION

I. summary _____

    A. first main point; same as I in body _____

    B. second main point; same as II in body _____

    C. third main point; same as III in body _____

II. motivation _____

III. closure _____

REFERENCES

1. _____

2. _____

3. _____

you in delivering the speech. Resist the temptation to use your preparation outline to deliver the speech. If you do use your preparation outline, you'll tend to read from the outline, instead of presenting an extemporaneous speech in which you attend to and respond to audience feedback.

Instead, construct a brief delivery outline that will assist rather than hinder your delivery of the speech. A sample delivery outline based on the full-sentence preparation outline presented on page 170 is presented in the Public Speaking Sample Assistant box on page 177.

Note first that the outline is brief enough so that you'll be able to use it effectively without losing eye contact with the audience. Notice too that the outline uses abbreviations (for example, S-D for self-disclosure) and phrases rather than complete sentences. This helps to keep the outline brief and also helps you to scan your message more quickly.

At the same time, however, the delivery outline is detailed enough to include all essential parts of your speech, including transitions. Be careful that you don't omit essential parts even if you're convinced that you couldn't possibly forget them. Normal apprehension may cause you to do exactly that.

This outline contains delivery notes specifically tailored to your own needs; for example, pause suggestions and guides to using visual aids.

The delivery outline is clearly divided into an introduction, body, and conclusion and uses the same numbering system as the preparation outline.

Rehearse with your delivery outline, not with your full-sentence preparation outline. This suggestion is simply a specific application of the general rule: Make rehearsals as close to the real thing as possible.

PHRASE/KEY-WORD DELIVERY OUTLINE

Public Speaking   *Sample Assistant*

Self-Disclosure

PAUSE!

LOOK OVER THE AUDIENCE!

INTRODUCTION

I. We've heard them:
   A. "I'm in love with my nephew."
   B. "My husband is not my baby's father."
   C. "I'm really a woman."

II. We've all S-D
   A. sometimes +, −, significant
   B. consequences = better decisions

III. 3 parts: (WRITE ON BOARD)
   A. nature of S-D
   B. rewards
   C. risks

[1st = type of communication]

PAUSE, STEP FORWARD

BODY

I. S-D: communication
   A. about self
   B. new
   C. hidden information

[knowing what self-disclosure is, now rewards]

II. 3 rewards
   A. self-knowledge

   B. communication effectiveness
   C. physiological health

[benefits substantial, there are also risks]

PAUSE!

III. 3 risks
   A. personal
   B. relationship
   C. professional

[summarize: S-D]

CONCLUSION

I. S-D = communication
   A. about self, new, and usually hidden
   B. rewards: increased self-knowledge, better communication, and improved health
   C. risks: personal, relational, and professional

II. S-D not only interesting, it's vital
   A. explore further "S-D" into www
   B. scholarly: Sandra Petronio's *Boundaries*

III. Should you S-D?
   A. yes
   B. no
   C. maybe

PAUSE!

ANY QUESTIONS?

A BRIEF NOTE ON ORGANIZATION AND FLEXIBILITY

Be careful that you don't allow your organization to destroy the flexibility that you need in delivering your speech—to prevent you from adjusting and adapting your speech to the ever-changing situation. To heighten your awareness of the need for flexibility, take the following self-test (developed from an idea by Martin & Rubin, 1994, 1995).

TEST YOURSELF

How Flexible Are You as a Public Speaker?

Visualize yourself in each of the following situations. Reflect for one minute on each situation, identifying as many different appropriate ways of handling the situation that you can think of in this one minute. Jot down brief abbreviations for each of the possibilities you think of. Record the number of ways you might appropriately handle each situation in the spaces provided.

____ **1.** You're preparing a speech on abortion and planning to use some posters on both sides of the issue. Unfortunately, the person who was going to lend you the posters went on vacation, and you now have no way of getting them. These were going to be great visual aids. What might you do?

____ **2.** Right in the middle of your speech on violence on television, a listener in the back row yells out in a perfect Austrian accent, "Hasta la vista, baby!" The entire class busts out laughing. What might you do?

____ **3.** While you are giving your speech, one of the audience members not only falls asleep but starts snoring so loudly that everyone begins to concentrate on the snoring rather than on what you're saying. What might you do?

____ **4.** In your speech on e-mail programs, you had planned to show the class three different programs. The first two went along without any mishaps. When you tried to show the third one, you got an error message that you didn't understand. What might you do?

____ **5.** One of your speech assignments requires that as part of your supporting material, you interview someone with special knowledge of your speech topic. You've developed a really great speech on the dangers of taking too many vitamins, and your interviewee is going to be a nurse who suffered from excess vitamins and has just written a book on the topic. Unfortunately, the nurse is called out of town for several weeks and won't be available for the interview. What might you do?

HOW DID YOU DO? The number of ways of handling each situation is a measure of your flexibility. The more ways you can think of, the more flexible you are.

WHAT WILL YOU DO? If possible, share your responses with others in small groups or with the class as a whole. You should find that any group is a lot more flexible than any one person; that is, the group as a whole will come up with more possibilities than would any one individual. Can you think of other situations in which flexibility would come in handy?

Essentials of Organizing Your Speech

This chapter has covered ways to organize the body of the speech; prepare the introduction, conclusion, and transitions; and outline the speech.

1. **Select your main points.**
   - Select the points that are most important to your thesis.
   - Combine those that have a common focus.
   - Select those that are most relevant to your audience.
   - Use few main points (two, three, or four work best).
   - Phrase your main points in parallel style.
   - Separate your main points avoiding any overlap.

2. **Organize your main points.**
   - In a **temporal** pattern your main ideas are arranged in a time sequence.
   - In a **spatial** pattern your main ideas are arranged in a space pattern—for example, left to right.
   - In a **topical** pattern your main ideas (equal in value and importance) are itemized.
   - In a **problem–solution** pattern your main ideas are divided into problems and solutions.
   - In a **cause–effect** pattern your main ideas are arranged into causes and effects.
   - In a **motivated sequence** pattern your main ideas are arranged into five steps: attention, need, satisfaction, visualization, and action.
   - Additional patterns include: **structure-function, comparison-and-contrast, pro-and-con (advantages and disadvantages), claim-and-proof, multiple-definition,** *Who? What? Why? Where? When?* and fact-fiction.
   - In selecting an organizational pattern, take into consideration the cultural backgrounds of your listeners, especially the extent to which they are from low-context or high-context cultures.

3. **Construct your introduction, conclusion, and transitions.**
   - Construct your introduction so that it:
     - Gains attention.
     - Establishes a connection among speaker, audience, and topic.
     - Orients the audience.
   - Construct your conclusion so that it:
     - Summarizes your speech or some aspect of it.
     - Motivates your audience.
     - Provides crisp closure.
   - Avoid the common problems of introductions and conclusions:
     - Don't apologize.
     - Don't rely on gimmicks.
     - Don't preface your introduction.
     - Don't introduce new material in your conclusion.
   - Use transitions to connect the parts of your speech and give your listeners guides to help them follow your speech. Use transitions:
     - Between the introduction and the body.
     - Among the main points.
     - Between the body and the conclusion.

4. **Construct your outline.**
   - Outlines may vary from complete sentence outlines to those with just key words and phrases. In constructing your outline:
     - Preface the outline with identifying data.
     - Outline the introduction, body, and conclusion as separate units.
     - Insert transitions in square brackets.
     - Append a list of references (if required).
     - Use a consistent set of symbols.
     - Use complete declarative sentences (for your preparation outline).

Essential Terms: Organizing Your Speech

Public Speaking Exercises

7.1 Generating Main Points

One of the skills in organizing a speech is to ask a strategic question of your thesis and from the answer to generate your main points. Below are 10 thesis statements suitable for a variety of informative or persuasive speeches. For each thesis statement, ask a question and generate two, three, or four main points that would be suitable for an informative or persuasive speech.
Here's an example to get you started:

Thesis statement: Mandatory retirement should (should not) be abolished.

Question: Why should mandatory retirement be (not be) abolished?

I. Mandatory retirement leads us to lose many of the most productive workers.

II. Mandatory retirement contributes to psychological problems of those forced to retire.

III. Mandatory retirement costs businesses economic hardship because they have to train new people.

1. Buy American.
2. Tax property assets owned by religious organizations.
3. Require adoption agencies to reveal the names of birth parents to all adopted children when they reach 18 years of age.
4. Permit condom distribution in all junior and senior high schools.
5. Permit gay men and lesbians to adopt children.
6. Ban all sales of furs from wild animals.
7. Make the death penalty mandatory for those convicted of selling drugs to minors.
8. Require all students at this college to take courses on women's issues.
9. Legalize soft drugs.
10. Grant full equality to gay men and lesbians in the military.

7.2 Constructing Introductions and Conclusions

Prepare an introduction and a conclusion for a speech on one of the theses listed. Be prepared to explain the methods you used to accomplish each of these aims.

1. College isn't for everyone.
2. Maximum sentences should be imposed even for first offenders of the drug laws.
3. Each of us should donate our organs to medicine after our death.
4. Laws restricting Sunday shopping should be abolished.
5. Suicide and its assistance by others should be legalized.
6. Gambling should be legalized in all states.
7. College athletics should be abolished.
8. Same-sex marriages should be legalized.
9. Divorce should be granted immediately when there's mutual agreement.
10. Privatization of elementary and high schools should be encouraged.

7.3 What Do You Say?

◆ **Using the Motivated Sequence**. Bette wants to give a speech opposing a proposed youth center, arguing that the way to fight youth crime is by mandating harsher sentences for all youth crimes. She wants to use the motivated sequence pattern.

- How might she gain attention?
- How might she demonstrate the need to establish harsher sentences?
- How might she demonstrate that if harsher sentences are handed down, youth crime will be reduced, thus satisfying the need?
- How might she visualize what it will be like with harsher sentences for all youth crimes; that is, if the need is satisfied?
- Bette wants to ask her audience to support harsher sentences for all youth crimes in a straw poll to be conducted next week. How might she phrase her action step?

◆ **Gender Expectations**. Papi is running for president of the local chapter of a construction workers' union. Papi is one of only five women in this entire local of more than 1,000 members, and she is the only woman running for this office. Papi wonders if she should mention the issue of gender in her speech announcing her intention to run. What would you advise Papi to do?

◆ **S–A–T Connection**. Kit, a former software engineer, is giving an informative speech on the way metasearch engines work. If the audience were your public speaking class, how might she establish a speaker–audience–topic connection?

◆ **Running Overtime**. Alice's speeches invariably run overtime. What would you advise Alice to do—aside from planning for the allotted time restrictions—if she gets a 30-second stop signal? Should she go directly to her conclusion? Should she apologize for going overtime and ask permission to continue? Should she just continue her speech?

Log*On!* MySpeechLab

Organizing Your Speech

A variety of template outlines for different types of speeches are available at MySpeechLab (www .myspeechlab.com), as is an exercise on organizing a scrambled outline. You'll also find it useful to view one or more of the video speeches and consider how these speakers organized their speeches and what you might do differently. Take a look especially at the speeches "Our Immigration Story" and the critique, Green Slime Tastes Good, which illustrates how to tie your conclusion to the introduction, and Tissue Engineering, which illustrates how to secure and maintain audience attention. Also look at the Explore activities on organization, transitions, developing key ideas, and Microsoft's outlining tool.

The Allyn & Bacon public speaking website (www.ablongman.com/pubspeak) provides a variety of aids for organizing your speech, choosing an organizational pattern, and preparing introductions and conclusions.

8 Wording Your Speech

Why Read This Chapter?

Because it will enable you to word your speech for greatest effectiveness by helping you to

- select words that will communicate your thoughts clearly, vividly, appropriately, and in a personal style

- phrase your sentences so that they are clear and memorable

When I read great literature, great drama, speeches, or sermons, I feel that the human mind has not achieved anything greater than the ability to share feelings and thoughts through language.

—James Earl Jones
American stage, film, and television actor and lecturer

Your success as a public speaker depends heavily on the way you express your ideas: on the words you select and the way you phrase your sentences. This chapter will focus on this crucial process of wording your speech, first explaining how language works and then suggesting ways to word and phrase your ideas for maximum impact and effectiveness.

How Language Works

Your use of language will greatly influence your ability to inform and persuade an audience. Five qualities of language are especially important: directness, abstraction, objectivity, orality, and accuracy.

In connection with this section, visit some of the online grammar guides to clarify anything about which you may not be sure. Among the many excellent sites are the grammar guides of Johns Hopkins University (www.welch.jhu.edu/publish/guides/html), California State University (www.calstatela.edu/library/styleman.html), and Colorado State University (http://writing.colostate.edu/references).

Language Varies in Directness

Consider the following sentences:

1A. We should all vote for Halliwell in the next election.

1B. Vote for Halliwell in the next election.

2A. It should be apparent that we should abandon the present system.

2B. Abandon the present system.

3A. Many people would like to go to Xanadu.

3B. How many of you want to go to Xanadu?

The B-sentences are clearly more direct than the A-sentences. Note, for example, that the B-sentences address the audience directly. The A-sentences are more distant, more indirect. Indirect sentences address only an abstract, unidentified mass of people. The sentences might as well address just anyone. In contrast, when you use direct sentences, you address your specific and clearly defined listeners.

Direct language, in sum, is explicit and forthright. To achieve **directness**, use active rather than passive sentences; say, "The professor invented the serum" rather than "The serum was invented by the professor." Use personal pronouns and personal references. Refer to your audience as "you" rather than "the audience" or "my listeners."

The preference for directness will vary considerably with the culture of the speaker and the audience. Many Asian and Latin American cultures, for example, stress the values of indirectness, largely because indirectness enables a person to avoid appearing criticized or contradicted and thereby losing face. In most of the United States, however, you're taught that directness is the preferred style. "Be up-front" and "tell it like it is" are commonly heard communication guidelines. Many Asian Americans and Latin Americans may, in fact, experience a conflict between the recommendation of style manuals to be direct and the cultural recommendation to be indirect.

LANGUAGE VARIES IN ABSTRACTION

Consider the following list of terms:

- entertainment
- film
- American film
- recent American film
- *Harry Potter and the Order of the Phoenix*

At the top is the general or abstract term *entertainment*. Note that *entertainment* includes all the other items on the list plus various other items—television, novels, drama, comics, and so on. *Film* is more specific and concrete. It includes all of the items below it as well as various other items, such as Indian film or Russian film. The term excludes, however, all entertainment that is not film. *American film* is again more specific than *film* and excludes all films that are not American. *Recent American film* further limits *American film* to a time period. *Harry Potter and the Order of the Phoenix* specifies concretely the one item to which reference is made.

Choose words from a wide range of levels of **abstraction**. At times a general term may suit your needs best; at other times a more concrete, specific term may serve better. Generally, the specific term is the better choice.

The more general term—in this case, *entertainment*—conjures up numerous different images. One person in the audience may focus on television, another on music, another on comic books, and still another on radio. To some, *film* may bring to mind the early silent films. To others, it brings to mind postwar Italian films. To still others, it recalls Disney's animated cartoons. So as you get more specific and less abstract, you more effectively guide the images that come to your listeners' minds. Specific rather than abstract language will aid you in both your informative and persuasive goals.

LANGUAGE VARIES IN OBJECTIVITY

The best way to explain how language varies in **objectivity**—in the degree to which it is factual and unemotional—is to introduce two new terms: **denotation** and **connotation**. The *denotative meaning* of a term is its objective meaning. This is the meaning that you'd find in a dictionary. This meaning points to specific references. Thus, the denotation of the word *book* is, for example, the actual book, a collection of pages bound together between two covers. The denotative meaning of *dog* is a four-legged canine; the denotative meaning of *kiss* is, according to the *Random House Dictionary*, "to touch or press with the lips slightly pursed in token of greeting, affection, reverence, etc."

Connotative meaning, however, is different. The connotative meaning is your affective, or emotional, meaning for the term. The word *book* may signify boredom or excitement. It may recall the novel you have to read or perhaps this textbook that you're reading right now. Connotatively, *dog* may mean friendliness, warmth, and affection. *Kiss* may, connotatively, mean warmth, good feeling, and happiness.

Seldom do listeners misunderstand the denotative meaning of a term. When you use a term with which the audience isn't familiar, you define it and thus make sure that the term is understood. Differences in connotative meanings, however, pose difficulties. For example, you may, use the term *neighbor*, intending to communicate security and friendliness. To some of your listeners, however, the term may connote unwanted intrusions, sneakiness, and nosiness. Notice that both you and your listeners would surely agree that denotatively *neighbor* means a person who lives near another person. What you and they disagree on—and what then leads to misunderstanding—is the connotation of the term.

Cultural differences add to the complexity and difficulty of accurately communicating meaning. The word *dog* will obviously mean one thing to a person from the United States, where *dog* signifies a "beloved pet," and quite another thing to a person from a culture where *dog* signifies "eating delicacy." *Beef* to a person from Kansas or Texas (where cattle provide much of the state's wealth) will mean something very different than *beef* does to a person from India (where the cow is a sacred animal).

As a speaker, consider the audience's evaluation of key terms before using them in your speech. When you're part of the audience, as in a public speaking class, you probably have a good idea of the meanings members have for various terms. When you address an audience very different from yourself, however, this prior investigation becomes crucial.

LANGUAGE VARIES IN ORALITY

Orality refers to the degree to which a communication style resembles that of informal conversation as opposed to the more formal style of writing. You don't speak as you write. The words and sentences you use differ. The major reason for this difference is that you compose speech instantly. You select your words and construct your sentences as you think of your ideas. There's very little time in between the thought and the utterance. When you write, however, you compose your thoughts after considerable reflection. Even then you probably often rewrite and edit as you go along. Because of this, written language has a more formal tone. Spoken language is more informal, more colloquial.

Generally, spoken language, or **oral style**, uses shorter, simpler, and more familiar words than does written language. Also, there's more qualification in speech than in writing. For example, when speaking you probably make greater use of such expressions as *although, however, perhaps,* and the like. When writing, you probably edit these out.

Spoken language has a greater number of self-reference terms (terms that refer to the speaker herself or himself): *I, me, our, us,* and *you.* Spoken language also has a greater number of "allness" terms such as *all, none, every, always, never.* When you write, you're probably more careful to edit out such allness terms, realizing that such terms are usually not very descriptive of reality.

Spoken language has more pseudo-quantifying terms (for example, *many, much, very, lots*) and terms that include the speaker as part of the observation (for example, "it seems to me that . . ." or "as I see it . . ."). Further, speech contains more verbs and adverbs; writing contains more nouns and adjectives.

Oral style and written language *should* differ. The main reason why spoken and written language should differ is that the listener hears a speech only once; therefore, speech must be *instantly intelligible*. The reader can reread an essay or look up an unfamiliar word; the reader can spend as much time as he or she wishes with the written page. The listener, however, must move at the pace set by the speaker. The reader may reread a sentence or paragraph if there's a temporary attention lapse; the listener doesn't have this option.

Research Link

THE WEB

In most cases, searching the World Wide Web efficiently requires the use of search engines and subject directories, plus some knowledge of how these tools operate. A *search engine* is a program that searches a database or index of Internet sites for the specific words you submit. Search engines search an enormous number of websites; they do not distinguish between reliable and unreliable information. A high school student's term paper may well be listed next to that of a world-famous scientist with no distinction between them. These search engines are easily accessed through your Internet browser, and both Netscape and Internet Explorer have search functions as a part of their own home pages; they also provide convenient links to the most popular search engines.

Some search engines are *meta–search engines*; these search the databases of a variety of search engines at the same time. These programs are especially useful if you want a broad search and you have the time to sift through lots of websites. Some of the more popular meta-search engines include Ask Jeeves at www.ask.com, Google at www.google.com, Dog Pile at www.dogpile.com, and Vivisimo at www.vivisimo.com. Other useful search engines (some of which also contain directories) include Yahoo! (www.yahoo.com), AltaVista (www.altavista.com), and Go (www.go.com).

In using search engines (and in searching many CD-ROM databases), you'll find it helpful to limit your search with *operators*—words and symbols that define relationships among the terms for which you're searching. Perhaps the most common are AND (or +), OR, NOT (or –), and quotation marks. Searching for *drugs AND violence* will limit your search to only those documents that contain both words—in any order. Searching for *drugs OR violence* will expand your search to all documents containing either word. And searching for *violence AND schools NOT elementary* will yield documents containing both *violence* and *schools* except those that contain the word *elementary*. Quotation marks around the phrase will yield only those sources that use the exact phrase; so, if you search for "drugs in New York City" it will identify only sources in which that exact phrase appears. Be careful when using quotes; if you searched with only the example just given, you'd miss articles that do not use the exact phrase but which still deal with the topic you're researching.

Another way to limit your topic and refine your search is to use a search engine that limits its search to only certain types of websites. For example, if you want to search for publications of the U.S. government, it will prove more efficient to search with Google's government search (www.usgov.google.com). With this search you'll retrieve only those websites that have a .gov domain, as already illustrated in the Research Link in Chapter 7 (The Government). If you want to search for blogs you can use Google's blog search (www.blogsearch.google.com).

You can also search the net by setting up alerts. For example, you can go to Google Alerts (www.google.com/alerts) and enter your speech topic and the kind of search you want (whether news, Web, news and Web, or groups) and how often you want to receive them (daily, weekly, or as-it-happens). You'll then receive in your e-mail "Google Alerts" with hot links to sites that include your speech topic. Yahoo offers a similar service (http://alerts.yahoo.com).

A *directory* is a list of subjects or categories of Web links. You select the category you're most interested in, then a subcategory of that, then a subcategory of that until you reach your specific topic. A directory doesn't cover everything; rather, the documents that it groups under its various categories are selected by the directory's staff members from those they deem to be especially worthwhile. Many search engines also provide directories, so you can use the method you prefer.

Learn about the search engines and directories that will help you find the information you need, and learn how to use them efficiently. Most search engines and directories work similarly, so you should be able to use essentially the same strategies with one that you use with another. However, each search engine and directory uses a somewhat different database; if you don't find what you want with one search engine or directory, try another.

The next Research Link, "E-mail, Newsgroups, Chat Groups, and Blogs," appears on page 207.

LANGUAGE VARIES IN ACCURACY

Language can reflect reality faithfully or unfaithfully. It can describe reality (as science tells us it exists) with great accuracy or with serious distortion. For example, we can use language to describe the many degrees that exist in, say, wealth, or we can describe wealth inaccurately in terms of two values, rich and poor. We can discuss these ways in which the accuracy of language may vary in terms of the five thinking errors central to the area of language study known as General Semantics (DeVito, 1974; Hayakawa & Hayakawa, 1990; Korzybski, 1933), now so much a part of critical thinking instruction (Johnson, 1991). These five errors are polarization, fact–inference confusion, allness, static evaluation, and indiscrimination.

Polarization

The term **polarization** refers to the tendency to look at the world in terms of opposites and to describe it in terms of extremes—good or bad, positive or negative, healthy or sick, intelligent or stupid, rich or poor, and so on. Polarization is often referred to as the "fallacy of either/or." So destructive is either/or thinking that the American Psychiatric Association identifies it as one of the major behavior characteristics of "borderline personality disorder"—a psychological disorder that lies between neurosis and psychosis and is characterized by unstable interpersonal relationships and confusion about identity.

Most people, events, and objects, of course, exist somewhere between the extremes of good and bad, health and sickness, intelligence and stupidity, wealth and poverty. Yet among all of us there's a strong tendency to view only the extremes and to categorize people, objects, and events in terms of these polar opposites.

Problems arise when polarization is used in inappropriate situations; for example, "The politician is either for us or against us." Note that these two options don't include all possibilities. The politician may be for us in some things and against us in other things, or may be neutral. Beware of speakers who imply and believe that two extreme classes include all possible classes—for example, that an individual must be pro–rebel forces or anti–rebel forces, with no other alternatives.

Fact–Inference Confusion

Before reading about facts and inferences, take the following self-test.

*T*EST YOURSELF

Can You Distinguish Facts from Inferences?

Carefully read the following report and the observations based on it. Indicate whether you think the observations are true, false, or doubtful on the basis of the information presented in the report. Write T if the observation is definitely true, F if the observation is definitely false, and ? if the observation may be either true or false. Judge each observation in order. Don't reread the observations after you've indicated your judgment, and don't change any of your answers.

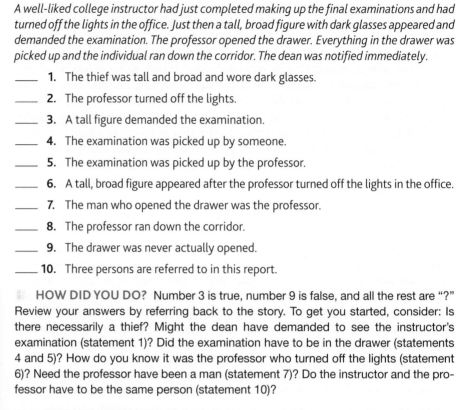

A well-liked college instructor had just completed making up the final examinations and had turned off the lights in the office. Just then a tall, broad figure with dark glasses appeared and demanded the examination. The professor opened the drawer. Everything in the drawer was picked up and the individual ran down the corridor. The dean was notified immediately.

_____ **1.** The thief was tall and broad and wore dark glasses.

_____ **2.** The professor turned off the lights.

_____ **3.** A tall figure demanded the examination.

_____ **4.** The examination was picked up by someone.

_____ **5.** The examination was picked up by the professor.

_____ **6.** A tall, broad figure appeared after the professor turned off the lights in the office.

_____ **7.** The man who opened the drawer was the professor.

_____ **8.** The professor ran down the corridor.

_____ **9.** The drawer was never actually opened.

_____ **10.** Three persons are referred to in this report.

HOW DID YOU DO? Number 3 is true, number 9 is false, and all the rest are "?" Review your answers by referring back to the story. To get you started, consider: Is there necessarily a thief? Might the dean have demanded to see the instructor's examination (statement 1)? Did the examination have to be in the drawer (statements 4 and 5)? How do you know it was the professor who turned off the lights (statement 6)? Need the professor have been a man (statement 7)? Do the instructor and the professor have to be the same person (statement 10)?

WHAT WILL YOU DO? There is, of course, nothing wrong with making inferences. When you hear inferential statements, however, treat them as inferences and not as facts. Be mindful of the possibility that such statements may prove to be wrong. As you read this next section, try to formulate specific guidelines that will help you distinguish facts from inferences.

In form or structure, facts and inferences are similar and can't be distinguished by any grammatical analysis. For example, you can say, "This proposal contains 17 pages" as well as "This proposal contains the seeds of its own self-destruction." Both sentences look similar in form, yet they're very different types of statements. You can observe the 17 pages, but how do you observe "the seeds of its own self-destruction"? Obviously, this isn't a descriptive but an inferential statement, a statement you make on the basis not only of what you observe, but on what you conclude.

In evaluating research, in presenting your information and arguments, and in listening to the speeches of others, beware of **fact–inference confusion**; be sure to distinguish between what is factual from what is inferential. Of course, there's nothing wrong with making inferences; the problem arises when you assume that an inference is a fact and treat it and behave as if it were a fact.

Allness

Because the world is infinitely complex, we can never know all or say all about anything—at least we can't logically say all about anything. Beware of speakers who fall into the error of **allness**—who present information as if it's all that there is or as if it's all you need to know to make up your mind, as in *There's only one way to save social security. Never let financial considerations get in the way of romance. Always be polite.*

Disraeli's observation, "to be conscious that you are ignorant is a great step toward knowledge," is an excellent example of a nonallness attitude. If, as a critical listener, you recognize that there's more to learn, more to see, and more to hear, you'll treat what the speaker says as part of the total picture, not the whole, or the final word.

Static Evaluation

Often when you form an abstraction of something or someone—when you formulate a verbal statement about an event or person—that statement remains static and unchanging. But, the object or person to whom it refers has changed. Everything is in a constant state of change.

To avoid the error of **static evaluation**, respond to the statements of speakers as if they contained a tag that identified the time frame to which they refer. Visualize each such statement as containing a date. Look at that date and ask yourself if the statement is still true today. Thus, when a speaker says that 10 percent of the population now lives at or below the poverty level, ask yourself about the date to which that statement applies. When were the statistics compiled? Does the poverty level determined at that time adequately reflect current conditions?

Indiscrimination

Nature seems to abhor sameness at least as much as vacuums. Nowhere in the universe can you find two things that are identical. Everything is unique. Language, however, provides you with common nouns (such as *teacher, student, friend, enemy, war, politician,* and *liberal*) that lead you to focus on similarities. Such nouns lead you to group all teachers together, all students together, all politicians together. These words divert attention away from the uniqueness of each individual, each object, and each event. **Indiscrimination**, then, is a thinking error that occurs when you focus on classes of individuals, objects, or events rather than on the unique individual, object, or event.

Of course, there's nothing wrong with classifying. No one would argue that classifying is unhealthy or immoral. On the contrary, it's an extremely useful method of dealing with any complex matter. Classifying helps us to deal with complexity. It puts order into our thinking. The problem arises from applying some evaluative label to that class, and then using that label as an "adequate" map for each individual in the group. Put differently, indiscrimination is a denial of uniqueness.

Beware, therefore, of speakers who group large numbers of unique individuals under the same label. Beware of speakers who tell you that "Democrats are . . .," that "Catholics believe . . . ." that "Mexicans will . . ." Ask yourself, which Democrats, how many Catholics, which Mexicans, and so on.

Fallacies of Language

Perhaps the clearest example of language inaccuracy is seen in the various **fallacies of language**, types of words that mislead listeners or hamper their ability to understand: weasel words, euphemisms, and jargon.

Consider Consider the language and style of the typical college textbook, including this one. How would you describe it in terms of directness, abstraction, objectivity, orality, and accuracy? How would you compare or contrast it with the language of the novel or short story?

Weasel words are words whose meanings are slippery and difficult to pin down (Pei, 1956; Hayakawa & Hayakawa, 1990). For example, a commercial claiming that Medicine M works "better than Brand X" doesn't specify how much better or in what respect Medicine M performs better. It's quite possible that it performs better in one respect but less effectively according to nine other measures. Other weasel words are "help," "virtually," "as much as," "like" (as in "it will make you feel like new"), and "more economical." Ask yourself, Exactly what is being claimed? For example, "What does 'may reduce cholesterol' mean? What exactly is being asserted?"

Euphemisms make the negative and unpleasant appear positive and appealing, as when a company calls the firing of 200 workers "downsizing" or "reallocation of resources." Justin Timberlake's reference to the highly publicized act with Janet Jackson during the 2004 Super Bowl as a "wardrobe malfunction" is another good example. Often euphemisms take the form of inflated language designed to make the mundane seem extraordinary, the common seem exotic ("the vacation of a lifetime," "unsurpassed vistas"). When things sound too good to be true, they probably are.

Jargon, the specialized language of a particular group or profession (for example, the lingo of the computer hacker), becomes doublespeak when used with people who aren't members of the group and who don't know this specialized language. Jargon often intimidates, and that's one reason it's often used to confuse others and to put them in disadvantaged positions.

Now that the general principles of language and style are understood, let's turn to some specific suggestions for improving your speech style, your words, and your sentences.

CHOOSING WORDS

Choose carefully the words you use in your public speeches. Choose words to achieve clarity, vividness, appropriateness, and a personal style.

CLARITY

Clarity in speaking style should be your primary goal. Here are some guidelines to help you make your speech clear.

Be Economical

Don't waste words. Two of the most important ways to achieve economy are to avoid redundancies and to avoid meaningless words. Notice the redundancies in the following expressions:

at 9 a.m. *in the morning*

we *first* began the discussion

the full *and complete* report

I *myself personally*

blue *in color*

*over*exaggerate

you, *members of the audience*

clearly unambiguous

approximately 10 inches *or so*

cash *money*

By withholding the italicized terms you eliminate unnecessary words. You thus move closer to a more economical and clearer style.

Use Specific Terms and Numbers

Picture these items:

- bracelet
- gold bracelet
- gold bracelet with a diamond clasp
- braided gold bracelet with a diamond clasp

Notice that as we get more and more specific, we get a clearer and more detailed picture. Be specific. Don't say *dog* when you want your listeners to picture a St. Bernard. Don't say *car* when you want them to picture a limousine. Don't say *television program* when you want them to think of *Lost*.

The same is true of numbers. Don't say "earned a good salary" if you mean "earned $90,000 a year." Don't say "taxes will go up" when you mean "taxes will increase 22 percent." Don't say "the defense budget was enormous" when you mean "the defense budget was $100 billion."

A Case of Ethics   QUALIFYING EVIDENCE

You're giving a speech on homelessness, and you want your listeners to contribute to the new homeless shelter that your community is building. In your research you discover (1) that the most recent statistics on the number of homeless people in your community are about 20 years old and (2) that although many community leaders are in favor of building this halfway house, a sizable number object. So you wonder: (1) Do you have to give the date the statistics were collected? (2) Can you say simply that community leaders favor the halfway house, without going into the fact that some don't favor it?

Ethical Choice Point *What would you do? More generally, what ethical obligations does a speaker have for qualifying evidence presented in a speech?*

Use Guide Phrases

Listening to a public speech is difficult work. Assist your listeners by using **guide phrases** to help them see that you're moving from one idea to another. Use phrases such as "now that we have seen how . . ., let us consider how . . ." and "my next argument . . . ." Terms such as *first, second, and also, although,* and *however* will help your audience follow your line of thinking.

Guide phrases are especially useful when your listeners aren't native speakers of the language you're speaking. And, of course, guide phrases will also prove valuable if you're speaking in a language that you have not fully mastered. The guide phrases will help compensate for the lack of language and speech similarity between speaker and audience.

Use Short, Familiar Terms

Generally, favor the short word over the long one. Favor the familiar word over the unfamiliar word. Favor the more commonly used term over the rarely used term. Say *harmless* rather than *innocuous, clarify* rather than *elucidate, use* rather than *utilize, find out* rather than *ascertain.*

Use Repetition and Restatement

Repetition and restatement will help listeners follow what you're saying and will make your speech clearer and more easily understood. These are not the same as redundancy, which involves using unnecessary words that don't communicate any information. **Repetition** means repeating something in exactly the same way, usually at different points in your speech. This will help your listeners better remember the idea and remind them of how it's connected with what you're now saying. **Restatement** means rephrasing an idea or statement in different words. This is especially helpful when the idea is new or even moderately complex. Expressing the same idea in two different ways helps clarify the concept.

Another type of restatement is the internal summary. Internal summaries—periodic summary statements or reviews of subsections of your speech—help listeners appreciate the speech as a progression of ideas and show them how one idea leads to another. Be careful not to overuse these techniques, however; you don't want to bore the audience by repeating material that doesn't need to be repeated.

Avoid Clichés

Clichés are phrases that have lost their novelty and part of their meaning through overuse. Avoid all clichés, which call attention to themselves because of their overuse. A few examples: "Tell it like it is," "free as a bird," "in the pink," "no sooner said than done," "tried and true," "for all intents and purposes," "it goes without saying," "few and far between," "no news is good news," and "mind over matter."

Distinguish Between Commonly Confused Words

Many words, because they sound alike or are used in similar situations, are commonly confused. Try the accompanying self-test; it covers 10 of the most frequently confused words.

TEST YOURSELF

Can You Distinguish Commonly Confused Words?

Underline the word in parentheses that you would use in each sentence.

_____ **1.** She (accepted, excepted) the award and thanked everyone (accept, except) the producer.

_____ **2.** The teacher (affected, effected) his students greatly and will now (affect, effect) a complete curriculum overhaul.

_____ **3.** Are you deciding (between, among) red and green or (between, among) red, green, and blue?

_____ **4.** I (can, may) scale the mountain but I (can, may) not reveal its hidden path.

_____ **5.** The table was (cheap, inexpensive) but has great style; the chairs cost a fortune but look (cheap, inexpensive).

_____ **6.** The professor (discovered, invented) uncharted lands and (discovered, invented) computer programs.

_____ **7.** He was (explicit, implicit) in his detailed description of the crime but made only (explicit, implicit) observations concerning the perpetrator.

_____ **8.** She was evasive and only (implied, inferred) that she'd seek a divorce. You can easily (imply, infer) her reasons.

_____ **9.** The wedding was (tasteful, tasty) and the food most (tasteful, tasty).

_____ **10.** The student seemed (disinterested, uninterested) in the test; in assigning grades the teacher was always (disinterested, uninterested).

HOW DID YOU DO? Here are the principles that govern correct usage. (1) Use _accept_ to mean "to receive" and _except_ to mean "with the exclusion of." (2) Use _to affect_ to mean "to have an effect or to influence," and _to effect_ to mean "to produce a result." (3) Use _between_ when referring to two items and _among_ when referring to more than two items. (4) Use _can_ to refer to ability and _may_ to refer to permission. (5) Use _cheap_ to refer to something that is inferior and _inexpensive_ to describe something that costs little. (6) Use _discover_ to refer to the act of finding something out or to learn something previously unknown, and use _invent_ to refer to the act of originating something new. (7) Use _explicit_ to mean "specific" and _implicit_ to describe something that's indicated but not openly stated. (8) Use _to imply_ to mean "to state indirectly" and to _infer_ "to mean to draw a conclusion." (9) Use _tasteful_ to refer to good taste and _tasty_ to refer to something that tastes good. (10) Use _uninterested_ to refer to a lack of interest, and use _disinterested_ to mean "objective or unbiased."

WHAT WILL YOU DO? Your use of language can greatly impact your persuasiveness. A word used incorrectly can lessen your credibility and general persuasiveness. Review your English handbook and identify other commonly confused words. Get into the habit of referring to a good dictionary whenever you have doubts about which word is preferred.

Carefully Assess Idioms

Idioms are expressions that are unique to a specific language. Perhaps the most interesting thing about idioms is that you can't deduce the meaning of an idiom from the individual words. You know the meaning of an idiom the way you know the meaning of a word. So, for example, you cannot gather the meaning of "kick the bucket" or "doesn't have a leg to stand on" from analyzing the individual words. Once you learn that "kick the bucket" means "die," the connection seems logical enough; but it's not a connection that you would have thought of merely by looking at the words. Similarly, once you learn that "he doesn't have a leg to stand on" means "he doesn't have a reasonable argument" or "he doesn't have an adequate defense," you can appreciate the idea behind the idiom—that is, that a position lacking reasonable arguments will collapse much as would a table (or a person) without legs.

The positive side of idioms is that they give your speech a casual and informal style; they make your speech sound like a speech and not like a written essay. The negative side of idioms is that they create problems for listeners who are not native speakers of your language. Many will simply not understand the meaning of your idioms. This problem is important, both because audiences are becoming increasingly intercultural and because the number of idioms we use is extremely high. If you're not convinced of this, read through any of the speeches in this text, especially in an intercultural group, and underline all idioms. You will no doubt find that you underline a great deal more than most people would have suspected.

Whether or not you speak English as a second language, you can learn a great deal about idioms from the websites devoted to ESL (for example, www.manythings.org/ or http://a4esl.org/). As you go through some of these websites consider what could supplement this chapter's discussions.

VIVIDNESS

Select words to make your ideas vivid and come alive in the minds of your listeners (Frey & Eagly, 1993; Meade, 2000).

Use Active Verbs

Favor verbs that communicate activity rather than passivity. The verb *to be*, in all its forms—*is, are, was, were, will be*—is relatively inactive. Try using verbs of action instead. Rather than saying, "The teacher was in the middle of the crowd," say, "The teacher stood in the middle of the crowd." Instead of saying, "The report was on the president's desk for three days," try, "The report sat (or slept) on the president's desk for three days." Instead of saying, "Management will be here tomorrow," consider "Management will descend on us tomorrow" or "Management jets in tomorrow."

Use Strong Verbs

The verb is the strongest part of your sentence. Instead of saying "He walked through the forest," consider such terms as *wandered, prowled, rambled*, or *roamed*. Consider whether one of these might not better suit your intended meaning. Consult a thesaurus for any verb you suspect might be weak. A good guide to identifying weak verbs is to look at your use of adverbs. If you use lots of adverbs, you may be using them to strengthen weak verbs. Consider cutting

Consider Consider the language of political speeches. What stylistic suggestions would you offer a political candidate giving a campaign speech to your public speaking class?

out the adverbs and substituting stronger verbs. Instead of *walked quickly* consider *ran, sped,* or *flew*; instead of *spoke softly* consider *whispered* or *murmured*.

Use Figures of Speech

Figures of speech are stylistic devices that have been a part of rhetoric since ancient times. Figures of speech help achieve vividness, in addition to making your speech more memorable and giving it a polished, well-crafted sound (Borchardt, 2006). But be careful not to overdo the use of figures of speech. If you do, your speech is likely to sound overly prepared and not as spontaneous as it should. With this caveat, here are some figures that you may wish to incorporate into your public speeches.

- **Alliteration**: the repetition of the same initial sound in two or more words as in "fifty famous flavors" or "the cool, calculating leader" or "the characteristics of credibility are competence, character, and charisma."

- **Hyperbole**: the use of extreme exaggeration, as in "He cried like a faucet" or "I'm so hungry I could eat a whale."

- **Irony**: the use of a word or sentence whose literal meaning is the opposite of that which is intended; for example, a teacher handing back failing examinations might say, "So pleased to see how hard you all studied."

- **Metaphor**: an implied comparison between two unlike things, as in "She's a lion when she wakes up" or "He's a real bulldozer" or as Shakespeare said in Hamlet, "I will speak daggers but use none." References to the legs of a table, the mouth of a river, and the arms of destiny also are metaphors, though we seldom think of them as such.

- **Simile**: like metaphor, compares two unlike objects but uses the words *like* or *as*; for example, "The manager is as gentle as a lamb," "Pat went through the problems like a high-speed drill," "Chris always acts like a weasel."

- **Synecdoche**: using a part of an object to stand for the whole object, as in "all hands were on deck," in which hands stands for "sailors" or "crew members"; or "green thumb" for "expert gardener."

- **Metonymy:** the substitution of a name for a title with which it's closely associated, as in "City Hall issued the following news release," in which City Hall stands for "the mayor" or "the city council."

- **Antithesis:** the presentation of contrary or polar opposite ideas in parallel form, as in "My loves are many, my enemies are few" or in Charles Dickens's opening to *A Tale of Two Cities*: "It was the best of times, it was the worst of times," or John F. Kennedy's "Ask not what your country can do for you; ask what you can do for your country."

- **Personification:** the attribution of human characteristics to inanimate objects—"This room cries out for activity" or "My car is tired."

- **Rhetorical questions:** questions that are used to make a statement or to produce a desired effect rather than secure an answer—"Do you want to be popular?" "Do you want to get well?"

- **Oxymoron:** a term that combines two normally opposite qualities: bittersweet, the silent roar, poverty-stricken millionaires, the ignorant genius, a war for peace or a peaceful war.

Use Imagery

Appeal to the senses through visual, auditory, and tactile **imagery**. Make us see, hear, and feel what you're talking about.

Visual Imagery. In describing people or objects, create images your listeners can see. When appropriate, describe such visual qualities as height, weight, color, size, shape, length, and contour. Let your audience see the sweat pouring down the faces of the coal miners; let them see the short, overweight executive in a pinstriped suit smoking a cigar. Here Stephanie Kaplan (Reynolds & Schnoor, 1991), a student from the University of Wisconsin, uses visual imagery to describe the AIDS Quilt:

> The Names Project is quite simply a quilt. It's larger than 10 football fields, and composed of over 9,000 unique 3-feet-by-6-feet panels each bearing a name of an individual who has died of AIDS. The panels have been made in homes across the country by the friends, lovers, and families of AIDS victims.

Auditory Imagery. Appeal to our sense of hearing by using terms that describe sounds. Let your listeners hear the car screeching, the wind whistling, the bells chiming, the angry professor roaring.

Tactile Imagery. Use terms referring to temperature, texture, and touch to create tactile imagery. Let your listeners feel the cool water running over their bodies and the punch of the fighter; let them feel the smooth skin of the newborn baby.

APPROPRIATENESS

Use language that is appropriate to you as the speaker. Also, use language that is appropriate to your audience, the occasion, and the speech topic. Here are some general guidelines to help you achieve this quality.

AN INFORMATIVE SPEECH

Public Speaking   *Sample Assistant*

This is an excellent informative speech, given by University of Texas at Austin student, Jillian Collum.

Speech Text

When Bangladesh achieved its independence in 1971, Vanderbilt University doctoral student Muhammad Yunus decided that it was time to go home. He soon found himself at Chittagong University, teaching complex economic theories involving the transfer of billions of dollars. However, as Yunus explained to Whole Foods Market team members in a March 2006 address, he couldn't help but notice the intense poverty that existed right outside the university's walls. So, Yunus decided to do something about it and in 1976, he struck his first blow in the battle against poverty, lending 42 people a combined total of $27.

The recipients used their loans so effectively that Yunus decided to start his own bank, called Grameen, which would give small loans to poor families for income-generating activities, such as buying a cow to sell its milk. Bahrain's *Gulf Daily News* of February 5, 2007 reports that 58% of the bank's borrowers have used their loans to rise out of poverty, a success rate so astonishing that it allowed Grameen to launch a global revolution.

The New York Times of October 14, 2006 asserts that microcredit, or the concept of giving small loans to individuals so that they can work to lift themselves out of poverty, now helps over 100 million of the world's most destitute people in more than 130 countries. And even the Nobel committee was impressed. In an October 13, 2006 press release, the committee awarded Muhammad Yunus the 2006 Nobel Peace Prize, noting that microcredit is an essential and powerful instrument in the worldwide fight against poverty. Because *The Toronto Star* of December 8, 2006, reveals that microcredit leaders plan to use the technique to help half a billion people rise out of poverty by the year 2015, we must examine how this macro-revolution in microcredit is changing the world.

Comments and Questions

Using a specific story is a good way to gain attention; we all seem interested in personal stories, especially when they're dramatic like this one.

Did the story gain your attention? In what other ways might the speaker have gained attention?

The speaker makes the point that a large group used the money (58%) to rise out of poverty. In what other ways might you have illustrated the fact that such a large group used the money to rise from poverty.

Here the speaker establishes the importance of the topic. Did it convince you that the topic and what the speaker was about to cover was worth your effort to listen? What specifically convinced you?

To do so, we will first explore the development of microcredit; next, discuss its rationale; and finally, look at the implications of this approach that is transforming lives a few dollars at a time.

MacLean's of November 27, 2006 states that two-thirds of the world's population is too poor to secure funds from traditional banks, which fear that they won't repay loans. Muhammad Yunus set out to prove that this view of the poor was completely wrong. In his previously cited speech, Yunus explains that Grameen looks at what a conventional bank does, and then does the opposite. Instead of rich customers, the bank seeks poor ones. Instead of big loans, it gives small ones. And instead of men, the bank more often chooses to loan to women, believing that money given to women is more likely to directly benefit families. According to *The International Herald Tribune* of October 14, 2006, today Grameen serves 6.6 million poor people in Bangladesh and enjoys a 98.5% repayment rate, almost twice as high as the average rate for traditional Bengali banks. Borrowers use their loans for income-generating activities, such as operating a small food stand or selling handmade crafts. And most astonishingly, *BusinessWeek* of November 27, 2006 notes that Grameen has reached this level of success even though it hasn't accepted any donations since 1995. Grameen remains self-sustaining much the same way traditional banks do—by taking in deposits and issuing loans.

While Muhammad Yunus's initial $27 loan to 42 Bengalis didn't amount to much, the microcredit revolution that this small act launched has changed the lives of millions. To better understand the rationale for this phenomenon, we'll discuss microcredit's driving principles and why the technique is so necessary.

Canada's *Hamilton Spectator* of November 13, 2006 reports that there are now more than 3,100 microcredit institutions worldwide. These groups provide average loans of $150, and more than 97% of the money they lend out is repaid. According to *The Arizona Daily Star* of November 3, 2006 this high repayment rate can be attributed to the group loan principle, in which five people from the community serve as each other's guarantors. Individual borrowers must repay their loans, or the entire group becomes ineligible for more funding. This provides a powerful incentive for individuals to pay on time and help each other

In this third part of the introduction the speaker provides an orientation to what will follow in the rest of the speech. You know from this that there will be three main parts of the speech: the development of microcredit, its rationale, and its implications.

Here the speaker explains her first main point: the development of microcredit. This gives those in the audience who didn't know much about this approach to loans and lending, a much better idea of what microcredit is and how it operates.

Throughout this speech the speaker uses a wide variety of sources. What source material do you find especially helpful? What types of source material would you have liked to see included here?

Here the speaker provides a transition from the first to the second main point. As a listener, you now know that you'll hear the rationale for microcredit and specifically that you'll hear about it in two parts: its principles and the reason this approach is so necessary.

You've been prepared to hear about the principles of microcredit. After reading this section on the principles, can you now identify the specific principles discussed by the speaker. If you can, what did the speaker do to help you remember them? If you can't, what might the speaker have done to ensure that you remember the principles?

Choosing Words **199**

meet their obligations. But the true genius of microcredit is that loans are given for income-generating activities that improve the lives of every member of the family. For example, *The Atlanta Journal-Constitution* of November 13, 2006 tells the story of Susan Wangui from Kenya. Abandoned by her parents and her husband after she contracted HIV, Wangui was forced to work as a prostitute to support her two children. But with a series of loans from a local microcredit institution, Wangui was able to start a clothes-mending business, a venture that has been profitable enough to allow her to move her children out of a slum and into a house with a floor and running water.

This section also provides a good example of explaining a concept in terms of abstract and general statements (for example, that 97% of the money is repaid) and then following these with specifics (for example, the story of Susan Wangui). This is almost always a useful technique for helping listeners see the issue as a generalization and as uniquely personal as well.

Microcredit is necessary because for many of its recipients, no reasonable alternatives exist. For example, *The New Yorker* of October 30, 2006 reveals that Latin America's largest microcredit institution, Compartamos, serves 500,000 people in Mexico, a country where over 70% of the population lacks access to traditional banks. In the absence of microcredit, poor individuals are forced to rely on loansharks. The Allentown, Pennsylvania *Morning Call* of December 7, 2006 explains that microcredit groups offer interest rates between 20% and 30%, compared to the 100% interest rates local moneylenders charge. In this way, microcredit provides a source of capital that families can actually afford to pay back, allowing them to improve their lives without getting trapped in an unmanageable cycle of debt.

Here the necessity for microcredit is considered, the second part of the second main idea. Notice that the speaker uses similar words in introducing these concepts as in previewing them in the introduction. This similarity in wording will help the audience follow the speaker.

Muhammad Yunus claims that one day the world will only see poverty in museums. While microcredit could make this a reality, it raises several implications for our views on social welfare, the economic role of women, and poverty.

Here the speaker provides a transition to the third major point, this one dealing with the implications of microcredit. As you can easily tell, the speaker will cover three implications—those pertaining to social welfare, the role of women, and poverty.

Microcredit could alter our outlook on social welfare. In his 1980 book *Free to Choose*, Nobel Prize winning economist Milton Friedman argues that the poor benefit more by being empowered to make their own decisions than they do from government handouts. The previously cited *International Herald Tribune* notes that microcredit reinforces Friedman's belief in free market capitalism by giving the poor control over how they generate income. The success of this approach could provide ammunition to those who rally against social welfare, strengthening attempts to abolish the so-called welfare state and the safety nets that it currently provides.

The first implication concerns social welfare. Notice that the speaker effectively establishes the credibility of her source, Milton Friedman, by recalling that he was a Nobel Prize–winning economist. In what other ways does the speaker establish credibility—her own as well as that of her sources?

Additionally, microcredit may not have the expected positive impact on women. According to an April 3, 2006 press release from the United Nations Department of Public Information, 80% of microcredit borrowers are women. Microcredit groups seek out female borrowers because they hope to empower women in traditionally patriarchal societies. However, the February 10, 2007 edition of India's *Economic and Political Weekly* argues that, sometimes, women are forced to hand their loans over to their husbands. The wife ends up worse off than when she started, because she is responsible for repaying the loan, but has not received any of its benefits. Thus, microcredit offers women a road to economic empowerment, but if male dominance in a given community is too deeply entrenched, microcredit may not be able to deliver on its promise.

Here we're jolted a bit. We assume that all microcredit is going to be positive but here the speaker notes a negative impact—it may make women more vulnerable not more empowered. Of course, this is an informative speech; it isn't designed to persuade you as it is to inform you.

Finally, microcredit could change our understanding of poverty. The 2005 documentary *Small Fortunes: Microcredit and the Future of Poverty* explains that one longstanding perception about the poor is that they just need to work harder. Yet, Pakistan's *The Nation* of December 6, 2006 states that microcredit's central message is that people are not poor because they lack ambition, but rather because traditional banking systems are "discriminatory and anti-poor." As microcredit continues to gain legitimacy, it could shift blame away from the impoverished and refocus our attention on the root causes of poverty—the very systems that perpetuate destitution in the first place.

We now know the speaker has come to the final point of the speech ("finally"), this one dealing with the implications of microcredit on poverty.

When awarding Muhammad Yunus the Nobel Prize, the committee noted, "Lasting peace can not be achieved unless large population groups find ways in which to break out of poverty."

After examining the development of microcredit, its rationale, and the implications of this movement, it seems that this poverty-fighting technique may be a step toward a more peaceful world. In the meantime, Yunus and other microcredit lenders will continue to spread the message that the poor are creditworthy. But the real challenge, in their eyes, is to continue to build banks that are people-worthy.

Here the speaker concludes the speech by clearly summarizing the main points of the speech: the development, rationale, and implications of microcredit. The speaker then stresses the importance of microcredit by calling it a poverty-fighting technique and that it may be a step toward a more peaceful world.

The speaker then recalls the introduction by getting back to Yunus and closes by noting the real challenge.

Speak on the Appropriate Level of Formality

The most effective public speaking style is (usually but not always) less formal than the written essay but more formal than conversation. One way to achieve an informal style—if this seems the appropriate style on the basis of your audience analysis—is to use contractions. Say *don't* instead of *do not*, *I'll* instead of *I shall*, and *wouldn't* instead of *would not*. Contractions give a public speech the sound and rhythm of conversation, a quality that most listeners react to favorably.

Use personal pronouns rather than impersonal expressions. Say "I found" instead of "it became evident," or "I will present three arguments" instead of "there are three main arguments."

Do remember, as noted elsewhere, that the expected and desirable level of formality will vary greatly from one culture to another.

Avoid Unfamiliar Terms

Avoid using terms the audience doesn't know. Avoid foreign and technical terms unless you're certain the audience is familiar with them. Similarly, avoid jargon (the technical vocabulary of a specialized field) unless you're sure the meanings are clear to your listeners. Some acronyms (NATO, UN, NOW, and CORE) are probably familiar to most audiences; most, however, are not. When you wish to use any of these types of expressions, fully explain their meaning to the audience.

Avoid Slang

Avoid **slang** or other expressions that risk offending audience members, embarrassing them, or making them feel you have little respect for them. Although your listeners may themselves use such expressions, they often resent their use by public speakers. So avoid any words or examples that may be considered "off-color."

Avoid Racist, Sexist, Ageist, and Heterosexist Terms

Avoid referring to culturally different groups with terms that carry negative connotations; be careful not to portray groups in stereotypical and negative ways.

Avoid racist language or any expressions that can be considered disparaging to members of a particular ethnic group. Using unintentionally **racist language**—qualifying someone with a racial identifier that is neither relevant nor necessary—is perhaps the most frequent mistake speakers make. For example, referring to a "Chicano professor" or an "African American mathematician" can imply that you're pointing to the rareness of Hispanics' being professors or of African Americans' being mathematicians.

Use nonsexist language. **Sexist language** is language that's derogatory to one gender (usually women). To avoid it, use gender-neutral terminology. Use "human" instead of "man" to include both sexes; use "she and he" instead of "he"; use "police officer" instead of "policeman" and "firefighter" instead of "fireman." Avoid sex-role stereotyping; for example, avoid making the hypothetical elementary school teacher female and the college professor male. Avoid referring to doctors as male and nurses as female. Avoid noting the gender of a professional with terms such as "lady lawyer" or "male nurse." When you're referring to a specific lawyer or nurse, the person's gender will become clear when you use the appropriate pronoun.

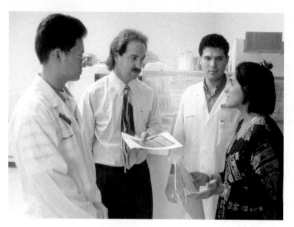

Consider Consider the use of sexist, racist, heterosexist and ageist language in public speaking. What problems might the use of such language create for the speaker? For audience members?

If you have any doubts as to the preferred gender-neutral term to use in your speech, visit online resources such as Rensselaer Polytechnic Institute's Writing Center (www.rpi.edu/dept/uc/writecenter/web/genderfair.html); Chicago–Kent College of Law's guide, which also contains exercises (www.kentlaw.edu/academics/lrw/grinker/LwTaGender_Neutral_Language.htm); James Cook University's site at www.jcu.edu.au/office/Policy/pubgen.htm; or Seton Hill University's site at http://jerz.setonhill.edu/writing/style/gender.html. UNESCO provides a 58-page booklet on gender-neutral language at http://unesdoc.unesco.org/images/0011/001149/114950mo.pdf.

Avoid ageist expressions or language that discriminates against people because of age. Avoid popular but insulting terms referring to older people—**ageist language** such as "old-timer," "little old lady," or "over the hill." As with racism, ageism also can creep in when you qualify or describe the abilities of an older person. For example, when you refer to a "quick-witted 75-year-old" or a "responsible teenager," you're indicating that those qualities are unusual in people in those age groups. You're saying that quick-wittedness and being 75 years old do not normally go together and that the fact that they do in this case merits special mention. You imply the same abnormality for the linking of "responsible" and "teenager." The problem with this is that using ageist expressions is simply wrong. There are many 80-year-olds who are extremely quick-witted and many 30-year-olds who aren't.

Avoid heterosexist language, language that disparages gay men and lesbians. As with racist language, **heterosexist language** can take the form of derogatory terms for lesbians and gay men as well as more subtle kinds of language usage. As with racist and sexist language, when you qualify a professional identifier—as in "gay athlete" or "lesbian doctor," you're in effect stating that athletes or doctors are not normally gay or lesbian. Also, you're making the affectional orientation more important than it probably should be in the context of, as in the examples, sports or medicine.

Once brought to awareness, most people recognize the moral legitimacy of using language that is inclusive and refraining from using racist, ageist, or heterosexist words or phrases. There are also rhetorical reasons for avoiding such language:

- It's likely to offend a significant part of your audience.
- It's likely to draw attention to itself and away from what you're saying.
- It's likely to reflect negatively on your own credibility.

Avoid Ethnic Expressions (Generally)

Ethnic expressions are words and phrases that are peculiar to a particular ethnic or language group. At times these expressions are known only by members of the ethnic group; at other times they are known more widely but still recognized as ethnic expressions.

When you are speaking to a multicultural audience, it's generally best to avoid ethnic expressions unless they're integral to your speech and you explain them. Such expressions often seem exclusionist—that is, they highlight the connection between the speaker and the members of that particular ethnic group and the lack of connection between the speaker and all others who are not members of that ethnic group. And, of course, ethnic expressions should never be used if you're not a member of the ethnic group.

If, on the other hand, you're speaking to an audience from one ethnic group and you're also a member of that group, then such expressions are fine. Politicians who run in districts in which they and the voters are of the same national origin or language community will frequently use ethnic terms or even phrases in the native language of the audience. In these cases ethnic expressions may well prove effective; they are part of the common language of speaker and audience and will help to stress your similarities with the audience.

Use Preferred Cultural Identifiers

Perhaps the best way to avoid sexism, racism, ageism, and heterosexism is to examine the **cultural identifiers** to use (and not to use) in talking about members of different cultures. As always, when in doubt, find out. The preferences and many of the specific examples identified here are drawn largely from the findings of the Task Force on Bias-Free Language of the Association of American University Presses (Schwartz, 1995). Although not everyone necessarily agrees with these recommendations; they're presented here—in the words of the Task Force—"to encourage sensitivity to usages that may be imprecise, misleading, and needlessly offensive" (Schwartz, 1995, p. ix). They're not presented so that you can "catch" someone being "politically incorrect" or label someone "culturally insensitive."

Generally, the term *girl* should be used only to refer to very young females and is equivalent to *boy*. Neither term should be used for people older than, say, 13 or 14. *Girl* is never used to refer to a grown woman, nor is *boy* used to refer to persons in blue-collar positions, as it once was. *Lady* is negatively evaluated by many because it connotes the stereotype of the prim and proper woman. *Woman* or *young woman* is preferred. *Older person* is preferred to *elder, elderly, senior,* or *senior citizen* (which technically refers to someone older than 65).

Generally, *gay* is the preferred term to refer to a man who has an affectional preference for other men and *lesbian* is the preferred term for a woman who has an affectional preference for other women. (*Lesbian* means "homosexual woman," so the phrase "lesbian woman" is redundant.) *Homosexual* refers to both gay men and lesbians but more often to a sexual orientation to members of one's own sex. *Gay* and *lesbian* refer to a lifestyle and not just to sexual orientation. *Gay* as a noun, although widely used, may prove offensive in some contexts; for example, in the remark "We have two gays on the team." Although used within the gay community in an effort to remove the negative stigma through frequent usage, the term *queer*—as in "queer power" or "queer studies"—is often resented when used by outsiders. Because most scientific thinking holds that sexuality is not a matter of choice, the term *affectional orientation* is preferred to *sexual preference* or *sexual status* (which are also vague) (Rogers, 2001; Wright, 1999).

Generally, most African Americans prefer *African American* to *black* (Hecht, Collier, & Ribeau, 1993), though *black* is often used with *white* and is used in a variety of other contexts (for example, Department of Black and Puerto Rican Studies, the *Journal of Black History*, and Black History Month). The American Psychological Association recommends that both terms be capitalized, but the *Chicago Manual of Style* (the manual used by most newspapers and publishing houses) recommends using lowercase. The terms *negro* and *colored*, although used in the names of some organizations (for example, the United Negro College Fund and the National Association for the Advancement of Colored People), are not used outside of these contexts.

White is generally used to refer to those whose roots are in European cultures and usually does not include Hispanics. Analogous to *African American* is the term *European American*. Few "European Americans," however, would want to be called that; most would prefer their national origins emphasized, as in, for example, *German American* or *Greek American*. This preference may well change as Europe moves into a more cohesive and united entity. *People of color*—a literary-sounding term that may be appropriate in public speaking, but is awkward in most conversations—is preferred to *nonwhite*, which implies that whiteness is the norm and nonwhiteness is a deviation from that norm. The same is true of the term *non-Christian*.

Generally, *Hispanic* is used to refer to anyone who identifies himself or herself as belonging to a Spanish-speaking culture. *Latina* (female) and *Latino* (male) refer to people with roots in Latin American countries such as the Dominican Republic, Nicaragua, or Guatemala. *Hispanic American* refers to U.S. residents whose ancestry is culturally Spanish and includes people of Mexican, Caribbean, and Central and South American origins. But in emphasizing a Spanish heritage, the term is really inadequate, because large numbers in the Caribbean and in South America have French or Portuguese roots. *Chicana* (female) and *Chicano* (male) refer to those with roots in Mexico, though it often connotes a nationalist attitude (Jandt, 2006) and is considered offensive by many Mexican Americans. *Mexican American* is preferred. "Anchor baby"—a derogatory term for a child born to an illegal immigrant in the United States (though used almost exclusively to refer to illegal immigrants from Mexico), who can now sponsor members of his or her family because the baby is a U.S. citizen—should obviously be avoided. Similarly, equating "illegal immigrants" with Mexicans, rather than recognizing the term as applying to citizens of any other country who enter the United States illegally, is naturally offensive and should be avoided.

Inuk (the plural is *Inuit*) was officially adopted at the Inuit Circumpolar Conference to refer to the indigenous peoples of Alaska, northern Canada, Greenland, and eastern Siberia. This term is preferred to *Eskimo* (a term the U.S. Census Bureau uses), which was applied to the indigenous peoples of Alaska by Europeans and derives from a term that means "raw meat eaters" (Maggio, 1997).

Indian technically should refer only to someone from India; it is incorrectly used when applied to citizens of other Asian countries or to the indigenous peoples of North America. *American Indian* or *Native American* is preferred, even though many Native Americans refer to themselves as "Indians" and "Indian people." The term *native American* (with a lowercase *n*) is most often used to refer to persons born in the United States. Although the term technically could refer to anyone born in North or South America, people outside the United States generally prefer more specific designations such as *Argentinean, Cuban,* or *Canadian*. The term *native* refers to a person born in a particular place and is distinguished from *stranger* or *foreigner*; it's not used to mean "someone having a less developed culture."

Muslim is the preferred form (rather than the older *Moslem*) to refer to a person who adheres to the religious teachings of Islam. *Quran* (rather than *Koran*) is the preferred term for the scriptures of Islam. The terms *Mohammedan* or *Mohammedanism* are not considered appropriate; they imply worship of Muhammad, the prophet, "considered by Muslims to be a blasphemy against the absolute oneness of God" (Maggio, 1997, p. 277).

Although there's no universal agreement, generally *Jewish people* is preferred to *Jews*; and *Jewess* (a Jewish female) is considered derogatory. *Jew* should be used only as a noun and is never correctly used as a verb or an adjective (Maggio, 1997).

When history was being written with a European perspective, Europe was taken as the focal point and the rest of the world was defined in terms of its location from Europe. Thus, Asia became "the east" or "the Orient" and Asians became *Orientals*—a term that is today considered inappropriate or "Eurocentric." Thus, people from Asia are *Asians*, just as people from Africa are *Africans* and people from Europe are *Europeans*.

In talking about people with disabilities, be especially careful to avoid terms that limit the person or define the person in terms of his or her impairment or disability. For example, avoid saying "the disabled person" or the "deaf person," and instead consider saying "the person with a disability"—or, better and more specifically, "the person with limited hearing." In addition, as with older people and different ethnic groups, scrupulously avoid any of the offensive derogatory terms that refer to various disabilities.

PERSONAL STYLE

Audiences favor speakers who speak in a **personal style** rather than in an impersonal way; who speak with them rather than at them.

Use Personal Pronouns

Say *I* and *me* and *he* and *she* and *you*. Avoid such impersonal expressions as *one* (as in "One is led to believe . . .") or "this speaker," or "listeners." These expressions distance the audience and create barriers rather than bridges. Use personal pronouns in addressing the audience: Say *you* rather than *students*; say *you'll enjoy reading . . .* instead of *everyone will enjoy reading*.

Use Questions

Ask the audience questions to involve them. In a small audience, you might even briefly entertain responses. In larger audiences, you might ask the question, pause to allow the audience time to consider their responses, and then move on. When you direct questions to your listeners, they feel a part of the public speaking transaction.

Create Immediacy

Immediacy is a connectedness, a relatedness with one's listeners. Immediacy is the opposite of disconnected and separated. Here are some suggestions for creating immediacy through language:

- Use personal examples.
- Use terms that include both you and the audience; for example, *we* and *our*.
- Use specific names of audience members when appropriate.
- Express concern for the audience members.

- Reinforce or compliment the audience.
- Refer directly to commonalities between you and the audience, for example, "We are all children of immigrants" or "We all want to see our team in the playoffs."
- Refer to shared experiences and goals; for example, "We all want, we all need a more responsive PTA."
- Recognize audience feedback and refer to it in your speech. Say, for example, "I can see from your expressions that we're all anxious to get to our immediate problem."

Books about words abound on the Internet and will prove helpful in your choice of words. Visit the Internet Public Library (www.ipl.org/ref) or the Reference Desk (www.refdesk.com) and search for dictionaries, thesauruses, and related wordbooks. Or see www.yourdictionary.com/, http://dictionary.cambridge.org/, or Merriam-Webster Collegiate Dictionary at www.m-w.com/dictionary.htm. One Look, at www.onelook.com/, enables you to search lots of dictionaries in a variety of languages. To get an idea of the differences among dictionaries, look up a few words, such as "rhetoric," "persuasion," or "style," in a few of these volumes.

PHRASING SENTENCES

Give the same careful consideration that you give to words to your sentences as well. Here are some guidelines to help you make your sentences clear and persuasive.

Use Short Sentences

Short sentences are more forceful and economical. They are easier to comprehend and they are easier to remember. Listeners don't have the time or the inclination to unravel long and complex sentences. Help them to listen more efficiently by using short rather than long sentences.

Use Direct Sentences

Direct sentences are easier to understand. They are also more forceful. Instead of saying, "I want to tell you of the three main reasons why we should not adopt Program A," say "We should not adopt Program A. I'm going to focus on three main reasons."

Use Active Sentences

Active sentences are easier to understand. They also make your speech seem livelier and more vivid. Instead of saying "The lower court's decision was reversed by the Supreme Court," say "The Supreme Court reversed the lower court's decision." Instead of saying "The proposal was favored by management," say "Management favored the proposal."

Use Positive Sentences

Positive sentences are easier to comprehend and remember. Notice how sentences **a** and **c** are easier to understand than sentences **b** and **d**.

Research Link

E-MAIL, NEWSGROUPS, CHAT GROUPS, AND BLOGS

E-mail may prove useful in public speaking in several ways. For example, you can write to specific people who may be experts in the topic you're researching. Internet services are now making it quite easy to locate a person's e-mail address. Try, for example, the Netscape people page—which you can access from Netscape's home page or by going to http://guide.netscape.com/guide/people.html—or Yahoo's directory (www.yahoo.com/search/people/) and their links to numerous other directories such as Yahoo's White Pages (www.yahoo.com/Reference/White-Pages/). Another useful people search tool is http://www.procd .com/hl/direct.htm. Also, try the sites that specialize in e-mail addresses such as Four11 (www.four11.com), Who Where? (www.whowhere.com), and Switchboard (www .switchboard.com). Four11 also provides a directory of regular telephone numbers as well as special directories for government personnel and for celebrities.

You can join a mailing list or listserv that focuses on the topic you're researching and learn from the collective insights of all members. In joining a listserv remember to lurk before contributing; get a feel for the group and for the types of messages they send. Read the FAQs to avoid asking questions that have already been answered.

Newsgroups are discussion forums for the exchange of ideas on a wide variety of topics. There are thousands of newsgroups on the Internet; you can post your messages, read the messages of others, and respond to the messages you read. Newsgroups are much like listservs, in that they bring together a group of people interested in communicating about a common topic. Some newsgroups also include messages from news services such as the Associated Press or Reuters. Newsgroups are useful to the public speaker for a variety of reasons. The most obvious reason is that newsgroups are sources of information; they contain news items, letters, and papers on just about any topic you can think of. An especially useful search engine for discussion groups is Google (http://groups .google.com/), although you can use any search engine to search for groups in which you might be interested.

Newsgroups that get news feeds are especially useful, because the information is so current and is likely to be more detailed than you'll find in newspapers. You're also likely to find a greater diversity of viewpoints than you'll encounter in, say, most newspapers or newsmagazines. Another advantage is that through newsgroups you can ask questions and get the opinions of others for your next speech. Newsgroups also provide an easily available and generally receptive audience to whom you can communicate your thoughts and feelings.

Chat groups, such as you'll find on the commercial Internet service providers (ISPs) and on the various social network sites such as Youtube (www.youtube.com), myface (www.myface.com), Facebook (www.facebook .com), and MySpace (www.myspace.com), enable you to communicate with others in real time. This is called *synchronous conversation*—as opposed to *asynchronous conversation*, in which there's a delay between message sending and message receiving.

Blogs are now extremely popular and often contain information that may be useful in public speaking. You can locate blogs most easily with a variety of search engines (for example, www.search.blogger.com or www .blogsearch.google.com). Like websites, blogs (web logs) vary greatly in their usefulness to the public speaker. Some blogs are just personal ramblings (perhaps useful for examples or illustrations), some guide you to additional online materials (useful for locating information you might not have found otherwise), and some contain the thoughts and ideas of experts in a wide variety of fields. Generally, don't assume that anything on a blog is reliable and accurate; check first.

The next Research Link, "Databases," appears on page 225.

a. The committee rejected the proposal.
b. The committee did not accept the proposal.
c. This committee works outside the normal company hierarchy.
d. This committee does not work within the normal company hierarchy.

Vary the Types of Sentences

The advice to use short, direct, active, and positive sentences is valid most of the time. Yet too many sentences of the same type or length will make your speech sound boring. Use variety while following (generally) the preceding advice. Here are a few special types of sentences that should prove useful, especially for adding variety, vividness, and forcefulness to your speech.

Parallel Sentences **Parallel sentences** convey ideas in parallel (similar, matching) style for ease of comprehension and memory. Note the parallelism in **a** and **c** and its absence in **b** and **d**.

a. The professor prepared the lecture, graded the examination, and read the notices.
b. The professor prepared the lecture, the examination was graded, and she read the notices.
c. Love needs two people to flourish. Jealousy needs but one.
d. Love needs two people. Just one can create jealousy.

Antithetical Sentences **Antithetical sentences** juxtapose contrasting ideas in parallel fashion. In his inaugural speech, President John F. Kennedy phrased one of his most often quoted lines in antithetical structure:

Ask not what your country can do for you; ask what you can do for your country.

Periodic Sentences In **periodic sentences** you reserve the key word until the end of the sentence. In fact, the sentence is not grammatically complete until you say this last word. For example, in "Looking longingly into his eyes, the old woman fainted," the sentence doesn't make sense until the last word is spoken.

Essentials of Wording Your Speech

In this chapter we looked at how language works and at how you can use language to better achieve your public speaking goals.

1. **Language varies** in several ways:
   - Directness and indirectness
   - Abstraction and specificity
   - Objectivity and subjectivity
   - Oral and written style
   - Accuracy and inaccuracy (including errors such as polarization, fact–inference confusion, allness, static evaluation, and indiscrimination)

2. In **choosing your words** to achieve an effective public speaking style, focus on the following qualities:
   - Clarity: Be economical; be specific; use guide phrases; use short, familiar terms; use repetition and restatement; avoid clichés; avoid misusing commonly confused words.
   - Vividness: Use active verbs; use strong verbs; use figures of speech; use imagery.
   - Appropriateness: Speak on the appropriate level of formality; avoid unfamiliar terms; avoid slang and vulgar terms; avoid racist, sexist, ageist, and heterosexist expressions; avoid ethnic expressions (generally); use preferred cultural identifiers.
   - Personal style: Use personal pronouns; ask questions; create immediacy.

3. In your **sentence construction** strive for clarity and forcefulness:
   - Use short rather than long sentences.
   - Use direct rather than indirect sentences.
   - Use active rather than passive sentences.
   - Use positive rather than negative sentences.
   - Vary the types and lengths of sentences, making use of parallel, antithetical, and periodic sentences.

Essential Terms: Wording Your Speech

abstraction **(p. 184)**
ageist language **(p. 202)**
alliteration **(p. 195)**
allness **(p. 189)**
antithesis **(p. 196)**
antithetical sentences **(p. 208)**
clarity **(p. 190)**
cliché **(p. 192)**
connotation **(p. 184)**
cultural identifiers **(p. 203)**
denotation **(p. 184)**
directness **(p. 183)**
ethnic expressions **(p. 202)**
euphemism **(p. 190)**
fact–inference confusion **(p. 188)**
fallacies of language **(p. 189)**

figures of speech **(p. 195)**
guide phrases **(p. 192)**
heterosexist language **(p. 202)**
hyperbole **(p. 195)**
idioms **(p. 194)**
imagery **(p. 196)**
immediacy **(p. 205)**
indiscrimination **(p. 189)**
irony **(p. 195)**
jargon **(p. 190)**
metaphor **(p. 195)**
metonymy **(p. 196)**
objectivity **(p. 184)**
oral style **(p. 185)**
oxymoron **(p. 196)**
parallel sentences **(p. 208)**

periodic sentences **(p. 208)**
personal style **(p. 205)**
personification **(p. 196)**
polarization **(p. 187)**
racist language **(p. 201)**
repetition **(p. 192)**
restatement **(p. 192)**
rhetorical question **(p. 196)**
sexist language **(p. 201)**
simile **(p. 195)**
slang **(p. 201)**
static evaluation **(p. 189)**
synecdoche **(p. 195)**
weasel words **(p. 190)**

Public Speaking Exercises

8.1 Making Concepts Specific

One of the major skills in public speaking is learning to make your ideas specific so that your listeners will understand exactly what you want them to understand. Here are 12 sentences. Rewrite each of the sentences making the italicized terms more specific.

1. The *teacher was discussing economics*.
2. The *player scored*.
3. No one in the *city* thought the *mayor* was right.
4. The *girl* and the *boy* each received *lots* of *presents*.
5. I read the *review* of the *movie*.
6. The *couple* rented a *great car*.
7. The *detective* wasn't much help in solving the *crime*.
8. The *dinosaur approached* the *baby*.
9. He *walked* up the *steep hill*.
10. *They* played *games*.
11. The *cat climbed* the *fence*.
12. The *large house* is in the *valley*.

8.2 Talking about Cultural Identities

Anonymously, on an index card, each class member should write one of his or her cultural identities (race, religion, nationality) and three strengths that the person feels a significant number of members of this cultural group possess. The cards should be collected, randomized, and read aloud. This brief experience—along with any discussion it generates—should make the following clear:

1. Not only do people have diverse cultural identities, but each individual has several such identities.
2. Each identity has its own perceived strengths. Even the "strengths" themselves may not be recognized as "strengths" by members of other cultures.
3. The most effective individual is likely to be the one who recognizes and welcomes the strengths of different cultures.

8.3 What Do You Say?

◆ **Offensive Language.** Chris wants to illustrate the negative effects of racist language by using these derogatory terms throughout his speech—to further drive home the point of the pain they can cause. If Chris were addressing your class, what advice would you give him?

◆ **Language Differences.** Greg, an anthropology professor, is to give an address on the topic of violence in schools twice in one day: first to the junior class at the local high school and later that day to the

Education Department of his college. If Greg is to be successful, how—if at all—should his language differ in these two situations?

◆ **Speaking Style.** As part of her second job interview at a most conservative brokerage house, Rochelle is asked to give a presentation to a group of analysts she would supervise (as well as to the management that will make the hiring decision). What advice would you give Rochelle concerning her speaking style? For example, should she strive for a personal or an impersonal style? Should she signal immedi-acy or distance? Would your advice differ if Rochelle were significantly older (or younger) than the group she'd be supervising?

◆ **Slang.** Tonya, a young college professor, is preparing to speak to an audience of high school juniors about going to Regional Community College and wonders if she should break the general rule against using slang. She figures that slang is the language of the students and imagines that they'd probably identify more with her if they felt she spoke their language. What would you advise Tonya to do?

Log*On!* MySpeechLab

Wording Your Speech

MySpeechLab (www.myspeechlab.com) for Chapter 8 offers a variety of aids for improving your use of language and style in public speaking: an extended example of "Oral and Written Style"; suggestions for using "Humor in Public Speaking"; exercises on "Rephrasing Clichés"; and "Metaphors, Similes, and Public Speaking." Examine one or two of the video speeches for the use of language and the way the speakers apply (or fail to apply) the principles explained in this chapter. An earlier version of the informative speech included in this unit is available on MySpeechLab. You might find it interesting to compare the two versions. Which do you prefer? Do both speeches follow the principles of public speaking equally well?

In addition, take a look at Martin Luther King Jr.'s "I Have a Dream," "Needleless Technology," and "Trauma Seal," all of which illustrate the effective use of words to create desired audience responses. Also, examine the Explore activities on language, including word choice, gender neutral words, word strategies, and transitions.

Presenting Your Speech

9

Why Read This Chapter?

Because it will enable you to deliver your speech with effective voice and action by helping you to:

- use your voice (volume, rate, pitch, and pauses, for example) to your best advantage

- use nonverbal communication (eyes, face, body posture, gestures, and movements) to further your purpose

- improve your public speaking delivery through systematic rehearsal

A good speaker is pointed and impassioned.

—Cicero (106–43 B.C.) Roman orator, rhetorical theorist, politician, and philosopher

If you're like most students, your greatest concern is not with limiting the topic or writing the outline; it's with delivery, the topic of this chapter. Here we'll focus on delivery skills that will help you achieve your purpose. After all, the best organized and researched speech, if delivered poorly, is not going to have the effect you want it to have.

METHODS OF PRESENTATION

Public speakers vary greatly in their methods of presentation. Some speak off-the-cuff, with no apparent preparation (impromptu); others read their speeches from the printed text (manuscript). Some construct a detailed outline and create the speech itself at the moment of delivery (extemporaneous).

Still others memorize their speeches, a method that is not recommended. The major disadvantage of a **memorized speech** is that you might forget your speech. In a memorized speech each sentence cues the recall of the following sentence. Thus, when you forget one sentence, you may forget the rest of the speech. Another disadvantage is that memorizing makes it virtually impossible to adjust to audience feedback. And if you're not going to adjust to feedback, you lose the main advantage of face-to-face contact.

Here we'll consider the impromptu, manuscript, and extemporaneous methods of presentation along with some general suggestions for using each method. These delivery suggestions—as you'll see—will also prove helpful in managing your apprehension. As you develop more control and comfort over your voice and bodily action in public speaking, you'll relax and feel more comfortable. These feelings will then help reduce your fear of public speaking.

SPEAKING IMPROMPTU

When you give an **impromptu speech**, you speak without any specific preparation or advance thinking. You and the topic meet for the first time, and immediately the speech begins. On some occasions you will not be able to avoid speaking impromptu. In a classroom, after someone has spoken, you may comment on the speech you just heard in a brief impromptu speech of evaluation. In asking or answering questions in an interview situation, you're giving impromptu speeches, albeit extremely short ones. At meetings you may find yourself speaking impromptu as you explain a proposal or defend a plan of action; these, too, are impromptu speeches. The ability to speak impromptu effectively depends on your general public speaking ability. The more proficient a speaker you are, the better you'll be able to function impromptu.

The impromptu experience provides excellent training in different aspects of public speaking, such as maintaining eye contact; responding to audience feedback; gesturing; organizing ideas; and developing examples, arguments, and appeals. The major disadvantage of speaking impromptu is that it does not permit attention to details of public speaking such as audience adaptation, research, and style.

When you are called upon to speak impromptu, the following suggestions should prove useful:

- Don't apologize. Everyone has difficulty speaking impromptu, and there's no need to emphasize any problems you may have.

- Don't express verbally or nonverbally any displeasure or any negative responses to the experience, the topic, the audience, or even yourself. Approach the entire task with a positive attitude and a positive appearance. It will help make the experience more enjoyable both for you and for your audience.

- When you have to speak impromptu, jot down two or three subtopics that you'll cover and perhaps two or three bits of supporting material that you'll use in amplifying these two or three subtopics.

- Develop your conclusion. It will probably be best to use a simple summary conclusion in which you restate your main topic and the subtopics that you discussed.

- Develop an introduction. Here it will probably be best simply to identify your topic and orient the audience by telling them the two or three subtopics that you'll cover.

SPEAKING FROM MANUSCRIPT

With a **manuscript speech**, you write out the entire speech, exactly as you want it to be heard by your audience, and read it to the audience. Because the manuscript method allows you to control exactly what you'll say, it may be the logical method to use in, say, politics, where an ambiguous phrase might prove insulting or belligerent and cause serious problems.

One of the major advantages of a manuscript speech is that you control the timing precisely. This is particularly important when you are delivering a speech that will be recorded (on television, for example). Also, there's no danger of forgetting an important point; everything is there for you on paper. Still another advantage is that the manuscript method allows you to use the exact wording you (or a team of speech writers) want. The most obvious disadvantage is that it's difficult to read a speech and sound natural and nonmechanical. Reading material from the printed page or a teleprompter with liveliness and naturalness is itself a skill that is difficult to achieve without considerable practice. Audiences don't like speakers to read their speeches. They prefer speakers who speak with them. Also, reading a manuscript makes it difficult to respond to feedback from your listeners. And when the manuscript is on a stationary lectern, as it most often is, it's impossible for you to move around. You have to stay in one place. The speech controls your movement or, rather, your lack of movement.

When speaking from manuscript, consider the following suggestions:

- Write out your speech with an eye to oral presentation. Try to hear what you write as you write.

- Mark up your manuscript with delivery notes. Write in pause points, especially important in manuscript speaking because of the tendency to read quickly. Underline or boldface key terms that you want to stress.

- Be sure to maintain eye contact. Even though you're reading from manuscript, you are still delivering a speech, and it should sound as natural and extemporaneous as possible. Rehearse your speech so that you can alternate looking at the manuscript with looking at the audience.

- Use large fonts that you'll be able to see easily without squinting or putting the manuscript up to your nose.

- Make page breaks coincide with natural breaks in the speech. Don't separate sentences or even main points on two different pages.

- Use only one side of the paper, and number the pages clearly to reduce any chance of losing your place.

- Even when speaking from manuscript, memorize your few opening lines and your closing lines. In this way you'll be able to maintain eye contact with the audience.

SPEAKING EXTEMPORANEOUSLY

An **extemporaneous speech** involves thorough preparation and a commitment to memory of the main ideas and their order (and, if you wish, your introduction and conclusion). There is, however, no commitment to exact wording for the remaining parts of the speech.

Extemporaneous delivery is useful in most speaking situations. Good college lecturers use the extemporaneous method. They prepare thoroughly and know what they want to say and in what order they want to say it, but they have given no commitment to exact wording.

One advantage of this method is that it allows you to respond easily to feedback. Should audience feedback suggest that a point needs clarification, for example, you can rephrase the idea or give an example. Extemporaneous delivery is the method that comes closest to conversation, a kind of "enlarged conversation." With this method you can move about and interact with the audience.

Here are a few guidelines for using the extemporaneous method—the method recommended for your classroom speeches and for most of the speeches you'll deliver throughout your life.

- Memorize the opening and closing lines; this will help you focus your complete attention on the audience and will put you more at ease. Similarly, memorize the main points and the order in which you'll cover them; this will free you from relying on your notes and will make you feel more in control of the speech and of the entire speech-making situation.

- Speak naturally. Listeners will enjoy your speech and believe you more if you speak as if you were conversing with a small group of people. Don't allow your delivery to call attention to itself. Your ultimate aim should be to deliver the speech so naturally that the audience won't even notice your delivery.

- Use delivery to reinforce your message. All aspects of your delivery—your voice, bodily action, and general appearance, for example—should work together to make your ideas instantly intelligible to your audience.

- Vary your delivery. Variety in voice and bodily action will help you maintain your listeners' attention. Vary your vocal volume and your rate of speaking. In a similar way, avoid standing in exactly the same position throughout the speech. Use your body to express your ideas, to communicate to the audience what is going on in your head.

- Create immediacy with delivery. Make your listeners feel that you're talking directly and individually to each of them: Maintain appropriate eye contact with the audience members, talk directly to your audience and not to your notes or to your visual aids, smile when it's appropriate and consistent with your speech purpose, and maintain a physical closeness that reinforces a psychological closeness (don't stand behind the desk or lectern).

- Be expressive. You can do this by allowing your facial muscles and your entire body to reflect and echo your inner involvement. Use gestures appropriately. Too few gestures may signal lack of involvement; too many may communicate uneasiness, awkwardness, or anxiety. Read carefully the feedback signals sent by your audience, and respond to these signals with verbal, vocal, and bodily adjustments.

The remaining sections of this chapter will explain how you can use your voice and your bodily action to most effectively communicate your thoughts and feelings. In conjunction with reading about what makes for effective presentation, visit American Rhetoric at www.americanrhetoric.com/speechbank.htm for lots of links to Internet sites containing full text, audio, and video versions of public speeches. Another valuable resource is the speech index at http://speeches .com/index.shtml. These sites as well as MySpeechLab (www.myspeechlab.com) will enable you to see effective delivery in action.

A PERSUASIVE SPEECH

Public Speaking *Sample Assistant*

Untitled [False Confessions]

Jessy Ohl

Kansas State University

Coached by Craig Brown, Bobby Imbody, and Erica Imbody

Assuming I don't violate the rules, I get 1,800 words to try and change the way you think and feel about some issue. My goal, in a sense, is to get you to confess that my point of view is the "truth" and to do so in around 10 minutes. But what if I really had no time limit, and could speak for say—20 hours? Twenty hours where you had to listen to me. I'd get to badger you, yell at you, no breaks, no judges' lounge, just 20

Here the speaker refers to the immediate occasion—the speech contest the speaker is now in—and then relates this situation to the topic of the speech; namely, coerced confessions. After you read the entire speech, return to this introduction and consider in what other ways the speaker might gain audience attention and introduce the topic of the speech.

hours of me. I'm not that bad to listen to for around 10 minutes, but after 20 hours, you'd be ready to sign whatever petition I put in front of you, or confess to practically any crime just to get me to shut up. And I wouldn't blame you. And neither would Kevin Fox. He cracked after only 14 hours. Kevin Fox wasn't a judge in a seriously overtime speech round. Instead, on December 13, 2004, he was a suspect in the murder of his three-year-old daughter Riley. After 14 straight hours of "aggressive persuasion," as the June 21, 2005, *Chicago Tribune* reported, he confessed. The problem is—he didn't do the crime. Only after DNA evidence surfaced did anyone take seriously his claim that he had been coerced into giving a false confession.

There is a fatal flaw with the U.S. legal system— it's too easy to promote and create false confessions. The *Journal of Psychological Science* of August 2005 found that as many as 1 in 5 faulty convictions are from false confessions. Now, you might think, I'm never even going to be in a position to be arrested, let alone give a false confession. OK, but every time someone else is convicted on the basis of a false confession, that means that you and I are still threatened by the real guilty party. It's time to stop the promotion of and abuse of false confessions. And to do so, in what I promise will take a lot less than 20 hours, we must first examine the damage created by false confessions, second explain why anybody would admit to a crime they didn't commit, and finally discover solutions to get our legal system back on track.

OK, there are going to be the occasional mistakes. But unfortunately, with false confessions they're more than occasional and they're creating damage throughout the process. The *Denver Post* of April 18, 2006, concludes that gross misjudgments in convictions due to coerced confessions create illegitimacy in all prosecutions. And these occurrences are unfortunately far from rare. So let's first look at the scope and then the damage created. The June 4, 2005, issue of *Psychology Today* finds that although it is nearly impossible to determine the exact number of false confessions nationwide, a 2003 review discovered 247 such instances in a single Illinois county over the past 10 years. The *Baltimore Sun* of April 26, 2005, points out that examples range from the juvenile,

Here the speaker clearly identifies the thesis: The legal system is flawed because it's too easy to create false confessions. The speaker then reinforces this thesis with the finding from a current article in the *Journal of Psychological Science* that 1 out of 5 confessions may be faulty—a statistic that gains our attention. If you were listening to this speech, would you accept this statistic, or would you want more evidence that this large a number of confessions are in fact false? If you would want additional evidence, what would that look like?

Notice how the speaker makes sure that the listeners understand the importance of this topic to them—the topic is not merely important in the abstract, but it's important to these specific audience members. If you were giving this speech to the members of your class, how would you establish the importance of the topic to them? Put differently, how would you answer their question, "Why should I listen to this speech?"

Here the speaker gives an orientation as to the major ideas to be discussed: the damage created by false confessions (the problem), why anyone would admit to a crime he or she didn't commit (some causes that help create the problem), and the ways to get the legal system back on track (the solution). Might this speech have been organized in another pattern? How might you reorganize this speech into the motivated sequence pattern?

This first point explains the problem: the frequency of false confessions and the damage that false confessions do to everyone. As a listener, are you convinced? If not, what would convince you?

to adult, to mentally disabled. But the real damage is what happens to those unjustly convicted and to the public; we think we are being protected. For example, Jon Kogut was sentenced to life in prison in 1985 when he confessed to murder. Mr. Kogut spent 17 years before forensic evidence cleared his name. That "solved case" is now a cold case.

An erroneous and problematic legal system that violates the rights of innocent people puts us in danger. The *Chicago Tribune* of June 18, 2005, claims that the United States' prosecution system is constructed in a way that rushes to conviction. But these hasty decisions are threatening the very fabric of justice. As Dr. Joseph Unekis put it in his 2005 book *People, Problems and Power,* the basic principle of the American legal system is the presumed innocence of the accused. You are innocent until proven guilty, not innocent until forced to confess.

I'm sure by now you're wondering one thing about false confessions. Why would you ever admit to a crime that you didn't commit? But remember, what if I had that 20 hours? How we think an interrogation works isn't what really happens. There are two explanations for false confessions: first, interrogation techniques, and second, human tolerance to persuasion. First, police officers are effectively trained to extract confessions, truthful or not. The *Wall Street Journal* of April 15, 2005, reports that "standard interrogation techniques are masterfully designed to leave people with almost no rational choice but confess." The *Christian Science Monitor* of July 20, 2005, explains that "Police can legally lie to suspects, claiming to have physical evidence or witnesses that don't exist." This explains the *Milwaukee Journal Sentinel's* November 7, 2004, account of the interrogation of a 14-year-old murder suspect. He was told by police that they had witnesses and if he didn't confess, he would be raped in prison and given the chair. After six hours with no parent or lawyer, he did confess. Only later was he found innocent.

The second cause for false confessions is the human tolerance to persuasion. Professor Saul Kassin from Williams College in Massachusetts told the *Wall Street Journal* on April 15, 2005, that under traumatic circumstances an individual will confess in order to ensure survival. Being innocent does not protect you from these limits. An experiment published in the winter 2005 edition

Here the speaker provides a transition to the second point, namely why anyone would falsely confess to a crime—a question the speaker already began to answer in the introduction. This transition, as all the transitions in this speech, cue the audience into what will be discussed next. Can you identify places in the speech where additional transitions might have been effective?

This second major idea is itself divided into two parts: interrogation techniques and human tolerance.

The argument that interrogation techniques are responsible for these false confessions is supported by the strength and credibility of the *Wall Street Journal* and the *Christian Science Monitor,* two highly respected newspapers. Would members of your class agree that these are respectable and credible sources of such information?

The story of the 14-year-old boy is a particularly dramatic example of how unethical interrogation techniques can produce false confessions. Would you have liked to hear more about this particular case? If so, what else might the speaker have included? As you read and respond to comments like this, however, remember the time limits the speaker is up against. If this example were to be increased in length, something else from the speech would have to be deleted. What might that be?

Notice that the next cause of false confessions, human tolerance, is clearly introduced. The audience knows to expect a discussion of how the limits of tolerance can produce such confessions.

of *Justice Denied* concluded that 69 percent of participants in the study signed a false confession that they destroyed a government property when confronted with fictitious evidence of their wrongdoing. Despite popular belief, we can all be coaxed into giving a false confession. Richard Ofshe, a sociology professor at the University of California at Berkeley, explained in *Newsday* of May 24, 2005, "most people believe that the innocent won't falsely confess unless they're tortured," but that "psychological coercion" can reduce you to "a state of hopelessness" where you believe confessing is the only alternative.

For example, after 50 hours of interrogation in a small windowless room, Corinthian Bell confessed to murder because he thought that if he told the police what they wanted to hear, they would release him. In the same way, if I legitimately threatened you with a 20-hour persuasion, you'd probably give me a good rank just to shut me up. The *St. Petersburg Times* of December 25, 2005, estimates that nearly 600 Floridians are wrongfully imprisoned, with false confession being both a leading and a preventable cause.

We need to do more to protect the innocent, and get truth back in our legal system. Therefore we will examine solutions on both the federal and personal level. First, on the federal level actions must be taken in order to make interrogations credible. The answer, according to the *New York Times* of April 11, 2006, is mandatory legislation that would require all interrogations to be recorded. Thus, Congress should pass the New York Bar Association's proposed legislation that would give all courtrooms a working history of the interrogation process. Our government must follow the example of Illinois, which as of August 2005 required all interrogations be recorded.

The good news is, cops actually like the idea. A 2004 survey by the Center of Wrongful Convictions found a 98 percent approval rating from the police department using this system. The bad news is that less than 1 percent of interrogation rooms across the country employ such technology. Once implemented this would allow jury members to judge the validity of the remarks and protect police officers who are merely trying to put criminals behind bars. Additionally, modifications must be made to the interrogation training received by police officers.

This speech contains a particularly good mixture of abstract and general information (for example, the statistic that 69 percent of participants in a study signed false confessions and the fact that a sociologist argued that this can happen to most people) along with specific and concrete examples (for example, the confession of Corinthian Bell). After presenting the specific example, the speaker then returns to more general statistics, noting that in Florida alone some 600 people are wrongfully imprisoned, often based on false confessions.

The speaker here returns to the thesis of the speech—the need to get the legal system back on track—and provides a transition to the third major point, the solution to this clearly demonstrated problem.

The speaker proposes several solutions to the problem. The first solution proposed is that all interrogations be recorded. Another solution is to modify the interrogation training of police officers. Notice, below, that the speaker doesn't leave the audience with solutions that they can do little about but instead suggests that they raise the issue with relevant candidates and contribute to the Center on Wrongful Convictions.

In nearly all cases false confessions are the product not of bad cops, but rather of good cops wielding bad techniques. The *Boston Globe* of November 27, 2005, believes that requiring interrogators to remain truthful can prevent false confessions and still trap guilty suspects. To help make this a reality, when election time rolls around, raise this issue with candidates running for District Attorney offices in your area. And you don't have to wait for an election to help. Make a tax-deductible donation to the Center on Wrongful Convictions at Northwestern University via their website. Your contributions support the center's mission to identify and rectify wrongful convictions.

Notice that the speaker uses a variety of newspapers, newsmagazines, and professional journals along with testimony from various people. What other supporting materials might the speaker have included?

On the personal level, you should also be ready to take steps to protect yourself. If you are ever arrested or even a suspect, realize, your best defense is to know your rights. In honor of the movie *Fight Club*, the rules of interrogation are as follows: Rule 1: Don't talk; rule 2: DON'T TALK. Don't say a word without a lawyer. The police can legally lie and attempt to deceive you. So don't talk. And finally, if you're on the other side of this situation, as a jury member, help eliminate the stereotype that a confession is synonymous with truth. If this were true, I would merely confess to being the sexiest speaker in the world.

Additional solutions on a more personal level also are suggested in the event that the audience member ever finds himself or herself a suspect or a juror. Did the inclusion of this personal-level material make you feel that the topic was really important to you? If not, what additional arguments would you have wanted?

Today we examined the problem and causes of false confessions in America, and discovered solutions to get truth back in our legal system. If after only 10 minutes of my persuasion you feel like you're ready to crack, think about what Kevin Fox went through before he signed a paper saying he murdered his daughter. And remember that a confessed "truth" will not necessarily set you free.

Here the speaker wraps up the speech by summarizing the three major ideas discussed (the problem, its causes, and proposed solutions) and closes by recalling the example used in the introduction.

Source: This speech is an edited version of the copy printed in Winning Orations of the Interstate Oratorical Association (Mankata, MN: Interstate Oratorical Association, 2006, pp. 25–27). Permission granted by the Interstate Oratorical Association, Mankato, MN 56001, Larry Schnoor, Executive Secretary.

EFFECTIVE VOCAL DELIVERY

Your voice and bodily action communicate some degree of power. In the context of public speaking, power refers to your control of the situation, your control of the presentation. The suggestions offered in the pages to follow are designed to give you that control as you present your speech to an audience. You may find it interesting as a preface to this discussion to examine your own power by taking the self-test that follows.

TEST YOURSELF

How Powerful Is Your Presentation Style?

Respond to the following statements with this three-point scale: (1) = People I know would probably say that this statement is often or frequently true of my voice and bodily action; (2) = People would say the statement is neither true nor false, that I'm in the middle; and (3) = People would say the statement is rarely or infrequently true of me.

_____ **1.** My speech is relatively hesitant with a lot of vocalized pauses ("ah," "um") and frequent long pauses.

_____ **2.** My speech makes use of lots of such terms as _maybe_, _perhaps_, and _possibly_ and of phrases such as "It seems to me that . . ." or "It may have happened. . . ."

_____ **3.** My speech is likely to use such statements as "I didn't read the entire article, but . . .," "Don't get my wrong, I'm not sexist, but . . .," or "I'm not hallucinating, hear me out. . . ."

_____ **4.** My bodily action is more random than focused.

_____ **5.** I generally don't maintain eye contact with the people I talk with.

_____ **6.** As a rule, I don't gesture when speaking.

▪ **HOW DID YOU DO?** As you can tell, the characteristics described in these statements contribute to an appearance of powerlessness. So if you gave yourself 1s and 2s, then your speech is likely to appear less powerful than if you gave yourself mostly 3s. Long and vocalized pauses (statement 1) make you seem unprepared and lacking in control over your material, and hence without power. Uncertainty expressions (statement 2) generally communicate a lack of conviction and a lack of certainty and may call into question the validity of your statements. And if you're giving a speech, you don't want the audience to think that you don't firmly believe in what you're saying. Disclaimers (statement 3) also make you seem unsure of yourself and may cast doubt on the strength of your beliefs. Random bodily movements (statement 4), like uncertainty expressions, give the impression that you're not sure of where you're going, that you may lack a sense of direction. Eye contact (statement 5), as you no doubt know, is often taken as a sign of honesty; so lack of eye contact may be perceived as a sign of dishonesty. Actually, research does not support that perception, but people will draw that conclusion anyway. Gesture (statement 6)—assuming it's appropriate and not excessive—displays your involvement in the situation and your certainty about what you're saying.

▪ **WHAT WILL YOU DO?** Try to relate the following discussions to your own style of speech and bodily action. You don't want to simply absorb a style that's alien to your personality, but you might want to look for areas where you can tweak your style in the direction of greater power and greater public speaking effectiveness.

You can achieve effective vocal delivery by mastering your volume, rate, pitch, articulation and pronunciation, and pauses. Let's look at each in turn.

VOLUME

The word **volume** refers to the relative intensity of the voice. (The word loudness refers to the hearer's perception of that relative intensity.) In an adequately controlled voice, volume will vary according to several factors. For example, the distance between you and your listeners, the competing noise, and the emphasis you wish to give an idea will all influence volume.

Problems with volume are easy to identify in others, though difficult to recognize in ourselves. One obvious problem is a voice that is too soft. When speech is so soft that listeners have to strain to hear, they'll soon tire of expending so much energy. On the other hand, a voice that is too loud will prove disturbing because it intrudes on listeners' psychological space; it also may communicate aggressiveness and give others the impression that you are difficult to get along with.

The most common problems are too little volume variation and variation that falls into an easily predictable pattern. If the audience can predict volume changes, they'll focus on that pattern and not on what you're saying.

Fading away at the end of sentences is particularly disturbing. Some speakers begin sentences in an appropriate volume but end them at an extremely low volume. Be careful to avoid this tendency; when finishing sentences, make sure the audience is able to hear at an appropriate volume.

Consider the delivery style of the average college professor. Does the professor speak impromptu, from manuscript, or extemporaneously? What delivery style do you find helps you, as a listener, maintain interest and attention?

RATE

Your speech **rate** is the speed at which you speak. About 150 words per minute seems average for speaking as well as for reading aloud. The problems with rate are speaking too fast or too slow, speaking with too little variation, or speaking with too predictable a pattern. If you talk too fast, you deprive your listeners of time they need to understand and digest what you're saying; they may simply decide not to spend the energy needed to understand your speech. If your rate is too slow, your listeners' attention may wander to matters unrelated to your speech. Speak at a pace that engages the listeners and allows them time for reflection without boring them.

Use variations in rate to call attention to certain points and to add variety. For example, if you speak of the dull routine of an assembly line worker at a rapid and varied pace, or of the wonder of a circus with no variation in rate, you're surely misusing this important vocal dimension. Again, if you're interested in and conscious of what you're saying, your rate variations should flow naturally and effectively.

PITCH

Pitch is the relative highness or lowness of your voice as perceived by your listener. More technically, pitch results from the rate at which your vocal cords vibrate. If they vibrate rapidly, listeners will perceive your voice as having a high pitch. If they vibrate slowly, they'll perceive it as having a low pitch.

Pitch changes often signal changes in the meanings of many sentences. The most obvious is the difference between a statement and a question. Thus, the difference between the declarative sentence "So this is the proposal you want me to support" and the question "So this is the proposal you want me to support?" is inflection or pitch. This, of course, is obvious. But note that depending on where the inflectional change is placed, the meaning of the sentence changes drastically. Note also that all of the following questions contain exactly the same words, but they each ask a different question when you emphasize different words:

- Is *this* the proposal you want me to support?
- Is this the proposal *you* want me to support?
- Is this the proposal you want *me* to support?
- Is this the proposal you want me to *support*?

The obvious problems with pitch are levels that are too high, too low, or too patterned. Neither of the first two problems is common in speakers with otherwise normal voices, and with practice you can correct a pitch pattern that is too predictable or monotonous. As you gain speaking experience, pitch changes will come naturally from the sense of what you're saying. Because each sentence is somewhat different from every other sentence, there should be a normal variation—a variation that results not from some predetermined pattern but rather from the meanings you wish to convey to the audience.

PAUSES

Pauses come in two basic types: filled and unfilled. Filled pauses are pauses in the stream of speech that you fill with vocalizations such as *er, um, ah, well,* and *you know.* Filled pauses are ineffective and will make you appear hesitant, unprepared, and unsure of yourself.

Unfilled pauses, silences interjected into the normally fluent stream of speech, can be effective in public speaking if used correctly. Here are just a few examples of places where unfilled pauses—silences of a second or two—should prove effective.

- Pause before beginning your speech. Don't start your speech as soon as you get to the front of the room; instead, position yourself so that you feel comfortable. Then scan the audience and begin your speech.
- Pause at transitional points to signal that you're moving from one part of the speech to another or from one idea to another.
- Pause at the end of an important assertion to give the audience time to think about the significance of what you're saying.
- Pause after asking a rhetorical question to let your listeners think about how they'd answer the question.
- Pause before an important idea. This will help signal that what comes next is especially significant.
- If there's a question period following your speech and you're in charge of it, pause after you've completed your conclusion and ask the audience if they have any questions. If there's a chairperson, pause after your conclusion, then nonverbally indicate to the chairperson that you're ready to entertain questions.
- If there's no period for questions and answers, pause after the last sentence of your conclusion, continue to maintain eye contact with the audience, and then walk, do not run, back to your seat. Once you are back in your seat, focus on the class activity taking place.

Consider the qualities of the effective voice. What makes a speaker's voice interesting and persuasive?

ARTICULATION AND PRONUNCIATION

Articulation and pronunciation are similar in that they both refer to enunciation, the way in which we produce sounds and words. Technically, the two processes do differ. **Articulation** consists of the movements the speech organs make as they modify and interrupt the air stream you send from the lungs. Different movements of these speech organs (for example, the tongue, lips, teeth, palate, and vocal cords) produce different sounds. **Pronunciation** is the production of syllables or words according to some accepted standard, as identified in any good dictionary. Our concern here is with identifying and correcting some of the most common problems associated with faulty articulation and pronunciation.

Articulation Problems

The three major articulation problems are omission, substitution, and addition of sounds or syllables. These problems occur both in native speakers of English and in speakers whose first language is not English. Fortunately, they can be easily corrected with informed practice.

Errors of Omission.   Omitting sounds or even syllables is a major articulation problem but one easily overcome with concentration and practice. Here are some examples:

Not This	This
gov-a-ment	gov-ern-ment
hi-stry	hi-story
wanna	want to
studyin	studying
a-lum-num	a-lum-i-num
comp-ny	comp-a-ny

Errors of Substitution. Substituting an incorrect sound for the correct one is another easily corrected problem. Among the most common errors are substituting "d" for "t" and "d" for "th."

Not This	This
wader	waiter
dese	these
ax	ask
undoubtebly	undoubtedly
beder	better
ekcetera	etcetera

Errors of Addition. When there are errors of addition, sounds are added where they don't belong. Some examples include:

Not This	This
acrost	across
athalete	athlete
Americer	America
idear	idea
filim	film
lore	law

If you make any of these errors, you can easily correct them. First, become conscious of your own articulation patterns (and of any specific errors you may be making). Then listen carefully to the articulation of prominent speakers (for example, broadcasters), comparing their speech patterns with your own. Practice the correct patterns until they become part of your normal speech behavior.

Pronunciation Problems

Among the most widespread pronunciation problems are putting the **accent** (stress or emphasis) on the wrong syllable and pronouncing sounds that should remain silent. Both of these pronunciation problems may result from learning English as a second language. For example, a person may use the accent system of his or her first language to pronounce words in English that may have a different accent system. Similarly, in many languages, all letters that appear in a word are pronounced in speech, whereas in English some letters are silent.

Errors of Accent. Here are some common examples of words accented incorrectly:

Not This	This
New Orleáns	New Órleans
ínsurance	insúrance
orátor	órator

Errors of Pronouncing Silent Sounds. For some words correct pronunciation means not articulating certain sounds, as in the following examples:

Not This	This
often	offen
homage	omage

Research Link

DATABASES

A database is simply an organized collection of information. Today there are a wide variety of research database packages available from an increasing number of vendors. These databases contain resources that you most likely will not be able to find on the Web without paying a fee. ProQuest, EBSCO, InfoTrac, WilsonWeb, and Search Premier are some of the names you'll probably run across in your exploration of databases. Each of these vendors package databases in different ways. Your college library will no doubt have purchased certain of these packages and will make them available to students and faculty for access from home or from the library without charge. Unfortunately, a log-in password is necessary to gain access to these databases, so if your college doesn't have what you need, you can't just go to the more extensive database of another college. Very likely, however, you'll find what you need at your own college library. If you don't, the best thing to do is to speak to your librarian, who will probably be able locate the information you need in an database to which you do have access.

Some databases focus on specific areas; for example, history (America: History and Life, Historical Abstracts), health (Medline, Health Source), or communication (Communication & Mass Media Complete, Sage: Communication Studies Collection). Some databases are combinations of a variety of specific databases and contain a variety of publications from the major disciplines. Some databases focus on scholarly articles published in professional journals by academic researchers and scientists. Other databases focus on popular articles in magazines and newspapers. There is almost sure to be a database on just about any topic you'll want to research.

Each library, however, subscribes to a somewhat different package of databases, so your access to these databases may be limited in some ways. The best advice is to find out the databases to which your college or local library subscribes and to which you'll have access. Then learn how they work, the ways you can search for information, the operators they use, and how you can print information or save retrieved information to disk. The more you learn about how the database works, the more efficient and effective your database searches will be.

In addition, depending on the specific package ordered with this textbook, you may have access to Research Navigator. This is a user-friendly, wide-ranging database with information organized by disciplines, along with access to the *New York Times* and the *Financial Times* (of London) and a variety of other useful research guides.

The next Research Link, "Integrating and Citing Research," appears on page 248.

Illinois	Illinoi
even-ing	eve-ning

The best way to deal with pronunciation problems is to look up in a good dictionary any words whose pronunciation you're not sure of. Learn to read the pronunciation key in your dictionary, and make it a practice to look up words you hear others use that seem to be pronounced incorrectly as well as words that you wish to use yourself but are not sure how to pronounce. The numerous online audio-dictionaries, of course, make this process even easier.

EFFECTIVE BODILY ACTION

You speak with your body as well as with your mouth. The total effect of the speech depends not only on what you say but also on the way you present it. It depends on your movements, gestures, and facial expressions as well as on your words. Eight aspects of bodily action are especially important in public speaking: eye contact, facial expression, posture, dress, gestures, movement, proxemics, and the use of notes.

EYE CONTACT

The most important single aspect of bodily communication is eye contact. The two major problems with eye contact are inappropriate eye contact and eye contact that does not cover the audience fairly. In much of the United States, listeners perceive speakers who don't maintain enough eye contact as distant, unconcerned, and less trustworthy than speakers who look directly at their audience. Consequently, it's generally best to maintain relatively focused eye contact with your audience. Use your eyes to communicate your concern for and interest in what you're saying and to convey your confidence and commitment. Avoid staring blankly through your audience or glancing over their heads, at the floor, or out the window. In other cultures—for example, in many Asian cultures—focused eye contact may prove embarrassing to audience members, so in such cultures, it's often best to politely scan the audience without locking eyes with specific listeners.

Involve all listeners in the public speaking transaction. Communicate equally with the members on the left and on the right, in both the back and the front. Eye contact will also enable you to secure audience feedback, to see if your listeners are interested or bored or puzzled. Use eye contact to gauge listeners' level of agreement and disagreement.

FACIAL EXPRESSION

Facial expressions are especially important in communicating emotions—anger and fear, boredom and excitement, doubt and surprise. If you feel committed to and believe in your thesis, you'll probably display your meanings appropriately and effectively.

Nervousness and anxiety, however, may at times prevent you from relaxing enough so that your emotions come through. Fortunately, time and practice will allow you to relax, and the emotions you feel will reveal themselves appropriately and automatically.

Generally, members of one culture will be able to recognize the emotions displayed facially by members of other cultures. But there are differences in what each culture considers appropriate to display in public. As discussed in Chapter 5, each culture has its own "display rules" (Ekman, Friesen, & Ellsworth, 1972). For example, Japanese Americans watching a stress-inducing film spontaneously displayed the same facial emotions as did other Americans when they thought they were unobserved. But when an observer was present, the Japanese Americans masked (tried to hide) their emotional expressions more than did the other Americans (Gudykunst & Kim, 1992).

POSTURE

When delivering your speech, stand straight but not stiff. Try to communicate a command of the situation without communicating the discomfort that is actually quite common for beginning speakers.

Avoid the common mistakes of posture: Avoid putting your hands in your pockets or clasping them in front or behind your back; and avoid leaning on the desk, the lectern, or the chalkboard. With practice you'll come to feel more at ease and will communicate this by the way you stand before the audience.

DRESS

Public speaking is usually a more formal type of communication than most others; try to dress accordingly.

First, discover what the accepted and appropriate attire for the occasion is. For your classroom speeches, you'll probably be fine if you dress as you might for a conference with the dean or chair of your department. That is, try to dress perhaps one level above your everyday attire.

Second, avoid excess in just about anything you can think of. Too much jewelry or especially wild colors are likely to call attention to your manner of dress instead of to what you're saying or who you are and what your competencies are.

Third, dress comfortably but not too casually. Comfortable clothing will make you feel more at ease and will help you to be yourself. If you're in doubt as to how casual you should be, err on the side of formality; wear the tie, high heels, or dress.

GESTURES

Gestures in public speaking help illustrate your verbal messages. We gesture for this purpose regularly in conversation. For example, when saying "Come here," you probably move your head, hands, arms, and perhaps your entire body to motion the listener in your direction. Your body as well as your verbal message say "Come here."

Avoid using your hands to preen, however. For example, avoid fixing your hair or adjusting your clothing; don't fidget with your watch, ring, or jewelry.

Effective bodily action is spontaneous and natural to you as the speaker, to your audience, and to your speech. If gestures seem planned or rehearsed, they'll appear phony and insincere. As a general rule, don't do anything with your hands that doesn't feel right for you; the audience will recognize it as unnatural. If you feel relaxed and comfortable with yourself and your audience, you'll generate natural bodily action without conscious or studied attention.

MOVEMENT

The word *movement* refers here to movements of your whole body. In public speaking it helps to move around a bit. Movement keeps both you and the audience more alert. Even when speaking behind a lectern, you can give the illusion of movement. You can step back or forward or flex your upper body so it appears that you're moving more than you are.

If you're using a lectern, you may wish to signal transitions by stepping to the side or in front of it and then behind it again as you move from one point to another. Generally, however, it's best to avoid too much or too little movement around the lectern. Too much movement may make you appear ill at ease, fidgety, or nervous, which in turn will detract from your credibility. Too little move-

Consider the qualities of effective bodily action. What characteristics help you understand and empathize with the speaker? What characteristics distract you?

ment may make you appear frightened or uninvolved, which also will work against your establishing credibility. For example, you may wish to lean over the lectern when, say, posing a question to your listeners or advancing a particularly important argument. But never lean on the lectern; never use it as support.

Avoid the three problems of movement: too little, too much, and too patterned. Speakers who move too little often appear strapped to the podium, afraid of the audience, or too uncommitted to involve themselves fully. With too much movement the audience begins to concentrate on the movement itself, wondering where the speaker will wind up next. With movement that is too patterned, the audience may become bored—too steady and predictable a rhythm quickly becomes tiring. The audience will often view the speaker as nonspontaneous and uninvolved.

Use whole-body movements to emphasize transitions and to emphasize the introduction of a new and important assumption, bit of evidence, or closely reasoned argument. Thus, when making a transition, you might take a step forward to signal that something new is coming.

$\mathcal{P}$ROXEMICS

Proxemics, or the way you use space in communication, can be a crucial factor in public speaking. Consider the spaces between you and your listeners and among the listeners themselves. If you stand too close to your listeners, they may feel uncomfortable, as if their personal space is being violated. If you stand too far away from your audience, you may be perceived as uninvolved, uninterested, or uncomfortable. Watch where your instructor and other speakers stand, and adjust your own position accordingly.

$\mathcal{U}$SING NOTES

For some speeches it may be helpful for you to use notes. As one public speaking consultant put it, "By using notes you are demonstrating that you 'plan your work and work your plan.' You are a well-organized speaker. You have more sense than to spend valuable time memorizing an entire presentation" (Fensholt, 2003, p. 66). To make the most effective use of notes, however, do keep in mind the following guidelines.

▪ **Keep notes to a minimum**. The fewer notes you take with you, the better off you'll be. One reason so many speakers bring notes with them is that they want to avoid the face-to-face interaction required. With experience, however, you should find this face-to-face interaction the best part of the public speaking experience.

Resist the normal temptation to bring with you the entire speech outline. You may rely on it too heavily and lose direct contact with the audience. Instead, compose a delivery outline (see pp. 174–177), using only key words. Bring this to the lectern with you—one side of an index card (5-by-8 cards work extremely well for most short speeches) or at most an $8\frac{1}{2}$-by-11 page should be sufficient. This will relieve anxiety over the possibility of forgetting your speech but will not be extensive enough to interfere with direct contact with your audience.

Ethics   CORRECTING ERRORS

During a speech on HIV infection, you mention that the rate of HIV infection in women has increased by 10 percent over the last several years. You meant to say that the rate had decreased, but—probably because of nervousness—you say exactly the opposite of what you intended. Even though no one asks you about this during the question-and-answer session following your speech, you wonder if you should correct yourself. The problem, you feel, is that if you do correct yourself, the audience may question your entire speech; and this could undercut a message that you feel very strongly about—that all people must take precautions to prevent HIV infection.

Ethical Choice Point *What is your ethical obligation in this case? More generally, what ethical responsibility does a speaker have to correct her or his mistakes?*

- **Use notes with "open subtlety."** Don't make your notes more obvious than necessary. At the same time, don't try to hide them. Don't gesture with your notes and thus make them more obvious than they need be; at the same time, don't turn away from the audience to steal a glance at them either. Use them openly and honestly but gracefully, with "open subtlety." To do this effectively, you'll have to know your notes intimately. Rehearse at least twice with the same notes that you'll take with you to the speaker's stand.

- **Don't allow your notes to prevent directness.** When using your notes, pause to look at them. Then regain eye contact with the audience and continue your speech. Don't read from your notes; just take cues from them. The one exception to this is an extensive quotation or complex set of statistics that you have to read; read it and then, almost immediately, resume direct eye contact with the audience.

REHEARSAL: PRACTICING AND IMPROVING DELIVERY

Through rehearsal you can develop delivery skills that will help you achieve the purposes of your speech. Rehearsal also will enable you to time your speech and to see how the speech will flow as a whole. Additionally, rehearsal will help you test out your presentation aids, detect any technological problems, and resolve them. And, of course, through rehearsal you'll learn your speech, so you'll know that you know your speech. With this knowledge should come greater confidence, and this confidence will help to reduce your apprehension.

The following procedures should assist you in achieving these goals.

REHEARSE THE SPEECH AS A WHOLE

Rehearse the speech from beginning to end. Don't rehearse the speech in parts. Rehearse it from getting out of your seat, through the introduction, body, and conclusion, to returning to your seat. Be sure to rehearse the speech with all the examples and illustrations (and audiovisual aids if any) included. This will enable you to connect the parts of the speech and to see how they interact with one another.

TIME THE SPEECH

Time the speech during each rehearsal. Make any necessary adjustments on the basis of this timing. If you're using computer presentation software, you'll be able to time your speech very precisely. Such software will also enable you to time the individual parts of your speech so you can achieve the balance you want—for example, you might want to spend twice as much time on the solutions as on the problems, or you might want to balance the introduction and conclusion so that each constitutes about 10 percent of your speech.

APPROXIMATE THE ACTUAL SPEECH SITUATION

Rehearse the speech under conditions as close as possible to those under which you'll deliver it. If possible, rehearse the speech in the same room in which you'll present it. If this is impossible, try to simulate the actual conditions as closely as you can—in your living room or even in a bathroom. If possible, rehearse the speech in front of supportive listeners; one study found that students who practiced their speeches before an audience received higher grades than those who practiced without an audience (Smith & Frymier, 2006). It's always helpful (especially for your beginning speeches) if your listeners are supportive rather than critical, but merely having listeners present during your rehearsal will further simulate the conditions under which you'll eventually speak. Get together with two or three other students in an empty classroom where you can each serve as speaker and listener.

INCORPORATE CHANGES AND DELIVERY NOTES

Don't interrupt your rehearsal to make notes or changes; if you do, you may never experience the entire speech from beginning to end. But do make any needed changes in the speech between rehearsals. While making these changes, note any words whose pronunciation or articulation you wish to check. Also, insert pause notations, "slow down" warnings, and other delivery suggestions into your outline.

If possible, record your speech (ideally, on videotape) so you can hear exactly what your listeners will hear: your volume, rate, pitch, articulation and pronunciation, and pauses. You'll then be in a better position to improve these qualities.

ℛEHEARSE OFTEN

Rehearse the speech as often as seems necessary. Two useful guides: (1) Rehearse the speech at least three or four times; less than this is sure to be too little. And (2) rehearse the speech as long as your rehearsals continue to produce improvements in the speech or in your delivery.

Essentials of Presenting Your Speech

In this chapter we looked at ways you can present your speech more effectively.

1. Three general **methods of presentation** are used in public speaking:
   - Impromptu: speaking without preparation; useful in certain aspects of public speaking
   - Manuscript: reading from a written text; useful when exact timing and wording are essential
   - Extemporaneous: speaking after thorough preparation and memorization of the main ideas; useful in most public speaking situations

2. Several key qualities make for **effective vocal delivery**:
   - Volume: Avoid speech that is overly soft, loud, or unvaried, and be sure not to fade away at ends of sentences.
   - Rate: Avoid speaking too fast, too slowly, with too little variation, or in too predictable a pattern.
   - Pitch: Avoid a pitch that is overly high, low, or monotonous, or that falls into too predictable a pattern.
   - Pauses: Use pauses to signal transitions between parts of the speech, give the audience time to think, allow listeners to ponder rhetorical questions, and signal the approach of especially important ideas.

   - Articulation and pronunciation: Errors of articulation and pronunciation include omission, substitution, and addition; using the wrong accent; and pronouncing silent sounds.

3. Seven aspects of **effective bodily action** are especially important:
   - Maintain eye contact.
   - Allow facial expressions to convey thoughts and feelings.
   - Use posture to communicate command of the speech experience.
   - Dress comfortably and at an appropriate level of formality.
   - Gesture naturally.
   - Move around a bit.
   - Position yourself neither too close to nor too far from the audience.
   - Use a few notes, but use them with "open subtlety" so that they don't prevent your maintaining direct contact with your audience.

4. Follow these **rehearsal guidelines**:
   - Rehearse the speech as a whole.
   - Time the speech.
   - Approximate the actual speech situation.
   - Incorporate changes and delivery notes.
   - Rehearse often.

Essential Terms: Presenting Your Speech

accent **(p. 224)**
articulation **(p. 223)**
extemporaneous speech **(p. 214)**
impromptu speech **(p. 212)**

manuscript speech **(p. 213)**
memorized speech **(p. 212)**
pauses **(p. 222)**
pitch **(p. 221)**

pronunciation **(p. 223)**
proxemics **(p. 228)**
rate **(p. 221)**
volume **(p. 220)**

Public Speaking Exercises

9.1 Communicating Vocally but Nonverbally

This exercise is designed to give you practice in communicating effectively with your voice and body. In this exercise a speaker recites the alphabet and attempts to communicate with each letter one of the following emotions: anger, nervousness, fear, pride, happiness, sadness, jealousy, satisfaction, love, or sympathy. The speaker should first number the emotions in random order so that he or she will have a set order to follow that is not known to the audience, whose task it will be to guess the emotions expressed.

As a variation, have the speaker go through the entire list of emotions twice: once facing the audience and employing any nonverbal signals desired, and once with his or her back to the audience and giving no nonverbal signals.

After the exercise is completed, consider some or all of the following questions:

1. What vocal cues help communicate the various emotions?

2. What bodily cues are useful in communicating these various emotions?

3. Are there gender display rules for effectively communicating some or all of these emotions? That is, are men and women expected to use different cues when communicating certain emotions?

9.2 Checking Your Pronunciation

Here are additional words that are often mispronounced. Consult a print or online dictionary (ideally, one with audio capabilities) and record the correct pronunciations here.

Words Often Mispronounced

abdomen	hierarchy
accessory	library
arctic	nausea
buffet	nuclear
cavalry	probably
clothes	prostate
costume	realtor
diagnosis	relevant
especially	repeat
espresso	salmon
February	sandwich
foliage	similar
forehead	strength
forte	substantive
herb	xenophobia

Mispronouncing words in public speaking may significantly impact on your credibility. Feeling unsure of how to pronounce a word in your speech also is likely to contribute to your communication apprehension.

9.3 What Do You Say?

◆ **Dressing for a Speech.** J. T. has to give three speeches on the same topic—school hate speech codes—to (1) the faculty of an exclusive prep school, (2) your class, and (3) the city council. J. T. wonders how to dress for these presentations. If you were an image consultant, what advice would you give for dressing in each of these three situations if J. T. were a man? If J. T. were a woman?

◆ **Speaking Volume.** After sitting through two rounds of speeches, Brad wonders if the class wouldn't be ready for a speech spoken at noticeably higher volume than normal—rather like television commercials, which are played louder than the regular broadcast. What would you advise Brad to do?

◆ **Citing Research.** Sharon wants to cite a recent research article she's read in *The New England Journal of Medicine*, and at the same time to establish the credibility of the article's author and of the journal itself. Using hypothetical data for this exercise, write out what an ideal oral citation of a research study from this journal would look like.

◆ **Unexpected Feedback.** Phyllis introduced her speech with a story she found extremely humorous and which made her laugh out loud as she relayed it to the audience. Unfortunately, the audience just didn't get it—not one smile in the entire audience. What (if anything) might Phyllis do now?

◆ **Technical Problems.** Victoria prepared a great slide show for her informative speech. Unfortunately, the projector that she needed to show the slides never arrived at the location of the speech. But she has to give the speech, and she has to (or must she?) explain something about what happened to her prepared slide show. What might Victoria say (if anything)?

Log*On*! **MySpeechLab**

Presenting Your Speech

Visit MySpeechLab (www.myspeechlab.com) and go to "Undertaking a Long-Term Delivery Program" for additional suggestions for improving your public speaking delivery and rehearsal. Two exercises will give you opportunities to practice using nonverbal signals to communicate: "Communicating Vocally but Nonverbally" and "Communicating Emotions Nonverbally." The video speeches will help you see both effective and ineffective delivery, especially in the contrasted speeches on "Untreated Depression" and "Brain Research on the Sexes." While at MSL and in connection with the Research Link on databases in this chapter, note the extensive database of research sources you have available and which you can search using key word or author name. Also take a look at Richard Nixon's resignation speech and Martin Luther King Jr.'s "I Have a Dream" (if you haven't viewed this already), as well as the two student speeches, "Choosing a Speech Topic" and "Needless Technology." All of these speeches will illustrate effective and ineffective speech presentation styles. You may also find it useful to take the practice tests on methods of delivery, effective vocal delivery and bodily action, and rehearsal.

Also visit the Allyn & Bacon public speaking website (www.ablongman.com/pubspeak) for a variety of delivery suggestions, including dressing for speaking, demonstrating dynamism, and the general modes of delivery.

10 Informing Your Audience

Why Read This Chapter?

Because it will enable you to convey information to an audience by helping you to:

- effectively inform an audience

- organize and develop speeches for describing (a person, object, event, or process), defining (a concept or theory), or demonstrating (how to do something or how something operates)

The beginning of wisdom is the definition of terms.

—Socrates (470–399 B.C.)
Greek philosopher,
Plato's teacher, and widely
considered the founder
of Western philosophy

One of the important types of speeches you'll be called upon to deliver is the informative speech, the subject of this chapter. We'll first look at the general goals of **informative speaking** and at some key principles for communicating information. Then we'll examine the varied types of informative speeches and see how you can develop each type most effectively.

GOALS OF INFORMATIVE SPEAKING

You can give an informative speech to serve a variety of goals. At the most obvious level, the goal of all informative speaking is to tell your listeners something they don't already know. But there are a variety of other, more specific goals that may motivate informative speaking. Reviewing these will help explain the nature and purpose of the informative speech.

One goal of informative speaking may be to introduce a topic that is totally new to the audience. A sales representative might demonstrate new surgical tools to a group of medical doctors or an inventor might explain an entirely new toy.

Another goal may be to clarify misconceptions that people have about something; say, the way an automobile or a cell phone works, or the ways in which graduate and professional schools select students, or the criteria for promotion of a college professor—all topics that many people think they understand but about which lots of misconceptions actually exist.

Still another goal is to demonstrate how to use information; the popular cooking shows are good examples of this type of speech. Many of the infomercials on television spend lots of time showing you how to use their new product—whether it's George Foreman's Grilling Machine, Joy Mangano's clothes hangers, or Ron Popeil's slow cooker, baldness fix, or roaster.

Perhaps the most popular goal is to communicate information about topics the audience knows something about but not a great deal; your goal here will be to enlarge the knowledge your listeners already have. Speeches on such topics as the way e-mail, spam, or pop-ups work or the rules of golf, tennis, or soccer would likely include information that the audience does not yet know.

As I write this, Microsoft's Vista operating system is making its debut and provides a good illustration of how the same topic can be pursued with different goals in mind. So let's say you want to give an informative speech on Vista.

- To an audience of dedicated Mac users, the information may be entirely new, so your goal will be to introduce a topic unknown to the audience.

- To an audience of dedicated Mac users who think there's little or no difference between the systems, you'll be clarifying misconceptions.

- To an audience of students using Windows, you may wish to demonstrate how to use the information—to explain, for example, the ways in which they can use Vista to accomplish a variety of tasks more efficiently.

- To an audience of Windows XP users, you'll be communicating about topics they know a lot about but augmenting their knowledge by discussing what's new in Vista.

As you can appreciate, a speech on Vista for dedicated Mac users would have to be different from a speech for XP users. Though both speeches would cover similar, and in some cases the same, material, you'd have to approach it very differently depending on the knowledge and experience of your listeners. With this basic principle in mind—a principle you see in operation every time you hear an effective classroom lecture, just as you see the principle violated in every ineffective lecture—we can look at several principles for communicating information.

PRINCIPLES OF INFORMATIVE SPEAKING

Once again, to communicate information is to tell your listeners something they don't know, something new. You may inform your audience about a new way of looking at old things or an old way of looking at new things. You may discuss a theory not previously heard of or a familiar concept not fully understood. You may talk about events that the audience may be unaware of or explain happenings they may have misconceptions about.

To complement your reading of this chapter, a variety of excellent websites devoted to informative speaking are available. Many public speaking courses maintain websites to help students find topics and develop informative speeches; for example, the Cincinnati State Technical and Community College (http://faculty.cinstate.cc.oh.us/gesellsc/publicspeaking/topics.html) and Colorado State University (http://writing.colostate.edu/references/speaking/infomod/index.cfm) both cover the purposes and types of informative speaking and offer lots of suggestions for developing and delivering informative speeches. Visit these sites or search for similar sites on "informative speaking" or "public speaking."

Regardless of what type of informative speech you intend to give, the following guidelines should help.

LIMIT THE AMOUNT OF INFORMATION

There's a limit to the amount of information that a listener can take in at one time. Resist the temptation to overload your listeners with information. Instead of enlarging the breadth of information you communicate, expand its depth. It's better to present two new items of information and explain these in depth with examples, illustrations, and descriptions than to present five items without this needed amplification. The speaker who attempts to discuss the physiological, psychological, social, and linguistic differences between men and women, for example, is clearly trying to cover too much and is going to be forced to cover these areas only superficially, with the result that little new information will be communicated. Even covering *one* of these areas completely is likely to prove difficult. Instead, select one subdivision of one area—say, language development or differences in language problems—and develop that in depth.

ADJUST THE LEVEL OF COMPLEXITY

As you know from attending college classes, information can be presented in very simple or very complex form. **Adjusting the level of complexity** on which you communicate your information is crucial. This adjustment should depend on the wide variety of factors considered throughout this book: the level of knowledge your audience has, the time you have available, the purpose you hope to achieve, the topic on which you're speaking, and so on. If you simplify a topic too much, you risk boring or, even worse, insulting your audience. On the other hand, if your talk is too complex, you risk confusing your audience and failing to communicate your message.

Generally, beginning speakers err by being too complex and not realizing that a 5- or 10-minute speech isn't long enough to make an audience understand sophisticated concepts or complicated processes. At least in your beginning speeches, try to keep it simple rather than complex. Make sure the words you use are familiar to your audience; alternatively, explain and define any unfamiliar terms as you use them. For example, remember that jargon and technical vocabulary familiar to the computer hacker may not be familiar to the person who still uses a typewriter. Always see your topic from the point of view of the audience; ask yourself how much they know about your topic and its particular terminology.

STRESS RELEVANCE AND USEFULNESS

Listeners remember information best when they see it as relevant and useful to their own needs or goals. Notice that as a listener you yourself regularly demonstrate this principle of **relevance and usefulness**. For example, in class you may attend to and remember the stages in the development of language in children simply because you'll be tested on the information and you want to earn a high grade. Or you may remember a given piece of information because it will help you make a better impression in your job interview, make you a better parent, or enable you to deal with relationship problems. Like you, listeners attend to information that will prove useful to them.

Consider the sales pitch for an item such as a new car. Although the purpose of the sales talk is obviously persuasive, you're likely to hear messages that appear almost entirely informative. How would you explain the relation beween information and persuasion in sales talks?

If you want the audience to listen to your speech, relate your information to their needs, wants, or goals. Throughout your speech, but especially in the beginning, make sure your audience knows that the information you're presenting is or will be relevant and useful to them now or in the immediate future. For example, you might say something like:

> We all want financial security. We all want to be able to buy those luxuries we read so much about in magazines and see every evening on television. Wouldn't it be nice to be able to buy a car without worrying about where you're going to get the down payment or how you'll be able to make the monthly payments? Actually, that is not an unrealistic goal, as I'll demonstrate in this speech. In fact, I'll show you several investment strategies that have enabled many people to increase their income by as much as 20 percent.

RELATE NEW INFORMATION TO OLD

Listeners will learn information more easily and retain it longer when you relate it to what they already know. So relate the new to the old, the unfamiliar to the familiar, the unseen to the seen, the untasted to the tasted. Here, for example, Betsy Heffernan, a student from the University of Wisconsin (Reynolds & Schnoor, 1991), relates the problem of sewage to a familiar historical event:

> During our nation's struggle for independence, the citizens of Boston were hailed as heroes for dumping tea into Boston Harbor. But not to be outdone, many modern day Bostonians are also dumping things into the harbor: five-thousand gallons of human waste every second. The New England Aquarium of Boston states that since 1900, Bostonians have dumped enough human sewage into the harbor to cover the entire state of Massachusetts chest deep in sludge. Unfortunately, Boston isn't alone. All over the country, bays, rivers, and lakes are literally becoming cesspools.

VARY THE LEVELS OF ABSTRACTION

You can talk about freedom of the press in the abstract by talking about the importance of getting information to the public, by referring to the Bill of Rights, and by relating a free press to the preservation of democracy. But you can also talk about freedom of the press on a low level of abstraction, a level that is specific and concrete; for example, you can describe how a local newspaper was prevented from running a story critical of the town council or how Lucy Rinaldo was fired from the *Accord Sentinel* after she wrote a story critical of the mayor.

Varying the **levels of abstraction**—combining high abstraction (the very general) and low abstraction (the very specific)—seems to work best. Too many generalizations without the specifics or too many specifics without the generalizations will prove less effective than the combination of abstract and specific.

Here, for example, is an excerpt from a speech on the homeless. Note that in the first paragraph we have a relatively abstract description of homelessness. In the second paragraph, we get into specifics. In the last paragraph the abstract and the concrete are connected.

> [Here the speaker begins with relatively general or abstract statements.] Homelessness is a serious problem for all metropolitan areas throughout the country. It's currently estimated that there are now more than 200,000 homeless in New York City alone. But what is this really about? Let me tell you what it's about.

[Here the speaker gets to specifics.] It's about a young man. He must be about 25 or 30, although he looks a lot older. He lives in a cardboard box on the side of my apartment house. We call him Tom, although we really don't know his name. All his possessions are stored in this huge box. I think it was a box from a refrigerator. Actually, he doesn't have very much, and what he has easily fits in this box. There's a blanket my neighbor threw out, some plastic bottles Tom puts water in, and some Styrofoam containers he picked up from the garbage from Burger King. He uses these to store whatever food he finds.

[The conclusion combines the general and the specific.] What is homelessness about? It's about Tom and 200,000 other "Toms" in New York and thousands of others throughout the rest of the country. And not all of them even have boxes to live in.

MAKE YOUR SPEECH EASY TO REMEMBER

The principles of public speaking (principles governing use of language, delivery, and supporting materials, for example) will all help your listeners remember your speech. If, for example, you stress interest and relevance—as already noted—the audience is more likely to remember what you say, because they will see it as important and relevant to their own lives. But here are a few extra suggestions.

- *Repeat the points you want the audience to remember.* Help your audience to remember what you want them to remember by repeating your most important points.
- *Use guide phrases.* Guide your audience's attention to your most memorable points by saying, for example, "the first point to remember is that . . . ," "the argument I want you to remember when you enter that voting booth is . . . ."
- *Use internal summary transitions.* Internal summary transitions will remind the audience of what you have said and how it relates to what is to follow. This kind of repetition will reinforce your message and help your listeners remember your main points.
- *Pattern your messages.* If the audience can see the logic of your speech, they'll be better able to organize what you say in their own minds. If they can see that you're following a temporal pattern or a spatial pattern, for example, it will be easier for them to retain more of what you say, because they'll have a framework into which they can fit what you say.
- *Focus audience attention.* The best way to focus the listeners' attention is to tell them to focus their attention. Simply say, "I want you to focus on three points that I will make in this speech. First, . . ." or "What I want you to remember is this: . . . ."

Now that the princples of information speaking have been identified, let's consider the main types of informative speeches. Different writers classify informative speeches in somewhat different ways (see Table 10.1 for additional classification systems). Here I'll use a simple three-part system:

- Speeches of *description* are speeches in which you describe an object (the human heart) or person (a genius, artist, or Picasso) or describe an event (a hurricane) or process (adopting a child).

TABLE 10.1 Additional Classifications of Informative Speeches

PUBLIC SPEAKING TEXTBOOKS	CLASSIFICATIONS	EXAMPLES
Stephen Lucas (2007) in *The Art of Public Speaking* uses a four-part classification:	1. Speeches about objects, persons, places, or things 2. Speeches about processes or series of actions 3. Speeches about events or happenings 4. Speeches about concepts, beliefs, or ideas	1. The contributions of a noted scientist or philosopher 2. An explanation of how to do something 3. The story of your first date 4. A review of theories of economics
George Grice and John Skinner (2007) in *Mastering Public Speaking* offer an eight-part system:	1. Speeches about people 2. Speeches about objects 3. Speeches about places 4. Speeches about events 5. Speeches about processes 6. Speeches about concepts 7. Speeches about conditions 8. Speeches about issues	1. Cesar Chavez, Margaret Mead 2. Electric cars, the Great Wall of China 3. Ellis Island, the Nile 4. The sinking of the Titanic, Woodstock festivals 5. Cartooning, waterproofing 6. Liberty, nihilism 7. McCarthyism, the civil rights movement 8. The use of polygraph tests, fetal tissue research
Rudolph and Kathleen Verderber in *The Challenge of Effective Speaking* (2006) offer a five-part system:	1. Speeches of description 2. Speeches of definition 3. Speeches of comparison and contrast 4. Speeches of narration 5. Speeches of demonstration	1. Speeches about objects, geographical features, settings, or images—a light bulb, holograph 2. Speeches that explain something by identi-fying its meaning—vegetarianism, plane 3. Speeches explaining how something is similar or different from other things—vegans and vegetarians 4. Speeches explaining something by recounting events, becoming a vegetarian 5. Speeches that explain how something is done, the stages of a process, or how something works—how to iron a shirt, the workings of a nuclear reactor

Sources: From Stephen E. Lucas, *The Art of Public Speaking, 9/e.* Copyright © 2007 by McGraw-Hill Education. Adapted by permission of the McGraw-Hill Companies. From Grice, George L. & John F. Skinner, *Mastering Public Speaking, 6/e.* Published by Allyn and Bacon, Boston, MA. Copyright © 2007 by Pearson Education. Adapted by permission of the publisher. From The Challenge of Effective Speaking (with CD-ROM and SpeechBuilder Express™/InfoTrac®) 13th edition by VERDERBER/ VERDERBER. 2006. Adapted with permission of Wadsworth, a division of Thomson Learning: www.thomsonrights.com. Fax 800-730-2215.

■ Speeches of *definition* are speeches in which you define a term (linguistics), a system or theory (evolution), or similar and dissimilar terms (nature/nurture, communism/socialism).

■ Speeches of *demonstration* are speeches in which you show how to do something (protecting yourself against identity theft) or how something works (search spiders).

Let's look first at the speech of description.

AN INFORMATIVE SPEECH

Public Speaking   *Sample Assistant*

This informative speech was delivered by Steve Zammit of Cornell University. In this speech Zammit informs his listeners about the nature of the electric heart and claims that the electric heart will significantly influence the treatment of heart problems.

THE ELECTRIC HEART

Steve Zammit

On February 21, 2000, David Letterman returned to the Late Show after his quadruple bypass with a list of the "Top 10 Things You Don't Want to Hear When You Wake Up from Surgery." They include: Number 2—"Hello Mr. Letterman . . . or should I say Miss Letterman?" and Number 1— "We did what we could, Mr. Letterman, but this is Jiffy Lube." But after the gags, Dave brought his doctors on stage and choked up as he thanked them for "saving my life."

One year later, the *New York Times* of February 1, 2001, announced conditional FDA approval for a medical device that will bring similar results to millions of heart patients. But rather than bypass a clogged artery, this revolutionary device bypasses the heart itself, thus fulfilling the life vision of 55-year-old scientist and heart surgeon Dr. David Lederman. Dr. David Lederman is the inventor of the [VA] Electric Heart.

The Electric Heart is a safe, battery-operated, permanent replacement that is directly implanted into the body. The February 12, 2001, *Telegram and Gazette* predicts that within one generation more than 10 million Americans will be living with terminal heart disease. For them, and for the 100,000 transplant candidates who pray for a new heart when only 2,000 are annually available, hope has been fleeting . . . until now.

So to learn why UCLA transplant surgeon Dr. Steven Marelli calls it the "Holy Grail of Heart

How effective was the introduction? What purposes did it accomplish? Would you have sought to accomplish any other purpose(s)? If so, what would you have said?

Note that the speech transcript shows the points at which visual aids [VA] are to be presented.

Does the speaker **stress relevance and usefulness** to maintain your attention? How would you have stressed relevance and usefulness?

What did you think of the way the speaker phrased the orientation to the major propositions of the speech? Did the orientation add clarity? Did it add humor?

Surgery," let's first plug into the heart's development and see how it works. Next, we'll flesh out its current status. So that finally we can see how the device's future impact will be heart-stopping.

In early 1982, Washington dentist Barney Clark's heart was stopping—literally. The world watched as Dr. Robert Jarvik implanted Clark with the first ever artificial heart. After 112 days marked by kidney failure, respiratory problems, and severe mental confusion, the heart stopped. It didn't take a rocket scientist to see that, as the *New York Times* of May 16, 1988, declared, artificial heart research was medical technology's version of Dracula. Basically, it sucked. Getting Dracula out of his coffin would require a little thinking outside the box. Enter Dr. David Lederman, who, in a happy coincidence, reported *Forbes* of April 17, 2000, is an actual rocket scientist. In fact, Lederman changed his career path in the early 1970s when he heard a lecture by a physicist who insisted artificial hearts would rise or fall based on fluid mechanics.

What functions did the Dracula example serve? Do you feel this was too flippant for a speech on such a serious topic? Do you feel it added the right note of levity?

Lederman's design can be likened to space flight in that the concept is easy, but the tiniest problems can prevent a launch or cause an explosion. *What separates the Electric Heart from Jarvik's earlier model is the development and implementation of space-age technology.* In particular, the *Pittsburgh Post-Gazette* of January 28, 2001, explains that an artificial heart must simultaneously weigh two pounds, be flexible enough to expand and contract, and be tough enough to absorb 40 million beats a year. The solution is a proprietary titanium compound called Angioflex, the first man-made material on earth that fits the mold.

How would you describe the **level of complexity** in this speech?

A typical heart pumps blood through constant muscular contractions regulated by the nervous system. [VA] But Lederman's model propels blood using an internal motor regulated by a microprocessor embedded inside the abdomen. A small external belt transmits energy through the skin to a copper coil, allowing the entire system to be continuously stimulated.

Although you can't see the visual aids the speaker used, you can imagine what they were. If you were listening to this speech, what would you have liked to have seen in these visuals?

When he returned last February, David Letterman was stimulated by a hospital gown–clad Robin Williams, who performed a zany strip tease. . . . I'll spare you the VA. But to see if Dr. Lederman is himself a tease, we must now evaluate his project's current status as well as the obstacles it faces.

Can you identify transitions the speaker used to connect the speech parts?

The *Houston Chronicle* of January 31, 2001, reveals that FDA approval of the Electric Heart was based on its wild success when implanted in animals. More than 100 cows have been recipients of the heart, and in Dr. Lederman's words, three hours after surgery, "I have seen the animals standing in their stalls munching hay, with their original hearts in a jar nearby." Sometime in early June, surgical teams will swap an Electric Heart for the failing one in five critically ill human patients, for what Dr. Lederman calls "the most public clinical trials in history." For those skeptics who argue it's a little early to break out the bubbly, Dr. Lederman adamantly agrees. He told the February 5, 2001, *Glasgow Herald*, "At first, you had the Wright brothers. Today, you can easily cross the Atlantic. Our heart is the equivalent of making the flight from Boston to New York," but the trip across the Atlantic is only a matter of time.

Despite the optimism, the beat will not go on until Dr. Lederman convincingly addresses two concerns about practicality. As the *British Medical Journal* of March 17, 2001, explains, organ transplant recipients must take expensive, nauseating drugs to prevent clotting and rejection. Fortunately, Angioflex's producer, Abiomed, revealed in a 2000 Securities and Exchange Commission filing that the material is perfectly seamless and can withstand over 20 years of abuse without cracking. No cracks, no place for clots to form. And since the Electric Heart is made of inert materials, UCLA transplant surgeon Dr. Steven Marelli told the February 7, 2001, *University Wire*, the body will not reject it, an observation confirmed by animal trials. Essentially, Electric Heart recipients will come back without expensive drug therapy.

Speaking of comebacks, just as David Letterman's return culminated in an Emmy nomination, Dr. Lederman will soon be picking up some awards of his own, due to the Electric Heart's impact on individuals and society. As transplant pioneer Robert Jarvik once said, "the artificial heart must not only be dependable, but truly forgettable." But during periods of increased energy demand—including making love—Jarvik's model required a user to be tethered to a power unit in the wall. Lederman's model, in the words of the February 2001 *GQ*, is "The Love Machine." As *GQ* observes, the internal battery can allow "unassisted" exercise for 30 minutes—every man's dream. But the *Boston*

As you read the speech, did you feel that the speaker successfully involved you in the speech? If not, what might the speaker have done to make you feel he was talking about you to you?

How effectively did the speaker integrate research into the speech?

Does the speaker **limit the amount of information** he communicates so that there is significant depth? Would you have done things differently?

Does the speaker successfully **relate new information** to old?

Globe of February 1, 2001, reveals that advances in battery technology eventually will allow a sleeping user to be charged for a full day—allowing recipients to emulate the Energizer Bunny in more ways than one.

But by normalizing life for individuals, the Electric Heart will be revolutionizing medicine in society. The March 26, 2001, *Los Angeles Times* notes that 400,000 Americans are diagnosed with heart failure each year. Add the number of other failing internal organs, as well as a glut of aging baby boomers, and we are a generation away from a crisis. To cope, some researchers have famously approached organ shortages by genetically engineering them to grow in a lab, a process that will still take years. But the Electric Heart is both more immediate, and carries none of the ethical entanglements of manipulating the human genome. As Dr. Ed Berger, vice president of Abiomed, explained in an April 2, 2001, telephone interview, Angioflex is so versatile, it could eventually be used to construct artificial kidneys and lungs.

Unfortunately, the *American Journal of Medicine* of February 1, 2001, reports that heart disease disproportionately strikes those in lower socioeconomic brackets, a group that often lacks access to advanced technology. But the April 19, 2001, *Boston Herald* predicts the procedure will eventually retail for about $25,000, the same as a traditional heart bypass. Coupled with the cost savings on drug treatment, the procedure should be affordably covered by most insurance companies, including Medicare. So whether rich or poor, young or old, resting or energized, the Electric Heart will be an equal opportunity lifesaver.

Although you can never mend a broken heart, Dr. Lederman has done the next best thing. By reviewing the Electric Heart's unusual development and current testing, we have seen its future impact on viewers around the world. On the night of his comeback, David Letterman put a human face on heart disease. But for thousands who find themselves in the comedian's shoes, laughter—and everything else—is insufficient medicine. But soon, Dr. David Lederman will reach audiences with a message of hope. For them, the Electric Heart will not just make the Top 10 List. It will be number one.

Source: Stephen Zammit, Cornell University. Reprinted with permission.

Of all the research cited in the speech, which did you think was the most effective? Which was the least effective? Why?

Did the speaker **vary the levels of abstraction** effectively, or would you have wished to hear more high-level or more low-level abstractions?

What influence did the research and its integration into the speech have on your image of the speaker's credibility?

How effective do you think the speech title, "The Electric Heart," was? What other titles might have worked?

What one thing will you remember most from this speech? Why will you remember this? That is, what did the speaker say that made this one thing most memorable?

How effective was the speaker's conclusion? What functions did the conclusion serve? What other functions might it have served?

Now that you've finished reading the speech (don't look back), what were the major propositions of the speech? What did you learn from this speech?

SPEECHES OF DESCRIPTION

In a **speech of description** you're concerned with explaining an object, person, event, or process. Here are a few examples:

Describing an Object or Person

- the structure of DNA
- the contributions of Benjamin Franklin
- the parts of a telephone
- the geography of Africa
- the hierarchy of a corporation
- the components of a computer system

Describing an Event or Process

- the attacks of September 11, 2001
- the events leading to war with Iraq
- organizing a bodybuilding contest
- how a book is printed
- purchasing stock online
- how a child acquires language

THESIS

The thesis of a speech, as explained in Chapter 4, is your single most important concept; it is what you most want your audience to remember. The thesis of a speech of description simply states what you'll describe in your speech; for example, *The child acquires language in four stages*, or *There are three steps to purchasing stock online*, or *Four major events led to the war with Iraq*.

MAIN POINTS

The main points of your speech are the major subdivisions of the thesis. You derive your main points from the thesis by asking strategic questions. For example, what are the four stages in child language acquisition? What are the three steps to purchasing stock online? What events led to the war with Iraq?

SUPPORT

Obviously you don't want simply to list your main points but to flesh them out—to make them memorable, interesting, and, most of all, clear. You do this by using a variety of materials that amplify and support your main ideas; you include examples, illustrations, testimony, statistics, and the like, as has already been explained. So, for example, in describing the babbling stage of language learning, you might give examples of babbling, the age at which babbling first

Consider the varied ways of describing an object, a person, or an event. Try, for example, to describe a room in your home without drawing any pictures. What types of descriptive categories would you use to describe yourself to someone who has never seen you, say, in a chat room conversation?

appears, the period of time that babbling lasts, or the differences between the babbling of girls and boys.

Because this is a speech of description, give extra consideration to the types of description you might use in your supporting materials. Try to describe the object or event with lots of different **descriptive categories**. With physical categories, for example, ask yourself questions such as these: What color is it? How big is it? What is it shaped like? How much does it weigh? What is its volume? How attractive/unattractive is it? Also consider social, psychological, and economic categories. In describing a person, for example, consider such categories as friendly/unfriendly, warm/cold, rich/poor, aggressive/meek, and pleasant/unpleasant.

Consider how you might use presentation aids. In describing an object or a person, show your listeners a picture; show them the inside of a telephone, pictures of the brain, the skeleton of the body. In describing an event or process, show them a diagram or flowchart to illustrate the stages or steps; for example, the steps involved in buying stock, in publishing a newspaper, in putting a parade together.

ORGANIZATION

Consider using a spatial or a topical organization when describing objects and people. Consider using a temporal pattern when describing events and processes. For example, if you were to describe the layout of Philadelphia, you might start from the north and work down to the south (using a spatial pattern). If you were to describe the achievements of Thomas Edison, you might select Edison's three or four major contributions and discuss each of these equally (using a topical pattern).

If you were describing the events leading up to Iraq war, you might use a temporal pattern, starting with the earliest and working up to the latest. A temporal pattern also would be appropriate for describing how a hurricane develops or how a parade is put together.

Consider the "Who? What? Where? When? and Why?" pattern of organization. These journalistic categories are especially useful when you want to describe an event or a process. For example, if you're going to describe how to purchase a house, you might want to consider the people involved (who?), the steps you have to go through (what?), the places you'll have to go (where?), the time or sequence in which each of the steps have to take place (when?), and the advantages and disadvantages of buying the house (why?).

Here are two examples of the bare bones of how a descriptive speech might look. In this first example, the speaker describes four suggestions for reducing energy bills. Notice that the speaker derives the main points from asking a question of the thesis.

General purpose: To inform.
Specific purpose: To describe how you can reduce energy bills.
Thesis: Energy bills can be reduced. (How can energy bills be reduced?)

 I. Caulk window and door seams.

 II. Apply weather stripping around windows and doors.

 III. Insulate walls.

 IV. Install storm windows and doors.

In this second example, the speaker describes the way in which fear works in intercultural communication.

General purpose: To inform.
Specific purpose: To describe the way fear works in intercultural communication.
Thesis: Fear influences intercultural communication. (How does fear influence intercultural communication?)

 I. We fear disapproval.

 II. We fear embarrassing ourselves.

 III. We fear being harmed.

In delivering such a speech a speaker might begin by saying:

Three major fears interfere with intercultural communication. First, we fear disapproval—from members of our own group as well as from members of the other person's group. Second, we fear embarrassing ourselves, even making fools of ourselves, by saying the wrong thing or appearing insensitive. And third, we may fear being harmed—our stereotypes of the other group may lead us to see its members as dangerous or potentially harmful to us.

Let's look at each of these fears in more detail. We'll be able to see clearly how they influence our own intercultural communication behavior.

Consider, first, the fear of disapproval. [The speaker would then amplify and support this fear of disapproval, giving examples of disapproval seen in his or her own experience, the testimony of communication theorists on the importance of such fear, research findings on the effects that such fear might have on intercultural communication, and so on.]

TABLE 10.2 The Oral Citation

Here are a few examples and notes on citing your sources in your speech. The written citations would be included at the end of your speech in a list of references. The American Psychological Association (APA) style is used here; additional help is available on Research Navigator (available through MSL at www.myspeechlab.com), which provides guidance for citing sources in reference lists and bibliographies using all major style manuals.

SOURCE TO BE CITED AND WRITTEN CITATION	ORAL CITATION	NOTES ON THE ORAL CITATION
Book Brownell, J. (2006). *Listening: Attitudes, principles, and skills*, 3rd ed. Boston: Allyn & Bacon.	Judi Brownell, an authority on listening and a professor at Cornell University, argues in *Listening: Attitudes, Principles, and Skills* that listening is . . .	Try to establish the importance of the book or the author to add weight to your argument.
Magazine Article Cloud, J. (2007, February 5). Yep, they're gay. *Time, 169* (6) 54.	A February 2006 article in *Time* magazine notes, and here I'm quoting the author, John Cloud, "Zoologists have known for many years that homosexuality isn't uncommon among animals."	If the magazine is well known, as is *Time*, it's sufficient to name the magazine. If it were less well known, then you might establish its credibility for your listeners by noting, for example, its reputation for fairness, its longevity, its well-known authors.
Newspaper Article Whitlock, C. (2007, March 12). Terrorists proving harder to profile. www.Washingtonpost.com, accessed March 12, 2007. If a letter to the editor or an editorial, then insert [Letter to the Editor] or [Editorial] after the article title.	An article in the online *Washington Post*, one of the world's great newspapers, dated March 12, 2007 reports that . . .	It sometimes helps to establish the credibility of the newspaper—some are more reputable than others. And always include reference to the date of the article. You should also indicate whether it was a regular news item or a letter to the editor or an editorial.
Encyclopedia Feminism (2007). In *Encyclopaedia Britannica*. Retrieved March 12, 2007, from Encyclopaedia Britannica Online: www.britannica.com/eb/article–9343946	The online version of the *Encyclopaedia Britannica*, accessed March 12, 2007, defines feminism as "the beliefs in the social, economic, and political equality of the sexes."	It isn't necessary to say "www.britannica.com." Your audience will know how to access the encyclopedia—especially if they're in this course.
Research Study Andrejevic, M. (2006). The discipline of watching: Detection, risk, and lateral surveillance. *Critical Studies in Media Communication, 23* (December), 391–407.	In the December 2006 issue of *Critical Studies in Media Communication*, one of the official journals of the National Communication Association, a research study conducted by Mark Andrejevic found that . . .	In citing a research study, make it clear that what you're reporting is from the primary source and not a magazine's summary of the research (that is, a secondary source).
Website New developments (2008, March 22). Retrieved May 14, 2008, from www.texas.gov. If an author is identified, then: Smith, C. (2008, March 17). The truth. Retrieved April 5, 2008, from www.hhhsmith.org.	The official State of Texas website, which you can access at www.texas.gov, contains the full text of the speeches on this issue; they all are in favor of . . .	Like blogs, websites vary in accuracy and credibility. Some are designed to sell a product or service, so their information may be suspect (it may also be quite accurate of course). A government (.gov domain), educational (.edu domain), or organizational (.org domain) website usually is more reliable and is more likely to be believed by an educated audience.

TABLE 10.2   **The Oral Citation**

Here are a few examples and notes on citing your sources in your speech. The written citations would be included at the end of your speech in a list of references. The American Psychological Association (APA) style is used here; additional help is available on Research Navigator (available through MSL at www.myspeechlab.com), which provides guidance for citing sources in reference lists and bibliographies using all major style manuals.

SOURCE TO BE CITED AND WRITTEN CITATION	ORAL CITATION	NOTES ON THE ORAL CITATION
Blog Sullivan, A. (2007, Jan 28). The Webb factor. http:time.blogs.com/daily_dish/, retrieved January 30, 2007.	Andrew Sullivan, the author of *The Conservative Soul*, in an article posted to his blog The Daily Dish—one of the most widely read blogs on the Internet—on January 28 of this year, had this to say about Webb . . .	Anyone can maintain a blog. If the blog is used for more than examples or illustrations, you need to establish the authority of the blogger and the date of the post you're citing.
Chat Room Conversation Seabiscuit (2007, May 4). Happiness. Retrieved June 8, 2008, from www.myheart.com.	One important insight on this issue was posted this week in a chat room by Seabiscuit.	Chat room conversation can give you good examples or ideas. Even if the conversation is no longer available, you need to credit the writer and indicate where you got the idea.
News Broadcast Charlie Rose (2008, May 4) interview with C. A. Smith, broadcast PBS.	In May of this year, Charlie Rose interviewed Smith on *The Nation* on PBS, and Smith agreed that . . .	It's helpful to name the network (rather than just say "a television news show said . . .") as well as the specific news show, the person being interviewed, and perhaps the interviewer. By naming all these, you create a clearer picture in the minds of your listeners and at the same time ensure accuracy.
Personal Interview Because this is not retrievable, this is not included in the reference list.	In an e-mail interview I conducted with James Wilder, the sheriff of Forest County, in September of this year, Wilder wrote that . . .	State how the interview was conducted—in person, by telephone, or through e-mail—and when this took place. Again, the currency of the date rather than the specific date is more important, so it's fine to say either "September of this year" or, say, "September 22."
Classroom Lecture Smith, R. (2007, September 16). History of American Public Address at Queens College.	In a lecture last week in History of American Public Address, Professor Russel Smith noted that . . .	Citations of classroom lectures should include the professor's name, the course, and the approximate time the comment was made.
Statistics Hurricane Information (2006, June 7). Retrieved from January 29, 2007, www.FedStats.gov. hurricane2.html.	FedStats—the online U.S. federal government's statistics website, which I accessed on Wednesday—provides sobering statistics on the devastation created by Katrina and Rita.	It's important with most statistics to stress the authority of the source that collected the statistics (.gov sites are more reliable than .com sites) and the recency of the statistics. Providing information on when you accessed the website will further help you establish the currency of the statistics.

Research Link

INTEGRATING AND CITING RESEARCH

Even the best and most extensive research would count for little if you didn't integrate it into your speech. By integrating and acknowledging your sources of information in your speech, you'll give fair credit to those whose ideas and research findings you're using, and you'll lessen the risk that anything you say can be interpeted as plagiarism (see pp. 11–12). At the same time you'll help establish your own reputation as a responsible researcher and thus increase your own credibility. Here are a few suggestions for integrating your research into your speech (additional suggestions are presented in Table 10.2, pp. 248–249):

Cite the Sources in Your Speech. Cite at least the author; if appropriate, cite the publication and the date. Check out some of the speeches reprinted in this book and on any of the many Internet sites, and note how the speakers have integrated their sources in the speech. In your written preparation outline, give the complete bibliographical reference.

Here is an example of how you might cite your source:

> *My discussion of the causes of anorexic nervosa is based on the work of Dr. Peter Rowan of the Priory Hospital in London. In an article titled "Introducing Anorexia Nervosa," which I last accessed on October 5, 2007, Rowan notes that "this is a disorder of many causes that come together." It's these causes that I want to cover in this talk.*

Although it's possible to overdo oral source citations—to give more information than listeners really need—there are even greater dangers in leaving out potentially useful source information. Because your speeches in this course are learning experiences, it will be better to err on the side of being more rather than less complete.

Integrate the Citation Smoothly. Avoid lead-in expressions such as "I have a quote here" or "I want to quote an example." Let the audience know that you're quoting by pausing before the quote, taking a step forward, or—to read an extended quotation—referring to your notes. If you want to state more directly that this is a quotation, you might do it this way:

> *Recently, Mary Kay Ash put this in perspective: [pause] "A woman can no more duplicate the male style of leadership than an American businessman can exactly reproduce the Japanese style."*

Include Written Citations in Outline. In addition to the oral citation, you'll most likely want to include a listing of your references in your preparation outline. In citing references, first find out what style manual is used in your class or at your school. Generally, it will be a style manual developed by the American Psychological Association (APA), the Modern Language Association (MLA), or the University of Chicago (*The Chicago Manual of Style*). Different colleges and even different departments within a given school often rely on different formats for citing research, which, quite frankly, makes a tedious process even worse.

Fortunately, a variety of websites provide guides to the information you'll need to cite any reference in your speech and will prove excellent complements to Table 10.2. For example, Purdue University offers an excellent site that covers APA and MLA style formats and provides examples for citing books, articles, newspaper articles, websites, e-mail, online postings, electronic databases, and more (http://owl.english.purdue.edu/handouts/research). Another excellent website is Capital Community College's Guide for Writing Research Papers (http://ccc.commnet.edu/apa/apa_index.htm). Guidelines for using the *Chicago Manual of Style* may be found at Ohio State's website (www.lib.ohio-state.edu/). This site provides guidance for citing all types of print and electronic sources. Another valuable source is the Columbia Guide to Online Style (www.columbia.edu/cu/cup/cgos/idx_basic.html), which provides detailed instructions and examples for citing e-mail, listserv, and newsgroup communications and even software programs and video games.

The next Research Link, "Evaluating Internet Resources," appears on page 270.

SPEECHES OF DEFINITION

What is leadership? What is a born-again Christian? What is the difference between sociology and psychology? What is a cultural anthropologist? What is safe sex? These are all topics for informative speeches of definition.

A *definition* is a statement of the meaning of a term. In giving a **speech of definition** (as opposed to using a definition as a form of supporting material, as explained in Chapter 6, pp. 116–118), you may focus on defining a term, defining a system or theory, or pinpointing the similarities and/or differences among terms or systems. A speech of definition may be on a subject new to the audience or may present a familiar topic in a new and different way. Here are a few examples:

Defining a Term

- What is a smart card?
- What is perjury?
- What is creativity?
- What is self-esteem?
- What is classism?
- What is political correctness?

Defining a System or Theory

- What is the classical theory of public speaking?
- What are the parts of a generative grammar?
- Buddhism: its major beliefs
- What is virtual reality?
- What is futurism?
- The "play theory" of mass communication

Defining Similar and Dissimilar Terms or Systems

- Football and soccer: What's the difference?
- What do Christians and Muslims have in common?
- Oedipus and Electra: How do they differ?
- Heredity and the environment
- Animal and human rights
- Visible and invisible web

THESIS

The thesis in a speech of definition is a statement identifying the term or system and your intention to define it or to contrast it with other terms; for example, *Christianity and Islam have much in common* or *You can search for information through key words or a directory.*

Consider the principles for defining a concept or system. What do college instructors do differently from speakers at community meetings when defining concepts? What principles do you see violated in speeches of definition?

MAIN POINTS

You derive the main points for a speech of definition by asking questions of your thesis; for example, What do Christianity and Islam have in common? How do text and online dictionaries differ? Each of your main points will then consist of, say, the factors that Christianity and Islam have in common or the several ways in which text and online dictionaries differ.

SUPPORT

Once you have each of your main points, support them with examples, testimony, and the like. For example, one of your main points in the Christianity–Islam example might be that both religions believe in the value of good works. You might then quote from the New Testament and from the Quran to illustrate this belief, or you might give examples of noted Christians and Muslims who exemplified this characteristic, or you might cite the testimony of religious leaders who talked about the importance of good works.

Because this is a speech of definition, you'll want to give special attention to all your definitions, as discussed earlier (Chapter 6, pp. 116–118).

ORGANIZATION

In addition to the obvious organizational pattern of multiple definitions, consider using a topical order, in which each main idea is treated equally. In either case, however, proceed from the known to the unknown. Start with what your audience knows and work up to what is new or unfamiliar. Let's say you want to explain the concept of phonemics (with which your audience is totally unfamiliar). The specific idea you wish to get across is that each phoneme stands for a unique sound. You might proceed from the known to the unknown and begin your definition with something like this:

> We all know that in the written language each letter of the alphabet stands for a unit of the written language. Each letter is different from every other letter. A *t* is different from a *g* and a *g* is different from a *b* and so on. Each letter is called a "grapheme." In English we know we have 26 such letters.
>
> We can look at the spoken language in much the same way. Each sound is different from every other sound. A *t* sound is different from a *d* and a *d* is different from a *k* and so on. Each individual sound is called a "phoneme."
>
> Now, let me explain in a little more detail what I mean by a "phoneme." . . .

Here are two examples of how you might go about constructing a speech of definition. In this first example the speaker explains the parts of a résumé and follows a spatial order, going from the top to the bottom of the page.

General purpose: To inform.
Specific purpose: To define the essential parts of a résumé.

Thesis:	There are four major parts to a résumé. (What are the four major parts of a résumé?)

I. Identify your career goals.

II. Identify your educational background.

III. Identify your work experience.

IV. Identify your special competencies.

In this second example the speaker selects three major types of lying for discussion and arranges these in a topical pattern.

General purpose:	To inform.
Specific purpose:	To define lying by explaining the major types of lying.
Thesis:	There are three major kinds of lying. (What are the three major kinds of lying?)

I. Concealment is the process of hiding the truth.

II. Falsification is the process of presenting false information as if it were true.

III. Misdirection is the process of acknowledging a feeling but misidentifying its cause.

In delivering such a speech, a speaker might begin the speech by saying:

A lie is a lie is a lie. True? Well, not exactly. Actually, there are a number of different ways we can lie. We can lie by concealing the truth. We can lie by falsification, by presenting false information as if it were true. And we can lie by misdirection, by acknowledging a feeling but misidentifying its cause.

Let's look at the first type of lie—the lie of concealment. Most lies are lies of concealment. Most of the time when we lie we simply conceal the truth. We don't actually make any false statements. Rather we simply don't reveal the truth. Let me give you some examples I overheard recently.

A Case of **Ethics**   USING ANOTHER'S WORK

In an economics course you took at another school, you received a handout that very clearly explained the relationship of interest rates to stock prices. Now you are planning to give a speech on that very topic, and you wonder how you can use this handout ethically.

Ethical Choice Point *Would it be ethical to use the handout to support one of your points without saying where you got it or who prepared it—to allow your audience to draw the conclusion that you prepared it yourself? If not, how might you use this handout effectively and ethically? More generally, what ethical guidelines should govern materials that a speaker presents to listeners but which were developed by someone else?*

SPEECHES OF DEMONSTRATION

Whether in using demonstration within a speech or in giving a speech devoted entirely to demonstration, you show the audience how to do something or how something operates. Here are some examples of topics of **speeches of demonstration**:

Demonstrating How to Do Something

- how to give mouth-to-mouth resuscitation
- how to drive defensively
- how to mix colors
- how to ask for a raise
- how to burglarproof your house
- how to use Excel to organize your finances

Demonstrating How Something Operates

- how the body maintains homeostasis
- how perception works
- how divorce laws work
- how e-mail works
- how a hurricane develops
- how a heart bypass operation is performed

THESIS

The thesis for a speech of demonstration identifies what you will show the audience how to do, or how something operates; for example, *E-mail works through a series of electronic connections from one computer to a server to another computer*, or *You can burglarproof your house in three different ways*, or *Three guidelines will help you get that raise.*

MAIN POINTS

You can then derive your main points by asking a simple How or What question of your thesis—How do these electronic connections work? What are the ways of burglarproofing a house? What are the guidelines for asking for a raise?

SUPPORT

You then support each of your main ideas with a variety of materials. For example, you might show diagrams of houses that use different burglarproofing methods, demonstrate how various locks work, or show how different security systems work.

Presentation aids are especially helpful in speeches of demonstration. Good examples of visual aids are the signs in restaurants demonstrating the Heimlich maneuver. These signs demonstrate the sequence of steps with pic-

Consider the television chefs as speakers giving speeches of demonstration. What do they do well as they demonstate their recipe? What suggestions for improvement would you make?

tures as well as words. The combination of verbal and graphic information makes it easy to understand this important process. In a speech on the Heimlich maneuver, however, it would be best to use only the pictures so that the written words would not distract your audience from your oral explanation.

ORGANIZATION

In most cases a temporal pattern will work best in speeches of demonstration. Demonstrate each step in the sequence in which it's to be performed. In this way, you'll avoid one of the major difficulties in demonstrating a process—backtracking. Don't skip steps, even if you think they're familiar to the audience. They may not be. Connect each step to the next with appropriate transitions. For example, in explaining the Heimlich maneuver, you might say,

> Now that you have your arms around the choking victim's chest, your next step is to. . . .
> Assist your listeners by labeling the steps clearly; for example, "the first step," "the second step," and so on.

Begin with an overview. It's often helpful when demonstrating to give a broad general picture and then present each step in turn. For example, suppose you were talking about how to prepare a wall for painting. You might begin with a general overview to give your listeners a general idea of the process, saying something like this:

> In preparing the wall for painting, you want to make sure that the wall is smoothly sanded, free of dust, and dry. Sanding a wall isn't like sanding a block of wood. So let's look at the proper way to sand a wall.

Here are two examples of the speech of demonstration. In this first example, the speaker explains the proper way to paint a wall by rag rolling. As you can see, the speaker uses a temporal organizational pattern and covers three stages in the order in which they would be performed.

General purpose: To inform.
Specific purpose: To demonstrate how to rag roll.
Thesis: Rag rolling is performed in three steps. (What are the three steps of rag rolling?)

   I. Apply the base coat of paint.

  II. Apply the glaze coat.

 III. Roll a rag through the wet glaze.

In the next example, the speaker identifies and demonstrates how to listen actively.

General purpose: To inform.
Specific purpose: To demonstrate three techniques of active listening.
Thesis: We can become active listeners. (How can we become active listeners?)

   I. Paraphrase the speaker's meaning.

  II. Express understanding of the speaker's feelings.

 III. Ask questions.

In delivering the speech, the speaker might begin by saying:

Active listening is a special kind of listening. It's listening with total involvement, with a concern for the speaker. It's probably the most important type of listening you can engage in. Active listening consists of three steps: paraphrasing the speaker's meaning, expressing understanding of the speaker's feelings, and asking questions.

Your first step in active listening is to paraphrase the speaker's meaning. What is a paraphrase? A paraphrase is a restatement in your own words of the speaker's meaning. That is, you express in your own words what you think the speaker meant. For example, let's say that the speaker said. . . .

Essentials of Informing Your Audience

This chapter considered the informative speech, first surveying some general principles, then examining three main types of informative speaking (speeches of description, definition, and demonstration).

1. Among the **goals of informative speaking** are:
   - to introduce new topics and issues
   - to clarify misconceptions
   - to demonstrate how to use information
   - to enlarge the audience's knowledge

2. Among the **principles of informative speaking** are these:
   - Limit the amount of information you communicate.
   - Adjust the level of complexity.
   - Stress the relevance and the usefulness of the information to your audience.
   - Relate new information to old.
   - Vary the levels of abstraction.
   - Make your speech easy to remember.

3. **Speeches of description** examine a process or procedure, an event, an object, or a person.

4. **Speeches of definition** define a term, system, or theory, or similarities and/or differences among terms.

5. **Speeches of demonstration** show how to do something or how something operates.

Essential Terms: Informing Your Audience

adjusting the level of complexity
(p. 236)
descriptive categories **(p. 246)**
informative speaking **(p. 235)**

levels of abstraction **(p. 238)**
relevance and usefulness **(p. 237)**
definition, speeches of **(p. 251)**

demonstration, speeches of
(p. 254)
description, speeches of **(p. 245)**

Public Speaking Exercises

10.1 Defining Terms

Select one of the following terms and define it, using at least three of the different types of definition considered in Chapter 6 (etymology, authority, negation, specific examples, or direct symbolism): *communication, love, friendship, conflict, leadership, audience.* You'll find it helpful to visit a few online dictionaries or thesauruses: http://c.gp.cs.cmu.edu:5103/prog/webster/; www.m-w.com/netdict.htm; http://humanities.uchicago.edu/forms_unrest/ROGET.html. A useful website containing links to varied types of dictionaries is www.bucknell.edu/~rbeard/diction.html.

10.2 A Two-Minute Informative Speech

Prepare and deliver a two-minute informative speech in which you do one of the following:

◆ **Explain a card game**: Explain the way a card game such as solitaire, poker, gin rummy, bridge, canasta, or pinochle is played.

◆ **Explain a board game**: Explain the way a board game such as chess, backgammon, Chinese checkers, Go, Othello, Scrabble, Yahtzee, or Monopoly is played.

◆ **Explain food preparation**: Explain how to make a pie, a soup, a western omelet, a pizza, roast beef, a dip, or a casserole (any kind you'd like).

◆ **Explain a sport**: Explain the way a sport such as football, baseball, basketball, hockey, soccer, tennis, or golf is played.

10.3 What Do You Say?

◆ **Unexpected Happenings**. Kate is the third speaker in a series of six. Unfortunately, the first speaker presented a really excellent speech on the same topic Kate is speaking on—how computer viruses work. What would you advise Kate to do if this speech were a classroom assignment? If this speech were to be given at a conference or community learning center?

◆ **Defining**. Juliet wants to give a speech defining the basic tenets of her religion. Some members of her audience have a fairly negative view of the religion; others hold positive views. Juliet wants to acknowledge her understanding of these diverse attitudes. What might Juliet say?

◆ **Informative Strategies**. Rose is planning to give an informative speech on defensive driving and is considering the strategies she might use. How might she introduce her speech? What organizational pattern might she use? What types of presentation aids might she use?

◆ **Demonstrating**. Sayid wants to demonstrate how e-mail works. The audience is probably mixed in terms of their knowledge of technology generally—some know a great deal, others very little. How might Sayid open his speech so that all audience members will want to listen?

LogOn! MySpeechLab

Informing Your Audience

Visit MySpeechLab (www.myspeechlab.com) for a brief discussion of "What Is Information?" to further clarify what is and what is not informative. View the demonstration speech, "Baking a Cake," for a variety of principles of informative speaking and for using visual aids as well as the speeches "Electoral College" and "CPR" (with a critique). This is also a good place to revisit the Outlining Wizard to help you fine tune the structure and organization of your information speeches.

Research Navigator (accessible through MSL and at www.researchnavigator.com) provides extensive guidance for citing sources and for writing endnotes and bibliographies in different formats and will prove an excellent complement to Table 10.2.

11 Persuading Your Audience

Why Read This Chapter?

Because it will enable you to influence an audience by helping you to:

- exert influence fairly and ethically through public speaking
- avoid engaging in fallacious reasoning yourself and recognize it in the speeches of others
- organize and develop speeches on facts, values, and policies that change your listeners' attitudes or move your listeners to action

How dangerous it always is to reason from insufficient data.

—Sherlock Holmes
Quintessential fictional
detective created by
Arthur Conan Doyle
(1859–1930)

The previous chapter focused on informative speaking; it examined the goals of such speaking, essential principles for communicating information, and the varied types of informative speeches. This chapter looks at persuasive speaking and follows a similar pattern: It will discuss the goals of persuasive speaking, essential principles of persuasion, and the varied types of persuasive speeches you might give.

There are a wide variety of websites that contain examples of persuasive speeches and that make perfect complements to this chapter. Visit, for example, the History Channel (www.historychannel.com/speeches), History and Politics Out Loud (www.hpol.org), C-Span (www.c-span.org/classroom/lang/speeches.asp), or American Rhetoric (www.americanrhetoric.com) and examine the speeches for the principles and strategies discussed in this chapter, for models of excellence, and for greater insight into the role of public speaking in society.

GOALS OF PERSUASIVE SPEAKING

Generally, the word **persuasion** refers to the process of influencing another person's attitudes, beliefs, values, and/or behaviors. Briefly, as discussed in Chapter 5, an *attitude* is a tendency to behave in a certain way. For example, if you have a positive attitude toward science fiction, then you're likely to watch science fiction movies or read science fiction books; if you have a negative attitude, you'll be likely to avoid such movies and books. A *belief* is a conviction in the existence or reality of something or in the truth of some assertion. For example, some believe that God exists, that democracy is the best form of government, or that soft drugs lead to hard drugs. A *value* is an indicator of what you feel is good or bad, ethical or unethical, just or unjust. Many people in your audience will positively value "college education" or "free speech" and negatively value "discrimination" or "war." In the context of persuasion, the word *behavior* refers to overt, observable actions such as voting for a particular person, contributing money to the Red Cross, or buying a hybrid automobile.

Your persuasive speeches may focus on your listeners' attitudes, beliefs, values, or behaviors. You may want to accomplish any one of the following three general goals of persuasive speaking:

- **To strengthen or weaken attitudes, beliefs, or values.** Persuasion often aims to strengthen audience views. For example, religious sermons usually seek to strengthen the existing beliefs of the audience. Similarly, many public service announcements try to strengthen existing beliefs about, say, recycling, smoking, or safe sex. At times, however, you may want to weaken the existing beliefs of the audience—to suggest that what they currently believe may not be entirely true. For example, you might want to weaken the favorable attitudes people might have toward a particular political party or policy. This type of speech is often used in combination with additional efforts designed to gradually weaken existing beliefs and ultimately to change them.

- **To change attitudes, beliefs, or values.** Sometimes you'll want to change your audience's thinking. You might want to change their attitudes about the college's no-smoking rules, to change their beliefs about television's influence on viewer violence, or to change their values about the efficacy of war.

- **To motivate to action.** Ultimately, your goal is to get people to do something—for example, to vote for one person rather than another, to donate money to a fund for the homeless, or to take a course in criminology.

Figure 11.1

The Persuasion Continuum

Any movement along the continuum would be considered persuasion.

Strongly in favor of same-sex marriage ___ : ___ : ___ : ___ : ___ : ___ : ___ Strongly opposed to same-sex marriage

It's useful to think of influence as occurring on a **persuasion continuum** ranging from one extreme to another. Let's say, to take one issue currently in the news, that you want to give a persuasive speech on same-sex marriage. You might visualize your audience as existing on a continuum ranging from strongly in favor to strongly opposed, as shown in Figure 11.1. Your task is to move your audience in the direction of your persuasive purpose. You can center your message on strengthening, weakening, or changing your listeners' attitudes, beliefs, or values about same-sex marriage; or you can center your message on moving the listeners to act—to protest, write letters, or sign a petition.

If your purpose is to persuade the audience to oppose same-sex marriage, then in Figure 11.1 any movement toward the right will be successful persuasion; if your purpose is to persuade listeners to support same-sex marriage, then any movement toward the left will be successful persuasion. Notice, however, that it's quite possible to give a speech in which you hope to move your listeners in one direction but actually to succeed in moving them in the other direction. This "negative persuasion" effect can occur, for example, when the audience perceives the speaker as dishonest or self-promoting.

Now that we've considered the general goals of persuasive speaking, let's turn to some principles that can help you become an effective persuader.

PRINCIPLES OF PERSUASIVE SPEAKING

You can become more successful in strengthening or changing attitudes or beliefs and in moving your listeners to action by following these guidelines for persuasive speaking.

ANTICIPATE SELECTIVE EXPOSURE

People listen in accordance with the **principle of selective exposure.** This principle or law has two parts: It states that (1) listeners actively seek out information that supports their opinions, beliefs, values, decisions, and behaviors; and (2) listeners actively avoid information that contradicts their existing opinions, beliefs, attitudes, values, decisions, and behaviors.

Of course, if you're very sure that your opinions and attitudes are logical and valid, then you may not bother to seek out supporting information. Similarly, you may not actively avoid contradictory messages. People exercise selective exposure most often when their confidence in their own opinions and beliefs is weak.

If you want to persuade an audience that holds attitudes different from your own, anticipate selective exposure operating and proceed inductively; that is, hold back on your thesis until you've given your evidence and argument. Only then relate this evidence and argument to your initially contrary thesis.

If you were to present them with your thesis first, your listeners might tune you out without giving your position a fair hearing. So become thoroughly familiar with the attitudes of your audience if you want to succeed in making these necessary adjustments and adaptations.

Let's say you're giving a speech on the need to reduce spending on college athletic programs. If your audience were composed of listeners who agreed with you and wanted to cut athletic spending, you might lead with your thesis. Your introduction might go something like this:

> Our college athletic program is absorbing money that we can more profitably use for the library, science labs, and language labs. Let me explain how the money now going to unnecessary athletic programs could be better spent in these other areas.

On the other hand, suppose you were addressing alumni who strongly favored the existing athletic programs. In this case, you might want to lead with your evidence and then state your thesis.

ASK FOR REASONABLE AMOUNTS OF CHANGE

The greater and more important the change you want to encourage in your audience, the more difficult your task will be. Put in terms of the continuum of persuasion introduced earlier, this principle suggests that you'll be more successful if you ask for small (rather than large) movements in the direction of your speech purpose. The reason is simple: As listeners we normally demand a greater number of reasons and a lot more evidence before we make important choices—such as, say, deciding to change careers, move to another state, or invest in stocks.

On the other hand, we may be more easily persuaded (and demand less evidence) on relatively minor issues—whether to take a course in "Small Group Communication" rather than "Persuasion" or to give to the United Heart Fund instead of the American Heart Fund.

Generally, people change gradually, in small degrees over a long period of time. Persuasion, therefore, is most effective when it strives for small changes and works over a period of time. For example, a persuasive speech stands a better chance when it tries to get a drinker to attend just one AA meeting rather than advocating giving up alcohol for life. If you try to convince your audience to change their attitudes radically or to engage in behaviors to which they're initially opposed, your attempts may backfire. In this type of situation, listeners may tune you out, closing their ears to even the best and most logical arguments.

So in your classroom speeches, set reasonable goals for what you want the audience to do. Remember you have only perhaps 10 minutes, and in that time you cannot move the proverbial mountain. Instead, ask for small, easily performed behaviors. Encourage your listeners to visit a particular website (perhaps even one dedicated to beliefs or values that they do not currently share), to vote in the next election, or to buy the new virus protection software.

When you are addressing an audience that is opposed to your position and your goal is to change their attitudes and beliefs, be especially careful to seek change in small increments. Let's say, for example, that your ultimate goal is to get an antiabortion group to favor abortion on demand. Obviously, this goal is too great to achieve in one speech. Therefore, strive for small changes. Here, for example, is an excerpt in which the speaker attempts to get an audience that opposes legal abortion to agree that at least some abortions should be legal. The speaker begins as follows:

> One of the great lessons I learned in college was that most extreme positions are wrong. Most of the important truths lie somewhere between the extreme opposites. And today I want to talk with you about one of these truths. I want to talk with you about rape and the problems faced by the mother carrying a child conceived in this most violent of all violent crimes we can imagine.

Notice that the speaker does not state a totally pro-choice position but instead focuses on one situation involving abortion and attempts to get the audience to agree that in some cases abortion should be legal.

When you have the opportunity to persuade your audience on several occasions (rather than simply delivering one speech), two strategies will prove helpful: the foot-in-the-door and door-in-the-face techniques.

Foot-in-the-Door Technique

As its name implies, the **foot-in-the-door technique** involves getting your foot in the door by requesting something small, something that your listeners will easily agree to. Once they agree to this small request, you then make your real request (Cialdini, 1984; Dejong, 1979; Freedman & Fraser, 1966; Pratkanis & Aronson, 1991). People are more apt to comply with a large request after they've complied with a similar but much smaller request. For example, in one study the objective was to get people to put a "Drive Carefully" sign on their lawn (a large request). When this (large) request was made first, only about 17 percent of the people were willing to agree. However, when this request was preceded by a much smaller request (to sign a petition), between 50 and 76 percent granted permission to install the sign. Agreement with the smaller request paves the way for the larger request and puts the audience into an agreeable mood.

Door-in-the-Face Technique

With the **door-in-the-face technique**, the opposite of foot-in-the-door, you first make a large request that you know will be refused and then follow it with a more moderate request. For example, your large request might be "We're asking people to donate $100 for new school computers." When this is refused, you make a more moderate request, the one you really want your listeners to comply with (for example, "Might you be willing to contribute $10?"). In changing from the large to the more moderate request, you demonstrate your willingness to compromise and your sensitivity to your listeners. The general idea here is that your listeners will feel that because you've made concessions, they should also make concessions and at least contribute something. Listeners will probably also feel that $10 is actually quite a small amount considering the initial request and are more likely to donate the $10 (Cialdini, 1984; Cialdini & Ascani, 1976).

IDENTIFY WITH YOUR AUDIENCE

If you can show your audience that you and they share important attitudes, beliefs, and values, you'll clearly advance your persuasive goal. Other similarities are also important. For example, in some cases similarity of cultural, educational, or social background may help you identify yourself with your audience. Be aware, however, that insincere or dishonest identification is likely to backfire and create problems. So avoid even implying similarities between yourself and your audience that don't exist.

As a general rule, never ask the audience to do what you have not done yourself; always demonstrate that you have done what you want the audience to do. If you don't, the audience will rightfully ask, "Why haven't you done it?" In addition, besides doing whatever it may be, show your listeners that you're pleased to have done it. For example, tell them of the satisfaction you derived from donating blood or from reading to blind students.

Consider the persuasive appeals that have been used on you recently. Were any of the foot-in-the-door or the door-in-the-face type?

BE CULTURALLY SENSITIVE

Cultural differences are especially important in persuasion; the appeals you'd use to influence one cultural group would not be the same you'd use for a different group. You can appreciate the importance of this by looking at five dimensions of culture with persuasive strategies in mind (Hofstede, 1997; Hall, 1976; Hall & Hall, 1987; Singh & Pereira, 2005).

Individualist and Collectivist Cultures

Before reading about individualist and collectivist cultures, take the accompanying self-test to give you some idea of your own individualist and collectivist leanings.

TEST YOURSELF

How Individualistic Are You?

Indicate how true or false the following statements are of you. Use the following scale: Almost always true = 1; more often true than false = 2; true about half the time and false about half the time = 3; more often false than true = 4; and almost always false = 5.

_____ **1.** My own goals rather than the goals of my group (for example, my extended family, my organization) are the more important.

_____ **2.** I feel responsible for myself and to my own conscience rather than for the entire group and to the group's values and rules.

_____ **3.** Success to me depends on my contribution to the group effort and the group's success rather than on my own individual success or on surpassing others.

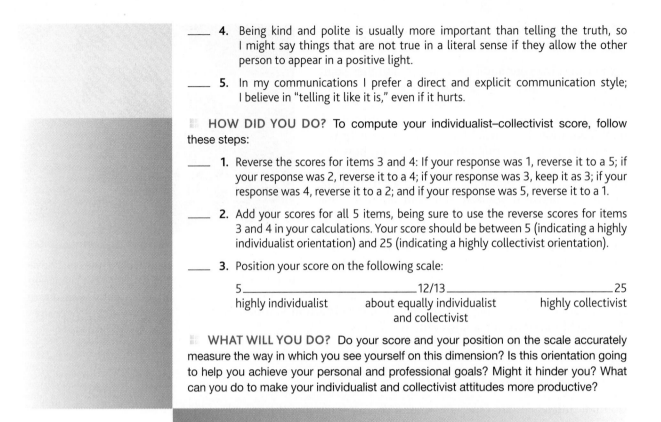

4. Being kind and polite is usually more important than telling the truth, so I might say things that are not true in a literal sense if they allow the other person to appear in a positive light.

5. In my communications I prefer a direct and explicit communication style; I believe in "telling it like it is," even if it hurts.

HOW DID YOU DO? To compute your individualist–collectivist score, follow these steps:

1. Reverse the scores for items 3 and 4: If your response was 1, reverse it to a 5; if your response was 2, reverse it to a 4; if your response was 3, keep it as 3; if your response was 4, reverse it to a 2; and if your response was 5, reverse it to a 1.

2. Add your scores for all 5 items, being sure to use the reverse scores for items 3 and 4 in your calculations. Your score should be between 5 (indicating a highly individualist orientation) and 25 (indicating a highly collectivist orientation).

3. Position your score on the following scale:

5_____12/13_____25
highly individualist   about equally individualist   highly collectivist
                        and collectivist

WHAT WILL YOU DO? Do your score and your position on the scale accurately measure the way in which you see yourself on this dimension? Is this orientation going to help you achieve your personal and professional goals? Might it hinder you? What can you do to make your individualist and collectivist attitudes more productive?

As you will recall from Chapter 3, some cultures emphasize the individual, individual success, and individual responsibility (individualist cultures such as the United States, Australia, United Kingdom, Netherlands, Canada, New Zealand, Italy, Belgium, Denmark, and Sweden), whereas in others the group (the group or family or organization) is more important than the individual (collectivist cultures such as Guatemala, Ecuador, Panama, Venezuela, Colombia, Indonesia, Pakistan, China, Costa Rica, and Peru). In appealing to members of individualistic cultures, you'll want to emphasize such themes as independence, nonconformity, and uniqueness. You'll also be well advised to stress your competence; if you don't, your listeners may assume it's because you don't have any. In a speech to members of a collectivist culture, on the other hand, successful appeals will emphasize the importance of family, of loyalty (to brand names or local organizations), and of national identity and pride (Han & Shavitt, 1994; Dillard & Marshall, 2003). In collectivist cultures, to stress your own competence or that of your corporation may prove insulting; it may be taken as a suggestion that your audience members are inferior or that their corporations are not as good as yours.

High- and Low-Power-Distance Cultures

In some cultures there is a large difference between those who have and those who don't have power (high-power-distance cultures such as Mexico, Brazil, India, and the Philippines); in some there is little difference (low-power-distance cultures such as Denmark, New Zealand, Sweden, and to a lesser extent the United States). When you are addressing members of a high-power-distance culture, references to important and prominent people and to what they believe and advocate will prove effective. In a low-power distance culture, however, these appeals will prove less effective than would, say, references to or testimonials from people much like the people you want to influence.

High- and Low-Uncertainty-Avoidance Cultures

In some cultures, people do little to avoid uncertainty and have little anxiety about not knowing what will happen next. In some other cultures, however, uncertainty is strongly avoided and there is much anxiety about uncertainty. Members of high-ambiguity-tolerance cultures don't feel threatened by uncertainty; such cultures include, for example, Singapore, Jamaica, Denmark, Sweden, Hong Kong, Ireland, Great Britain, Malaysia, India, Philippines, and the United States. Members of low-ambiguity-tolerance cultures do much to avoid uncertainty and have much anxiety about not knowing what will happen next; these cultures include, for example, Greece, Portugal, Guatemala, Uruguay, Belgium, El Salvador, Japan, Yugoslavia, Peru, France, Chile, Spain, and Costa Rica. Audiences high in uncertainty avoidance want information from experts (or supported by experts)—they want to know very clearly where they can go for information and guidance. These audiences also value tradition, so appeals to the past will prove effective. Audiences low in uncertainty avoidance are more ready to accept the new and the different.

Masculine and Feminine Cultures

Some cultures emphasize stereotypically masculine values of strength, status, and success; examples include Japan, Austria, Venezuela, Italy, Switzerland, Mexico, Ireland, Jamaica, Great Britain, and Germany. Other cultures emphasize stereotypically feminine values of intimacy, relationships, and fidelity; for example, Sweden, Norway, Netherlands, Denmark, Costa Rica, Yugoslavia, Finland, Chile, Portugal, and Thailand. The message here is clear; audience members with "masculine" cultural beliefs will be motivated by appeals to achievement, adventure, and enjoyment and will welcome the "hard sell." Listeners from cultures high in "femininity" will be motivated by "soft sell" appeals and by appeals to harmony and aesthetic qualities.

High- and Low-Context Cultures

As noted earlier in connection with the discussion of speech organization (Chapter 7, pp. 155–156), in some cultures information is part of the context and does not have to be verbalized explicitly; these high-context cultures are also collectivist, as seen in the Japanese, Arabic, Latin American, Thai, Korean, Apache, and Mexican cultures. In low-context cultures, which are also individualist cultures, information is made explicit and little is taken for granted. Low-context cultures include those of Germany, Sweden, Norway, and the United States. Listeners from high-context cultures will favor appeals that are indirect and implied; listeners from low-context cultures will want detail, directness, and explicitness.

*U*SE LOGICAL APPEALS

Logical, emotional, and credibility appeals all can be effective means to persuade an audience, and we'll look at all three. However, we'll start with the most effective: **logical appeals.** When a speaker persuades listeners with logical arguments—focusing on facts and evidence rather than on emotions or credibility claims—the listeners are more likely to remain persuaded over time and are more likely to resist counterarguments that may come up in the future

(Petty & Wegener, 1998). We'll look at the three main categories of logical appeals, then at the dangers of pseudo-arguments.

Reasoning from Specific Instances and Generalizations

In **reasoning from specific instances** (or examples), you examine several specific instances and then conclude something about the whole. This form of reasoning, known as induction, is useful when you want to develop a general principle or conclusion but cannot examine the whole. For example, you sample a few communication courses and conclude something about communication courses in general; you visit several Scandinavian cities and conclude something about the whole of Scandinavia. Critically analyze reasoning from specific instances by asking the following questions.

- **Were enough specific instances examined?** Two general guidelines will help you determine how much is enough. First, the larger the group you wish covered by your conclusion, the greater the number of specific instances you should examine. If you wish to draw conclusions about members of an entire country or culture, you'll have to examine a considerable number of people before drawing even tentative conclusions. On the other hand, if you're attempting to draw a conclusion about a bushel of 100 apples, sampling a few is probably sufficient.

- Second, the greater the diversity of items in the class, the more specific instances you will have to examine. Some classes or groups of items are relatively homogeneous, whereas others are more heterogeneous; this will influence how many specific instances constitute a sufficient number. Pieces of spaghetti in boiling water are all about the same; thus, sampling one usually tells you something about all the others. On the other hand, communication courses are probably very different from one another, so valid conclusions about the entire range of communication courses will require a much larger sample.

- **Are there significant exceptions?** When you examine specific instances and attempt to draw a conclusion about the whole, take into consideration the exceptions. Thus, if you examine the GPA of computer science majors and discover that 70 percent have GPAs above 3.5, you may be tempted to draw the conclusion that computer science majors are especially bright. But what about the 30 percent who have lower GPAs? How much lower are these scores? This may be a significant exception that must be taken into account when you draw your conclusion and would require you to qualify your conclusion in significant ways. Exactly what kind of or how many exceptions will constitute "significant exceptions" will depend on the unique situation.

Reasoning from Causes and Effects

In **reasoning from causes and effects**, you may go in either of two directions. You may reason from cause to effect (from observed cause to unobserved effect) or from effect to cause (from observed effect to unobserved cause). In testing reasoning from cause to effect or from effect to cause, ask yourself the following questions.

- **Might other causes be producing the observed effect?** If you observe a particular effect (say, high crime or student apathy), you need to ask if

Consider the rallies you've witnessed or been a part of. How would you describe the types of appeals (logical, emotional, credibility) used at rallies?

causes other than the one you're postulating might be producing these effects. Thus, you might postulate that poverty leads to high crime, but there might be other factors actually causing the high crime rate. Or poverty might be one cause but not the most important cause. Therefore, explore the possibility of other causes' producing the observed effects.

- **Is the causation in the direction postulated?** If two things occur together, it's often difficult to determine which is the cause and which is the effect. For example, a lack of interpersonal intimacy and a lack of self-confidence often occur in the same person. The person who lacks self-confidence seldom has intimate relationships with others. But which is the cause and which is the effect? It might be that the lack of intimacy "causes" low self-confidence; it might also be, however, that low self-confidence "causes" a lack of intimacy. Of course, it might also be that some other previously unexamined cause (a history of negative criticism, for example) might be producing both the lack of intimacy and the low self-confidence.

Reasoning from Sign

Reasoning from sign involves drawing a conclusion on the basis of the presence of clues or symptoms that frequently occur together. Medical diagnosis is a good example of reasoning by sign. The general procedure is simple. If a sign and an object, event, or condition are frequently paired, the presence of the sign is taken as proof of the presence of the object, event, or condition. For example, fatigue, extreme thirst, and overeating serve as signs of hyperthyroidism, because they frequently accompany the condition. In reasoning from sign, ask yourself these questions.

- **Do the signs necessitate the conclusion drawn?** Given extreme thirst, overeating, and the like, how certain may you be of the "hyperthyroid" conclusion? With most medical and legal matters we can never be absolutely certain, but we can be certain beyond a reasonable doubt.

- **Are there other signs that point to the same conclusion?** In the thyroid example, extreme thirst could be brought on by any number of factors. Similarly, the fatigue and the overeating could be attributed to other causes. Yet taken together, the three signs seem to point to only one reasonable diagnosis. Generally, the more signs that point toward the conclusion, the more confidence you can have that it's valid.

- **Are there contradictory signs?** Are there signs pointing toward contradictory conclusions? For example, if the butler had a motive and a history of violence (signs supporting the conclusion that the butler was the murderer) but also had an alibi (a sign pointing to the conclusion of innocence), then the conclusion of guilt would have to be reconsidered or discarded.

Avoiding Pseudo-Argument

Reasoning or attempts at reasoning are not always as logical as the above discussion may have implied. In many instances would-be persuaders use what might be called pseudo-logic: arguments that appear to address issues but really don't. Here are 10 such pseudo-arguments (Lee & Lee, 1972, 1995; Pratkanis & Aronson, 1991; Herrick, 2004). Learn to spot pseudo-arguments in the speeches of others, and be sure to avoid them in your own speeches.

- **Anecdotal evidence.** Often you'll hear people use **anecdotal evidence** to "prove" a point: "Women are like that; I know, because I have three sisters." "That's the way Japanese managers are; I've seen plenty of them." One reason this type of "evidence" is inadequate is that it relies on too few observations; it's usually a clear case of overgeneralizing on the basis of too few instances. A second reason anecdotal evidence is inadequate is that one person's observations may be unduly clouded by his or her own attitudes and beliefs; your personal attitudes toward women or the Japanese, for example, may influence your perception of their behaviors.

- **Straw man**. A **straw man** argument (like a man made of straw) is a contention that's easy to knock down. In this fallacy a speaker creates an easy-to-destroy simplification of an opposing position (that is, a straw man) and then proceeds to smash it. But, of course, if the opposing case were presented fairly and without bias, it wouldn't be so easy to demolish.

- **Appeal to tradition.** Often used as an argument against change, the **appeal to tradition** simply claims that some proposed innovation is wrong or should not be adopted because it was never done before. This pseudo-argument is used repeatedly by those who don't want change. But, of course, the fact that something has not been done before says nothing about its value or whether or not it should be done now.

- **Bandwagon.** In the **bandwagon** fallacy, often referred to as an argument *ad populum* (to the people), the speaker tries to persuade the audience to accept or reject an idea or proposal because "everybody's doing it" or because the "right" people are doing it. The speaker urges you to jump on this large and popular bandwagon—or be left out by yourself. This is a popular technique in political elections; campaigns trumpet the results of polls in an effort to get undecided voters to jump on the bandwagon of the leading candidate. After all, you don't want to vote for a loser.

- **Testimonial.** The **testimonial** technique involves using the image associated with some person to secure your approval (if you respect the person) or your rejection (if you don't respect the person). This is the technique of advertisers who use people dressed up to look like doctors or plumbers or chefs to sell their products. Sometimes this technique takes the form of using only vague and general "authorities," as in "experts agree," "scientists say," "good cooks know," or "dentists advise."

Transfer. In **transfer** the speaker associates her or his idea with something you respect (to gain your approval) or with something you detest (to gain your rejection). For example, a speaker might portray a proposal for condom distribution in schools as a means for "saving our children from AIDS" (to encourage acceptance) or as a means for "promoting sexual promiscuity" (to encourage disapproval). Sports-car manufacturers try to get you to buy their cars by associating them with high status and sex appeal; promoters of exercise clubs and diet plans attempt to associate them with health, self-confidence, and interpersonal appeal.

Plain folks. Using the **plain folks** device, the speaker identifies himself or herself with the audience. The speaker is good—the "reasoning" goes—because he or she is one of the people, just plain folks like everyone else. Of course, the speaker who presents himself or herself as plain folks often is not. And even if he or she is plain folks, it has nothing to do with the issue under discussion.

Card-stacking. In the pseudo-argument known as **card-stacking**, the speaker selects only evidence and arguments that support his or her case and may even falsify evidence or distort facts to better fit the case. Despite these misrepresentations, the speaker presents the supporting materials as "fair" and "impartial."

Thin entering wedge. In the **thin entering wedge** pseudo-argument, a speaker argues against a proposal or new development on the grounds that as a "thin entering wedge" it will open the floodgates to all sorts of catastrophes (Chase, 1956). Though often based on no evidence, this argument has been used throughout history to oppose change. Some examples are "wedge" claims that school integration and interracial marriage will bring the collapse of American education and society, same-sex unions will destroy the family, computers will lead to mass unemployment, and banning smoking in all public places will lead to the collapse of the restaurant industry.

Agenda-setting. In **agenda-setting** a speaker contends that XYZ is the issue and that all others are unimportant and insignificant. This kind of fallacious appeal is heard frequently, as in "Balancing the budget is the key to the city's survival" or "There's only one issue confronting elementary education in our largest cities, and that is violence." In almost all situations, however, there are many issues and many sides to each issue. Often the person proclaiming that X is the issue really means, "I'll be able to persuade you if you focus solely on X and ignore the other issues."

*U*SE EMOTIONAL APPEALS

Emotional appeals, or appeals to your listeners' feelings, needs, desires, and wants, also can be powerful means of persuasion (Wood, 2000). Specifically, when you use motivational appeals, you appeal to those forces that energize, move, or motivate people to develop, change, or strengthen their attitudes or

Research Link

EVALUATING INTERNET RESOURCES

As you research your topic, keep in mind that anyone can "publish" on the Internet, making it essential that you subject everything you find on the Net to critical analysis. An article on the Internet can be written by world-renowned scientists or by elementary school students; by fair and objective reporters or by people who would spin the issues to serve their own political, religious, or social purposes. It's not always easy to tell which is which. Here are five questions to ask concerning the (1) qualifications, (2) currency, (3) fairness, (4) sufficiency, and (5) accuracy of Internet resources (as well as information from print media, from interpersonal interaction, or from film and electronic media).

Qualifications. Does the author have the necessary credentials? For example, does the author have a background in science or medicine to write authoritatively on health issues? Do an Internet search using the biography sites already discussed (see the Research Link in Chapter 6, p. 120), or simply enter the author's name in your favorite search engine and check on the author's expertise.

Currency. When was the information published? When were the sources cited in the article written? Generally, the more recent the material, the more useful it will be. With some topics—for example, unemployment statistics, developments in AIDS research, tuition costs, stem cell research, or attitudes toward the war, same-sex marriage, or organized religion—the currency of the information is crucial to its usefulness, simply because these things change so rapidly. Other topics, such as historical or literary subjects, may well rely on information that was written even hundreds of years ago. Even here, however, new information frequently sheds light on events that happened in the far distant past. To ensure currency, check important figures in a recent almanac, in a newspaper, or at a frequently updated Internet source such as Federal Statistics at www.fedstats.gov. At the same time, it's often helpful to simply search for more recent information, updating your facts and figures as necessary.

Fairness. Does the author of the material present the information fairly and objectively, or is there a bias favoring one position? Some websites, although objective on the surface, are actually organs of some political, religious, or social organization; so it's often useful to go to the home page and look for information on the nature of the organization sponsoring the website. Reviewing a range of research in the area will help you see how other experts view the issue. It will also enable you to see if this author's view of the situation takes into consideration all sides of the issue and if these sides are represented fairly.

Sufficiency. Is the information presented sufficient to establish the claim or conclusion? The opinion of one dietitian is insufficient to support the usefulness of a particular diet; statistics on tuition increases at five elite private colleges are insufficient to illustrate national trends in tuition costs. Generally, the broader your conclusion, the greater the information you'll need to meet the requirements for sufficiency. If you want to claim the usefulness of a diet for all people, then you're going to need a great deal of information from different populations—men and women, old and young, healthy and sickly, and so on.

Accuracy. Is the information presented accurate? Of course, determining accuracy is not easy, but the more you learn about your topic, the more able you'll be to judge the accuracy of information about the topic. Is the information primary or secondary (see the Research Link in Chapter 4, p. 72)? If it's secondary information, you may be able to locate the primary source material (often a hot link in the Internet article or a reference at the end of a printed text). Check to see if the information is consistent with information found in other sources and if the recognized authorities in the field accept this information.

Major textbook and trade book publishers go to enormous effort to ensure the accuracy of what appears in print or on their websites, so the information they provide is generally reliable. Some publishers, however, are arms of special interest groups with specific agendas. If this is the case with one of your sources, try to balance this publisher's perspective with information that represents other views of the issue. If an article appears in a journal sponsored by a major academic organization such as the American Psychological Association or the National Communication Association, you can be pretty sure that experts in the field have carefully reviewed the article before publication. Again, if an article appears in a well-respected major newspaper like the *New York Times*, the *Washington Post*, or the *Wall Street Journal*, or in any of the major newsmagazines or news networks (or online on their websites), you can be pretty sure that the information is accurate. Of course, these claims of accuracy are generalizations; errors do occur even in the most respected publications. Both academic journals and newspapers have printed fraudulent articles, though these instances are rare.

The next Research Link, "Museum Collections and Exhibits," appears on page 309.

ways of behaving. For example, one motive might be the desire for status. This desire might motivate someone to enter a high-status occupation or to dress a certain way.

Developed in the late 1960s, one of the most useful analyses of human motives remains Abraham Maslow's fivefold **hierarchy of needs**, reproduced in Figure 11.2 below (Benson & Dundis, 2003; Hanley & Abell, 2002; Kiel, 1999; Maslow, 1970). One of the assumptions contained in this theory is that people seek to fulfill the needs at the lowest level first. Only when those needs are satisfied do the needs at the next level begin to influence behavior. For example, people would not concern themselves with the need for security or freedom from fear if they were starving (if their need for food had not been fulfilled). Similarly, they would not be concerned with friendship if their need for protection and security had not been fulfilled. The implication for you as a speaker is that you have to know what needs of your audience are unsatisfied. These are the needs you can appeal to in motivating them.

Here are several useful motivational appeals organized around Maslow's hierarchy. As you review these, try to visualize how you would use each one in your next speech.

Physiological Needs

In many parts of the world, and even in parts of the United States, the basic physiological needs of people are not fully met and thus, as you can appreciate, are powerful motivating forces. Lech Walesa, former leader of the Polish

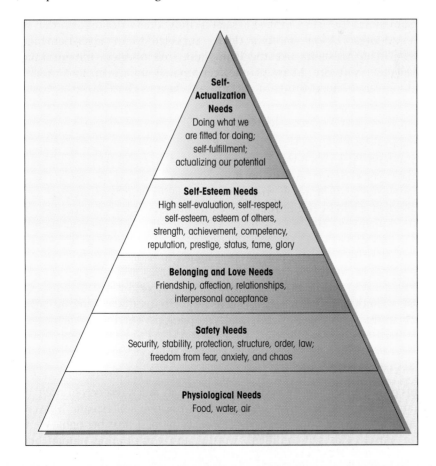

Figure 11.2
Maslow's Hierarchy of Needs

How would you describe the satisfied and unsatisfied needs of members of your public speaking class? Which of these needs would, according to Maslow, be most motivating for your class?

Source: Based on Abraham Maslow, *Motivation and Personality.* New York: HarperCollins, 1970.

Solidarity Party, recognized this when he wrote: "He who gives food to the people will win." In many of the poorest countries of the world, the speaker who promises to meet fundamental physiological needs is the one the people will follow. Most college students in the United States, however, have their physiological needs for food, water, and air well satisfied, so these issues will not prove helpful in motivating and persuading them. In other words, if they already have sufficient food, they won't need it and therefore won't be motivated to get it.

Safety Needs

Those who do not have their basic safety and freedom-from-fear needs met will be motivated by appeals to security, protection, and freedom from physical harm and from psychological distress. You see appeals to this need in advertisements for burglar protection devices for home and car, in political speeches promising greater police protection on the streets and in schools, and in the speeches of motivational gurus who promise psychological safety and freedom from anxiety. Freedom from anxiety also seems to be the motive many psychic services use in their ads, which promise that the services can tell you what is really going on (with, say, your romantic partner) as well as what will happen in the future. With this information, the ads imply, you'll be free of the anxiety that a lack of knowledge brings. You'll also learn what you should do—break off your relationship, move to the West Coast, or take that new job. The fact that this "information" is totally without any factual basis seems not to deter people from spending millions of dollars on psychics.

Sometimes the safety motive is seen in individuals' desire for order, structure, and organization—motives clearly appealed to in advertisements for personal data assistants like the Palm Pilot, cell phones, and information management software. Many people fear what is unknown, and order and structure seem to make things predictable and hence safe.

Belonging and Love Needs

Belonging and love needs are extremely powerful and comprise a variety of specific motives. For example, most people are motivated to love and be loved. For most persons, love and its pursuit occupy a considerable amount of time and energy. If you can teach your audience how to be loved and how to love, your audience will be not only attentive but also grateful.

As humans we also want affiliation—friendship and companionship. We want to be a part of a group, despite our equally potent desire for independence and individuality. Notice how advertisements for singles clubs, cruises, and dating services appeal to this need for affiliation. On this basis alone they successfully gain the attention, interest, and participation of thousands. Again, affiliation and group membership seem to assure us that we are in fact worthy creatures. If we have friends and companions, surely we are people of some merit.

Self-Esteem Needs

"In his private heart," wrote Mark Twain, "no man much respects himself." And perhaps because of this, we have a need for positive **self-esteem**: a favorable self-image, a view of ourselves that casts us in the best possible light. We want to see ourselves as self-confident, worthy, and contributing human beings.

Inspirational speeches, speeches of the "you're the greatest" type, never seem to lack receptive and suggestible audiences.

Self-esteem derives, at least in part, from the approval of others (something that is important in all cultures but especially in collectivist cultures). Most people are concerned not only with peer approval but also with approval from family, teachers, elders, and even children. And beyond contributing to positive self-esteem, approval from others also promotes the attainment of related goals. For example, if you have peer approval, you probably also have influence. If you have approval, you're likely to have status. In addressing your audience's desire for approval, however, avoid being too obvious. Few people want to be told that they need or desire approval.

People also want power, control, and influence. First, they want to have power over themselves—to be in control of their own destiny, to be responsible for their own successes. As Ralph Waldo Emerson put it, "Can anything be so elegant as to have few wants, and to serve them one's self?"

Many people also want to have power over other persons, to be influential. Similarly, they may want to increase control over their environment and over events and things in the world. Because of this you'll motivate your listeners when you make them see that they can increase their power, control, and influence if they learn what you have to say or do as you suggest.

People want to achieve in whatever they do. You want to be a successful student. You also want to achieve as a friend, as a parent, as a lover. This is why books and speeches that purport to tell people how to be better achievers are so successful. At the same time, of course, you also want others to recognize your achievements as real and valuable. In using the achievement motive, be explicit in stating how your speech, ideas, and recommendations will contribute to the listeners' achievements. At the same time, recognize that different cultures will view achievement very differently. To some achievement may mean financial success, to others it may mean group popularity, to still others it may mean security. Show your listeners how what you have to say will help them achieve the goals they seek, and you'll likely have an active and receptive audience.

Although they often deny it, most people are motivated to some extent by the desire for financial gain—for what money can buy, for what it can do. Concern for lower taxes, for higher salaries, and for fringe benefits all are related to the money motive. Show the audience that what you're saying or advocating will make them money, and they'll listen with considerable interest—much as they read the get-rich-quick books that constantly flood the bookstores.

Self-Actualization Needs

At the top of Maslow's hierarchy is the self-actualization motive. According to Maslow (1970), this motive influences attitudes and behaviors only after all other needs are satisfied. Because these other needs are very rarely all satisfied, the time spent appealing to self-actualization needs might be better spent on other motives. And yet it seems that regardless of how satisfied or unsatisfied your other desires may be, you have a desire to self-actualize, to become what you feel you're fit for. If you see yourself as a poet, you must write poetry. If you see yourself as a teacher, you must teach. Even if you don't pursue these as occupations, you nevertheless have a desire to write poetry or to teach. Appeals to self-actualization needs—to the yearning "to be the best you can be"—encourage listeners to strive for their highest ideals and are often welcomed by the audience.

Listening to Emotional Appeals

Emotional appeals are all around you, urging you to do all sorts of things—usually to buy a product or to support a position or cause. As you listen to these inevitable appeals, consider the following:

- Emotional appeals do not constitute proof. No matter how passionate the speaker's voice or bodily movement, no matter how compelling the language, passion does not prove the case a speaker is presenting.

- Feelings are not open to public inspection. You really can't tell with certainty what the speaker is feeling. The speaker may, in fact, be using facial management techniques or clever speechwriters to communicate emotions without actually feeling them.

- Emotional appeals may be used to divert attention from the lack of real evidence. If emotional appeals are being used to the exclusion of argument and evidence, or if you suspect that the speaker seeks to arouse your emotions so you forget that there's no evidence, ask yourself why.

- Emotional appeals may be to high or low motives. A speaker can arouse feelings of love and peace but also feelings of hatred and war. In asking for charitable donations, an organization may appeal to high motives such as your desire to help those less fortunate than you, or to lower motives such as guilt and fear.

- Be especially on the lookout for the appeal to pity (what logicians call *argumentum ad misericordiam*), as in "I really tried to write the speech, but I've been having terrible depression and find it difficult to concentrate."

A Case of **Ethics**   USING FEAR APPEALS

You're an elementary school teacher and are required to teach your eighth-grade class the unit on sex education. Your objective, which is mandated by the state syllabus but also is consistent with your own feeling, is to get students to avoid sexual relationships until they are much older. But you know from talking with students that many of them intend to have sexual relationships at the earliest opportunity; in fact, some are currently sexually active. You wonder if it would be ethical to use fear appeals to scare the students about the potential dangers of sex. For example, you could show them photos of people with advanced cases of sexually transmitted diseases, youngsters living in poverty because they now have children to support, and so on. Your purpose, you feel, is a noble one; but you wonder if the means to achieve that end are ethical.

Ethical Choice Point What would you do in this situation as you tried to balance accuracy with advocacy of ideas that you believed would benefit your audience? More generally, what ethical guidelines should govern the use of appeals to fear? Would you advocate different guidelines for audiences composed of adults and audiences composed of children?

*U*SE CREDIBILITY APPEALS

Your **credibility** is the degree to which your audience regards you as a believable spokesperson. If your listeners see you as competent and knowledgeable, of good character, and charismatic or dynamic, they will find you credible. As a result, you'll be more effective in changing their attitudes or in moving them to do something. Credibility is not something you have or don't have in any objective sense; rather, it's a function of what the audience thinks of you.

What makes a speaker credible will vary from one culture to another. In some cultures people would see competence as the most important factor in, say, their choice of a teacher for their preschool children. In other cultures the most important factor might be the goodness or morality of the teacher or perhaps the reputation of the teacher's family.

At the same time, each culture may define each of the factors in credibility differently. For example, "character" may mean following the rules of a specific religion in some cultures and following the individual conscience in others. To take another example, the Quran, the Torah, and the New Testament will be ascribed very different levels of credibility depending on the religious beliefs of the audience. And this will be true even when all three religious books say essentially the same thing on a given point.

Before reading any farther about the ways to establish your credibility, you may wish to take the self-test "How Credible Are You?"

*T*EST YOURSELF

How Credible Are You?

Respond to each of the following phrases to indicate how you think members of your class see you when you deliver a public speech. Use the following scale: Definitely true = 5; probably true = 4; neither true nor untrue = 3; probably untrue = 2; and definitely untrue = 1.

_____ **1.** Knowledgeable about the subject matter

_____ **2.** Experienced

_____ **3.** Informed about the subject matter

_____ **4.** Fair in the presentation of material (evidence and argument)

_____ **5.** Concerned with the audience's needs

_____ **6.** Consistent over time on the issues addressed in the speech

_____ **7.** Assertive in personal style

_____ **8.** Enthusiastic about the topic and in general

_____ **9.** Active rather than passive

HOW DID YOU DO? This test focuses on the three qualities of credibility—competence, character, and charisma—and is based on a large body of research (for example, McCroskey, 2001; Riggio, 1987). Items 1 to 3 refer to your perceived competence: How competent or capable do you seem to the audience when you give a public speech? Items 4 to 6 refer to your perceived character: Does the audience see you as a good and moral person? Items 7 to 9 refer to your perceived charisma: Does the audience see you as dynamic and active rather than as static and passive? Total scores will range from a high of 45 to a low of 9. If you scored relatively high (say around 32 or higher), then you feel your audience sees you as credible. If you scored relatively low (say below 27), then you feel your audience sees you as lacking in credibility.

WHAT WILL YOU DO? Think about how you might go about increasing your credibility. What specific steps can you take to change any audience perception with which you may be unhappy? Are there specific things you can do to strengthen your competence, character, and/or charisma? A good source to consult is Ronald Riggio's (1987) *The Charisma Quotient* (New York: Dodd).

Competence

Your perceived **competence** is the knowledge and expertise an audience thinks you have. The more knowledge and expertise the audience sees you as having, the more likely the audience will believe you. Similarly, you're likely to believe a teacher or doctor if you think he or she is knowledgeable on the subject at hand. You can demonstrate your competence to your audience in a variety of ways.

Tell Listeners of Your Competence Let the audience know of any special experience or training that qualifies you to speak on this specific topic. If you're speaking on communal living and you've lived on a commune yourself, then say so in your speech. Tell the audience of your unique personal experiences when these contribute to your credibility.

This recommendation to tell listeners of your competence generally applies to most audiences you'll encounter in the United States. But in some cultures—notably collectivist cultures such as those of Japan, China, and Korea, for example—to stress your own competence or that of your corporation may be taken as a suggestion that your audience members are inferior or that their corporations are not as good as yours. In other cultures—notably individualist cultures such as those of Scandinavia, the United States, and western Europe, for example—if you don't stress your competence, your listeners may assume it's because you don't have any.

Cite a Variety of Research Sources Make it clear to your audience that you've thoroughly researched your topic. Do this by mentioning some of the books you've read, the persons you've interviewed, the articles you've consulted. Weave these references throughout your speech. Don't bunch them together at one time.

Stress the Competencies of Your Sources If your audience isn't aware of them, then emphasize the particular competencies of your sources. In this way it becomes clear to the audience that you've chosen your sources carefully so as to provide the most authoritative sources possible. For example, saying simply, "Senator Cardova thinks..." does nothing to establish the senator's credibility. Instead, consider saying something like "Senator Cardova, who headed the finance committee for three years and was formerly a professor of economics at MIT, thinks. . . ."

Character

An audience will see you as credible if they perceive you as being someone of high moral **character**, someone who is honest, and someone they can trust. When an audience perceives your intentions as good for them (rather than for your own personal gain), they'll think you credible and they'll believe you. You can establish your high moral character in a number of ways.

Stress Fairness   If delivering a persuasive speech, stress that you've examined both sides of the issue (if indeed you have). If you're presenting both sides, then make it clear that your presentation is accurate and fair. Be particularly careful not to omit any argument the audience may already have thought of—this is a sure sign that your presentation isn't fair or balanced. Tell the audience that you would not advocate a position if you did not base it on a fair evaluation of the issues.

Stress Concern for Audience   Make it clear to the audience that you're interested in their welfare rather than seeking self-gain. If the audience feels that you are "out for yourself," they'll justifiably downgrade your credibility. Make it clear that the audience's interests are foremost in your mind. Tell your audience how the new legislation will reduce *their* taxes, how recycling will improve *their* community, how a knowledge of sexual harassment will make *their* workplace more comfortable and stress free.

Stress Concern for Enduring Values   We view speakers who are concerned with small and insignificant issues as less credible than speakers who demonstrate a concern for lasting truths and general principles. Thus, make it clear to the audience that your position—your thesis—is related to higher-order values; show them exactly how this is true.

Here, for example, Kofi Annan, in giving his farewell speech as secretary general of the United Nations on September 19, 2006, stressed his concern for enduring values (www.UN.org, accessed February 27, 2007):

> Yes, I remain convinced that the only answer to this divided world must be a truly United Nations. Climate change, HIV/AIDS, fair trade, migration, human rights—all these issues, and many more, bring us back to that point. Addressing each is indispensable for each of us in our village, in our neighborhood, and in our country. Yet each has acquired a global dimension that can only be reached by global action, agreed and coordinated through this most universal of institutions.

Charisma

Charisma is a combination of your personality and dynamism as seen by the audience. An audience will perceive you as credible (and believable) if they like you and if they see you as friendly and pleasant rather than aloof and reserved. Similarly, audiences favor the dynamic speaker over the hesitant, nonassertive speaker. They'll perceive you as less credible if they see you as shy, introverted, and soft-spoken rather than as an extroverted and forceful individual. (Perhaps people feel that a dynamic speaker is open and honest in presenting herself or himself but that a shy, introverted individual may be hiding something.) As a speaker there's much that you can do to increase your charisma and hence your perceived credibility.

Demonstrate a Positive Outlook   Show the audience that you have a positive orientation to the public speaking situation and to the entire speaker–

audience encounter. We see positive and forward-looking people as more credible than negative and backward-looking people. Stress your pleasure at addressing the audience. Stress hope rather than despair; stress happiness rather than sadness.

Demonstrate Enthusiasm The lethargic speaker, the speaker who somehow plods through the speech, is the very opposite of the charismatic speaker. Try viewing a film of Martin Luther King Jr. or Billy Graham speaking—they're totally absorbed with the speech and with the audience. They're excellent examples of the enthusiasm that makes a charismatic speaker.

Be Emphatic Use language that is emphatic rather than colorless and indecisive. Use gestures that are clear and decisive rather than random and hesitant. Demonstrate a firm commitment to the position you're advocating; the audience will be much more likely to agree with a speaker who believes firmly in the thesis of the speech.

Listening to Credibility Appeals

When you listen to credibility appeals, evaluate them critically. Here are three questions you'll find helpful to ask in assessing credibility appeals:

- Is the dimension of credibility used relevant to the issue at hand? For example, are the politician's family members (nice though they may be) relevant to his or her position on gun control or social security or immigration? Is the politician's former military service (or the lack of it) relevant to the issue being discussed?

- Are credibility appeals being used instead of argument and evidence? In typical examples of invalid credibility appeals, speakers may emphasize their educational background (to establish "competence"), appear at religious rituals (to establish "moral character"), or endeavor to present themselves as take-charge, alpha-type individuals (to demonstrate "charisma"). When done to divert attention from the issues or to mask the absence of evidence, such appeals are meaningless.

- Are the credibility appeals true? The actor who advertises toothpaste dressed as a dentist is still an actor doing a modeling job, not a dentist. Too often people unconsciously attribute credibility to a performance because of a uniform. Even when the endorser is a real dentist, remember that this dentist is getting paid for the endorsement. Although this doesn't necessarily make the endorsement false, it does (or should) make you wonder.

Avoiding Character Attacks

In addition, become conscious of fallacious strategies that focus on attacking the person. Be alert for fallacies like the following in the speeches of others, and eliminate them from your own reasoning:

- **Personal interest. Personal interest** attacks may take either of two forms. In one form the speaker disqualifies someone from having a point of view because he or she isn't directly affected by an issue or proposal or doesn't have firsthand knowledge; for example, a speaker might dismiss an argument on abortion merely because it was made by a man. In another form the speaker disqualifies someone because he or she will benefit in some way from a proposal. For example, arguing that someone is rich, middle class, or poor and thus will benefit greatly from a proposed tax cut does not mean that the argument for the tax cut is invalid. The legitimacy of an argument can never depend on the gender (or culture) of the individual. Nor can it depend on the gain that a person may derive from the position advocated. The legitimacy of an argument can be judged only on the basis of the evidence and reasoning presented.

- **Character attacks.** Often referred to as ad hominem arguments, **character attacks** involve accusing another person (usually an opponent) of some wrongdoing or of some character flaw. The purpose is to discredit the person or to divert attention from the issue under discussion. Arguments such as "How can we support a candidate who has smoked pot [or avoided the military]?" or "Do you want to believe someone who has been unfaithful on more than one occasion?" are often heard in political discussions but probably have little to do with the logic of the argument.

- **Name-calling.** In **name-calling**, often referred to as "poisoning the well," the speaker gives an idea, a group of people, or a political philosophy a bad name ("bigoted," "soft on terrorism,") to try to get listeners to condemn an idea without analyzing the argument and evidence. The opposite of name-calling is the use of "glittering generalities," in which the speaker tries to make you accept some idea by associating it with things you value highly ("democracy," "free speech," "academic freedom"). By using these "virtue words," the speaker tries to get you to ignore the evidence and simply approve of the idea.

MOTIVATE YOUR LISTENERS

If you want to persuade your listeners, you have to motivate them to believe or to act in some way. One way to motivate, as explained in Chapter 7 (pp. 163–174), is to use the motivated sequence—the organizational structure in which you gain your listeners' attention, demonstrate that a need exists, demonstrate how that need can be satisfied by their believing or doing what you say, showing them what things will be like if the need is satisfied as you suggested, and urging them to do something to solve the problem.

Table 11.1 summarizes the motivated sequence as a persuasive strategy and will help you develop your speeches whether they deal with questions of fact, value, or policy—the topics to which we now turn.

PERSUASIVE SPEECHES ON QUESTIONS OF FACT

Questions of fact concern what is or is not true, what does or does not exist, what did or did not happen. Some questions of fact are easily answered. These include many academic questions you're familiar with: Who was Aristotle? How many people use the Internet to get news? When was the first satellite launched? Questions of fact also include more mundane questions: What's on television? When is the meeting? What's Jenny's e-mail address? You can easily find answers to these questions by looking at some reference book, finding the relevant website, or asking someone who knows the answer.

TABLE 11.1   The Motivated Sequence as a Persuasive Strategy

STEP	PURPOSE	AUDIENCE QUESTION SPEAKER SHOULD ANSWER	AUDIENCE RESPONSE YOU WANT TO AVOID	IDEAL AUDIENCE RESPONSE	SPEECH MATERIALS TO USE	CAUTIONS TO OBSERVE
Attention	Focus listeners' attention on you and your message.	Why should I listen? Why should I use my time listening?	This is boring. This is irrelevant. This is of no interest to me.	This sounds interesting. Tell me more.	Attention-gaining materials (pp. 158–159).	Make attention relevant to speech topic.
Need	Demonstrate that there is a problem that affects them.	Why do I need to know or do anything?	I don't need to hear this. Things are fine now. This won't benefit me.	Ok, I understand; there's a problem.	Supporting materials (examples, statistics, testimony) (pp. 113–141).	Don't over-dramatize the need.
Satisfaction	Show listeners how they can satisfy the need.	How can I do anything about this?	I really can't do anything. It's beyond my control.	I can change things.	Supporting materials, pp. 113–141; logical, motivational, and ethical appeals.	Answer any objections listeners might have to your plan.
Visualization	Show listeners what their lives will be like with the need satisfied.	How would anything be different or improved?	I can't see how anything would be different. Nothing's going to change.	*Wow!* Things look a lot better this way.	Motivational appeals, pp. 269–273; illustrations and language high in imagery.	Be realistic; don't visualize the world as perfect once your listeners do as you suggest.
Action	Urge listeners to do something to solve the problem.	What can I do to effect this change?	I can't do anything. I'll be wasting my time and energy.	Let me sign up. Here's my contribution. I'll participate in the campaign.	Motivational appeals, pp. 269–273; specific language.	Be specific. Ask for small attitude changes and easily performed behaviors.

The questions of fact that we deal with in persuasive speeches are a bit different. Although these questions also have answers, the answers are not that easy to find and in fact may never be found. The questions concern controversial issues for which different people have different answers. Daily newspapers and Internet websites abound in questions of fact. For example, on July 21, 2007, Google News (www.googlenews.com) contained articles suggesting such questions of fact as these: Is Iran supporting the militias in Iraq? Did Attorney General Alberto Gonzales pressure then-Attorney General John Ashcroft to recertify President Bush's domestic surveillance program? Has North Korea complied with its promise to dismantle its nuclear plant? Is National Basketball referee Tim Donaghy guilt of betting on the games and providing information to others? Will no-smoking rules save lives? Did FEMA fail in New Orleans? Are the courts in the United States being politicized? Is human activity altering the world's rainfall patterns? Is Apple's iPhone vulnerable to hackers?

THESIS

For a persuasive speech on a question of fact, you'll formulate a thesis on the basis of a factual statement such as:

- This company has a glass ceiling for women.
- The plaintiff was slandered (or libeled or defamed).
- The death was a case of physician-assisted suicide.
- Gay men and lesbians make competent military personnel.
- Television violence leads to violent behavior in viewers.

If you were preparing a persuasive speech on, say, the first example given above, you might phrase your thesis as "This company discriminates against women." Whether or not the company does discriminate is a question of fact; clearly the company either does or does not discriminate. Whether you can prove it does or it doesn't, however, is another issue.

MAIN POINTS

Once you've formulated your thesis, you can generate your main points by asking the simple question "How do you know this?" or "Why would you believe this is true (factual)?" The answers to one of these questions will enable you to develop your main points. The bare bones of your speech might then look something like this:

General purpose: To persuade.
Specific purpose: To persuade my listeners that this company discriminates against women.
Thesis: This company discriminates against women. (How can we tell that this company discriminates against women?)

I. Women earn less than men.

II. Women are hired less often than men.

III. Women occupy fewer managerial positions than men.

Make sure that you clearly connect your main points to your thesis in your introduction, when introducing each of the points, and again in your summary. Don't allow the audience to forget that the lower salaries that women earn directly supports the thesis that this company discriminates against women.

SUPPORT

Having identified your main points, you will then begin searching for information to support them. Taking the first point, you might develop it something like this:

I. Women earn less than men.

  A. Over the past five years, the average salary for editorial assistants was $6,000 less for women than it was for men.

  B. Over the past five years, the entry-level salaries for women averaged $4,500 less than the entry-level salaries for men.

  C. Over the past five years, the bonuses earned by women were 20 percent below the bonuses earned by men.

Consider the rallies you've witnessed or been a part of. How would you describe the types of appeals (logical, emotional, credibility) used at rallies?

The following speech focuses entirely on a question of fact; the thesis itself is a question of fact. In other speeches, however, you may want just one of your main points to center on a question of fact. So, for example, let's say you're giving a speech advocating that the military give gay men and lesbians full equality. In this case, one of your points might focus on a question of fact: You might seek to establish that gay men and lesbians make competent military personnel. Once you've established that, you'd then be in a better position to argue for equality in military policy.

In a speech on questions of fact, you'll want to emphasize logical proof. Facts are your best support. The more facts you have, the more persuasive you'll be in dealing with questions of fact. For example, the more evidence you can find that women earn less than men, the more convincing you will be in proving that women do in fact earn less and, ultimately, that women are discriminated against.

Use the most recent materials possible. The more recent your materials, the more relevant they will be to the present time and the more persuasive they're likely to be. Notice, in our example, that if you said that in 1980 women earned on average $13,000 less than men, it would be meaningless in proving that the company discriminates against women *now*.

ORGANIZATION

Speeches on questions of fact probably fit most clearly into a topical organizational pattern, in which each reason for your thesis is given approximately equal weight. Notice, for example, that the outline of the speech under "Main Points" (p. 281) uses a topical order: Each of the reasons pointing to discrimination is treated as an equal main point.

A Persuasive Speech

Public Speaking *Sample Assistant*

Here is an excellent persuasive speech. "The Home of the Slaves," given by Jayme Meyer of the University of Texas at Austin at the American Forensic Association's National Individual Events tounament in 2004. The speech is used here with the permission of Jayme Meyer.

THE HOME OF THE SLAVES

Jayme Meyer

History books tell us that slavery ended after the Civil War. Try telling that to Andrea. At the age of 4, she was sold by her mother and enslaved for 12 years. Locked in a basement with 16 other children, the *New York Times Magazine* of January 25, 2004, explains, Andrea was raped almost every night while her owner got rich. Tragically, Andrea and her companions were not victims of an inadequate Third World government, but, according to the September 2003 *National Geographic*, they are among the almost 150,000 slaves currently held here in the United States.

Unlike the slaves of our early history, these slaves are lured to America with false promises of a better life through well-paying jobs or marriage. But as the *Boston Globe* of April 17, 2003, elaborates, once they arrive, these immigrants are forced to work in "brothels, sweatshops, fields, or private homes." And the terror doesn't stop there. The *San Antonio Express News* of April 3, 2003, reveals that slavery is now the third-largest source of money for organized crime, generating $19 billion annually, money that is often used for other criminal activity, including drug trafficking and arms smuggling, producing more crime for all of us to deal with here at home.

So in order to break this cycle of slavery, we must first, explore the extent of slavery in the United States; next, understand why this problem keeps us in chains; and finally, implement some solutions to what John Miller of the U.S. State Department calls in the *Washington Post* of January 1, 2004, "the emerging human rights issue of the 21st century."

This is a particularly dramatic story designed to gain attention and to suggest the topic of the speech. Did it gain your attention? If not, what else might the speaker have done?

Is 150,000 people a lot? How might the speaker have dramatized this number and made it more significant to an audience of college students?

This elaboration continues to dramatize the situation of modern slavery and presents it as a problem for the listeners. Was the speaker successful in convincing you that this is a problem for society and for you? If not, what else might the speaker have done to convince you that this problem really affected you personally?

Here the speaker provides an excellent orientation to the speech and identifies the three major sections of the speech: (1) the present state of slavery in the United States, (2) the reasons this is a problem, and (3) ways of solving the problem.

The organizational pattern is also identified; the first two sections present the problem and the third presents the

The 13th Amendment was supposed to end slavery in December 1865, but even today slaves are forced into the U.S. and slavery fosters additional crime. Kristiina Kangaspunta of the United Nations tells the Associated Press of May 13, 2003, that the United States is now one of the top three human trafficking destinations in the world, with most slaves originating from Thailand, Russia, or the Ukraine. The January 25, 2004, *New York Times Magazine* explains that traffickers promise slaves better lives in the U.S. as waiters, actors, models or nannies. But after tricking them into paying their own way into Mexico, the traffickers smuggle them across the border and force them into a nightmare world of brutality. According to the U.S. Department of State's *Trafficking in Persons Report* of June 11, 2003, slaves are exposed to appalling working conditions, sexually transmitted diseases from rape and forced prostitution, poor nutrition, and even torture. For instance, four girls between the ages of 14 and 17 were recently discovered working in an underground brothel in Plainfield, New Jersey. The same *New York Times Magazine* described the conditions when the police found them: the emaciated girls slept on rotting mattresses, used a doorless, filthy bathroom, and were surrounded by morning-after pills and abortion-inducing medications.

Although we may not personally be enslaved, all of us are affected by America's slave trade. According to the summer/fall 2003 *Brown Journal of World Affairs*, the profits made from slavery are often invested in the mainstream economy, giving criminal networks more power because of their immense wealth. And the more they make, the more we're affected. As M2 Presswire of October 14, 2003, explains, crime syndicates use the billions of dollars generated by slavery to fund other criminal activities, including drug trafficking, arms smuggling, and money laundering. While 150,000 slaves suffer the immediate evils of slavery, all of us are endangered by its long-term implications.

We pride ourselves on our freedoms, but 150,000 people within our borders are denied theirs because of slavery's lucrative nature and ineffective legislation. The *Agence France Presse* of August 1, 2003, reports the results of an International Labour Organization study: modern-day slavery is "more lucrative . . . than drug trafficking." As the aforementioned *Trafficking in Persons Report*

solution. In what other ways could this speech have been organized?

Here the speaker begins to explain the current state of slavery and makes us see it as a horrendous crime.

The speaker continues to introduce current material from reliable sources and makes us feel he is well prepared and knowledgeable, which adds to his credibility.

The speaker makes a great effort to make the topic of these enslaved individuals significant for a group of listeners who are probably quite comfortable and secure. Did the speaker succeed in making you feel that this problem affects you? If not, what else might the speaker have done?

Here the speaker moves from general statements about slavery to a specific case of four girls. Moving from the abstract to the specific is a useful technique for making your listeners understand and feel the problem.

The speaker cleverly answers the potential audience question ("Why should this concern me?") by relating the problem to one that creates additional crime from which we all suffer. Was the speaker successful in getting you to feel that this is important to you? How much do you care about these other problems—drug trafficking, arms smuggling, and money laundering? If you don't care very much, what might the speaker have done to make you care?

What has the speaker done throughout this speech to identify with the audience? What else might the speaker have done?

reveals, slave owners make up to thousands of dollars for each child laborer and tens of thousands for each brothel worker. And, as a February 24, 2004, article on the Florida State University Web page notes, "unlike drugs, humans can be recycled . . . so it's a better investment for the traffickers." And according to the *National Geographic* of September 2003, countless people take advantage of its lucrative nature: Juan, Ramiro, and Jose Ramos forced men and women from Mexico to pick fruit in Florida. Sardar and Nadira Gasanov made women from Uzbekistan work in strip clubs in West Texas. Louisa Satia and Kevin Nanji tricked a 14-year-old girl from Cameroon into working as their private servant in Maryland after raping her and imprisoning her in their house—and the list goes on.

And unfortunately, current laws are simply not strong enough. The Trafficking Victims Protection Act of 2000 has done a good job of protecting some victims, giving former slaves temporary U.S. visas and offering protection from their traffickers. But helping victims after they are discovered doesn't get to the root of the problem; getting traffickers off the streets would. The *San Antonio Express News* of April 3, 2003, states that while $60 million per year is spent on the cause, only 75 traffickers were actually prosecuted in 2000, simply not enough for the problem that Assistant Secretary of State Richard Armitage tells the *Weekly Standard* of October 6, 2003, will "outstrip the illicit trade in guns and narcotics within a decade."

We thought we abolished slavery in 1865, but the fight obviously is not over. Action from the UN and the United States government, as well as our own attention, can help protect those who have lost all freedom. The United Nations needs to follow through with its international database of human trafficking. As a UN press release of May 16, 2003, states, the database, now consisting of about 3,000 cases, tracks the "countries of origin, transit and destination of trafficked persons." This database needs to be continuously updated in order to give governments accurate information to prosecute those who traffic human beings. The U.S. government needs to work in conjunction with the UN to help populate the database, and then must utilize the information once it is available. This database will help us find a way to stop the flow of slaves into the United States, allowing us to get to the root of the problem.

Would selective exposure play a role in this speech? If so, what could the speaker do to **anticipate selective exposure?**

What kinds of **logical appeals** does the speaker use in this speech? How effective are they?

Again, the speaker cleverly weaves in specific examples along with the generalizations and gives the problem a human face.

What types of **emotional appeals** can you find throughout this speech? How effective are they? How might they have been made even more effective?

This first sentence is an interesting but subtle transition between the problem, already discussed, and the solution, which is about to be discussed. Would you have preferred a more obvious and direct transition?

Does the speaker convince you that the United Nations can help in combating this problem?

Once this information is acquired, United States lawmakers must also take swift action. The Trafficking Victims Protection Act of 2000 was definitely a good first step. However, it needs to refocus its funding on the prosecution of traffickers. To reach this goal, more money obviously needs to be spent. According to Mohamed Matted, codirector of the Protection Project at Johns Hopkins University, in his testimony to the House Committee on International Relations on June 24, 2003, this can be done by confiscating traffickers' assets. This money could be used to fund prosecution of other traffickers as well as provide restitution for the victims.

The second part of the solution concerns lawmakers. Does the speaker make an effective case for the role that laws and lawmakers must play in human trafficking?

What types of **credibility appeals** can you identify throughout this speech? Would you have used credibility appeals differently? What would you have said?

Finally, you and I easily can play our part in abolishing slavery by going to the American Anti-Slavery Group's website at iAbolish.com. Next time you are online, become an e-abolitionist by signing antislavery petitions and joining the site's Freedom Action Network. The Network will send you weekly e-mail newsletters to keep you informed and to alert you to antislavery events in your area. We have condemned past slavery and those who allowed it to persist. But now it's our turn to stand up for what we know is right and help abolish the slavery that plagues our time.

The third part of the solution is to act on a personal level, specifically to participate in a particular Internet group devoted to the speech's ultimate aim—the elimination of human slavery. Is this something you might do after reading this speech? If not, what might the speaker have said to move you to action?

Is the speaker asking for **reasonable amounts** of **change?** If not, what correction would you suggest?

Even though Andrea has been free for about 5 years, so are those who tortured her for 12. Fearing retribution, she's in constant hiding, dealing with the daily trauma from her years of forced servitude. But after understanding the extent of modern-day slavery and discussing how it came about, we can implement solutions to help people like Andrea see for themselves that we do live in the land of the free, not the home of the slave.

Here the speaker returns to the introduction, and you know that he is nearing the end of his speech.

The speaker here summarizes the main points that were introduced in the introduction and developed throughout the speech.

Now that you've read the entire speech, what would you have titled it if it had been prepared for presentation in your public speaking class?

PERSUASIVE SPEECHES ON QUESTIONS OF VALUE

Questions of value concern what people consider good or bad, moral or immoral, just or unjust. Google News (July 21, 2007), for example, identified such questions of value as these: Are the proposed changes to Medicare beneficial? What should be the legacy of Tammy Faye [Bakker] Messner? What is the value of stopping North Korea's nuclear program? Should the Food and

Drug Administration have approved the new breast cancer drug? Was Tony Blair a good choice for Mideast envoy? Will increasing the minimum wage help workers (businesses)? Should safeguards be developed to protect consumer privacy on the Internet? Should circumcision be promoted to slow the spread of AIDS? Should Cindy Sheehan have been arrested during her call for President Bush's impeachment? Should the state of Washington have instituted the Domestic Partnership Law? Should Calgary paramedics be permitted to strike? Is funding faith-based education a good idea?

Speeches on questions of value will seek to strengthen audiences' existing attitudes, beliefs, or values. This is true of much religious and political speaking; for example, people who listen to religious speeches usually are already believers, so these speeches strive to strengthen the beliefs and values the people already hold. In a religious setting, the listeners already share the speaker's values and are willing to listen. Speeches that seek to change audience values are much more difficult to construct. Most people resist change. When you try to get people to change their values or beliefs, you're fighting an uphill (though not necessarily impossible) battle.

Be sure that you define clearly the specific value on which you're focusing. For example, let's say that you're developing a speech to persuade high school students to attend college. You want to stress that college is of value, but what type of value do you focus on? The financial value (college graduates earn more money than nongraduates)? The social value (college is a lot of fun and a great place to make friends)? The intellectual value (college will broaden your view of the world and make you a more critical and creative thinker)? Once you clarify the type of value on which you'll focus, you'll find it easier to develop the relevant points. You'll also find it easier to locate appropriate supporting materials.

THESIS

Theses devoted to questions of value might look something like this:

- The death penalty is unjustifiable.
- Bullfighting is inhumane.
- Discrimination on the basis of affectional orientation is wrong.
- Chemical weapons are immoral.
- Human cloning is morally justified.
- College athletics minimize the importance of academics.

MAIN POINTS

As with speeches on questions of fact, you can generate the main points for a speech on a question of value by asking a strategic question of your thesis, such as "Why is this good?" or "Why is this immoral?" For example, you can take the first thesis given above and ask, "Why is the death penalty unjustifiable?" The answers to this question will give you the speech's main points. The body of your speech might then look something like this:

General purpose: To persuade.
Specific purpose: To persuade my listeners that the death penalty is unjustifiable.

Thesis: The death penalty is unjustifiable. (Why is the death penalty unjustifiable?)

I. The criminal justice system can make mistakes.

II. The death penalty constitutes cruel and unusual punishment.

III. No one has the moral right to take another's life.

SUPPORT

To support your main points, search for relevant evidence. For example, to show that mistakes have been made in capital punishment cases, you might itemize three or four high-profile cases in which people were put to death and later, through DNA, found to have been innocent.

At times, and with certain topics, it may be useful to identify the standards you would use to judge something moral or justified or fair or good. For example, in the "bullfighting is inhumane" speech, you might devote your first main point to defining when an action can be considered inhumane. In this case, the body of your speech might look like this:

I. An inhumane act has two qualities.

    A. It is cruel and painful.

    B. It serves no human necessity.

II. Bullfighting is inhumane.

    A. It is cruel and painful.

    B. It serves no necessary function.

Notice that in the example of capital punishment, the speaker aims to strengthen or change the listeners' beliefs about the death penalty. The speaker is not asking the audience to do anything about capital punishment, but merely to believe that it's not justified. However, you might also use a question of value as a first step toward persuading your audience to take some action. For example, once you got your listeners to see the death penalty as unjustified, you might then ask them to take certain actions—perhaps in your next speech—to support an anti–death penalty politician, to vote for or against a particular proposition, or to join an organization fighting against the death penalty.

ORGANIZATION

Like speeches on questions of fact, speeches on questions of value often lend themselves to topical organization. For example, the speech on capital punishment cited earlier uses a topical order. But even within this topical order there is another level of organization, an organization that begins with those items on which there is the least disagreement or opposition and moves on to the items on which your listeners are likely to see things very differently. It's likely that even listeners in favor of the death penalty would agree that mistakes can be made; and such listeners probably would be willing to accept evidence that mistakes have in fact been made, especially if you cite reliable statistical evidence and expert testimony. By starting with this issue, you secure initial agreement and can use that as a basis for approaching areas where you and the audience are more likely to disagree.

PERSUASIVE SPEECHES ON QUESTIONS OF POLICY

When you move beyond a focus on value to urging your audience to do something about an issue, you're then into a question of policy. For example, in a speech designed to convince your listeners that bullfighting is inhumane, you'd be focusing on a question of value. If you were to urge that bullfighting should therefore be declared illegal, you'd be urging the adoption of a particular policy.

Items on Google News (July 21, 2007) that suggested questions of policy included these: How can flooding be prevented? What should be the policy of search engines regarding behaviorally targeted ads? How can prison overcrowding best be reduced? What can be done to improve communication between medical professionals and their older patients? What should be the policy concerning paramedics going on strike? What policy should the National Basketball Association adapt regarding betting by members? How should the United States treat Iran (or North Korea)? What safeguards should be developed to protect consumer privacy on the Internet?

Questions of policy concern what should be done, what procedures should be adopted, what laws should be changed; in short, what policy should be followed. In some speeches you may want to defend or promote a specific policy; in others you may wish to argue that a current policy should be discontinued.

THESIS

Persuasive speeches frequently revolve around questions of policy and may use theses such as the following:

- Hate speech should be banned on college campuses.
- Our community should adopt a zero tolerance policy for guns in schools.
- Abortion should be available on demand.
- Music CDs should be rated for violence and profanity.
- Medical marijuana should be legalized.
- Smoking in cars should be banned.

As you can tell from these examples, questions of policy almost invariably involve questions of values. For example, the argument that hate speech should be banned at colleges is based on the value judgment that hate speech is wrong. To argue for a zero tolerance policy on guns in schools implies that you think it's wrong for students or faculty to carry guns to school.

MAIN POINTS

You can develop your speech on a question of policy by asking a strategic question of your thesis. With policy issues, the question will be "Why should this policy be adopted?" or "Why should this policy be discontinued?" or "Why is this policy better than what we now have?" Taking our first example, we might ask, "Why should hate speech be banned on campus?" From the answers to this question, you would develop your main points, which might look something like this:

I. Hate speech encourages violence against women and minorities.

II. Hate speech denigrates women and minorities.

III. Hate speech teaches hate instead of tolerance.

SUPPORT

You would then support each main point with a variety of supporting materials that would convince your audience that hate speech should be banned from college campuses. For example, you might cite the websites put up by certain groups that advocate violence against women and minority members, or quote from the lyrics of performers who came to campus. Or you might cite examples of actual violence that had been accompanied by hate speech or hate literature.

In some speeches on questions of policy, you might simply want your listeners to agree that the policy you're advocating is a good idea. In other cases you might want them to do something about the policy—to vote for a particular candidate, to take vitamin C, to diet, to write to their elected officials, to participate in a walkathon, to wear an AIDS awareness ribbon, and so on.

ORGANIZATION

Speeches on questions of policy may be oganized in a varety of ways. For example, if the existing policy is doing harm, consider using a cause-to-effect pattern. If your policy is designed to solve a problem, consider the problem–solution pattern. For example, in a speech advocating zero tolerance for guns in school, the problem–solution pattern would seem appropriate; your speech would be divided into two basic parts:

I. Guns are destroying our high schools. (problem)

II. We must adopt a zero tolerance policy. (solution)

Questions of policy are often well suited to organization with the motivated sequence. Here is an example how a talk about hate speech might employ the motivated sequence:

ATTENTION

I. Here are just a few of the examples of hate speech I collected right here on campus.

[Show slides 1–7]

NEED

II. Hate speech creates all sorts of problems.

A. Hate speech encourages violence.

B. Hate speech denigrates women and minorities.

C. Hate speech teaches intolerance.

SATISFACTION

III. If we're to build an effective learning environment, hate speech must go.

VISUALIZATION

IV. Banning hate speech will help us build an environment conducive to learning.

   A. Students will not fear violence.

   B. Women and minorities will not feel as if they are second-class citizens.

   C. Tolerance can replace intolerance.

ACTION

V. Sign my petition urging the administration to take action, to ban hate speech.

If you're persuading your listeners that one policy will be more effective than another (say, that a new policy will be better than the present policy), then a comparison-and-contrast organization might work best. Here you might divide each of your main points into two parts—the present policy and the proposed plan—so as to effectively compare and contrast them on each issue. For example, the body of a speech urging a new health care plan might look something like this:

I. The plans are different in their coverage for psychiatric problems.

   A. The present plan offers nothing for such problems.

   B. The proposed plan treats psychiatric problems with the same coverage as physical problems.

II. The plans differ in their deductibles.

   A. The present plan has a $2,000 deductible.

   B. The proposed plan has a $500 deductible.

III. The plans differ in the hospitalization allowances.

   A. In the present plan two days are allowed for childbirth; in the proposed plan four days are allowed.

   B. In the present plan all patients are assigned to large wards; in the proposed plan all patients are assigned to semiprivate rooms.

Essentials of Persuading Your Audience

In this chapter we looked at the persuasive speech: its goals, the principles of persuasion, and the three main types of persuasive speeches.

1. **Persuasive speaking** has three general **goals**:
   - To strengthen or weaken attitudes, beliefs, or values
   - To change attitudes, beliefs, or values
   - To motivate to action

2. Among the important **principles for persuasive speaking** are:
   - Anticipate selective exposure.
   - Ask for reasonable amounts of change.
   - Identify with your audience.
   - Be culturally sensitive.
   - Use logical appeals.
   - Use emotional appeals.
   - Use credibility appeals.
   - Motivate your listeners.

3. Persuasive speeches on **questions of fact** focus on what is or is not true. In a speech on a question of fact:
   - Emphasize logical proof.
   - Use the most recent materials possible.
   - Use highly competent sources.
   - Clearly connect your main points to your thesis.

4. Speeches on **questions of value** focus on issues of good and bad, justice or injustice. In designing

speeches to strengthen or change attitudes, beliefs, or values:

- Define clearly the specific value on which you're focusing.
- Begin with shared assumptions and beliefs, then progress gradually to areas of disagreement.
- Use sources that the audience values highly.

5. Speeches on **questions of policy** focus on what should or should not be done, what procedures should or should not be adopted. In designing speeches to move listeners to action:

- Prove that the policy is needed.
- Emphasize that the policy you're supporting is practical and reasonable.
- Show your listeners how the policy will benefit them directly.
- When asking for action, ask for small, easily performed, and very specific behaviors.
- Use an organizational pattern that best fits your topic.

Essential Terms: Persuading Your Audience

agenda-setting **(p. 269)**
anecdotal evidence **(p. 268)**
appeal to tradition **(p. 268)**
bandwagon **(p. 268)**
card-stacking **(p. 269)**
character **(p. 277)**
character attacks **(p. 279)**
charisma **(p. 277)**
competence **(p. 276)**
credibility **(p. 275)**
door-in-the-face technique **(p. 262)**

emotional appeals **(p. 269)**
foot-in-the-door technique **(p. 262)**
hierarchy of needs **(p. 271)**
logical appeals **(p. 265)**
name-calling **(p. 279)**
personal interest **(p. 278)**
persuasion **(p. 259)**
persuasion continuum **(p. 260)**
plain folks **(p. 269)**
questions of fact **(p. 279)**
questions of policy **(p. 289)**

questions of value **(p. 286)**
reasoning from causes and effects **(p. 266)**
reasoning from sign **(p. 267)**
reasoning from specific instances **(p. 266)**
selective exposure **(p. 260)**
straw man **(p. 268)**
testimonial **(p. 268)**
thin entering wedge **(p. 269)**
transfer **(p. 269)**

Public Speaking Exercises

11.1 Developing Persuasive Strategies

The objective of this exercise is to stimulate the discussion of persuasive strategies on a variety of contemporary cultural issues. The exercise may be completed individually, in small groups, or with the entire class.

What persuasive strategies would you use to convince your class of the validity of either side in any of the following points of view? For example, what persuasive strategies would you use to persuade your class members that interracial adoption should be encouraged or discouraged? These points of view are simplified for purposes of this exercise and shouldn't be taken to suggest that the viewpoints given here are complete descriptions of these complex issues.

Point of View: Interracial Adoption. Those in favor of interracial adoption argue that the welfare of the child—who might not get adopted if made to wait for someone of the same race—must be considered first. Adoption (regardless of race) is good for the child and therefore is a positive social process. Those opposed to interracial adoption argue that children need to be raised by those of the same race if they are to develop self-esteem and become functioning members of their own ethnic group. Interracial adoption is therefore a negative social process.

Point of View: Gay Men and Lesbians in the Military. Those in favor argue that gay men and lesbians should be accorded exactly the same rights and privileges as heterosexuals—no more, no less; equality means equality for all. Those opposed argue that gay men and lesbians will undermine the image of the military and will make heterosexuals uncomfortable.

Point of View: Affirmative Action. Those in favor of affirmative action argue that because of the injustices in the way certain groups (racial, national, gender) were treated, they should now be given preferential treatment to correct the imbalance caused by social injustices. Those opposed to affirmative action argue that merit must be the sole criterion for promotion, jobs, entrance to graduate schools, and so on, and that affirmative action is just reverse racism; one form of injustice cannot correct another form of injustice.

11.2 Questions of Fact, Value, and Policy

Understanding how purposes and theses can be identified from a wide variety of questions of fact, value, and policy will help you construct more effective speeches. To develop this understanding, select a newspaper (Sunday's edition will work best), a weekly newsmagazine, or an Internet news site and identify the questions of fact, value, and policy covered in this one issue (as was done in this chapter). From these select one question of fact, value, or policy and develop a general purpose, a specific purpose, and a thesis that would be appropriate for a speech in this class. Then identify the two or three main ideas that you might want to develop based on this thesis.

11.3 Constructing Motivational Appeals

Here are five theses you might use or hear in a persuasive speech. Select one of these and develop two or three motivational appeals that you might use in a speech to members of this class.

- Universal health care is a human right.
- Same-sex marriage should be legalized in all 50 states.
- Capital punishment should be declared illegal.
- Smoking should be banned throughout the entire college (buildings and grounds).
- Tenure for college teachers should be abolished.

11.4 Establishing Credibility

Acquiring facility in establishing a person's credibility is essential in a wide variety of persuasive speeches. To work on this helpful skill, select a person—an authority on any topic you'd like—and develop a minibiography of this person that you might use in a speech to establish this person's competence, character, and charisma. You may find it helpful to review the Research Link on Biographical Material in Chapter 6 (p. 120).

11.5 What Do You Say?

- **Magnitude of Change.** Charlie wants to get his listeners to contribute four hours a week to the college's program in which volunteers help high school students prepare for college. How would you suggest that Charlie use the foot-in-the-door technique? How might he use the door-in-the-face technique? Which strategy do you think would work best if your class were the audience?
- **Negative Audience.** Alan is planning to give a speech in favor of the college's restricting access to certain lifestyle websites. Alan knows that his audience is opposed to his position, so he wonders what types of arguments will work best. What advice would you give Alan?
- **Persuasive Appeals.** Jake wants to give a speech urging listeners to vote for a proposed new required curriculum. He wants to use both logical and emotional appeals. If Jake were speaking to your class, what logical and what emotional appeals would you advise him to use?
- **Establishing Credibility.** Evelyn is planning a speech on baseball. She fears, however, that simply because she's a woman, her audience is not going to perceive her as credible—even though she knows more about baseball than any other person in the room. What would you advise Evelyn to do to establish her credibility?
- **Assessing Questions of Fact.** Judith wants to give her persuasive speech on a question of fact (media violence leads to violent behavior). If the audience were your public speaking class, what main points might Judith develop?
- **Developing Main Points for a Speech on a Question of Value.** Berta wants to develop her persuasive speech against using animals to test cosmetics. If she were giving this speech to your class, how might Berta phrase a thesis, and what might her main points be?
- **Selecting Arguments.** Rose is preparing a persuasive speech on a question of policy, arguing that owners of phone-in psychic advice services should be prosecuted for fraud. What types of arguments would Rose need if she were presenting this speech to your class?

Log*On!* MySpeechLab

Persuading Your Audience

Visit MySpeechLab (www.myspeechlab.com) for additional insights into the nature of persuasion and into the strategies of persuasive speaking; see "Principles of Motivation"; "Additional Motivational Appeals"; "How You Form Credibility Impressions"; "General Guidelines for Communicating Credibility"; "Thinking Critically about Persuasive Speaking"; "Evaluating the Adequacy of Reasoning"; "Analyzing Arguments: The Toulmin Model"; "Comparative Credibility Judgments"; and "Gender, Credibility, and the Topics of Public Speaking." A self-test on the ethics of persuasion is presented in "When Is Persuasion Unethical?" An excellent persuasive speech by Upendri Gunasekera, "The Perils of Philanthropy," also appears here along with annotations and questions for analysis.

Several excellent video persuasive speeches are available. See, for example, "Chicago Mass Transit" and "Commercialization of Religion" for examples of the principles of persuasion. You may also wish to examine "Mandatory Minimums," which uses the motivated sequence as an organizational pattern.

Also see the practice tests for the goals of and guidelines for persuasive speaking and on speeches of fact, value, and policy. You may also want to consult the Outlining Wizard for help with organizing your persuasive speeches.

12 Speaking on Special Occasions

Why Read This Chapter?

Because it will enable you to develop additional types of public speeches by helping you to:

- prepare and present a variety of special occasion speeches, including speeches designed to secure goodwill, to praise another person, to present or accept an award, or to honor or celebrate some occasion

- present a group's thinking in a variety of public speaking formats

- apply special occasion insights and guidelines to all kinds of speeches

"Where shall I begin, please your majesty?" she asked. "Begin at the beginning," the King said, very gravely, "and go on till you come to the end: then stop."

—Lewis Carroll (1832–1898)
Mathematician, logician, and author, most famous for his *Alice in Wonderland*

In addition to the many varieties of informative and persuasive speeches, there are several types of speeches usually called "special occasion speeches," with which you'll want to achieve some familiarity. In this chapter we'll consider speeches to introduce someone, to present or accept an award, to secure goodwill or apologize, to dedicate something, to congratulate a graduating class (the commencement speech), to eulogize someone, to bid farewell, or to toast. We'll also look at some of the ways in which you might present the thinking of a group to an audience after the group has brainstormed or problemsolved. We'll conclude the chapter with a look at the role of culture in the special occasion speech.

THE SPEECH OF INTRODUCTION

Chapter 2 (see Public Speaking Sample Assistant on pp. 34–36) illustrated the speech designed to introduce you or another person to an audience. The aim of that speech is to help listeners learn something about you or another person. The **speech of introduction** considered here is a bit different and is usually designed to introduce a speaker or a topic area which a series of speakers will address. For example, before a speaker addresses an audience, another speaker often sets the stage by introducing both the speaker and the topic. At conventions, where a series of speakers address an audience, a speech of introduction might introduce the general topic on which the speakers will focus and perhaps provide connecting links among the several presentations.

In a speech of introduction, your main purpose is to gain the attention and arouse the interest of the audience. Your speech should pave the way for favorable and attentive listening. The speech of introduction is basically informative and follows the general patterns already discussed for the informative speech. The main difference is that instead of discussing a topic's issues, you discuss who the speaker is and what the speaker will talk about. In your speeches of introduction, follow these general principles:

- Establish the significance of the speech. Focus the audience's attention and interest on the main speaker and on the importance of what the speaker will say.

- Establish relevant connections among the speaker, the topic, and the audience, and answer your listeners' inevitable question: Why should we listen to this speaker on this topic?

- Stress the speaker's credibility (see Chapter 11) by telling the audience what has earned this speaker the right to speak on this topic to this audience.

- Speak in a style and manner that is consistent with the main speech. Introduce the speaker with the same degree of formality that will prevail during the actual speech. Otherwise, the speaker will have to counteract an inappropriate atmosphere created by the speech of introduction.

- Be brief (relative to the length of the main speech). If the main speech is to be brief—say, 10 to 20 minutes—your introduction should be no longer than 1 or 2 minutes. If, on the other hand, the main speech is to be an hour long, then your introduction might last 5 to 10 minutes or even longer.

■ Don't cover the substance of the topic the speaker will discuss. Also remember that clever stories, jokes, startling statistics, or historical analogies, which are often effective in speeches of introduction, will prove a liability if the main speaker intended to use this same material.

■ Don't oversell the speaker or topic. Present the speaker in a positive light, but don't create an image that the speaker will find impossible to live up to.

THE SPEECH OF PRESENTATION OR ACCEPTANCE

We'll consider speeches of presentation and speeches of acceptance together, both because they're frequently paired and because the same general principles govern both types of speeches. In a **presentation speech** you seek to (1) place an award or honor in some kind of context and (2) give the award an extra air of dignity or status. A speech of presentation may focus on rewarding a colleague for an important accomplishment (being named Teacher of the Year) or on recognizing a particularly impressive performance (winning an Academy Award). It may honor an employee's service to a company or a student's outstanding grades or athletic abilities.

The **acceptance speech** is the other side of this honoring ceremony. Here the recipient accepts the award and attempts to place the award in some kind of context. At times the presentation and the acceptance speeches are rather informal and amount to a simple "You really deserve this" and an equally simple "Thank you." At other times—for example, in the presentation and acceptance of a Nobel Prize—the speeches are formal and are prepared in great detail and with great care. Such speeches are frequently reprinted in newspapers throughout the world. Somewhere between these two extremes lie average speeches of presentation and acceptance.

In your speeches of presentation, follow these two principles:

■ State the reason for the presentation. Make clear why this particular award is being given to this particular person.

■ State the importance of the award. The audience (as well as the group authorizing or sponsoring the award) will no doubt want to hear something about this. You might point out the importance of the award by referring to the previous recipients (assuming they're well known to the audience), emphasizing the status of the award (assuming that it's a prestigious award), or describing the award's influence on previous recipients.

In preparing and presenting your speech of acceptance, follow these three principles:

■ Thank the people responsible for giving you the award—the academy members, the board of directors, the student body, your teammates.

■ Acknowledge those who helped you achieve the award. Be specific without being overly detailed.

■ Put the award into personal perspective by telling the audience what the award means to you right now and perhaps what it will mean to you in the future.

Consider the acceptance speech. What would you say in accepting an award for the most improved public speaker in the class? What would you say in presenting the award to someone else?

For fun and for further insight into the acceptance speech, log on to the Academy Award Acceptance Speech Generator (http://www.chickenhead.com/stuff/oscar/index.asp).

Here is an exceptionally moving and provocative acceptance speech that clearly illustrates how closely tied together are the speaker, audience, and occasion. This is the acceptance speech by actor Elizabeth Taylor on receiving the Jean Hersholt Humanitarian Award, given for her work on behalf of people with AIDS. The speech was transcribed from television.

I have been on this stage many times as a presenter. I have sat in the audience as a loser. And I've had the thrill and the honor of standing here as a winner. But, I never, ever thought I would come out here to receive this award.

It is the highest possible accolade I could receive from my peers. And for doing something I just have to do, that my passion must do.

I am filled with pride and humility. I accept this award in honor of all the men, women, and children with AIDS who are waging incredibly valiant battles for their lives—those to whom I have given my commitment, the real heroes of the pandemic of AIDS.

I am so proud of the work that people in Hollywood have done to help so many others, like dearest, gentle Audrey. And while she is, I know, in heaven, forever guarding her beloved children, I will remain here as rowdy an activist as I have to be and, God willing, for as long as I have to be. [Applause]

Tonight I am asking for your help. I call upon you to draw from the depths of your being, to prove that we are a human race, to prove that our love outweighs our need to hate, that our compassion is more compelling than our need to blame, that our sensitivity to those in need is stronger than our greed, that our ability to reason overcomes our fear, and that at the end of each of our lives we can look back and be proud that we have treated others with the kindness, dignity, and respect that every human being deserves.

Thank you and God bless.

Here is another speech of acceptance, this one written for the scene depicting John Nash's acceptance of the 1994 Nobel Prize in Economic Sciences in the 2001 movie *A Beautiful Mind.* (http://www.americanrhetoric.com /MovieSpeeches/moviespeechabeautifulmind.html, accessed February 6, 2004): The speech was delivered by actor Russell Crowe.

Thank you. I've always believed in numbers and the equations and logics that lead to reason. But after a lifetime of such pursuits, I ask, "What truly is logic? Who decides reason?" My quest has taken me through the physical, the metaphysical, the delusional—and back. And I have made the most important discovery of my career, the most important discovery of my life: It is only in the mysterious equations of love that any logic or reasons can be found. I'm only here tonight because of you [his wife, Alicia]. You are the reason I am. You are all my reasons.

THE SPEECH TO SECURE GOODWILL

The **goodwill speech** is part information and part persuasion. On the surface, the speech informs the audience about a product, company, profession, institution, or person. Beneath this surface, however, lies a more persuasive purpose: to heighten the image of a person, product, or company—to create a more positive attitude toward this person or thing. Many speeches of goodwill have a further persuasive purpose: to get the audience ultimately to change their behavior toward the person, product, or company.

A special type of goodwill speech is the speech of self-justification, in which the speaker seeks to justify his or her actions to the audience. Political figures do this frequently. Richard Nixon's "Checkers Speech," his Cambodia-bombing speeches, and, of course, his Watergate speeches are clear examples of speeches of self-justification. Edward Kennedy's Chappaquiddick speech, in which he attempted to justify what happened when Mary Jo Kopechne drowned, is another example. In securing goodwill, whether for another person or for yourself, consider the following suggestions:

- Demonstrate the contributions that deserve goodwill. Show how the audience may benefit from this company, product, or person. Or at least—in the speech of self-justification—show that the listeners have not been hurt; or, if they have been hurt, that the injury was unintentional.

- Stress uniqueness. In a world dominated by competition, the speech to secure goodwill must stress the uniqueness of the specific company, person, profession, situation, and so on. Distinguish your subject clearly from all others; otherwise, any goodwill you secure will be spread over the entire field.

- Establish credibility. Speeches to secure goodwill must also establish credibility, thereby securing goodwill for the individual or commodity. To do so, concentrate on those dimensions of credibility discussed in Chapter 11. Demonstrate that the person is competent, of good intention, and of high moral character.

- Don't be obvious. The effective goodwill speech looks, on the surface, very much like an objective informative speech. It will not appear to ask for goodwill, except on close analysis.

A particularly effective example of the speech to secure goodwill—perhaps the classic in the world of business—is the following speech by Lee Iacocca, former CEO of Chrysler Corporation, Iacocca was presented with a particularly difficult problem: Chrysler was accused of disconnecting odometers so that cars would appear to be new despite 40 miles of road testing. This was not a particularly horrible offense; most car buyers know that their cars are put through various tests. Yet it presented Iacocca with a credibility problem. He met this head on with a series of print and television advertisements in which he admitted the error of judgment and spelled out what he would do to correct it.

Testing cars is a good idea. Disconnecting odometers is a lousy idea. That's a mistake we won't make again at Chrysler. Period.

—*Lee Iacocca*

Let me set the record straight.

1. For years, spot checking and road testing new cars and trucks that come off the assembly line with the odometers disengaged was standard industry practice. In our case, the average test mileage was 40 miles.
2. Even though the practice wasn't illegal, some companies began connecting their odometers. We didn't. In retrospect, that was dumb. Since October 1986, however, the odometer of every car and truck we've built has been connected, including those in the test program.
3. A few cars—and I mean a few—were damaged in testing badly enough that they should not have been fixed and sold as new. That was a mistake in an otherwise valid quality assurance program. And now we have to make it right.

What we're doing to make things right.

1. In all instances where our records show a vehicle was damaged in the test program and repaired and sold, we will offer to replace that vehicle with a brand new 1987 Chrysler Corporation model of comparable value. No ifs, ands, or buts.
2. We are sending letters to everyone our records show bought a vehicle that was in the test program and offering a free inspection. If anything is wrong because of a product deficiency, we will make it right.
3. Along with free inspection, we are extending their present 5-year or 50,000-mile protection plan on engine and powertrain to 7 years or 70,000 miles.
4. And to put their minds completely at ease, we are extending the 7-year or 70,000-mile protection to all major systems: brakes, suspension, air conditioning, electrical, and steering.

The quality testing program is a good program. But there were mistakes and we were too slow in stopping them. Now they're stopped. Done. Finished. Over.

Personally, I'm proud of our products. Proud of the quality improvements we've made. So we're going to keep right on testing. Because without it we couldn't have given America 5-year, 50,000-mile protection five years ahead of everyone else. Or maintained our warranty leadership with 7-year, 70,000-mile protection. I'm proud, too, of our leadership in safety-related recalls.

But I'm not proud of this episode. Not at all.

As Harry Truman once said, "The buck stops here." It just stopped. Period.

Another type of goodwill speech is the speech of **apology**, a speech in which the speaker apologizes for some transgression and tries to restore his or her credibility. A particularly dramatic example of this type of speech, given by President William Jefferson Clinton, is presented here. The speech was given to the nation on August 17, 1998, after Clinton testified to a grand jury about a variety of issues. The issue that the nation and the media focused on, however, was the president's affair with a White House intern, Monica Lewinsky, including the extent to which he misled the country and the question of whether he obstructed justice. This speech was almost universally criticized for not expressing enough of an apology, for not asking for forgiveness, and for attacking the opposition rather than taking responsibility. The speech is presented in the Public Speaking Sample Assistant below. (If you wish to learn more about this speech and some of the critical reactions to it, visit *The American Communication Journal* online at www.uark.edu/~aca and go to Volume Two, Issue Two [February, 1999].)

SPEECH TO SECURE GOODWILL (APOLOGY)

Public Speaking   *Sample Assistant*

Good evening. This afternoon in this room, from this chair, I testified before the Office of Independent Counsel and a grand jury. I answered their questions truthfully, including questions about my private life, questions no American citizen would ever want to answer.

Still I must take complete responsibility for all my actions, both public and private. And that is why I am speaking to you tonight.

As you know, in a deposition in January, I was asked questions about my relationship with Monica Lewinsky. While my answers were legally accurate, I did not volunteer information. Indeed I did have a relationship with Miss Lewinsky that was not appropriate. In fact, it was wrong.

It constituted a critical lapse in judgment and a personal failure on my part for which I am solely and completely responsible.

But I told the grand jury today, and I say to you now, that at no time did I ask anyone to lie, to hide or destroy evidence, or to take any other unlawful action.

I know that my public comments and my silence about this matter gave a false impression. I misled people. Including even my wife. I deeply regret that.

I can only tell you I was motivated by many factors. First, by a desire to protect myself from the embarrassment of my own conduct. I was also very concerned about protecting my family. The fact that these questions were being asked in a politically inspired lawsuit which has since been dismissed was a consideration too.

In addition, I had real and serious concerns about an independent counsel investigation that began with private business dealings 20 years ago—dealings, I might add, about which an independent federal agency found no evidence of any wrongdoing by me or my wife over two years ago.

The independent counsel investigation moved on to my staff and friends. Then into my private life. And now the investigation itself is under investigation. This has gone on too long, cost too much, and hurt too many innocent people.

Now this matter is between me, the two people I love most—my wife and our daughter—and our God. I must put it right. And I am prepared to do whatever it takes to do so.

Nothing is more important to me personally, but it is private. And I intend to reclaim my family life for my family. It's nobody's business but ours. Even presidents have private lives. It is time to stop the pursuit of personal destruction and the prying into private lives and get on with our national life.

Our country has been distracted by this matter for too long, and I take my responsibility for my part in all of this. That is all I can do. Now it is time, in fact it is past time, to move on. We have important work to do, real opportunities to seize, real problems to solve, real security matters to face.

And so tonight I ask you to turn away from the spectacle of the past seven months, to repair the fabric of our national discourse and to return our attention to all the challenges and all the promise of the next American century.

Thank you for watching and good night.

THE SPEECH OF DEDICATION

The **dedication speech** is designed to give some specific meaning to, say, a new research lab, a store opening, or the start of the building of a bridge. This speech is usually given at a rather formal occasion. You'll need to do some research on exactly what it is that is being dedicated. For example, if it's a bridge, then you'll want to learn something about why the bridge was built, when it was constructed, and who designed it. In preparing a dedication speech, consider the following suggestions:

- State the reason you're giving the dedication; for example, identify the connection you have to the project.
- Explain exactly what is being dedicated; for example, the opening of the bridge linking Roosevelt Island to Manhattan.
- Tell the audience who is responsible for the project; for example, who designed the bridge, who constructed it, who paid for it.
- Explain why this project is significant—what advantages it will create. For example, describe the relevance the bridge has to your audience; that is, what changes will occur as a result of this bridge and how the bridge will benefit your listeners.

THE COMMENCEMENT SPEECH

The **commencement speech** recognizes and celebrates the end of some training period, such as the listeners' school or college years. The commencement speech is designed to congratulate and inspire the recent graduates and is often intended to mark the transition from school to the next stage in life. Usually the person asked to give a commencement speech is a well-known personality. The speakers at college graduations—depending on the prestige of the institution—are often important men and women in the world: presidents, senators, religious leaders, Nobel Prize winners, famous scientists, and people

---

A Case of ⚖ Ethics TELLING THE TRUTH

You'll be delivering the commencement speech to a graduating class at the high school you attended. In all honesty, you thought the education you received was horrible; the teachers were unconcerned, the science and computer labs were 30 years old, and all the money went to sports and athletic programs.

Ethical Choice Point You want to criticize the poor educational training the high school provided and urge students to approach college with a new perspective. Given that a commencement speech is usually a positive, congratulatory exercise, you wonder if you should present this negative picture. And yet you don't want to be dishonest. What should you do?

---

of similar accomplishment. Or a commencement speech may be given by a student who has achieved some exceptional goal; for example, the student with the highest grade point average or the winner of a prestigious award. In giving a commencement speech, consider the following:

- Organize the speech in a temporal pattern, beginning with the past, commenting on the present, and projecting into the future.
- Do your research. Learn something about the school, the student body, the goals and ambitions of the graduates, and integrate these into your speech.
- Be brief. Recognize that your audience has other things on their minds— the graduation party, for example—and may become restless if your speech is too long.
- Congratulate the graduates—but also congratulate the parents, friends, and instructors who also contributed to this day.
- Offer the graduates some kind of motivational message, some guidance, some suggestions for taking their education and using it in their lives.
- Offer your own good wishes to the graduates.

THE SPEECH OF INSPIRATION

A great many special occasion speeches aim to inspire the audience, as you've seen in the speeches already covered. Some speeches, however, are designed primarily to inspire; raising the spirits of an audience is their primary objective. Many religious speeches are of this type. Similarly, speeches that corporate leaders give to stockholders when introducing a new product or a new CEO, for example, would be designed to inspire investors. A commanding officer might give a speech of inspiration to the troops before going into battle. And of course there are the speeches of professional motivational speakers who seek to arouse the audience to feel better about themselves by organizing their lives, taking chances, giving up drugs, or doing any of a variety of things.

Before reading some suggestions for preparing and presenting an **inspirational speech,** consider the following speech by Nikki Giovanni. This is a particularly

SPEECH OF INSPIRATION

Public Speaking *Sample Assistant*

This inspirational speech was delivered by Nikki Giovanni on April 17, 2007.

We are Virginia Tech.

We are sad today, and we will be sad for quite a while. We are not moving on, we are embracing our mourning.

We are Virginia Tech.

We are strong enough to stand tall tearlessly, we are brave enough to bend to cry, and we are sad enough to know that we must laugh again.

We are Virginia Tech.

We do not understand this tragedy. We know we did nothing to deserve it, but neither does a child in Africa dying of AIDS, neither do the invisible children walking the night away to avoid being captured by the rogue army, neither does the baby elephant watching his community being devastated for ivory, neither does the Mexican child looking for fresh water, neither does the Appalachian infant killed in the middle of the night in his crib in the home his father built with his own hands being run over by a boulder because the land was destabilized. No one deserves a tragedy.

We are Virginia Tech.

The Hokie Nation embraces our own and reaches out with open heart and hands to those who offer their hearts and minds. We are strong, and brave, and innocent, and unafraid. We are better than we think and not quite what we want to be. We are alive to the imaginations and the possibilities. We will continue to invent the future through our blood and tears and through all our sadness.

We are the Hokies.

We will prevail.

We will prevail.

We will prevail.

We are Virginia Tech.

impressive inspirational speech given by Virginia Tech faculty member and poet Giovanni after 32 students and faculty were killed at the college on April 16, 2007.

- In a speech of inspiration, demonstrate your oneness with the audience. Try to show in some way that you and your listeners have significant similarities. Notice in this accompanying speech the repeated use of "we": It makes listeners feel connected to the speaker.

- Demonstrate your own intense involvement, the kind of intensity you want your audience to show. You cannot make others feel emotions if you don't feel them yourself. The photo on page 304 aptly captures Giovanni's intensity, as does the language of the speech.

- Stress emotional appeals. Inspiring an audience has to do more with emotions than with logic. Use appeals that are consistent with the nature of the event. In Nikki Giovanni's speech you see appeals to pity, loyalty to friends and institution, and empathy for others.

- Stress the positive. Especially, end your speech on a positive note. Inspirational speeches are always positive. Note the positiveness in Giovanni's speech: "We will prevail. We will prevail. We will prevail."

Consider the inspirational speeches you've heard—the photo is of poet and professor Nikki Giovanni delivering the speech on p. 303 after the shooting tragedy at Virginia Tech in 2007. What appeals move you most easily? What appeals have little effect on you?

THE EULOGY

The **eulogy** is a speech of tribute in which you seek to praise someone who has died. In the eulogy you attempt to put the person's life and contributions in perspective and show them in a positive light. This type of speech is often given at a funeral or at the anniversary of the person's birth or death. This is not the time for a balanced appraisal of the individual's life. Rather, it's a time for praise. In developing the eulogy, consider the following:

- Relate the person whose life you're celebrating to yourself, to those in the audience—and, if appropriate, to the larger audience—for example, the scientific community, the world of book lovers, or those who have devoted their lives to peace.

- Be specific; show that you really knew the person or know a great deal about the person. The best way to do that is to give specific examples from the person's life. Then combine the specifics with the more general so that the audience can see these specifics as being a part of some larger whole—for example, after you mention the several books that an author wrote, frame the author's contribution in a more general way within the mystery genre or contemporary poetry genre.

- Make the audience see that this person is deserving of the praise you are bestowing on him or her by explaining what this person accomplished and how this person influenced—for example—the world of patient care, the design of safer cars, and so on.

- Show the audience what they can learn from this individual.

An especially moving eulogy appears in the accompanying Public Speaking Sample Assistant box.

Public Speaking *Sample Assistant*

EULOGY

This eulogy was written and delivered by Bernard J. Brommel, a professor of communication and a family therapist, at the funeral of his sister.

A complete text of this eulogy is available at www.myspeechlab.com.

Today we gather to honor the memory of Florence who is at rest from her labors and we rejoice in knowing her love and good deeds remain with us, the living. It's an honor to speak on behalf of her family, especially seven wonderful sons, her husband Bill, my siblings, and our Aunt/ Stepmother, Florence, who was her namesake.

Florence set an example for courage, drive, responsibility, patience, honesty, tolerance, and countless other virtues. Most of all, she set for us an example of how to love, both as a giver and a receiver of it. It took so little to please her and evoke that quiet smile of appreciation. Gentle and kind, never loud or outspoken, she supported each of us by her nurturing nature and that rare ability, seldom found in many humans, to listen without judging. It's easy to understand why it was her heart that kept her alive in the last weeks. Everything in her system failed, but not her heart! Her physical heart was symbolic of her loving heart that reached each of us and was the last to go.

As the oldest of nine, she grew up with far more responsibility than most children. She grew up at the side of her mother as a constant helper. I remember her stirring cakes at five or six; there were no mixes then! She churned butter by hand, washed thousands of dishes, milk pails, diapers, and scrubbed those splintered floors. Mama was frequently ill or having difficult pregnancies. Florence took over! No wonder Florence could later in life manage a bank.

Three years ago this week we buried Dad. Two themes characterized his life: one, that it was a hard life but it got easier, and a second one, work—work—work. Florence's life experiences were similar. In our time Florence represented what has happened to women in transition—a transition for women from a domestic life to combining a professional life with raising a large family. She married at 18. She never planned a career; it just evolved out of necessity! Like her mother, or favorite aunt, Dolly, she might have preferred staying home with her sons. There were no maternity leaves; she saved her two-week vacations to coincide with delivery dates, and then back to work to keep the groceries on the table.

For us, the living, that have loved Florence, it's so hard to accept her death from cancer. Sixty-one years isn't long enough for this gentle soul, but God has called her and we have to accept His decision.

To each of her sons, I express my admiration for the way you helped look after your mom, not only in illness but throughout the years. You stayed out of trouble and made life easier for her because you did. In the hospital, Louie, you rubbed her feet and talked to her about her fears. Greg and Mike, each of you stopped by at noon hour or after work. David—you probably knew your mother best and always brought a special smile to her parched lips. To Will, the farmer, who she said was the loudest of her quiet boys. You could tell that he loved his mom whenever their eyes met. To John and Bob, identical twins who only their mother knew from day one the differences between the two of you. You knew how special you were to her. Finally to my siblings—the time has come for us to say farewell to Florence. Weren't we blessed with a great sister who left us with so much joy to remember? Thanks, Bill, for your love for our sister. Florence will have the last words. I asked her what she wanted me to say on this occasion and she, through tears, said, "Tell each of those at my funeral, 'I love you and I'll miss you, but I'm OK!'"

THE FAREWELL SPEECH

In the **farewell speech** you say goodbye to an organization or to colleagues and signal that you're moving on. In this speech you'll want to express your positive feelings to those you're leaving. Generally, the farewell speech is given after you've achieved some level of distinction within a company or other group or organization that you're now leaving. In developing a farewell speech, consider the following:

- Thank those who made life interesting, helped you in your position, taught you essential principles, and so on.
- Set your achievements in a positive light, but do it modestly.
- Express your enjoyment of the experience. This is a time for positive reflection, not for critical evaluation, so put aside the negative memories, at least for this speech.
- If appropriate, state your reason for leaving and your plans for the future.
- Express good wishes to those who remain.
- Offer some words of wisdom that you learned and that you now want to pass on to those remaining.

Here is an example of a farewell speech, delivered by Cal Ripken Jr. on his retirement from baseball (http://www.americanrhetoric.com/speeches/calripkenjr.htm, accessed February 6, 2004):

> As a kid, I had this dream.
> And I had the parents that helped me shape that dream.
> Then, I became part of an organization, the Baltimore Orioles—the Baltimore Orioles, to help me grow that dream. Imagine playing for my hometown team for my whole career.
> And I have a wife and children to help me share and save the fruits of that dream.
> And I've had teammates who filled my career with unbelievable moments.
> And you fans, who have loved the game, and have shared your love with me.
> Tonight, we close a chapter of this dream—my playing career.
> But I have other dreams.
> You know, I might have some white hair on top of this head—well, maybe on the sides of this head. But I'm really not that old.
> My dreams for the future include pursuing my passion for baseball. Hopefully, I will be able to share what I have learned. And, I would be happy if that sharing would lead to something as simple as a smile on the face of others.
> One question I've been repeatedly asked these past few weeks is, "How do I want to be remembered?" My answer has been simple: to be remembered at all is pretty special.
> I might also add that if, if I am remembered, I hope it's because, by living my dream, I was able to make a difference.
> Thank you.

THE TOAST

The **toast** is a brief speech designed to celebrate a person or an occasion. You might, for example, toast the next CEO of your company, a friend who just got admitted to a prestigious graduate program, or a colleague on the occasion of a promotion. Often toasts are given at weddings or at the start of a new venture. The toast is designed to say hello or good luck in a relatively formal sense. In developing your toast consider the following:

- Be brief; realize that people want to get on with the festivities and don't want to listen to an overly long speech.

- Focus attention on the person or persons you're toasting, not on yourself.

- Avoid inside jokes that only you and the person you're toasting understand; remember that the toast is not only for the benefit of the person you're toasting but for the audience as well.

- When you raise your glass in the toast—an almost obligatory part of toasting—make the audience realize that they should drink and that your speech is at an end.

PRESENTING THE GROUP'S THINKING

Often you'll find yourself as a member of a small group, brainstorming ideas or solving a problem. At times the thinking of the small group needs to be presented to a larger audience; for example, when a small group of workers investigate a new wage and benefits proposal and then report back to the entire union membership, or when representatives of university academic departments report their proposals to the administration or to the entire university.

Let's begin by looking at some general guidelines for presenting groups' ideas to wider audiences; then we'll examine some more specific suggestions for various group formats.

GENERAL SPEAKING GUIDELINES

If a group develops a solution to a problem, it will generally seek some way to put this solution into operation. Often it's necessary to convince others that the solution is workable and cost effective. Try these suggestions:

- Present the solution in a nonthreatening manner. New solutions often frighten people. For example, if your solution might lead people to feel insecure about their jobs, then alleviate these worries before you try to explain the solution in any detail. As a general rule it's best to proceed slowly, especially if you anticipate objections or hostility from your listeners.

- Present new solutions tentatively. In the excitement of inspiration, you may not have thought through all of the practical implications of your proposed solution. If you present your ideas tentatively and they're shown to be impractical or unworkable, you will be less hurt psychologically and—most important—more willing to present new solutions again.

- In many instances it will prove helpful to link changes to well-known problems in the organization. For example, if you're going to ask employees to complete extensive surveys, then show them how this extra work will correct a long-standing problem and benefit them and the organization.

- Say why you think the solution will work. Give the advantages of your plan over the existing situation and explain why you think your solution should be implemented. The patterns for organizing a public speech (see Chapter 7) will help you make an effective presentation.

Consider the importance of presenting the group's thinking. What principles should speakers be sure to follow to achieve clarity and accuracy?

■ State the negatives (there usually are some with most ideas) as you understand them—and, of course, explain why you think the positives outweigh any potential drawbacks.

■ Show how your solution is directly related to the needs and interests of those whom the solution will affect. Show others how your solution will benefit them.

SPEAKING IN THE PANEL GROUP

In a **panel** the group members are cast in the role of "experts" and participate informally and without any set pattern of who speaks when. The procedure is similar to that of any small group interaction, except that the panel is discussing the issue before an audience; the audience is present but does not participate in the actual discussion. Normally a moderator guides the discussion.

A variation is the two-panel format, with an expert panel and a lay panel. The expert panel consists of the members who participated in the group and who ideally are more knowledgeable than the lay panel members. The topic is then discussed as the lay and the expert panel members interact. This is the format followed by many talk shows, such as those featuring Jerry Springer and Oprah Winfrey. On these shows the moderator is the host (Springer, Winfrey). The "expert panel" is the group of guests (the dysfunctional family, the gossip columnists, the political activists). And the lay panel consists of the members of the studio audience who ask questions or offer comments.

Here are a few suggestions for making the panel format more effective:

■ As moderator, always treat panel members and their questions with respect. You'll notice this on the popular talk shows: No matter how stupid the question may be, the moderator treats it as serious, though often restructuring it just a bit so that it makes more sense. Treat questions objectively; don't try to bias either a question or its answer through your verbal or nonverbal responses.

■ As a panel member, speak in short turns. The group's interaction should resemble a conversation rather than individual public speeches. Resist the temptation to tell long stories or go into too much detail.

■ Try to spread the conversation around the group. Generally, try to give each member the same opportunity to speak.

SPEAKING IN THE SYMPOSIUM AND TEAM PRESENTATIONS

In a **symposium** each member delivers a prepared presentation, a public speech. All speeches are addressed to different aspects of a single topic. The symposium leader introduces the speakers, provides transitions from one speaker to another, and may provide periodic summaries.

In a **team presentation**, a format popular in business settings, two or three members of a group will report the group's findings to a larger group. In some situations team presentations may amount to "position papers" and may

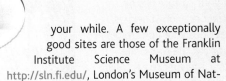

MUSEUM COLLECTIONS AND EXHIBITS

Not too long ago, museums weren't even included in research discussions; good museums were so far away from most people that the possibility of visiting any given museum was remote. Now, however, you have the world of museums literally at your fingertips. Every museum collects all sorts of information pertaining to its major focus; for example, to natural history, science, or art (see, for example, the website for one of the world's greatest art museums, the Metropolitan Museum of Art, at www.metmuseum.org/home.asp). Visiting a few museum websites is well worth your while. A few exceptionally good sites are those of the Franklin Institute Science Museum at http://sln.fi.edu/, London's Museum of Natural History at www.nhm.ac.uk, and the Smithsonian Institution at www.si.edu/. An especially good site if you don't know what museum you'd like to visit is www.comlab.ox.ac.uk/archive/other/museums/usa.html, where you will find links to museums, archives, and galleries throughout the United States.

So take a break and visit the Smithsonian or any of the numerous art, science, or history online museums. Have fun.

---

include both majority and minority reports, as at the Supreme Court. Or if, say, a group considered a range of new scheduling systems, members of a team might each present one of the proposed systems and the advantages and disadvantages of each.

Here are a few suggestions for making symposia and team presentations more effective:

- Coordinate your presentations very carefully. Team presentations and symposia are extremely difficult to synchronize. Make sure that everyone knows exactly what he or she is responsible for. Make sure there's no (or very little) overlap among the presentations.

- Much as you would rehearse a public speech, try to rehearse these presentations and their coordination. This is rarely possible to do in actual practice, but it is very helpful to "rehearse" mentally or imaginatively, going through the proceedings in your mind in advance.

- Adhere carefully to time limits. If you speak for more time than allotted, that time will be deducted from the minutes available to a later speaker. As you can appreciate, violating time limits will severely damage the entire group's presentation.

- Provide clear transitions between the presentations. Internal summaries work especially well as connectives between one speech and the next: "Now that Judy has explained the general proposal, Peter and Margarita will explain some of the advantages and disadvantages of the proposal. First, we'll hear from Peter with the advantages and then from Margarita with the disadvantages."

A variation of the symposium is the **symposium–forum**, which consists of a symposium (with prepared speeches, as just explained) and a **forum**, with questions from the audience and responses by the speakers. The leader introduces the speakers and moderates the question-and-answer session. The suggestions for making these presentations more effective are essentially the same as for the panel and the symposium.

Consider the influence that your culture has on special occasion speeches. What does your culture teach you about the toast, the eulogy, the speech of dedication, or the speech of acceptance or presentations?

ORAL AND WRITTEN REPORTS

In many cases the small group leader will make a presentation of the group's findings, recommendations, or decisions to some larger group—for example, to the class as a whole, the entire student body, the board of directors, the union membership, or the heads of departments.

Depending on the specific situation, these reports may be similar to speeches of information or speeches of persuasion. For example, if you are the group leader, your task may be simply to inform the wider group of the findings or recommendations of your committee—the proposed ways to increase morale, the new pension scheme, the new developments in competing organizations. In other cases your report will be largely persuasive; for example, you may need to convince the larger group to provide increased funding so that your group's recommendations can be implemented.

In some situations both a brief oral report and a more extensive written report are required. A good example is the press conference. At a press conference you deliver an oral report to members of the press, who also receive a written report. The press will then question you for further details. In some cases you may want to use a computer-assisted presentation and prepare handouts of your slides, your speaker's notes, or selected slides with space for your listeners to write notes (see Chapter 6). Here are a few suggestions for more effective oral and written reports.

- Write the written report as you would a term paper, and from that develop a summary of the report in the form of a public speech, following the 10 steps explained in Chapter 2 and elaborated throughout this text.

- Don't read the written report. Even though the oral and the written report may cover essentially the same content, they're totally different in development and presentation. The written report is meant to be read; the oral report is meant to be listened to.

- In some instances it's helpful to distribute the written report and to use your oral presentation to highlight the most essential aspects of the report. Listeners may then refer to the report as you speak—a situation not recommended for most public speeches.

In some instances you might distribute the written report only after you have completed your oral report. Generally, however, people don't like this procedure; they prefer the option of thumbing through the report as they listen or reserving reading until after they've heard the oral report.

Now that you've finished the first part of your public speaking training—the remaining training will likely come from your experience with your own speeches and from listening to the speeches of others—you may wish to look at your public speaking satisfaction and compare it to what you remember at the beginning of this course.

TEST YOURSELF

How Satisfying Is Your Public Speaking Experience?

Respond to each of the following statements by recording the number best representing your feelings during your last speech, using this scale: Strongly agree = 1, moderately agree = 2, slightly agree = 3, neutral = 4, slightly disagree = 5, moderately disagree = 6, and strongly disagree = 7.

_____ **1.** The audience let me know that I was speaking effectively.

_____ **2.** My speech accomplished nothing.

_____ **3.** I would like to give another speech like this one.

_____ **4.** The audience genuinely wanted to get to know me.

_____ **5.** I was very dissatisfied with my speech.

_____ **6.** I was very satisfied with my speech.

_____ **7.** The audience seemed very interested in what I had to say.

_____ **8.** I did not enjoy the public speaking experience.

_____ **9.** The audience did not seem supportive of what I was saying.

_____ **10.** The speech flowed smoothly.

HOW DID YOU DO? To compute your score, follow these steps:

1. Add the scores for items 1, 3, 4, 6, 7, and 10.
2. Reverse the scores for items 2, 5, 8, and 9 so that 7 becomes 1, 6 becomes 2, 5 becomes 3, 4 remains 4, 3 becomes 5, 2 becomes 6, and 1 becomes 7.
3. Add the reversed scores for items 2, 5, 8, and 9.
4. Add the totals from steps 1 and 3 to yield your communication satisfaction score.

You may interpret your score along the following scale:

10	20	30	40	50	60	70
Extremely satisfying	Quite satisfying	Fairly satisfying	Average	Fairly unsatisfying	Quite unsatisfying	Extremely unsatisfying

How accurately do you think this scale captures the satisfaction you derive from public speaking?

WHAT WILL YOU DO? As you become a more successful and effective public speaker, your satisfaction is likely to increase. What specific actions can you take to increase your satisfaction?

Adapted with permission from Hecht, M. (1978). The conceptualization and measurement of interpersonal communication satisfaction. *Human Communication Research*, 4, 253–264. This test was adapted for public speaking from the conversational satisfaction test and is used with the permission and suggestions of the author.

THE SPECIAL OCCASION SPEECH IN CULTURAL PERSPECTIVE

Like all forms of communication, the special occasion speech must be developed with a clear understanding of the influence of culture. For example, the discussion of the speech of introduction suggested that you not oversell the speaker; excessive exaggeration is generally evaluated negatively in much of the United States. On the other hand, exaggerated praise often is expected in some Latin cultures.

Similarly, the discussion of the speech of goodwill suggested that you present yourself as being worthy of the goodwill rather than as a supplicant begging for it. In some cultures, however, this attitude might be seen as arrogant and disrespectful to the audience. In some Asian cultures, for example, pleading for goodwill would be seen as suitably modest and respectful of the audience.

In introducing or in paying tribute to someone, consider the extent to which you wish to focus on the person's contribution to the group or to individual achievement. An audience with a predominantly collectivist orientation (see Chapter 3) will expect to hear group-centered achievements, whereas an audience of predominantly individualist orientation will expect to hear more individually focused achievements.

Culture also will influence the way in which an acceptance speech should be framed. Not surprisingly, collectivist cultures would suggest that you give a lot of credit to the group, whereas individualist cultures would suggest that taking self-credit is appropriate when it's due. Thus, if you were accepting an award for a performance in a movie, an extreme collectivist orientation would lead you to give great praise to others and to claim that without others you never could have accomplished what you did. An extreme individualist orientation would lead you to accept the award and the praise for yourself; after all, you did it! In the media business, as you see from the numerous televised award shows, everyone gives thanks to almost everyone connected with the project. That's the custom; the collectivist form of expression has become the norm, at least in the context of show business.

Essentials of Speaking on Special Occasions

This chapter discussed special occasion speeches, highlighting a variety of specific types, and placed special occasion speeches in a cultural context.

1. The **speech of introduction** introduces another speaker or series of speakers. In this speech: Establish a connection among speaker, topic, and audience; establish the speaker's credibility; be consistent in style and manner with the major speech; be brief; avoid covering what the speaker intends to discuss; and avoid overselling the speaker.

2. The **speech of presentation** explains why the presentation is being made, and the speech of acceptance expresses thanks for the award. In the speech of presentation, state the reason for the presentation and state the importance of the award. In the **speech of acceptance**, thank those who gave the award, thank those who helped, and state the meaning of the award to you.

3. The **speech to secure goodwill** attempts to secure or, more often, to regain the speaker's place in the listeners' good graces. In this speech: Stress benefits the audience may derive; stress uniqueness; establish your credibility and the credibility of the subject; avoid being obvious in securing goodwill; and avoid pleading for goodwill.

4. The **speech of dedication** gives specific meaning to some event or object. In this speech: Explain why you're giving the speech; explain what is being dedicated; state who is responsible for the event or object; and say why this is significant, especially to your specific listeners.

5. The **commencement speech** celebrates the end of some training period. In this speech: Consider the values of a temporal organizational pattern; learn something about the training organization and demonstrate this knowledge in your speech; be brief; congratulate the larger audience, not only those who went through the training; offer some motivational message; and offer your own good wishes.

6. The **inspirational speech** aims to inspire the audience, to lead listeners to think in a positive direction. In this speech you demonstrate your connection with the audience and your intense involvement using emotional appeals and stressing the positive.

7. The **eulogy** seeks to praise someone who has died. In this speech: Show the connection between yourself and the person you're eulogizing; be specific; combine specifics with the general; stress that the person is deserving of your praise; and show your listeners what they can learn from this person.

8. The **farewell speech** signals a transition between what was and what will be. In this speech: Thank those who helped you; portray the positives of the past; explain your reasons for making the transition; and offer some words of wisdom, some motivational message.

9. The **toast** celebrates a person or an occasion. In the toast: Be brief; focus attention on the person or event you're toasting; avoid references that listeners may not understand; and make it clear that this is the end of your speech when you raise your glass.

10. Among the formats that typically involve **public presentations of group conclusions** are the panel, the symposium (or symposium–forum) and team presentations, and oral and written reports

11. The special occasion speech needs to be developed with an awareness of the **cultural norms and rules** specific to the occasion and to the audience members. Especially relevant here is the distinction between individualist and collectivist cultures.

Essential Terms: Speaking on Special Occasions

acceptance speech **(p. 296)**
apology **(p. 300)**
commencement speech **(p. 301)**
dedication speech **(p. 301)**
eulogy **(p. 304)**
farewell speech **(p. 306)**
goodwill speech **(p. 298)**
inspirational speech **(p. 302)**

forum **(p. 309)**
panel **(p. 308)**
presentation speech **(p. 296)**
speech of introduction **(p. 295)**
symposium **(p. 308)**
symposium–forum **(p. 309)**
team presentation **(p. 308)**
toast **(p. 306)**

Public Speaking Exercises

12.1 Developing the Speech of Introduction

Prepare a speech of introduction approximately two minutes in length. For this experience you may assume that the speaker you introduce will speak on any topic you wish. Do, however, assume a topic appropriate to the speaker and to your audience—your class. You may wish to select your introduction from one of the following suggestions:

1. Introduce a historical figure to the class.
2. Introduce a contemporary religious, political, or social leader.
3. Prepare a speech of introduction that someone might give to introduce you to your class.
4. Introduce a famous media (film, television, radio, recording, writing) personality—alive or dead.
5. Introduce a series of speeches debating the pros and cons of a cultural emphasis in college courses.

12.2 Developing the Speech of Presentation/Acceptance

Form pairs. One person should serve as the presenter and one as the recipient of a particular award or honor. Each pair can select a situation from the list presented below or make one up themselves. The presenter should prepare and present a two-minute speech in which she or he presents one of the awards to the other person. The recipient should prepare and present a two-minute speech of acceptance.

1. Academy Award for best performance.
2. Gold watch for service to the company.
3. Ms. or Mr. America.
4. Five million dollars for the college library.
5. Award for contributions to intercultural under-standing.
6. Book of the Year award.
7. Mother (Father) of the Year award.
8. Honorary Ph.D. in communication for outstanding contributions to the art.
9. Award for outstanding achievement in architecture.
10. Award for raising a prize hog.

12.3 Developing the Speech to Secure Goodwill

Prepare a speech approximately three to five minutes in length in which you attempt to secure the goodwill of your audience toward one of the following:

1. Your college (visualize your audience as high school seniors).
2. A particular profession or way of life (teaching, religious life, nursing, law, medicine, bricklaying, truck driving, etc.).
3. This course (visualize your audience as college students who have not yet taken this course).
4. The policies of a particular foreign country now in the news.
5. A specific multinational corporation.

12.4 What Do You Say?

◆ **Presenting an Award.** Betty has been asked to present the award for Recording Artist of the Year to a certain performer (select your own favorite). The speech is to last no longer than one minute (approximately 150 words). What would you advise Betty to say?

◆ **Securing Goodwill.** Ignacio has been asked by his catering firm—which was cited by the Board of Health for several health violations a year ago—to present to the local Board of Education the firm's case for the catering contract for the entire elementary school district. The board members agree to hear Ignacio but are generally reluctant to hire his firm because of its history of unsafe practices. What advice would you give Ignacio for his speech, in which he'll try to secure goodwill (and another chance)?

◆ **Speech of Apology.** If you had been CEO of Ford Motors when the company was confronted with the evidence of defective tires on certain SUVs, what kind of announcement would you have issued?

LogOn! MySpeechLab

Visit MySpeechLab (www.myspeechlab.com) for an extended example of a eulogy, President William Clinton's farewell address; Martin Scorsese's acceptance speech for the John Huston Award for Artists' Rights; and an exercise, "Developing the Speech of Tribute." A number of special occasion speeches are available on video at MSL, including an award acceptance speech, a eulogy for Peanuts creator Charles Schultz, a nomination speech, an oral report, and a wedding toast. Also available are critiques of the acceptance speech and the wedding toast. In addition, practice tests are offered for a variety of special occasion speeches.

For those who wish more information on small group communication to complement the discussion of "Presenting the Group's Thinking" in this chapter, two complete chapters from my *Essentials of Human Communication*, 6th edition (2008) are available on MSL: "Small Group Communication" and "Members and Leaders in Small Group Communication."

Glossary

abstraction A general concept derived from a class of objects; a partial representation of some whole; the quality of abstractness, or non-concreteness.

abstraction process The process by which a general concept is derived from specifics; the process by which some (never all) characteristics of an object, person, or event are perceived by the senses or included in some term, phrase, or sentence.

accent The stress or emphasis placed on a syllable when it is pronounced.

acceptance speech A speech in which the speaker accepts an award or honor of some kind and attempts to place the award in some kind of context.

active listening A process of putting together into some meaningful whole the listener's understanding of the speaker's total message—the verbal and the nonverbal, the content and the feelings.

agenda-setting A fallacy or pseudo-argument in which a speaker contends that only certain issues are important and others are not—in an attempt, for example, to focus attention on the strong points of a plan and divert attention from the weak points.

alliteration A figure of speech in which the initial sound in two or more words is repeated.

allness The assumption that all can be known or is known about a given person, issue, object, or event.

analogy Comparison of two things; analogies may be literal (in which items from the same class are compared) or figurative (in which items from different classes are compared).

anecdotal evidence A fallacious persuasive tactic in which the speaker offers specific examples or illustrations as "proof."

antithesis A figure of speech in which contrary ideas are presented in parallel form, as in Charles Dickens's opening lines in *A Tale of Two Cities*: "It was the best of times, it was the worst of times."

apology A type of excuse in which you acknowledge responsibility for the behavior, generally ask forgiveness, and claim that the behavior will not happen again.

appeal to tradition A fallacy often used as an argument against change, as when a speaker claims that a proposed plan should not be adopted because it was never done before.

articulation The movements of the speech organs as they modify and interrupt the air stream from the lungs, forming sounds.

assimilation A process of message distortion in which messages are reworked to conform to our own attitudes, prejudices, needs, and values.

attention The process of responding to a stimulus or stimuli; usually some consciousness of responding is implied.

attitude A predisposition to respond for or against an object, person, or position.

audience A group of people listening to the same message or speech.

audience analysis The process of discovering useful information about the listeners so that a speech may be better tailored to this specific group of people.

bandwagon A persuasive technique in which the speaker tries to gain compliance by saying that "everyone is doing it" and urges you to jump on the bandwagon.

belief Confidence in the existence or truth of something; conviction.

bias Preconceived ideas that predispose you to interpret meaning on the basis of these ideas rather than on the basis of the evidence and argument.

brainstorming A technique for generating ideas either alone or, more usually, in a small group.

card-stacking A fallacy in reasoning in which the speaker selects only the evidence and arguments that support the case, and may even falsify evidence and distort the facts to better fit the case; despite these misrepresentations, the speaker presents the supporting materials as "fair" and "impartial."

causes and effects, reasoning from A form of reasoning in which you reason that certain effects are due to specific causes or that specific causes produce certain effects.

channel The vehicle or medium through which signals are sent.

character One of the qualities of **credibility**; an individual's honesty and basic nature; moral qualities.

character attacks A fallacy—often referred to as *ad hominem*—in which a speaker accuses another person (usually an opponent) of some serious wrongdoing or of some serious character flaw that has nothing to do with the issues under discussion in an attempt to discredit the person or to divert attention from the issues.

charisma One of the qualities of **credibility**; an individual's dynamism or forcefulness.

cliché An overused expression that has lost its novelty and part of its meaning and that calls attention to itself because of its overuse; "tall, dark, and handsome" as a description of a man is a cliché.

collectivist culture A culture in which the group's goals rather than the individual's are given primary importance and where, for example, benevolence, tradition, and conformity are given special emphasis. Opposed to **individualistic culture**.

commencement speech A speech given to celebrate the end of some training period, often at school graduation ceremonies.

communication apprehension Fear or anxiety over communicating; may be trait apprehension (a fear of communication generally, regardless of the specific situation) or state apprehension (a fear that is specific to a given communication situation).

competence One of the qualities that undergird personal **credibility**; encompasses a person's ability and knowledge.

connotation The feeling or emotional aspect of meaning, generally viewed as consisting of the evaluative (for example, good/bad), potency (strong/weak), and activity (fast/slow) dimensions; the associations of a term. See also **denotation**.

context The physical, psychological, social, and temporal environment in which communication takes place.

credibility The degree to which a receiver perceives the speaker to be believable; **competence**, **character**, and **charisma** (dynamism) are credibility's major dimensions.

criticism The reasoned judgment of some work; although often equated with faultfinding, criticism can involve both positive and negative evaluations.

culture The relatively specialized lifestyle of a group of people—consisting of their values, beliefs, artifacts, ways of behaving, and ways of communicating—that is passed on from one generation to the next.

database An organized collection of information.

dedication speech A special occasion speech in which you commemorate the opening or start of a project.

definition, speech of An informative speech devoted to explaining the meaning of a concept.

delivery outline A brief outline of a speech that the speaker uses during the actual speech presentation.

demonstration, speech of A speech in which the speaker shows the audience how to do something or how something operates.

denotation Referential meaning; the objective or descriptive meaning of a word. See also **connotation**.

description, speech of A speech in which you explain an object, person, event, or process.

directness A quality of speech in which the speaker's intentions are stated clearly and directly.

door-in-the-face technique A persuasive strategy in which the speaker first makes a large request that will be refused and then follows with the intended and much smaller request.

emotional appeals Persuasive strategies designed to influence the emotions of the audience.

empathy The feeling of another person's feeling; feeling or perceiving something as another person does.

ethics The branch of philosophy that deals with the rightness or wrongness of actions; the study of moral values.

ethnocentrism The tendency to see others and their behaviors through our own cultural filters, often as distortions of our own behaviors; the tendency to evaluate the values and beliefs of our own culture more positively than those of another culture.

eulogy A speech of tribute in which the speaker praises someone who died.

euphemism A polite word or phrase used to substitute for some taboo or otherwise offensive term; often used as a persuasive strategy to make the negative appear positive.

extemporaneous speech A speech that is thoroughly prepared and organized in detail and in which certain aspects of style are predetermined.

fact, questions of Questions that concern what is or is not true, what does or does not exist, what did or did not happen; questions that, potentially at least, have answers.

fact–inference confusion A misevaluation in which a person makes an inference, regards it as a fact, and acts upon it as if it were a fact.

farewell speech A speech designed to say goodbye to a position or to colleagues and to signal that you're moving on.

figures of speech Stylistic devices and ways of expressing ideas that are used to achieve special effects.

flexibility The ability to adjust communication strategies on the basis of the unique situation.

foot-in-the-door technique A persuasive strategy in which the speaker first asks for something small (to get a foot in the door) and then, once a pattern of agreement has been achieved, follows with the real and larger request.

forum A question-and-answer period that often follows a public speech or small group presentation.

goodwill speech A special occasion speech in which the speaker seeks to make the image of a person, product, or company more positive.

heterosexist language Language that assumes all people are heterosexual and thereby denigrates lesbians and gay men.

hierarchy of needs A view of human needs that argues that certain basic needs (e.g., for food and shelter) have to be satisfied before higher-order needs (e.g., for self-esteem or love) can be effective in motivating listeners.

high-context culture A culture in which much of the information in communication is in the context or in the person rather than explicitly coded in the verbal messages. **Collectivist cultures** are generally high-context. Opposed to **low-context culture**.

hyperbole A figure of speech in which something is exaggerated for effect but is not intended to be taken literally.

immediacy A quality of interpersonal effectiveness; a sense of contact and togetherness; a feeling of interest in and liking for the other person.

impromptu speech A speech given without any explicit prior preparation.

indiscrimination A misevaluation that results when someone categorizes people, events, or objects into a particular class and responds to them only as members of the class; a person's failure to recognize that each individual is unique.

individualist culture A culture in which the individual's rather than the group's goals and preferences are given primary importance. Opposed to **collectivist culture**.

informative speech A speech designed to communicate information to an audience rather than to persuade.

introduction, speech of A speech designed to introduce the speaker himself or herself to an audience or a speech designed to introduce another speaker or group of speakers.

irony A figure of speech employed for special emphasis, in which a speaker uses words whose literal meaning is the opposite of the speaker's actual message or intent.

jargon The technical language of any specialized group, often a professional class, which is unintelligible to individuals not belonging to the group; "shop talk."

listening An active process of receiving messages sent orally; this process consists of five stages: receiving, understanding, remembering, evaluating, and responding.

logical appeals Persuasive appeals that focus on facts and evidence rather than on emotions or credibility.

low-context culture A culture in which most of the information in communication is explicitly stated in the verbal messages. **Individualist cultures** are usually low-context cultures. Opposed to **high-context culture**.

manuscript speech A speech designed to be read verbatim from a script.

message Any signal or combination of signals that serves as a **stimulus** for a receiver.

metaphor A figure of speech in which there is an implied comparison between two unlike things; for example, "That CEO is a jackal."

motivated sequence An organizational pattern for arranging the information in a discourse to motivate an audience to respond positively to the speaker's purpose.

name-calling An often-used fallacy in which the speaker gives an idea a derogatory name to try to get you to condemn the idea without analyzing the argument and evidence.

noise Anything that interferes with a person's receiving a message as the source intended the message to be received. Noise is present in a communication system to the extent that the message received is not the message sent.

nonverbal communication Messages without words; communication by means of space, gestures, facial expressions, touching, vocal variation, and silence, for example.

oral style The style of spoken discourse that, when compared with written style, consists of shorter, simpler, and more familiar words; more qualification, self-reference terms, allness terms, verbs and adverbs; and more concrete terms and terms indicative of consciousness of projection—for example, "as I see it."

outline A blueprint or pattern for a speech.

panel A small group presentation format in which participants speak informally and without any set pattern.

pauses Silent periods in the normally fluent stream of speech. Pauses are of two major types: filled pauses (interruptions in speech that are filled with such vocalizations as "er" or "um") and unfilled pauses (silences of unusually long duration).

personal interest A persuasive fallacy that attempts to divert attention from the issues and arguments in one of two ways: (1) The speaker argues that the opponent should be disqualified because he or she isn't directly affected by the proposal or doesn't have firsthand knowledge, or (2) the speaker tries to disqualify someone because he or she will benefit in some way from the proposal.

personification A figure of speech in which human characteristics are attributed to inanimate objects for special effect; for example, "After the painting, the room looked cheerful and energetic."

persuasion The process of influencing attitudes and behavior.

persuasive speech A speech designed to strengthen or change the attitudes or beliefs of the audience or to move them to take some kind of action.

pitch The highness or lowness of the vocal tone.

plain folks An often-used fallacy in which the speaker presents himself or herself as one of the people, just "plain folks" like everyone else, even when that image is false or is not relevant to the issue at hand.

polarization A form of fallacious reasoning in which only two extremes are considered; also referred to as "black-or-white" or "either/or" thinking or a two-valued orientation.

policy, questions of Questions that focus on what should be done (the policy that should be adopted).

pronunciation The production of syllables or words according to some accepted standard; as presented, for example, in a dictionary.

proxemics The study of the communicative function of space; the study of how people unconsciously structure their space—the distance between people in their interactions, the organization of space in homes and offices, and even the design of cities.

public speaking Communication in which the source is one person and the receiver is an audience of many persons.

racist language Language that denigrates or is derogatory toward members of a particular race.

rate The speed at which you speak, generally measured in words per minute.

reliability A quality of research or support that can be counted on as accurate and trustworthy.

rhetorical question A figure of speech in which a question is asked to make a statement rather than to secure an answer.

selective exposure, principle of A principle of persuasive that argues that listeners actively seek out information that supports their opinions, beliefs, and values while actively avoiding information that would contradict these opinions, beliefs, and values.

self-esteem The value you place on yourself; your self-evaluation; usually refers to the positive value a person places on himself or herself.

sexist language Language derogatory to one gender, usually women.

sign, reasoning from A form of reasoning in which the presence of certain signs (clues) are interpreted as leading to a particular conclusion.

simile A figure of speech in which a speaker compares two unlike things using the words *like* or *as*.

slang Language used by special groups that is not considered proper by the general society; language made up of the argot, cant, and jargon of various groups and known by the general public.

specific instances, reasoning from A form of reasoning in which several specific instances are examined and then a conclusion about the whole is formed.

static evaluation An orientation that fails to recognize that the world is characterized by constant change; an attitude that sees people and events as fixed rather than as constantly changing.

straw man An argument (like a person made of straw) that is set up only to be knocked down. In this fallacy a speaker creates a "straw man"—an easy-to-destroy simplification of the opposing position—and then proceeds to demolish it.

symposium A small group presentation format in which each member of the group delivers a relatively prepared talk on some aspect of the topic. Often combined with a **forum**.

symposium–forum A moderated group presentation with prepared speeches on various aspects of a topic, followed by a question-and-answer session with the audience.

systematic desensitization A theory and technique for dealing with a variety of fears (such as communication apprehension) in which you gradually desensitize yourself to behaviors you wish to eliminate.

testimonial A persuasive and often fallacious technique in which the speaker uses the authority or image of some positively evaluated person to gain your approval or of some negatively evaluated person to gain your rejection.

thesis The main assertion of a message—for example, the theme of a public speech.

thin entering wedge A persuasive fallacy in which a speaker argues against a position on the grounds that it is a thin entering wedge that will open the floodgates to all sorts of catastrophes, though there is no evidence to support such results.

toast A brief speech designed to celebrate a person or an occasion.

transfer A persuasive technique in which a speaker associates an idea with something you respect to gain your approval or with something you dislike to gain your rejection.

transitions Words, phrases, or sentences that connect the parts of a speech and that serve as guides to help listeners follow the speaker's train of thought.

tree diagrams A method for illustrating how a topic may be divided into its various parts.

value Relative worth of an object; a quality that makes something desirable or undesirable; ideals or customs about which we have emotional responses, whether positive or negative.

value, questions of Questions that focus on the goodness or badness, the morality or immorality of an act.

volume The relative loudness of the voice.

weasel words Words whose meanings are difficult (slippery like a weasel) to pin down to specifics.

References

Alessandra, T. (1986). How to listen effectively. *Speaking of success* [videotape series]. San Diego, CA: Levitz Sommer Productions.

Allan, K., & Burridge, K. (2007). *Forbidden words: Taboo and the censoring of language*. Cambridge, UK: Cambridge University Press.

Allen, R. L. (1997, October 6). People—the single point of difference—listening to them. *Nation's Restaurant News, 31*, 130.

Arliss, Laurie P. (1991). *Gender communication*. Englewood Cliffs, NJ: Prentice-Hall.

Axtell, R. E. (1990). *Do's and taboos of hosting international visitors*. New York: Wiley.

Axtell, R. E. (1993). *Do's and taboos around the world* (3rd ed.). New York: Wiley.

Ayres, J. (1986). Perceptions of speaking ability: An explanation for stage fright. *Communication Education, 35*, 275–287.

Ayres, J. (2005, April). Performance visualization and behavioral disruption: A clarification. *Communication Reports, 18*, 55–63.

Ayres, J., & Hopf, T. S. (1992). Visualization: Reducing speech anxiety and enhancing performance. *Communication Reports, 5*, 1–10.

Ayres, J., & Hopf, T. S. (1993). *Coping with speech anxiety*. Norwood, NJ: Ablex.

Ayres, J., Hopf, T., & Ayres, D. M. (1994, July). An examination of whether imaging ability enhances the effectiveness of an intervention designed to reduce speech anxiety. *Communication Education, 43*, 252–258.

Barker, L. L. (1990). *Communication* (5th ed.). Englewood Cliffs, NJ: Prentice-Hall.

Barker, L. L., Edwards, R., Gaines, C., Gladney, K., & Holley, F. (1980). An investigation of proportional time spent in various communication activities by college students. *Journal of Applied Communication Research, 8*, 101–109.

Bates, D. G., & Fratkin, E. M. (1999). *Cultural anthropology* (2nd ed.). Boston: Allyn & Bacon.

Beatty, M. J. (1988). Situational and predispositional correlates of public speaking anxiety. *Communication Education, 37*, 28–39.

Beck, A. T. (1988). *Love is never enough*. New York: Harper & Row.

Bellafiore, D. (2005). *Interpersonal conflict and effective communication*. Retrieved July 6, 2007, from www.drbalternatives.com/articles/cc2.html.

Benson, S. G., & Dundis, S. P. (2003, September). Understanding and motivating health care employees: Integrating Maslow's hierarchy of needs, training and technology. *Journal of Nursing Management, 11*, 315–320.

Bok, S. (1978). *Lying: Moral choice in public and private life*. New York: Pantheon.

Borchardt, J. K. (2006, November). Harness the power of metaphors. *Writer, 119*, 28–30.

Brownback, S. (1998, May 15). Free speech: Lyrics, liberty and license. *Vital Speeches of the Day, 64*, 454–456.

Brownell, J. (2006). *Listening: Attitudes, principles, and skills* (3rd ed.). Boston: Allyn & Bacon.

Burgoon, J. K., & Bacue, A. E. (2003). Nonverbal communication skills. In J. O. Greene & B. R. Burleson (Eds.), *Handbook of communication and social interaction skills* (pp. 179–220). Mahwah, NJ: Erlbaum.

Burke, K. (1950). *A rhetoric of motives*. New York: Prentice-Hall.

Butler, M. M. (2005). Communication apprehension and its impact on individuals in the work place. Howard University. *Dissertation Abstracts International: A. The Humanities and Social Sciences, 65* (9-A), 3215.

Chang, H. C., & Holt, G. R. (1996, Winter). The changing Chinese interpersonal world: Popular themes in interpersonal communication books in modern Taiwan. *Communication Quarterly, 44*, 85–106.

Chase, S. (1956). *Guides to straight thinking, with 13 common fallacies*. New York: HarperCollins.

Cialdini, R. T. (1984). *Influence: How and why people agree to things*. New York: Morrow.

Cialdini, R. T., & Ascani, K. (1976). Test of a concession procedure for inducing verbal, behavioral, and further compliance with a request to give blood. *Journal of Applied Psychology, 61*, 295–300.

Coates, J., & Cameron, D. (1989). *Women, men, and language: Studies in language and linguistics*. London: Longman.

Dalton, J. (1994, March 1). The character of readiness. *Vital Speeches of the Day, 60*, 296–299.

deBono, E. (1967). *Lateral thinking*. New York: Harper Paperbacks.

deBono, E. (1976). *Teaching thinking*. New York: Penguin.

Dejong, W. (1979). An examination of self perception mediation of the foot in the door effect. *Journal of Personality and Social Psychology, 37*, 2221–2239.

DeVito, J. A. (1974). *General semantics: Guide and workbook* (Rev. ed.). DeLand, FL: Everett/Edwards.

DeVito, J. A. (1996). *Brainstorms: How to think more creatively about communication (or about anything else)*. Boston: Allyn & Bacon.

Dillard, J. P., & Marshall, L. J. (2003). Persuasion as a social skill. In J. O. Greene & B. R. Burleson (Eds.),

Handbook of communication and social interaction skills (pp. 479–514). Mahwah, NJ: Erlbaum.

Dwyer, K. K. (2005). *Conquer your speech anxiety* (2nd ed.). Belmont, CA: Wadsworth.

Eisenberg, N., & Strayer, J. (1987). *Empathy and its development*. New York: Cambridge University Press.

Ekman, P., Friesen, W. V., & Ellsworth, P. (1972). *Emotion in the human face: Guidelines for research and an integration of findings*. New York: Pergamon Press.

Ellis, A. (1988). *How to stubbornly refuse to make yourself miserable about anything, yes anything*. Secaucus, NJ: Lyle Stuart.

Emmert, P. (1994). A definition of listening. *Listening Post, 51*, 6.

Feinstein, D. (2006, October 23). *Gang violence: An environment of fear*. Speech delivered at the Gang Summit hosted by the U.S. Department of Justice. Retrieved from http://feinstein.seate.gov/public.

Fensholt, M. (2003, June). There's nothing wrong with taking written notes to the podium. *Presentations, 17*, 66.

Floyd, J. J. (1985). *Listening: A practical approach*. Boston: Allyn & Bacon.

Fraser, B. (1990, April). Perspectives on politeness. *Journal of Pragmatics, 14*, 219–236.

Freedman, J., & Fraser, S. (1966). Compliance without pressure: The foot-in-the-door technique. *Journal of Personality and Social Psychology, 4*, 195–202.

Frey, K. J., & Eagly, A. H. (1993, July). Vividness can undermine the persuasiveness of messages. *Journal of Personality and Social Psychology, 65*, 32–44.

Gamble, T. K., & Gamble, M. W. (2003). *The gender communication connection*. Boston: Houghton Mifflin.

Glucksberg, S., & Danks, J. H. (1975). *Experimental psycholinguistics: An introduction*. Hillsdale, NJ: Erlbaum.

Goss, B., Thompson, M., & Olds, S. (1978). Behavioral support for systematic desensitization for communication apprehension. *Human Communication Research, 4*, 158–163.

Grice, G. L., & Skinner, J. F. (2007). *Mastering public speaking* (6th ed.). Boston: Allyn & Bacon.

Gudykunst, W. B., & Kim, Y. Y. (Eds.). (1992). *Readings on communication with strangers: An approach to intercultural communication*. New York: McGraw-Hill.

Gudykunst, W., & Nishida, T. (1984). Individual and cultural influence on uncertainty reduction. *Communication Monographs, 51*, 23–36.

Gudykunst, W., Yang, S., & Nishida, T. (1985). A cross-cultural test of uncertainty reduction theory: Comparisons of acquaintance, friend, and dating relationships in Japan, Korea, and the United States. *Human Communication Research, 11*, 407–454.

Hall, E. T. (1976). *Beyond culture*. Garden City, NY: Doubleday.

Hall, E. T., & Hall, M. R. (1987). *Hidden differences: Doing business with the Japanese*. New York: Doubleday.

Hall, J. A. (2006). Women's and men's nonverbal communication: Similarities, differences, stereotypes and origins. In V. Manusov & M. L. Patterson (Eds.), *The Sage handbook of nonverbal communication* (pp. 201–218). Thousand Oaks, CA: Sage.

Hammond, R. A., & Axelrod, R. (2006, December). The evolution of ethnocentrism. *Journal of Conflict Resolution, 50*, 926–936.

Han, S. P., & Shavitt, S. (1994). Persuasion and culture: Advertising appeals in individualistic and collectivist societies. *Journal of Experimental Social Psychology, 30*, 326–350.

Hanley, S. J., & Abell, S. C. (2002, Fall). Maslow and relatedness: Creating an interpersonal model of self-actualization. *Journal of Humanistic Psychology, 42*, 37–56.

Harris, M., & Johnson, O. (2000). *Cultural anthropology* (5th ed.). Boston: Allyn & Bacon.

Hayakawa, S. I., & Hayakawa, A. R. (1990). *Language in thought and action* (5th ed.). New York: Harcourt Brace Jovanovich.

Hecht, M. L., Collier, M. J., & Ribeau, S. (1993). *African American communication: Ethnic identity and cultural interpretation*. Thousand Oaks, CA: Sage.

Hendry, J. (1995). *Wrapping culture: Politeness, presentation, and power in Japan and other societies*. New York: Oxford University Press.

Hensley, C. W. (1994, March 1). Divorce—the sensible approach. *Vital Speeches of the Day, 60*, 317–319.

Henslin, J. M. (2000). *Essentials of sociology: A down-to-earth approach* (3rd ed.). Boston: Allyn & Bacon.

Herrick, J. A. (2004). *Argumentation: Understanding and shaping arguments*. State College, PA: Strata Publishing.

Higgins, J. M. (1994). *101 creative problem solving techniques*. New York: New Management Publishing.

Himle, J. A., Abelson, J. L., & Haghightgou, H. (1999, August). Effect of alcohol on social phobic anxiety. *American Journal of Psychiatry, 156*, 1237–1243.

Hofstede, G. (1997). *Cultures and organizations: Software of the mind*. New York: McGraw-Hill.

Holmes, J. (1995). *Women, men and politeness*. New York: Longman.

Jaffe, C. (2007). *Public speaking: Concepts and skills for a diverse society* (5th ed.). Belmont, CA: Wadsworth.

Jaksa, J. A., & Pritchard, M. S. (1994). *Communication ethics: Methods of analysis* (2nd ed.). Belmont, CA: Wadsworth.

James, D. L. (1995). *The executive guide to Asia–Pacific communications*. New York: Kodansha International.

Jandt, F. E. (2000). *Intercultural communication* (3rd ed.). Thousand Oaks, CA: Sage.

Johannesen, R. L. (1996). *Ethics in human communication* (5th ed.). Prospect Heights, IL: Waveland Press.

Johnson, K. G. (Ed.). (1991). *Thinking creatically: Thinking creatively, thinking critically*. Concord, CA: International Society for General Semantics.

Kiel, J. M. (1999, September). Reshaping Maslow's hierarchy of needs to reflect today's educational and managerial philosophies. *Journal of Instructional Psychology, 26*, 167–168.

Korzybski, A. (1933). *Science and sanity: An introduction to non-Aristotelian systems and General Semantics*. Concord, CA: International Society for General Semantics.

Kramarae, C. (1981). *Women and men speaking*. Rowley, MA: Newbury House.

Lee, A. M., & Lee, E. B. (1972). *The fine art of propaganda.* San Francisco: International Society for General Semantics.

Lee, A. M., & Lee, E. B. (1995, Spring). The iconography of propaganda analysis. *ETC.: A Review of General Semantics, 52,* 13–17.

Lucas, S. E. (2007). *The art of public speaking* (9th ed.) New York: McGraw-Hill.

Lustig, M. W., & Koester, J. (2006). *Intercultural competence: Interpersonal communication across cultures* (5th ed.). New York: Allyn & Bacon.

Mackay, H. B. (1991, August 15). How to get a job. *Vital Speeches of the Day, 57,* 656–659.

Maggio, R. (1997). *Talking about people: A guide to fair and accurate language.* Phoenix, AZ: Oryx Press.

Marien, M. (1992, March 15). Education and learning in the 21st century. *Vital Speeches of the Day, 58,* 340–344.

Martin, M. M., & Rubin, R. B. (1994, Winter). Development of a communication flexibility measure. *The Southern Communication Journal, 59,* 171–178.

Martin, M. M., & Rubin, R. B. (1995). A new measure of cognitive flexibility. *Psychological Reports, 76,* 623–626.

Maslow, A. (1970). *Motivation and personality.* New York: HarperCollins.

Matsumoto, D. (2006). Culture and nonverbal communication. In V. Manusov & M. L. Patterson (Eds.), *The Sage handbook of nonverbal communication* (pp. 219–235). Thousand Oaks, CA: Sage.

Maxwell, J. (1987, September 1). Economic forecasting. *Vital Speeches of the Day, 53,* 685–686.

McCroskey, J. C. (2001). *An introduction to rhetorical communication* (8th ed.). Boston: Allyn & Bacon.

McKerrow, R. E., Gronbeck, B. E., Ehninger, D., & Monroe, A. H. (2000). *Principles and types of speech communication* (14th ed.). Boston: Allyn & Bacon.

Meade, C. H. (2000). The misunderstood vividness effect: Roles in which vividness can enhance persuasion. University of Georgia. *Dissertation Abstracts International: B. The Physical Sciences and Engineering, 61* (January), 3323.

Midooka, K. (1990, October). Characteristics of Japanese style communication. *Media, Culture and Society, 12,* 477–489.

Nelson, A. (1986, June 1). The sanctuary movement. *Vital Speeches of the Day, 52,* 482–485.

Neuliep, J. W., Chaudoir, M., & McCroskey, J. C. (2001). A cross-cultural comparison of ethnocentrism among Japanese and United States college students. *Communication Research Reports, 18,* 137–146.

Nordahl, H. M., & Wells, A. (2007). *Changing beliefs in cognitive therapy.* New York: Wiley.

Osborn, A. (1957). *Applied imagination* (Rev. ed.). New York: Scribners.

Pearson, J. C., West, R., & Turner, L. H. (1995). *Gender and communication* (3rd ed.). Dubuque, IA: William C. Brown.

Pei, M. (1956). *Language for everybody.* New York: Pocket Books.

Perkins, D. F., & Fogarty, K. (2006). Active listening: A communication tool. Retrieved January 31, 2007, from http://edis.ifas.ufl.edu.

Peterson, H. (Ed.). (1965). *A treasury of the world's great speeches.* New York: Simon & Schuster.

Petty, R. E., & Wegener, D. T. (1998). Attitude change: Multiple roles for persuasion variables. In D. T. Gilbert, S. T. Fiske, & G. Lindzey (Eds.), *The handbook of social psychology* (4th ed., Vol. 1, pp. 323–390). New York: McGraw-Hill.

Pratkanis, A., & Aronson, E. (1991). *Age of propaganda: The everyday use and abuse of persuasion.* New York: W. H. Freeman.

Rankin, P. (1929). Listening ability. *Proceedings of the Ohio State Educational Conference's Ninth Annual Session.*

Reynolds, C. L., & Schnoor, L. G. (Eds.). (1991). *1989 championship debates and speeches.* Normal, IL: American Forensic Association.

Richardson, M. M. (1995, January 15). Taxation with representation. *Vital Speeches of the Day, 61,* 201–203.

Richmond, V. P., & McCroskey, J. C. (1998). *Communication: Apprehension, avoidance, and effectiveness* (5th ed.). Boston: Allyn & Bacon.

Riggio, R. E. (1987). *The charisma quotient.* New York: Dodd, Mead.

Rodman, G. (2001). *Making sense of media: An introduction to mass communication.* Boston: Allyn & Bacon.

Rogers, C. (1970). *Carl Rogers on encounter groups.* New York: Harrow Books.

Rogers, L. (2001). *Sexing the brain.* New York: Columbia University Press.

Salopek, J. (1999, September). Is anyone listening? *Training and Development, 53,* 58.

Schnoor, L. G. (Ed.). (1994). *1991 and 1992 championship debates and speeches.* River Falls, WI: American Forensic Association.

Schnoor, L. G. (Ed.). (2000). *Winning orations of the Interstate Oratorical Association.* Mankato, MN: Interstate Oratorical Association.

Schnoor, L. G. (Ed.). (2006). *Winning orations of the Interstate Oratorical Association.* Mankato, MN: Interstate Oratorical Association.

Schwartz, M., and the Task Force on Bias-Free Language of the Association of American University Presses. (1995). *Guidelines for bias-free writing.* Bloomington: Indiana University Press.

Singh, N., & Pereira, A. (2005). *The culturally customized web site.* Oxford, UK., Elsevier Butterworth-Heinemann.

Smith, T. E., & Frymier, A. B. (2006, February). Get 'real': Does practicing speeches before an audience improve performance? *Communication Quarterly, 54,* 111–125.

Sojourner, R. J., & Wogalter, M. S. (1998). The influence of pictorials on the comprehension and recall of pharmaceutical safety and warning information. *International Journal of Cognitive Ergonomics, 2,* 93–106.

Sprague, J., & Stuart, D. (2008). *The speaker's handbook* (8th ed.). Belmont, CA: Wadsworth.

Steil, L. K., Barker, L. L., & Watson, K. W. (1983). *Effective listening: Key to your success.* Reading, MA: Addison-Wesley.

Stephan, W. G., & Stephan, C. W. (1992). *Improving intergroup relations.* Thousand Oaks, CA: Sage.

Tannen, D. (1990). *You just don't understand: Women and men in conversation.* New York: Morrow.

Verderber, R. F., & Verderber, K. S. (2006). *The challenge of effective speaking* (13th ed.). Belmont, CA: Wadsworth.

von Oech, R. (1990). *A whack on the side of the head: How you can be more creative* (Rev. ed.). New York: Warner.

Watts, R. J. (2004). *Politeness.* Cambridge, UK: Cambridge University Press.

Watzlawick, P. (1978). *The language of change: Elements of therapeutic communication.* New York: Basic Books.

Watzlawick, P., Beavin, J., & Jackson, D. D. (1967). *Pragmatics of human communication: A study of interactional patterns, pathologies, and paradoxes.* New York: Norton.

Werner, E. K. (1975). *A study of communication time.* Master's thesis, University of Maryland, College Park.

Cited in A. Wolvin & C. Coakley. (1988). *Listening* (3rd ed.). Dubuque, IA: William C. Brown.

Westbrook, D., Kennerley, H., & Kirk, J. (2007). *An introduction to cognitive behavior therapy: Skills and applications.* Thousand Oaks, CA: Sage.

Withers, L. A., & Vernon, L. L. (2006, January). To err is human: Embarrassment, attachment, and communication apprehension. *Personality and Individual Differences 40,* 99–110.

Wolpe, J. (1957). *Psychotherapy by reciprocal inhibition.* Stanford, CA: Stanford University Press.

Wolvin, A. D., & Coakley, C. G. (1996). *Listening.* Dubuque, IA: William C. Brown.

Wood, W. (2000). Attitude change: Persuasion and social influence. *Annual Review of Psychology, 51,* 539–570.

Wright, W. (1999). *Born that way: Genes–behavior–personality.* New York: Knopf.

Young-Hong, Z. (2004, May). A study of group counseling for dispelling communication apprehension of undergraduates. *Chinese Journal of Clinical Psychology, 12,* 156–157.

Index

Page numbers followed by *t* or *f* indicate tables and figures, respectively.

Credits

Photo Credits

Text Credits